Lecture Notes in Computer Science   10457

Commenced Publication in 1973
Founding and Former Series Editors:
Gerhard Goos, Juris Hartmanis, and Jan van Leeuwen

More information about this series at http://www.springer.com/series/7408

Editors
Ezio Bartocci
TU Wien
Vienna
Austria

Yliès Falcone
Université Grenoble Alpes, Inria,
   Laboratoire d'Informatique de Grenoble
Grenoble
France

ISSN 0302-9743   ISSN 1611-3349 (electronic)
Lecture Notes in Computer Science
ISBN 978-3-319-75631-8   ISBN 978-3-319-75632-5 (eBook)
https://doi.org/10.1007/978-3-319-75632-5

Library of Congress Control Number: 2018933096

LNCS Sublibrary: SL2 – Programming and Software Engineering

Cover illustration: Automata-based and rewrite-based runtime verification. Created by Yliès Falcone. Used with permission.

Printed on acid-free paper

This Springer imprint is published by the registered company Springer International Publishing AG part of Springer Nature
The registered company address is: Gewerbestrasse 11, 6330 Cham, Switzerland

Ezio Bartocci · Yliès Falcone (Eds.)

Lectures on Runtime Verification

Introductory and Advanced Topics

Springer

Preface

Runtime verification (RV) is a lightweight, yet rigorous, formal method for the monitoring and analysis of the runtime behavior of software and hardware systems. RV complements classic exhaustive verification techniques (such as model checking and theorem proving) with a more practical approach that analyzes a single execution trace of a system. At the price of a limited execution coverage, RV can give very precise information on the runtime behavior of the monitored system. RV is now widely employed in both academia and industry both before system deployment, for testing, verification, and debugging purposes, and after deployment to ensure reliability, safety, robustness, and security.

The interest in this field of research has grown since 2001 when the first international workshop on RV was organized. This venue has occurred each year since then, becoming a conference in 2010. In 2014, we initiated the International Competition on Runtime Verification (CRV) with the goal of fostering the comparison and evaluation of software runtime verification tools. In the same year, an European scientific network for the Cooperation in Science and Technology (COST) on "Runtime Verification Beyond Monitoring (ARVI)" was approved and funded within the European framework program Horizon 2020. ARVI currently includes the participation of scientists from 26 European countries and Australia. In 2016, together with other partners of ARVI, we also started to organize the first of a series of schools on RV. Our aim is to train researchers from academia and industry introducing them first to the basic concepts and then to the advanced topics in this exciting research area.

The idea of this volume originated from the need to have a book for students to support their training with several tutorials on different aspects of RV. The volume has been organized in seven chapters and the topics covered include an introduction on runtime verification, dynamic analysis of concurrency errors, monitoring events that carry data, runtime error reaction and prevention, monitoring of cyber-physical systems, runtime verification for decentralized and distributed systems, and an industrial application of runtime verification techniques in financial transaction systems.

Each paper has been reviewed by two reviewers and the editors. The editors would like to thank the reviewers: Thomas Arts, Ebru Aydin Gol, Andreas Bauer, Christian Colombo, Raymond Hu, Jan Kofron, Zhaodan Kong, Laura Nenzi, Gordon Pace, Rahul Purandare, Giles Reger, Oleg Sokolsky, Shmuel Ur.

November 2017

Ezio Bartocci
Yliès Falcone

Contents

Introduction to Runtime Verification

Ezio Bartocci[1]($\boxtimes$), Yliès Falcone[2], Adrian Francalanza[3], and Giles Reger[4]

[1] TU Wien, Vienna, Austria
ezio.bartocci@tuwien.ac.at
[2] Univ. Grenoble Alpes, Inria, CNRS, Grenoble INP,
Laboratoire d'Informatique de Grenoble, 38000 Grenoble, France
[3] University of Malta, Msida MSD 2080, Malta
[4] University of Manchester, Manchester, UK

Abstract. The aim of this chapter is to act as a primer for those wanting to learn about Runtime Verification (RV). We start by providing an overview of the main specification languages used for RV. We then introduce the standard terminology necessary to describe the monitoring problem, covering the pragmatic issues of monitoring and instrumentation, and discussing extensively the monitorability problem.

1 Introduction

The field of Runtime Verification (RV) has been, and is still, referred to by many names such as runtime monitoring, trace analysis, dynamic analysis etc. The term *verification* implies a notion of *correctness* with respect to some property. This is somewhat different from the term *monitoring* (the other popular term) which only suggests that there is some form of behaviour being observed. Some view the notion of monitoring as being more specific than that of verification as they take it to imply some interaction with the system, whereas verification is passive in nature. At this early point in this chapter we would like to note that the community is not in agreement about the various meanings of certain terminology, such as the difference between *runtime verification* and *runtime monitoring*. We take a popular interpretation in this chapter, but the reader will most likely encounter alternative views in the literature.

RV is a lightweight, yet rigorous, formal method that complements classical exhaustive verification techniques (such as model checking and theorem proving) with a more practical approach that analyses a single execution trace of a system. At the price of a limited execution coverage, RV can give very precise information on the runtime behaviour of the monitored system. The system considered can be a software system, hardware or cyber-physical system, a sensor network, or any system in general whose dynamic behaviour can be observed. The archetypal analysis that can be performed on runtime behaviour is to check for correctness of that behaviour. This is also the main activity considered in this chapter. However, there are many other analyses (e.g., falsification analysis [22]) or activities (e.g., runtime enforcement [80]) that can be performed, as it will be discussed elsewhere in this book. RV is now widely employed in both academia and industry both

© Springer International Publishing AG, part of Springer Nature 2018
E. Bartocci and Y. Falcone (Eds.): Lectures on Runtime Verification, LNCS 10457, pp. 1–33, 2018.
https://doi.org/10.1007/978-3-319-75632-5_1

before system deployment, for testing, verification, and debugging purposes, and after deployment to ensure reliability, safety, robustness and security.

The RV field as a self-named community grew out of the RV workshop established in 2001, which became a conference in 2010 and occurs each year since then. In 2014, we have initiated the international Competition on Runtime Verification (CRV) [17,23] with the aim to foster the comparison and evaluation of software runtime verification tools. In the same year, a European scientific network for the COoperation in Science and Technology (COST) on *Runtime Verification beyond Monitoring (ARVI)* was approved and funded within the European framework programme Horizon 2020. ARVI currently includes the participation of scientists from 26 European countries and Australia. In 2016, together with other partners of ARVI, we have also started to organise the first of a series of Schools on RV.

However, it is worth noting that the research on monitoring techniques has been around for a very long time and it is present in other communities where it is not referred to in the same terms as it is here, even if the process is the same.

In this chapter we introduce the field of RV covering the basic concepts and the standard notions of monitoring. We have not attempted to make a full survey of all related work, but we refer to the main relevant literature [77,100,112,140].

When considering how to check whether the runtime behaviour of a system conforms to some specification there are three necessary steps to be taken:

1. *Specifying (Un)Desired System Behaviour.* Section 2 considers how system behaviour can be abstracted in terms of events and traces and how specification languages can be used to describe properties of such traces.
2. *Generating a Monitor from a Specification.* Section 3 considers the monitoring problem and various issues that must be dealt with during monitoring.
3. *Connecting a Monitor to a System.* Section 4 considers how various *instrumentation* approaches can be used to extract the information necessary for monitoring from a running system.

We are also interested in the question of *what can and cannot be monitored*; this is addressed in Sect. 5. Even though this question seems more theoretical, it determines what sorts of properties can be handled with runtime verification. We provide an overview of all the chapters of this book in Sect. 6 and we conclude in Sect. 7.

2   Formal Specification of the System Behaviour

This section introduces the reader to different formal approaches to describe the expected behaviour of a system. We start by presenting various abstractions enabling to reason about the system behaviour at different level of detail. We then present some specification languages after having discussed first some general properties of these formalisms.

Example 1 (Traffic Lights). Throughout this section we choose as our running example a traffic light system. This system consists of three lights of different colors: *green, red, yellow*. We then consider how to specify the expected behaviour of such a system using different formalisms.

2.1 The Abstract Notion of Behaviour

When we consider the behaviour of a system we are referring to the way the system changes over time, by updating some internal state, taking some internal or external action, or affecting the environment in some way. We typically describe this behaviour in terms of the observations we can make about it. There are two general kinds of observations we can make: either we inspect some snapshots of the current *state* of the system at a particular time, or we record certain *actions* or *state changes* made by the system (where the system in question may include the environment). Below we describe how we will abstract systems in terms of the observations (events) we can make about them over time (giving a trace) and how we describe behaviour using these abstractions.

Events. We will call any kind of observation about the system an *event*. In the simple case an event is a name for something that can happen, for example lightTurnsGreen, lightBrightnessIs80 or pedestrianButtonPressed. In the more complex case an event could be structured, containing data values of interest. We do not cover this complex case here, but it is discussed in Chap. 3 [102].

Note that we make a distinction between events as syntactic elements and what they denote semantically. For example, an event temperatureLimit may correspond to a sensor detecting that the temperature is at or above 20 °C. We separate the representation of this event and the process of recording/detecting and reporting it (Sect. 4 describes how we practically observe systems).

In this presentation events are discrete atomic entities, but there are two alternative views that are taken in various work. Firstly, some work considers an event as having a *duration*, i.e., a start and end time. This can be easily translated into the setting where events are atomic by introducing associated start and end events. For example, we might have the event *lightGreen* at one level of abstraction, but *lightGreenOn* and *lightGreenOff* at another level of abstraction. Secondly, in languages specified over *continuous time* events can be viewed as *signals* that can be queried for a value. We discuss this setting in more detail later. Where an alternative interpretation of event is being taken we will be explicit in the text.

We call *alphabet* the set of the system's observable events of interest. We stress *of interest* as there are potentially an infinite number of different ways of describing an event, but typically we are only interested in a small (at least usually finite) set of such events. It is clear that the choice of events is fundamental in how much information we have about a system and the properties we can describe. Events can be defined at different levels of abstraction and be related to the internal or external behaviour. They may cover the whole system or one specific part, and may not correspond directly with existing components or actions defined in the system. The choice of events is part of the specification process and will depend on what the end goal is.

We note that this choice of abstracting systems in terms of *events* rather than *states* is a distinction that is different from (but compatible with) the work of model checking. As with many things, not all work in RV uses the event abstraction and some work may view an execution as a sequence of observed states.

Traces. We use events to abstract a particular observation about a system. We abstract the behaviour of a single run of a system as a *trace*, which is a (finite) sequence of events (or sets of events) [129].

Clearly, an observable trace of a system must be *finite*, but it is sometimes useful to think about the possible *infinite* behaviours of a system. As discussed later, when viewing a trace as a finite prefix of some possible infinite behaviour we can ask whether the finite prefix can be extended to some acceptable infinite trace. Another key choice in structuring a trace is whether each point in the trace consists of a single event or a set of events. The single event view is often more straightforward, but it does not easily allow for settings where multiple observations may occur concurrently (and it does not make sense to coalesce them) or the exact ordering of events within a particular time frame is unclear (or unhelpful to enforce). This choice may seem arbitrary, but it has an impact on the interpretation of specifications as those languages assuming a single event at a time implicitly include extra axioms, i.e., seeing one event precludes seeing any other. Finally, different approaches treat the notion of *time* differently. The order of events in a trace gives a qualitative notion of time, but it does not immediately capture any quantitative distance (in time) between events. We discuss the different approaches for embedding time into traces later.

Properties and Specifications. A *property* of a system can be abstractly described as a (possibly infinite) set of traces. A *specification* is a concrete (textual) object describing a property and therefore it denotes a set of traces. We have chosen to distinguish properties from specifications as the distinction can be important. However, this distinction is not universal in the literature. Note that the full behaviour, or intended behaviour, of a system may be given as a property. However, this will always be restricted by the event abstractions chosen and it is usually not the aim to describe total behaviour but key behaviour at a level of abstraction that is useful.

Using this separation we can have many specifications for a single property, but a property is unique and independent of a specification language. If the specification language is ambiguous (e.g., English) then the specific property being described may not be clear. Dealing with such ambiguities is a common issue in the specification process. Generally we expect a *specification language* to be unambiguous, at least in terms of the traces its specifications denote. We note that most work in the area conflate the notions of property and specification, and we may do so here. This is due to the fact the specification is the only object that exists concretely and it is often used to represent its underlying property.

A somewhat alternative distinction that some make between property and specification is that a property describes a unit of behaviour whilst a specification may capture many properties.

Much of the activity of RV considers *explicit* properties captured in some specification language. However, there are also many *implicit* properties covered by the field. A notable example of an implicit property is *deadlock avoidance* (see Chap. 2 [115]). When monitoring this property the property itself is not written in a specification language; instead specific ad-hoc algorithms are written to detect a violation of the property. Other examples of implicit properties are memory safety and bounds checking.

2.2   General Specification Language Features

In the following we discuss general features of specification languages used for runtime verification. We do not aim to present a taxonomy of languages, but instead aim to introduce some general concepts and terminology that is helpful when discussing such languages. See [101] for a more in-depth discussion of such features.

Executable versus Declarative. In some specification languages (e.g., state machines) the specification is directly executable whereas in other languages (e.g., temporal logic) it is more common to generate an executable object (monitor) from the specification. Languages where specifications are executable tend to have more straightforward monitoring algorithms. However, executable specifications also tend to be more low-level (operational) and less able to capture properties at a high level of abstraction. For example, it is usually more straightforward to combine specifications written declaratively, e.g., if the temporal logic formula φ_1 represents the normal behaviour of a traffic light system and formula φ_2 represents some special behaviour to be seen if a special emergency event occurs then the total behaviour should be $\varphi_1 \vee (\text{emergency} \rightarrow \varphi_2)$. With automata this would either require monitoring mechanisms to allow the monitoring of multiple automata, or a construction on the automata leading to a complex automata that is difficult to read.

Prefix Closure. Consider the property that the yellow light is never on immediately after the red light. We might try to specify this using the regular expression

$$((\text{green} \mid \text{yellow})^* \text{red}^+ \text{green})^*$$

but under the standard semantics this does not accept the trace green yellow red. Our intention is for all *prefixes* of the describe language to be accepted. Such properties are *safety* properties and are common in system specification. Some specification languages assume prefix-closure, although most do not.

When Language ≠ Property. Typically, a concrete specification denotes a set of traces. Sometimes, for usability reasons, it might be useful for this language to not directly describe the property being specified, but be implicitly related to it. Therefore, this is less a feature of a language and more a feature of its usage. We give two examples here:

1. *Polarity.* A specification may capture *good* (desired, positive) behaviour or *bad* (undesired, negative) behaviour. Consider again the above property that the yellow light is never on immediately after the red light. Any trace *not* satisfying this property would match the regular expression

$$(\text{red} \mid \text{green} \mid \text{yellow})^* \text{ red yellow}$$

which is, arguably, easier to read. When good behaviour is described a match represents *validation* of the desired property, whereas matching a specification describing bad behaviour represents a *violation* of that property.

2. *Suffix Matching.* Consider again the above property, the expression (red | green | yellow)* represents all possible traces and is, in some sense, redundant. In the interests of readability it would be more concise to simply write the expression

$$\text{red yellow}$$

and let it be understood that matching this expression against the *suffix* of a trace *violates* the desired property.

Finite versus Infinite. Some specification languages are more suited to specifying sets of finite traces (e.g., state machines) whereas other are more suited to specifying sets of infinite traces (e.g., temporal logic). As observations at runtime are necessarily finite this often leads to a mapping from a semantics over infinite traces to one over finite traces.

Time. As mentioned above, a totally ordered trace gives a qualitative notion of time, but not a quantitative one. Specification languages whose specifications denote such traces also only capture this qualitative notion of time. Notice that this qualitative notion is fragile as properties making use of this make assumptions about the level of abstraction events will be recorded at. Consider the property that the green light should be followed by the red light. Unless we are careful, the following two traces would not satisfy this property:

$$\tau_1 = \text{green green red} \qquad \tau_2 = \text{green pedestrianButtonPressed red}$$

Furthermore, if we want to check that the green light is on for 30 s it would be necessary to sample this light at a particular frequency and count the number of events seen. As discussed below, there are various methods for integrating quantitative notions of time into a specification language. Most commonly this is via explicit *clocks* in executable languages, or explicit *intervals* in declarative ones. With this quantitative notion one can now say how long the green light should be on and how soon the red light should come on once it goes off.

Data and Quantification. A specification language may view events as atomic symbols or as structures containing *data*. Languages that consider data may do so in various ways, but this tends to be dependent on the underlying formalism. Temporal logics may be extended by standard notions of quantification [25,53,70], quantification over the *active domain* [28,97,144], or (more recently) with freeze quantifiers [20, 21, 26, 64]. An alternative approach is the use of *parametric trace slicing* [52, 130] to add a form of data quantification to a range of otherwise propositional formalisms (e.g., regular expressions and state machines). Specification languages making use of state machines often include the idea of transitions being labelled with guards and assignments [12, 59]. Finally, some formalisms, such as stream languages [82] and rule systems [16], have data manipulating features as standard. Chapter 3 considers such languages in more detail.

2.3 Specific Specification Languages

This section focusses on particular (families of) specification languages used for runtime verification. Figure 1 formalises a typical light sequence property of traffic lights in various basic languages described in this section.

Temporal Logic. The most common family of specification languages used for runtime verification is temporal logic with the most basic and usual variant being *linear temporal logic* (LTL) [127].

Linear Temporal Logic (LTL). Future-time LTL introduces two basic modal operators: *Next* is written $\circ\varphi$ and means that φ is true at the next point of the trace; and *Until* is written $\varphi_1 \; \mathcal{U} \; \varphi_2$ and means that φ_1 is true from the current point of the trace until φ_2 is true. These operators are used to define two (often more frequently used) operators: *Always* is defined as $\Box\varphi \equiv \varphi \; \mathcal{U} \; false$ and means that φ should be true on every step of the trace from the current one onwards; and *Eventually* is defined as $\Diamond\varphi \equiv \neg\Box\neg\varphi$ and means that φ is true at some point in the trace from the current point onwards. Some variations of LTL also introduce a notion of *Weak Until* that does not require φ_2 to eventually hold, only that φ_1 holds until it does (i.e., this may be infinitely often).

Past-time LTL has symmetric operators looking into the past e.g., *Previous* (•) as the dual of *Next* and *Since* ($\mathcal{S}$) as the dual of *Until*. However, things are not quite this simple due to the finite nature of the past. It is typical to introduce a notion of *Weak Previous* (•̂) that is always true at the first state; it is then possible to define $\bullet\varphi = \neg\hat{\bullet}\neg\varphi$. It is common to consider a setting where both future-time and past-time operators are available.

In the runtime verification setting it is typical to consider *finite* traces only. As LTL has an infinite trace semantics it is necessary to provide an alternative finite

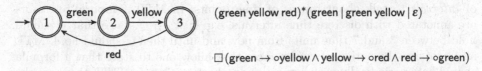

Fig. 1. Illustrating the traffic light sequence property using a state machine, regular expression, and linear temporal logic formula.

trace semantics to deal with the end of trace. There are two main approaches to this:

- Providing an alternative semantics ensuring that $\Box\varphi$ is true at the end of a trace and $\Diamond\varphi$ is false. One way of achieving this is to add the dual of *Weak Previous* i.e., *Weak Next* and set up the semantics to preserve the identify $\Box\varphi = \varphi \wedge \hat{\circ}\varphi$. However, it is more common to define an alternative semantics directly without introducing $\hat{\circ}$ (see, for example, the early work in [131]).
- The finite trace is a finite prefix of some infinite trace. The truth of a formula on this finite prefix is defined by the possible *extensions* of that prefix i.e., it is true if all extensions make it true. This necessitates a multi-valued verdict domain. This idea is captured in LTL_3 [29] where a third verdict ? is given where some extensions are failing and some succeeding. This is called *impartiality* and means that some formulas (e.g., $\Box a$) can never be satisfied (there are always bad extensions) and dually some can never be violated (e.g., $\Diamond a$). These ideas relate to the notion of *monitorability*, discussed later.

There is an additional dimension that crosscuts both approaches, that of *anticipation*. The general idea is that if every extension of a finite trace leads to a single verdict then this verdict should be given to that finite trace. In the case where a purely finite trace semantics is given, the notion of anticipation is often captured by splitting the verdict domain into two forms of verdicts: strong verdicts reflecting an anticipatory result (all extensions) and weak verdicts reflecting the verdict to be given if the trace were to finish at the current point [12,16].

Interval Temporal Logic. In LTL formulas are given over states or events i.e., distinct points in time. An alternative view, taken by interval temporal logic [48, 147], is to reason over *intervals*, i.e. pairs of points in time. Formulas in this logic may then use binary relations comparing intervals e.g. whether their start/end points are ordered, or whether one interval overlaps with, or is contained within, another. This presentation is generally not strictly more expressive than LTL as translations have been given into LTL [132].

Variants with Time. Standard temporal logics take a *qualitative* view of time i.e. they place an ordering on events but do not relate those events to the quantitative time line they occur within. There exist variants of LTL that add a notion of quantitative time via the extension of the underlying model (trace) with timestamps and an extension of the language constructs. Two notable variants are metric temporal logic [145] and timed LTL [30] which both use the notion of *intervals* to talk about ranges of time points. In MTL, temporal operators are annotated with discrete time intervals, e.g. $\varphi \, \mathcal{U}_{[3,7]} \, \psi$ states that ψ should hold between 3 and 7 time units from now and until then φ should hold. MTL also contains the notion of *congruences* that allow one to state that a formula should hold periodically with respect to an absolute time. In TLTL there are the additional constructs $\triangleleft_a \in I$, indicating that the time since a last occurred lies within the interval I, and $\triangleright_a \in I$, indicating that the time until a next occurs lies within the interval I. Whilst these variants of LTL alter the model of traces to include information about time and extend temporal operators to make use of this, they remain inherently regular.

More Expressive Variants. We consider further extensions of LTL that increase the expressiveness of the logic as examples of how more complex properties could be captured. There is a rich literature in extending LTL in various ways and this discussion is not meant to be exhaustive.

The first is CaReT [3] which extends LTL with a (context-free) language of *calls* and *returns*. The language is extended with reserved symbols `call` and `ret` annotated with labels for the modules being entered or exited. The temporal operators are then separated into global and abstract forms where the abstract versions reason over the so-called abstract successors of the current position which skips behaviour belonging to nested calls.

Next, one may consider adding *fixed-point operator* to the language, as is done in Eagle [14, 95]. As examples, the maximum fixed point equation $vx.a \wedge x$ and minimum fixed-point equation $\mu x.a \vee \circ x$ capture the behaviour of $\Box a$ and $\Diamond a$ respectively. Such equations allow behaviour to be defined recursively, which allows context-free behaviour to be captured. In the Eagle setting, the difference between minimum and maximum fixed points is most important when given a finite trace semantics, as it clearly defines what should happen at this boundary.

In [37] Bollig et al. introduce *frequency Linear-time Temporal* (fLTL) which replaces $\mathscr{U}$ with $\mathscr{U}^c$ where c is a rational number between 0 and 1. The formula $\varphi \, \mathscr{U}^c \, \psi$ means that φ holds *with frequency* c until ψ holds, meaning that when $c = 1$ this coincides with the standard interpretation of *Until*. The effect of this addition is that fLTL can capture non context-free properties.

As a more exotic example of an expressive variant of LTL is given by Baader et al. [11] who describe a runtime verification approach for a temporal description logic that combines LTL with the ALC description logic. As well as allowing description logic axioms to replace axioms, this approach considers the idea of reasoning with *incomplete* information about the trace.

Signal Temporal Logic. Another important temporal logic in the runtime verification domain is the setting where the trace is not a discrete sequence of events but a collection of *signals* where a signal is a function from a set of real time points to a value domain. This a setting typically assumed in *hardware monitoring* and comes with its own rich set of specification languages. The standard such language is *Signal Temporal Logic* [119] which includes *signal predicates* of the form $f(x_1[t], \ldots, x_n[t]) > 0$ where f is some function and $x_i[t]$ is the value of the ith signal at time t. One can use such predicates to define operators to capture the rising and falling edges of a signal. A further defining feature of this logic is the lack of next operator, due to a dense interpretation of time meaning that there is no notion of next state. A consequence of this is that *Until* is typically interpreted with the left operand holding for all times *after* the current point (up until the right operand holds).

Spatial Temporal Logics. As we live in a cyberworld where interacting software and hardware components are generally spatially distributed (i.e., smart grids, robotics teams), temporal logics may be not sufficient to capture also topological spatial requirements. For this reason, in the past five years, there has been a great effort to extend STL for expressing not just temporal, but also spatiotemporal requirements. Examples include *Spatial-Temporal Logic* (SpaTeL) [96], the *Signal Spatio-Temporal Logic* (SSTL) [19,123] and the *Spatio-Temporal Reach and Escape Logic* (STREL) [18].

Hyperproperties. A growing area of interest in RV is that of *hyperproperties* i.e., properties on sets of traces rather than on single traces. There have been various extensions of standard temporal logics to this setting [55] and some have been considered in the context of runtime verification.

Regular Expressions. A popular declarative language for describing sets of strings in computer science is the regular expression. These have received attention in the runtime verification community, but less attention than temporal logics. We do not spend time describing regular expressions (which should be familiar), but note that they are sometimes used alongside the notion of *suffix-matching* for violations (e.g., in the work of `tracematches` [2]). Later we point out work that combines regular expressions and temporal logic as they are declarative approaches with different advantages. Whilst regular expressions have been extended with a quantitative notion of time [7] and to handle data words [113], such extensions have not received much interest in runtime verification.

State Machines. Whilst temporal logic and regular expressions are important *declarative* languages for specification they require *monitor synthesis* techniques to produce an executable monitor, which is usually described as some form of state machine. Conversely, state machines have the advantage of being directly executable. As for regular expressions, we do not cover the standard definition of a state machine here, but note that various runtime verification approaches make use of this formalism e.g. [59]. Such approaches do not necessarily agree on exact semantics, but follow the same approach. Areas where approaches may differ include the semantics of completion (what to do if no transition exists), the introduction of various special states, and whether states have explicit output. They may also extend state machines with clocks [59] or deal with extended finite state machines [12]. Some approaches [126] also deal with UML state charts as a state machine representation.

Beyond Regular. The previous languages were typically regular in nature (with some exceptions). There are also more expressive languages available. This space has not been as well explored, which perhaps suggests that the need for more expressive specification languages is not there, or that such languages have not been accepted for other reasons such as usability.

Grammars and String Rewriting. The obvious non-regular language is that of context-free grammars. The key application for such expressiveness is to capture the notion of calls and returns in programs (which can already be handled in the above CaReT logic). A generalised form of grammar is a string rewriting system, which allows arbitrary rewrite rules on strings. Such systems are Turing-complete. JavaMOP [120] includes both context-free grammars and string-rewriting systems as so-called *plugin* languages.

Rule Systems. Another powerful formalism is the rule system. In this setting, conditional rules are used to rewrite a set of facts i.e. by adding and removing facts from the set. By predicating a rule on a particular fact, it is then possible to use rules to effectively turn other rules on and off. This setting was first explored in the RuleR system [16] and has been continued in the recent work on LogFire [99].

Stream Languages. An alternative approach is to view the trace as one or more *streams* and to define *stream equations* over these streams to produce new streams, which may themselves be the subject of further stream equations. This approach makes computing values (rather than verdicts) over traces straightforward. An early example in this space is LOLA [82].

Other Approaches. The above covers the more standard runtime verification approaches. However, there have been various other languages utilised in the field that have received only a little attention. For example, Calder and Sevegnani [43] have utilised a process algebra to perform runtime verification of wireless networks, and Majma et al. [118] make use of coloured petri-nets in their runtime verification of a pacemaker. Recent work [88] makes use of Hennessy-Milner Logic with recursion (μHML) to describe monitors and explore the monitoring problem in general.

Combinations. Some specification approaches consider combinations of various languages previously described. Such work aims to find good compromises between the various advantages and disadvantages of different languages.

Mixing temporal logic and regular expressions. A popular combination is to add regular expressions to temporal logic. Such a combination typically increases expressiveness (as LTL is *star-free regular*) and make the language more suitable for expressing certain properties involving sequences of events. Examples of combinations include Sugar/PSL [85], RLTL [111], SALT [31], LDL [62], and MDL [27].

Many in One. TraceContract [15] provides an internal Scala DSL that supports temporal logic, rule systems, and state machines. As previously mentioned, the JavaMOP tool [120] includes the notion of *plugin* languages which allows users to describe instrumentation in one common language and then use different specification languages over declared events. Supported plugin languages include finite state machines, extended regular expressions, context free grammars, past and future linear temporal logic, CaReT, and string rewriting systems.

Translations. As well as combinations of approaches, there are also a number of cases where translations exist between languages. An early example is the embedding of LTL into the very expressive Eagle logic [13]. Other examples include the translation of domain specific languages into more standard logics for runtime verification (e.g. [42]. A recent example is the translation of first-order temporal logic into quantified event automata [130].

2.4   Summary

This section has introduced abstractions and languages for describing system behaviour. One conclusion one can draw from this section is that there are a vast number of different ways to describe system behaviour and there is no conclusive silver bullet. Research into specification languages for runtime verification is ongoing and there are many languages that we have not been able to mention in this short summary.

3   From Specifications to Monitors

So far we have spoken about how to *specify* desired or undesired system behaviour i.e. a property of a system. In this section we consider the runtime analysis that checks whether a system satisfies or violates a property. We begin by discussing the typical monitoring setup

3.1   The Monitoring Setup

As depicted in Fig. 2, a typical RV monitoring setup consists of three main components, namely the system-under-scrutiny, the monitor and the instrumentation mechanism. The collective unit encompassing these three components is

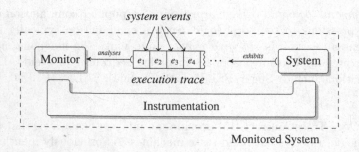

Fig. 2. The basic monitoring setup

then often referred to as the *monitored system*. The previous section discussed how we abstract a system being monitored and here we briefly describe what we mean by a *monitor* and the role of *instrumentation* (although practical instrumentation techniques are discussed in Sect. 4).

Monitors (execution monitors [134]) are computational entities that execute along side a system so as to *observe* its runtime behaviour and possibly determine whether a property is satisfied or violated from the exhibited (system) execution. When sufficient system behaviour is observed, a monitor may reach a *verdict* (e.g., acceptance or rejection). This verdict is normally assumed to be *definite*, *i.e.*, it cannot be retracted or revised, and is typically communicated to some higher-level entity responsible for handling monitor detections (*e.g.*, the user or some other supervising software component). Whereas few guarantees are expected of the system under scrutiny, in a monitoring setup, monitors are generally considered part of the trusted computing base (TCB) [86,109,134] and should manifest a level of correctness themselves. For instance, the verdicts produced by monitors should relate, in some sense, to the property being checked for (*e.g.*, a detected violation should only be flagged by a monitor when the system violates the property being checked) and monitors are also normally expected to interfere minimally (if at all) with the execution of the system under scrutiny. For this reason, monitors are usually generated by *automated synthesis procedures* that take a syntactic representation of the property as input and return the executable code of the monitor as a result. Apart from assisting and expediting monitor construction, automated monitor syntheses mitigate problems associated with the correctness of the monitor itself by standardizing monitor code and giving more scope for a formal treatment of their correctness.

Instrumentation is the computational plumbing that connects the execution of a system under scrutiny with the analysis performed by the monitor. It typically concerns itself with two aspects of the monitoring process. First, instrumentation determines what aspects of the system execution are made visible (to the monitor) for analysis. As depicted in Fig. 2, instrumentation records the relevant information from the computation of a running system (*e.g.*, program variable reads/writes, method/function calls and returns, memory management operations such as allocations and deallocations, lock acquisitions and releases, and communication operations such as channel inputs and outputs) and records them as system *events*. Event recording may either consist of redirecting and filtering out existing visible system behaviour, or it may involve extracting aspects of system behaviour that were previously not observable, transforming a black-box system into a grey-box one. The recorded events are then reported to the monitor in the form of an ordered stream called an *execution trace* (of events), which would normally correspond to the same notion introduced in the previous section. Instrumentation usually guarantees that the event order in the execution trace corresponds to the order in which the respective computational step occurred. However, there are cases such as in distributed settings where only a *partial ordering* of events can be reliably reported to the monitor.

Second, instrumentation also dictates how the system and the monitor execute in relation to one another in a monitoring setup. For instance, instrumentation may require the system to terminate executing before the monitor starts running, or interleave the respective executions of the system and the monitor that share a common execution thread. In concurrent settings, the system and monitor typically have their own execution threads, and instrumentation may dictates how tightly coupled these executions need to be. The instrumentation may either require that the respective threads to execute synchronously regulated by a global (symbolic) clock [78], or else allow threads to execute asynchronously to one another and then specify synchronisation points between the respective executions. The latter organisation may, in turn, impinge on the timeliness of monitor detections in relation to when the system exhibits a violation to the property being monitored for [46].

Monitoring setups need not necessarily be to confined to the structure and functionality depicted in Fig. 2. In *Monitor-Oriented Programming* (MOP) [49,50], monitoring is envisaged more as a code design principle advocating for the separation of concerns between the core functionality of a system and ancillary functionality that deals with aspects such as safety, security, reliability and robustness. Code is thus organised as a layered architecture where the innermost core consists of the plain-vanilla system, and the outer layers are made up of monitors observing the execution of the inner layers and reacting to these observations [46]. In MOP, monitors typically do more than just analyse execution traces and raise detections; they may suppress observable behaviour from the inner-layers or filter stimuli coming from outer layers [35,81,114], or inject adaptation actions affecting the structure and future behaviour of the inner layers [45,60,94].

3.2   Monitor Synthesis and Deployment Design Choices

In general, monitoring setups come in various shapes and sizes, and might differ slightly from the clean conceptual view presented in Fig. 2. In what follows, we overview a few of the possible variations commonly encountered in the literature.

Offline, Online, Synchronous and Asynchronous Monitoring. In offline monitoring (or logging) the analysis is carried out *after* the system executes. Relevant system events are recorded as an execution trace inside a permanent data store (*e.g.*, a file) which is then passed on to the monitor for analysis. Since the execution of the monitor is independent of that of the executing system, an offline analysis is less intrusive and certain constraints such as low monitor runtime overheads do not apply. Offline monitoring also benefits from the fact that the captured execution trace typically describes complete executions, which allows for global trace analyses—these often require backwards traversal [131].

By contrast, online monitoring is performed *during* system execution. It addresses one of the main disadvantages of its offline counterpart, namely that of *late detections*: a violation to a property is only discovered once the system execution terminates, potentially missing the opportunity to mitigate the damage resulting from that violation. Online monitoring operates within tighter constraints such as working with partial executions (*i.e.,* up to the current execution point), stringent requirements for low overheads and, because of this, the need to perform the analysis in incremental fashion.

The simultaneous execution of the system and the monitor may be performed in a variety of ways. At one extreme, *synchronous* online monitoring instruments the system and monitor to execute in lock-step: every time the system generates an event, it waits for the monitor to process it before proceeding with its execution (monitors are by nature passive entities and their execution depends on systems to generate events). At the other extreme, *asynchronous* online monitoring detaches the execution of the monitor from that of the system. This approach is less intrusive on system execution when compared to synchronous monitoring, typically leading to lower overheads [44], but may still yield a degree of late detections (especially when the underlying platform does not guarantee fair executions between the monitor and the system). Due to this, cross-breed approaches that fall on the spectrum in between these two approaches are used to obtain the best of both worlds; consult [47] for a comprehensive survey on this spectrum of approaches.

Monolithic, Decentralised, Orchestrated and Choreographed Monitor Approaches. There are a number of strategies for synthesising monitors from a particular specification. By far, the most common approach is to synthesise a single monitor that represents the entire specification as one monolithic block (*e.g.,* [30]). Increasingly however, new synthesis strategies are being explored. For instance, the work in [8,33,93,117,122] synthesise concurrently executing monitors to better exploit the underlying parallel hardware consisting of multiple processing units whereas the work in [9,32,68,69,79] synthesise component-based monitors to better localise analysis due to multiple event sources and heterogeneous hardware. Distribution is another important aspect affecting the monitor synthesis. In general, there are two main strategies for coordinating the monitoring activity across the various distributed locations. Orchestration relies on a single coordinating entity to gather, order and analyse events whereas a choreographed approach disseminates these tasks across a number of monitors [56,91]. Whereas orchestration is typically simpler to synthesise, thus easier to get right, choreography is more attuned to the characteristics of distributed computing, leading to lower network traffic and a higher degree of fault tolerance [68]. This topic is discussed further in a dedicated chapter.

Inlining Monitor Code Versus Monitor Code Separation. Monitoring can be either inlined [51,71,138] or consolidated as a separate code unit with events of interest being sent to it (often referred to as outlined). Figure 2 describes more of a conceptual view rather than the actual implementation, and covers both alternatives. In multi-threaded settings, inlining of inter-thread monitoring requires a *choreographed* setup [91,138] whereas keeping monitor code separate also affords a centralised *orchestrated* solution. Monitor inlining tends to yield lower overheads and is generally more expressive because it has full access of the system code [71]. By contrast, having monitoring as a separate unit minimally alters the code of the monitored system (all the decision branching is performed inside the monitor), is less error-prone (orchestration tends to be easier to program than monitor choreographies and is harder to tamper with), allows monitor computation to be offloaded to other machines [57], and facilitates compositional analysis whereby monitors may be more readily treated in isolation [1,86,87,90].

4   Instrumentation

The term *instrumentation* refers to the mechanism employed to probe and to extract signals, traces of events and other information of interest from a software or hardware system during its execution.

The instrumentation is an important phase in runtime verification setup enabling monitors to be hooked on to the system. The choice of instrumentation techniques depends on the type of system to be monitored. For example, monitoring hardware system may require probing mixed-analog signals using physical wires, while for software the instrumentation method is strictly related to the programming language in which the software is implemented or to the low-level language in which it is compiled (i.e., bytecode, assembly, etc.). In the following we further explain these concepts in two dedicated sections for hardware and software instrumentation.

4.1   Hardware Instrumentation

The increased level of integration, complexity and functionality of the new generation of analog/mixed-signal (AMS) and digital system-on-chip (SoC) technology demands for always new efficient and effective methods to observe and to analyze SoC behaviour both at the physical and at the operational level [4,5,104,105,125,133,135–137].

Due to the complexity of their design, the simulation of such systems is becoming very time-consuming and expensive. For this reason, simulation is generally complemented with design emulation that uses dedicated acceleration platforms such as Field Programmable Gate Arrays (FPGAs) to implement the design under test in hardware. Thus, monitoring the behaviour of an emulated design is an important task supporting the verification of the pre-silicon design. Figure 3 shows two examples of hardware instrumentation in such scenarios [104]. In the first case (a) the emulated design and the monitor are two independent pieces of hardware. They both share the same source of external clock. The available digital and analog output pins of the emulated design are hooked with physical wires to the hardware monitor. The analog signals are transformed into digital ones using an analog-to-digital (ADC) converter. The obtained signals are then processed synchronously using also a dedicated hardware implementing a monitor. An oscilloscope is employed to observe the verdict of the monitor at

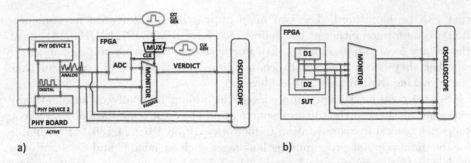

Fig. 3. Monitoring design under test: (a) the hardware monitor is external to the design under test sharing the same clock generator; (b) the emulated design is implemented together with the monitor in the same hardware.

runtime. In the second case (b) both the monitor and the design are implemented using the same hardware.

However, simulation and emulation are not able to cover all the aspects of the physical hardware and in particular the software related aspects. In order to check software related problems, large multiprocessor architectures usually require many cycles of executions. In such cases either simulation or emulation may result in too complex and expensive tasks to perform. For this reason, modern SoC have embedded test functionalities, providing a dedicated debug interface [143] called JTAG (also referred as the IEEE Specification 1149.1).

JTAG is a test architecture equipped with a serial interface and other debugging features enabling to sample snapshots of individual SoC pin signals and to drive specific output signals. JTAG is nowadays the most popular standard for on-chip instrumentation. Many modern processor architectures such as ARM, x86, MIPS are using JTAG protocol as the foundation for complex data/instruction tracing and debugging. The JTAG port enables the control over the processor that can be halted, single stepped or run freely. However, the possibility to halt the processor running real-time applications can introduce delays in the normal execution altering important timing constraints of the system. For this reason, some designs enable debuggers to access only registers and data buses without the need of halting the processors. Special dedicated on-chip circular memory buffers called *embedded trace buffers* (EBU) [143] can be employed to store compressed trace information enabling non-intrusive observation of the program trace [63]. We refer the reader to [143] for a detailed survey of other hardware instrumentation techniques.

4.2 Software Instrumentation

Software instrumentation (SI) is a well-established method employed in many applications including software profiling, performance analysis, optimization, testing and runtime verification. SI consists in adding extra code to track the execution of particular software components and to output an execution trace that can be monitored. The two main approaches for software instrumentation are performed either at the *source code level* [10,36,107,124,139,141] or at the *binary level* [34,40,110,116,121]. Furthermore, SI can be *static* or *dynamic* whether they occur before (i.e., compilation-/link-time) or at execution time (i.e., tracking dynamically linked libraries).

Source code instrumentation consists in adding manually or automatically extra instructions to the software source files before the compilation. Nowadays, there are several instrumentation frameworks [10,36,107,124,139,141] available for the main popular programming languages such as Java, C and C++, or even mobile platforms running on Android [61,67,73,74]. For example, *aspect-oriented programming* (AOP) environments usually provide static weaving mechanisms that enable to add at compile-time an additional behaviour to the existing source code without modifying the original source code. The key idea (see Fig. 4) is to apply special instructions and code segments (called *advices*) contained in a specification file (*aspect*) that indicate what methods (called *pointcuts*) should be handled by the aspect code. For example, it is possible to specify how to add some additional code to log all the function calls when the function's name starts with a particular prefix. An *aspect weaver* is then the component responsible to process the *advice* instructions and *weave* them together with original source files, generating the final source code that is compiled into an executable. Although in many AOP frameworks the weaving is generally performed statically at the level of source code, there are also cases such as in AspectWerkz [39] where the weaving can occur also dynamically at level of bytecode.

SI is generally limited by the execution coverage. This means that if some parts of the instrumented code are not reachable during the execution, the instrumentation will not provide any information. Furthermore, SI generally introduces a computational overhead that changes the timing-related behaviour of the instrumented program. This could be unacceptable in applications where preserving real-time constraints is extremely important to meet safety critical requirements. In the worst case scenario the overhead of SI may be also the responsible of timing related *Heisenbugs* [84,146], bugs that disappear or are altered in the instrumented program. For all these reasons, in the last decade, there has been a great effort to develop new approaches [6,38,83,84,98,103] for controlling and mitigating the computational overhead due to SI.

These approaches generally employ sampling-based techniques that reduce the overhead by selecting only a limited and controlled number of events. However, sampling-based techniques are prone to introduce gaps in the output trace, leading to uncertainty in the monitoring result. To quantify such uncertainty, a possible approach (developed in [24,106,142]) is to learn statistical models of the monitored system and to use them to "fill in" sampling-induced gaps in event sequences, and then computing the probability that the property of interest is satisfied or violated.

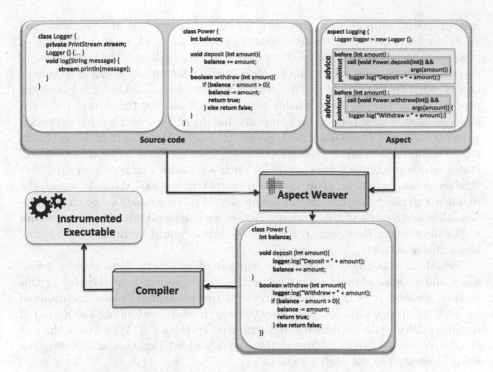

Fig. 4. Example of instrumentation of the Java source code with AspectJ.

5   Monitorability: What Can We Monitor?

In this section, we discuss the (notion of) monitorability of properties. Informally, studying the monitorability of a property consists in determining whether or not a property is monitorable, that is, determining whether it is worth monitoring that property at runtime. Intuitively, it is worth monitoring a property if, during monitoring, the monitor can still provide an evaluation (in the form of a verdict) of the current execution and one can avoid situations in which a monitor would inevitably provide inconclusive verdicts.

When using a formalism to write properties (specifying the expected system behaviour), one of the questions that arise is whether all properties that are expressible in this formalism can be monitored. Thus, the monitorability question naturally depends on the specification formalism. Moreover, monitorability also depends on the nature of the decision procedure implemented by a runtime monitor. At runtime, a monitor tries to assign a verdict to the current *observation* σ (which is by nature finite) by determining whether σ is a model or not of the monitored property. Hence, when using a formalism with a semantics over infinite sequences (that is, the models of the properties are infinite executions), monitorability issues arise when relating finite sequences to infinite ones. To intuitively illustrate this issue, consider the two properties "predicate p always holds" and "whenever predicate p holds, predicate q holds in the future". For the first property, suppose that a monitor for this property has in so far observed an execution wherein all observed states predicate p held. In this situation, a monitor is useful because one can later obtain a state leading to the falsification of p and a monitor could detect that an observation wherein p does not hold cannot be extended to the correct infinite correct executions (which are models of the property) wherein predicate p holds at every position. For the second property, suppose that a monitor for this property has in so far observed an execution wherein whenever predicate p held, predicate q held on the next position. Then, suppose that this monitor observes predicate p and receives a certain number of states where predicate q does not hold. Such a monitor can not determine that this sequence cannot be continued to a correct execution. What is worse, the monitor can not relate this execution nor any of its continuations to the infinite ones that are models of the property. Hence, we can see intuitively that it is not worth monitoring that property and the monitor would be doomed producing inconclusive verdicts.

Based on the above informal description of monitorability, several definitions and visions of monitorable properties were proposed. In the rest of this section, we first present the definitions and the associated characterisations of monitorable properties. We note recent research efforts extending the notion of monitorability to decentralised and distributed systems [68]. We focus in the rest of this section to monitorability in the centralised setting, that is following the setup presented in the earlier sections.

5.1 Definitions of Monitorability

Monitoring to detect bad behaviors. The first definition of monitorability was given by Kim et al. [108]. In their definition, monitoring is purposed to detect violations of properties. They consider safety properties over infinite executions. Since for any safety property, any bad (infinite) execution has a finite prefix that cannot be extended to a correct execution, it is possible to detect any violation of a safety property with a finite sequence. However, the detection of such bad prefixes should be computable. Hence, a property $\varphi \subseteq \Sigma^\omega$ is said to be monitorable if $\Sigma^* \setminus \mathrm{pref}(\varphi)$ is co-recursively enumerable, where $\mathrm{pref}(\varphi)$ is the set of prefixes of φ.

Monitoring to detect good and bad behaviors. Pnueli and Zaks later generalised the notion of monitorability [128]. The underlying principles behind their definition are twofold: a monitor can be also used to detect good behaviours, and a monitor should be running only if it has the possibility to reach a verdict. In their definition, a monitor is purposed to determine whether the current execution leads to infinite continuations that are models of the monitored property. A monitor can then determine a verdict whenever either every continuation of the current observation is a model or every continuation is a counter-example of the monitored property. Moreover, it is worth monitoring as long as the monitor can find a verdict with a possible continuation of the observed sequence.

More precisely, their definition of monitorability comes as follows. For a property $\varphi \subseteq \Sigma^\omega$, and given the current execution $\sigma \in \Sigma^*$, φ is said to be positively determined by σ if all (infinite) continuations of σ satisfy φ. Conversely, Pnueli and Zaks also define the notion of negative determinacy. Whenever an execution σ positively (resp. negatively) determines a property φ, a monitor for φ associates verdict $\top$ (resp. $\bot$) with σ. Then, φ is said to be σ-monitorable, if σ has a continuation such that φ is either positively or negatively determined by this continuation. Finally, a property is monitorable if it is σ-monitorable, for any $\sigma \in \Sigma^*$.

We note that in [65], Diekert and Leucker provide an equivalent topological definition of monitorability. Given a property to monitor φ over some alphabet Σ and an execution sequence $\sigma \in \Sigma^*$, φ is monitorable at σ (alternatively σ-monitorable) if every open set O_σ containing σ has a subset SO_σ such that either $SO_\sigma \subseteq \varphi$ or $SO_\sigma \subseteq (\Sigma^* \setminus \varphi)$, which one can understand as σ has a continuation that positively or negatively determines φ. And then φ is monitorable if it is monitorable at every $\sigma \in \Sigma^*$.

Monitoring with a parameterised verdict domain. The previous definition of monitorability implicitly uses the 3-valued truth-domain $\{\bot, ?, \top\}$ where $\bot$ and $\top$ are final verdicts (i.e., assigned once and never changed) and verdict ? is emitted by the monitor for other sequences (i.e., those not allowing it to reach a final verdict). Falcone et al. argue that in some situations, one may monitor only to detect satisfactions or violations in separation [76]. Hence, they parameterised the definition of monitorability by a truth-domain $\mathbb{B}$ that contains at least one final verdict.

Monitoring with a semantics for finite executions. To account for the situations where the monitored program stops before the monitor is able to reach a final verdict (i.e., when the last verdict is ?), Falcone et al. introduce a notion of monitorability taking finite executions into account [76]. The definitions requires the specification formalism to be endowed with a semantics over finite sequences including verdicts $\top_c$ and $\bot_c$ used to indicate that the property is *currently true* and *currently false*, respectively. An execution sequence evaluates to $\top$ and $\bot$ as in the definition of Pnueli et al. [128], and it evaluates to $\top_c$ (resp. $\bot_c$) as long as no definitive verdict has been found and the current execution sequence satisfies (resp. does not satisfy) the property. Intuitively, for a property to be monitorable, the evaluations of the property on correct and incorrect finite executions should differ so that a monitor is able to detect in a sound manner the situations in which it should emit a final verdict.

Monitoring for a branching-time logic. Francalanza et al. [89,90] study the problem of monitoring for branching-time logics and define μ-HML a reformulation of μ-calculus as a branching-time logic with least and greatest fix-points. Monitorability of a formula in this logic amounts to being able to synthesise a sound monitor that is able to detect all violations or all satisfactions of the formula. A salient aspect of this body of work is the identification of a maximally-expressive syntactic subset of the logic whereby any monitorable property is guaranteed to be expressible within this syntactic subset (similar maximality guarantees are also given in the context of LTL in [54]). More importantly, the branching nature of the logic considered gives scope for considering monitoring setups that depart from the classic setup consisting of one system execution generating a single trace, since alternative setups may extend the set of monitorable properties.

5.2 Characterisations of Monitorable Properties

We now report on the existing characterisations of monitorable properties. Characterising monitorable properties as a class of properties is important because, when specifying a system, it allows determining the monitorability of the specified property just by determining the class to which the property belongs (for instance using the syntactic elements used to construct the property).

Characterisation for the definition in [108]. Kim et al. directly define monitorable properties as the class of safety properties such that the set of prefixes is co-recursively enumerable.

Characterisation for the definition in [128]. The definition of monitorability in [128] is the most studied one. Bauer et al. [29,30] prove that the set of monitorable properties in the sense of [128] is a (strict) superset of the union of safety and co-safety properties. Falcone et al. [75,76] prove that the set of monitorable properties in the sense of [128] is a (strict) super set of the set of obligation properties (which are formed by finite conjunctions and disjunctions of safety and co-safety properties). They also prove that adding additional verdicts to the definition of monitorability in [128] does not allow monitoring more properties. Later in [65], Diekert and Leucker enunciate the same results as in [76] from a topological perspective. They additionally prove that any countable union/disjunction or any countable intersection/conjunction of monitorable sets/properties is also monitorable. In [66] Diekert et al. study the complexity of deciding monitorability. They show that (i) deciding whether a Büchi automaton defines a monitorable property is PSPACE-complete, and (ii) deciding whether an LTL formula defines a monitorable property is PSPACE-hard and EXPSPACE-easy.

Characterisation for the definition in [76]. Falcone et al. [76] prove that the set of monitorable properties in the sense of [76] forms a strict subset of obligation properties. They also prove that the definition in [76] allows monitoring any (linear-time) property when used with truth-domain $\{\bot, \bot_c, \top_c, \top\}$.

6   Overview of the Book

The idea of this book originated from the need to support the students' training with tutorials covering different aspects of RV. The volume has been organised into seven chapters. This chapter can be considered a primer to the field and necessary knowledge for the rest of this book.

The second chapter [115] is dedicated to the detection of concurrency errors raised in concurrent programming. It presents how dynamic analysis techniques can be used for the detection and localisation of data races, atomicity violations, and deadlocks.

The third chapter [102] shows to adapt early-stage runtime verification frameworks wherein events are names to events that carry date. It shows how adding data to events complexifies the specification language and the underlying monitoring algorithms. It also provides an overview of five specification formalisms and associated monitoring algorithms.

The fourth chapter [80] presents how runtime monitors can be used to prevent and react to failures to increase the dependability of systems. In particular, it presents the two main techniques for such purposes, namely runtime enforcement and healing failures, respectively.

The fifth chapter [22] revolves around the techniques for the monitoring of specifications on cyber-physical systems. The behaviour of cyber-physical systems is modelled by continuous state variables interleaved with discrete events. The chapter presents state-of-the-art techniques for using qualitative and quantitative monitoring techniques either during simulation or when the system is running. The chapter also provides example applications and compares exiting tools.

The sixth chapter [92] tackles the emerging and important topics of decentralised monitoring and distributed monitoring. The chapter identifies the distinguishing features of decentralised and distributed systems and classifies the existing approaches along these features.

The seventh chapter [58] is dedicated to the application of runtime verification to industrial systems and more particularly on financial transaction systems. This chapter places runtime verification in the development lifecycle of a software. It interestingly describes some of the properties that can be useful in real-life applications. Moreover, it reports on some of the lessons learned by the authors and outlines some of the challenges to address for RV to become an industrial practice.

7 Conclusion

We have provided a brief introduction to the field of runtime verification covering four major topics: how to specify system behaviour, how to setup monitoring, how to perform instrumentation, and what the limitations of monitoring are. We refer the reader to the other chapters in this book and other introductions to RV [18,72,112] for further details on the topic.

Acknowledgment. All the authors acknowledge the support of the ICT COST Action IC1402 Runtime Verification beyond Monitoring (ARVI). Ezio Bartocci acknowledges the Austrian National Research Network (nr. S 11405-N23) SHiNE funded by the Austrian Science Fund (FWF).

References

1. Aceto, L., Achilleos, A., Francalanza, A., Ingólfsdóttir, A.: Monitoring for silent actions. In: FSTTCS. LIPIcs, vol. 93, pp. 43:1–43:14 (2017, to appear)
2. Allan, C., Avgustinov, P., Christensen, A.S., Hendren, L., Kuzins, S., Lhoták, O., de Moor, O., Sereni, D., Sittampalam, G., Tibble, J.: Adding trace matching with free variables to AspectJ. SIGPLAN Not. **40**(10), 345–364 (2005)
3. Alur, R., Etessami, K., Madhusudan, P.: A temporal logic of nested calls and returns. In: Jensen, K., Podelski, A. (eds.) TACAS 2004. LNCS, vol. 2988, pp. 467–481. Springer, Heidelberg (2004). https://doi.org/10.1007/978-3-540-24730-2_35
4. Amiar, A., Delahaye, M., Falcone, Y., du Bousquet, L.: Compressing microcontroller execution traces to assist system analysis. In: Schirner, G., Götz, M., Rettberg, A., Zanella, M.C., Rammig, F.J. (eds.) IESS 2013. IAICT, vol. 403, pp. 139–150. Springer, Heidelberg (2013). https://doi.org/10.1007/978-3-642-38853-8_13
5. Amiar, A., Delahaye, M., Falcone, Y., du Bousquet, L.: Fault localization in embedded software based on a single cyclic trace. In: IEEE 24th International Symposium on Software Reliability Engineering, ISSRE 2013, Pasadena, CA, USA, 4–7 November 2013, pp. 148–157. IEEE Computer Society (2013)
6. Arnold, M., Vechev, M.T., Yahav, E.: QVM: an efficient runtime for detecting defects in deployed systems. In: Proceedings of OOPSLA 2008: The 23rd Annual ACM SIGPLAN Conference on Object-Oriented Programming, Systems, Languages, and Applications, pp. 143–162. ACM (2008)
7. Asarin, E., Caspi, P., Maler, O.: Timed regular expressions. J. ACM **49**, 2002 (2001)
8. Attard, D.P., Francalanza, A.: A monitoring tool for a branching-time logic. In: Falcone, Y., Sánchez, C. (eds.) RV 2016. LNCS, vol. 10012, pp. 473–481. Springer, Cham (2016). https://doi.org/10.1007/978-3-319-46982-9_31
9. Attard, D.P., Francalanza, A.: Trace partitioning and local monitoring for asynchronous components. In: Cimatti, A., Sirjani, M. (eds.) SEFM 2017. LNCS, vol. 10469, pp. 219–235. Springer, Cham (2017). https://doi.org/10.1007/978-3-319-66197-1_14
10. Avgustinov, P., Christensen, A.S., Hendren, L.J., Kuzins, S., Lhoták, J., Lhoták, O., de Moor, O., Sereni, D., Sittampalam, G., Tibble, J.: abc: an extensible AspectJ compiler. Trans. Aspect-Oriented Softw. Dev. I **3880**(3880), 293–334 (2006)
11. Baader, F., Bauer, A., Lippmann, M.: Runtime verification using a temporal description logic. In: Ghilardi, S., Sebastiani, R. (eds.) FroCoS 2009. LNCS (LNAI), vol. 5749, pp. 149–164. Springer, Heidelberg (2009). https://doi.org/10.1007/978-3-642-04222-5_9
12. Barringer, H., Falcone, Y., Havelund, K., Reger, G., Rydeheard, D.: Quantified event automata: towards expressive and efficient runtime monitors. In: Giannakopoulou, D., Méry, D. (eds.) FM 2012. LNCS, vol. 7436, pp. 68–84. Springer, Heidelberg (2012). https://doi.org/10.1007/978-3-642-32759-9_9
13. Barringer, H., Goldberg, A., Havelund, K., Sen, K.:. Program monitoring with LTL in EAGLE. In: 18th International Parallel and Distributed Processing Symposium (IPDPS 2004), Abstracts Proceedings, 26–30 April 2004, Santa Fe, New Mexico, USA (2004)

14. Barringer, H., Goldberg, A., Havelund, K., Sen, K.: Rule-based runtime verification. In: Steffen, B., Levi, G. (eds.) VMCAI 2004. LNCS, vol. 2937, pp. 44–57. Springer, Heidelberg (2004). https://doi.org/10.1007/978-3-540-24622-0_5
15. Barringer, H., Havelund, K.: TRACECONTRACT: a scala DSL for trace analysis. In: Butler, M., Schulte, W. (eds.) FM 2011. LNCS, vol. 6664, pp. 57–72. Springer, Heidelberg (2011). https://doi.org/10.1007/978-3-642-21437-0_7
16. Barringer, H., Rydeheard, D.E., Havelund, K.: Rule systems for run-time monitoring: from Eagle to RuleR. J. Log. Comput. **20**(3), 675–706 (2010)
17. Bartocci, E., Bonakdarpour, B., Falcone, Y.: First international competition on software for runtime verification. In: Bonakdarpour, B., Smolka, S.A. (eds.) RV 2014. LNCS, vol. 8734, pp. 1–9. Springer, Cham (2014). https://doi.org/10.1007/978-3-319-11164-3_1
18. Bartocci, E., Bortolussi, L., Loreti, M., Nenzi, L.: Monitoring mobile and spatially distributed cyber-physical systems. In: Proceedings of MEMOCODE 2017: The 15th ACM-IEEE International Conference on Formal Methods and Models for System Design, pp. 146–155. ACM (2017)
19. Bartocci, E., Bortolussi, L., Milios, D., Nenzi, L., Sanguinetti, G.: Studying emergent behaviours in morphogenesis using signal spatio-temporal logic. In: Abate, A., Šafránek, D. (eds.) HSB 2015. LNCS, vol. 9271, pp. 156–172. Springer, Cham (2015). https://doi.org/10.1007/978-3-319-26916-0_9
20. Bartocci, E., Corradini, F., Merelli, E., Tesei, L.: Model checking biological oscillators. Electr. Notes Theor. Comput. Sci. **229**(1), 41–58 (2009)
21. Bartocci, E., Corradini, F., Merelli, E., Tesei, L.: Detecting synchronisation of biological oscillators by model checking. Theor. Comput. Sci. **411**(20), 1999–2018 (2010)
22. Bartocci, E., Deshmukh, J., Donzé, A., Fainekos, G., Maler, O., Nickovic, D., Sankaranarayanan, S.: Specification-based monitoring of cyber-physical systems: a survey on theory, tools and applications. In: Bartocci, E., Falcone, Y. (eds.) Lectures on Runtime Verification. LNCS, vol. 10457, pp. 135–175. Springer, Cham (2018)
23. Bartocci, E., Falcone, Y., Bonakdarpour, B., Colombo, C., Decker, N., Havelund, K., Joshi, Y., Klaedtke, F., Milewicz, R., Reger, G., Rosu, G., Signoles, J., Thoma, D., Zalinescu, E., Zhang, Y.: First international competition on runtime verification: rules, benchmarks, tools, and final results of CRV 2014. Int. J. Softw. Tools Technol. Transf. (2017)
24. Bartocci, E., Grosu, R., Karmarkar, A., Smolka, S.A., Stoller, S.D., Zadok, E., Seyster, J.: Adaptive runtime verification. In: Qadeer, S., Tasiran, S. (eds.) RV 2012. LNCS, vol. 7687, pp. 168–182. Springer, Heidelberg (2013). https://doi.org/10.1007/978-3-642-35632-2_18
25. Basin, D.A., Klaedtke, F., Müller, S., Zalinescu, E.: Monitoring metric first-order temporal properties. J. ACM **62**(2), 15:1–15:45 (2015)
26. Basin, D., Klaedtke, F., Zălinescu, E.: Runtime verification of temporal properties over out-of-order data streams. In: Majumdar, R., Kunčak, V. (eds.) CAV 2017. LNCS, vol. 10426, pp. 356–376. Springer, Cham (2017). https://doi.org/10.1007/978-3-319-63387-9_18
27. Basin, D., Krstić, S., Traytel, D.: Almost event-rate independent monitoring of metric dynamic logic. In: Lahiri, S., Reger, G. (eds.) RV 2017. LNCS, vol. 10548, pp. 85–102. Springer, Cham (2017). https://doi.org/10.1007/978-3-319-67531-2_6
28. Bauer, A., Küster, J.-C., Vegliach, G.: The ins and outs of first-order runtime verification. Form. Methods Syst. Des. **46**(3), 286–316 (2015)

29. Bauer, A., Leucker, M., Schallhart, C.: The good, the bad, and the ugly, but how ugly is ugly? In: Sokolsky, O., Taşıran, S. (eds.) RV 2007. LNCS, vol. 4839, pp. 126–138. Springer, Heidelberg (2007). https://doi.org/10.1007/978-3-540-77395-5_11

30. Bauer, A., Leucker, M., Schallhart, C.: Runtime verification for LTL and TLTL. ACM Trans. Softw. Eng. Methodol. **20**(4), 14:1–14:64 (2011)

31. Bauer, A., Leucker, M., Streit, J.: SALT—structured assertion language for temporal logic. In: Liu, Z., He, J. (eds.) ICFEM 2006. LNCS, vol. 4260, pp. 757–775. Springer, Heidelberg (2006). https://doi.org/10.1007/11901433_41

32. Bauer, A.K., Falcone, Y.: Decentralised LTL monitoring. Form. Methods Syst. Des. **48**(1–2), 49–93 (2016)

33. Berkovich, S., Bonakdarpour, B., Fischmeister, S.: Runtime verification with minimal intrusion through parallelism. Form. Methods Syst. Des. **46**(3), 317–348 (2015)

34. Bernat, A.R., Miller, B.P.: Anywhere, any-time binary instrumentation. In: Proceedings of PASTE 2011: The 10th ACM SIGPLAN-SIGSOFT Workshop on Program Analysis for Software Tools, pp. 9–16. ACM (2011)

35. Bielova, N., Massacci, F.: Do you really mean what you actually enforced?: edited automata revisited. Int. J. Inf. Secur. **10**(4), 239–254 (2011)

36. Bodden, E., Havelund, K.: Racer: effective race detection using AspectJ. In: Proceedings of ISSTA 2008: The 2008 International Symposium on Software Testing and Analysis, ISSTA 2008, pp. 155–166. ACM (2008)

37. Bollig, B., Decker, N., Leucker, M.: Frequency linear-time temporal logic. In: Proceedings of the 6th International Symposium on Theoretical Aspects of Software Engineering (TASE 2012), Beijing, China, pp. 85–92. IEEE Computer Society Press (2012)

38. Bonakdarpour, B., Navabpour, S., Fischmeister, S.: Sampling-based runtime verification. In: Butler, M., Schulte, W. (eds.) FM 2011. LNCS, vol. 6664, pp. 88–102. Springer, Heidelberg (2011). https://doi.org/10.1007/978-3-642-21437-0_9

39. Bonér, J.: What are the key issues for commercial AOP use: how does AspectWerkz address them? In: Proceedings of the 3rd International Conference on Aspect-Oriented Software Development, AOSD 2004, Lancaster, UK, 22–24 March 2004, pp. 5–6. ACM (2004)

40. Bruening, D., Garnett, T., Amarasinghe, S.P.: An infrastructure for adaptive dynamic optimization. In: Proceedings of CGO 2003: The 1st IEEE/ACM International Symposium on Code Generation and Optimization, pp. 265–275. IEEE Computer Society (2003)

41. Bultan, T., Sen, K. (eds.): Proceedings of the 26th ACM SIGSOFT International Symposium on Software Testing and Analysis. ACM, New York (2017)

42. Calafato, A., Colombo, C., Pace, G.J.: A controlled natural language for tax fraud detection. In: Davis, B., Pace, G.J.J., Wyner, A. (eds.) CNL 2016. LNCS (LNAI), vol. 9767, pp. 1–12. Springer, Cham (2016). https://doi.org/10.1007/978-3-319-41498-0_1

43. Calder, M., Sevegnani, M.: Process algebra for event-driven runtime verification: a case study of wireless network management. In: Derrick, J., Gnesi, S., Latella, D., Treharne, H. (eds.) IFM 2012. LNCS, vol. 7321, pp. 21–23. Springer, Heidelberg (2012). https://doi.org/10.1007/978-3-642-30729-4_2

44. Cassar, I., Francalanza, A.: On synchronous and asynchronous monitor instrumentation for actor-based systems. In: Proceedings 13th International Workshop on Foundations of Coordination Languages and Self-Adaptive Systems. Electronic Proceedings in Theoretical Computer Science, Rome, Italy, 6th September 2014, vol. 175, pp. 54–68. Open Publishing Association (2015)
45. Cassar, I., Francalanza, A.: Runtime adaptation for actor systems. In: Bartocci, E., Majumdar, R. (eds.) RV 2015. LNCS, vol. 9333, pp. 38–54. Springer, Cham (2015). https://doi.org/10.1007/978-3-319-23820-3_3
46. Cassar, I., Francalanza, A.: On implementing a monitor-oriented programming framework for actor systems. In: Ábrahám, E., Huisman, M. (eds.) IFM 2016. LNCS, vol. 9681, pp. 176–192. Springer, Cham (2016). https://doi.org/10.1007/978-3-319-33693-0_12
47. Cassar, I., Francalanza, A., Aceto, L., Ingólfsdóttir, A.: A survey of runtime monitoring instrumentation techniques. In: PrePost@iFM. EPTCS, vol. 254, pp. 15–28 (2017)
48. Cau, A., Zedan, H.: Refining interval temporal logic specifications. In: Bertran, M., Rus, T. (eds.) ARTS 1997. LNCS, vol. 1231, pp. 79–94. Springer, Heidelberg (1997). https://doi.org/10.1007/3-540-63010-4_6
49. Chen, F., Roşu, G.: Towards monitoring-oriented programming: a paradigm combining specification and implementation. In: ENTCS, pp. 106–125. Elsevier (2003)
50. Chen, F., Roşu, G.: Java-MOP: a monitoring oriented programming environment for Java. In: Halbwachs, N., Zuck, L.D. (eds.) TACAS 2005. LNCS, vol. 3440, pp. 546–550. Springer, Heidelberg (2005). https://doi.org/10.1007/978-3-540-31980-1_36
51. Chen, F., Roşu, G.: MOP: an efficient and generic runtime verification framework. In: OOPSLA, pp. 569–588. ACM Press (2007)
52. Chen, F., Roşu, G.: Parametric trace slicing and monitoring. In: Kowalewski, S., Philippou, A. (eds.) TACAS 2009. LNCS, vol. 5505, pp. 246–261. Springer, Heidelberg (2009). https://doi.org/10.1007/978-3-642-00768-2_23
53. Chomicki, J.: Efficient checking of temporal integrity constraints using bounded history encoding. ACM Trans. Database Syst. **20**(2), 149–186 (1995)
54. Cini, C., Francalanza, A.: An LTL proof system for runtime verification. In: Baier, C., Tinelli, C. (eds.) TACAS 2015. LNCS, vol. 9035, pp. 581–595. Springer, Heidelberg (2015). https://doi.org/10.1007/978-3-662-46681-0_54
55. Clarkson, M.R., Finkbeiner, B., Koleini, M., Micinski, K.K., Rabe, M.N., Sánchez, C.: Temporal logics for hyperproperties. In: Abadi, M., Kremer, S. (eds.) POST 2014. LNCS, vol. 8414, pp. 265–284. Springer, Heidelberg (2014). https://doi.org/10.1007/978-3-642-54792-8_15
56. Colombo, C., Falcone, Y.: Organising LTL monitors over distributed systems with a global clock. Form. Methods Syst. Des. **49**(1–2), 109–158 (2016)
57. Colombo, C., Francalanza, A., Mizzi, R., Pace, G.J.: polyLARVA: runtime verification with configurable resource-aware monitoring boundaries. In: Eleftherakis, G., Hinchey, M., Holcombe, M. (eds.) SEFM 2012. LNCS, vol. 7504, pp. 218–232. Springer, Heidelberg (2012). https://doi.org/10.1007/978-3-642-33826-7_15
58. Colombo, C., Pace, G.J.: Industrial experiences with runtime verification of financial transaction systems: lessons learnt and standing challenges. In: Bartocci, E., Falcone, Y. (eds.) Lectures on Runtime Verification. LNCS, vol. 10457, pp. 211–232. Springer, Cham (2018)

59. Colombo, C., Pace, G.J., Schneider, G.: LARVA – safer monitoring of real-time java programs (tool paper). In: Proceedings of SEFM 2009: The Seventh IEEE International Conference on Software Engineering and Formal Methods, pp. 33–37. IEEE Computer Society (2009)
60. Coppo, M., Dezani-Ciancaglini, M., Venneri, B.: Self-adaptive monitors for multiparty sessions. In: PDP, pp. 688–696. IEEE Computer Society (2014)
61. Daian, P., Falcone, Y., Meredith, P., Şerbănuţă, T.F., Shiriashi, S., Iwai, A., Rosu, G.: RV-Android: efficient parametric android runtime verification, a brief tutorial. In: Bartocci, E., Majumdar, R. (eds.) RV 2015. LNCS, vol. 9333, pp. 342–357. Springer, Cham (2015). https://doi.org/10.1007/978-3-319-23820-3_24
62. De Giacomo, G., Vardi, M.Y.: Linear temporal logic and linear dynamic logic on finite traces. In: Proceedings of the Twenty-Third International Joint Conference on Artificial Intelligence, IJCAI 2013, pp. 854–860. AAAI Press (2013)
63. Decker, N., Gottschling, P., Hochberger, C., Leucker, M., Scheffel, T., Schmitz, M., Weiss, A.: Rapidly adjustable non-intrusive online monitoring for multi-core systems. In: Cavalheiro, S., Fiadeiro, J. (eds.) SBMF 2017. LNCS, vol. 10623, pp. 179–196. Springer, Cham (2017). https://doi.org/10.1007/978-3-319-70848-5_12
64. Decker, N., Thoma, D.: On freeze LTL with ordered attributes. In: Jacobs, B., Löding, C. (eds.) FoSSaCS 2016. LNCS, vol. 9634, pp. 269–284. Springer, Heidelberg (2016). https://doi.org/10.1007/978-3-662-49630-5_16
65. Diekert, V., Leucker, M.: Topology, monitorable properties and runtime verification. Theor. Comput. Sci. **537**, 29–41 (2014)
66. Diekert, V., Muscholl, A., Walukiewicz, I.: A note on monitors and Büchi automata. In: Leucker, M., Rueda, C., Valencia, F.D. (eds.) ICTAC 2015. LNCS, vol. 9399, pp. 39–57. Springer, Cham (2015). https://doi.org/10.1007/978-3-319-25150-9_3
67. El-Harake, K., Falcone, Y., Jerad, W., Langet, M., Mamlouk, M.: Blocking advertisements on android devices using monitoring techniques. In: Margaria, T., Steffen, B. (eds.) ISoLA 2014. LNCS, vol. 8803, pp. 239–253. Springer, Heidelberg (2014). https://doi.org/10.1007/978-3-662-45231-8_17
68. El-Hokayem, A., Falcone, Y.: Monitoring decentralized specifications. In: Bultan and Sen [41], pp. 125–135
69. El-Hokayem, A., Falcone, Y.: THEMIS: a tool for decentralized monitoring algorithms. In: Bultan and Sen [41], pp. 372–375
70. Emerson, E.A.: Temporal and modal logic. In: van Leeuwen, J. (ed.) Handbook of Theoretical Computer Science, Volume B: Formal Models and Sematics (B), pp. 995–1072. MIT Press, Cambridge (1990)
71. Erlingsson, U.: The inlined reference monitor approach to security policy enforcement. Ph.D. thesis, Cornell University (2004)
72. Falcone, Y., Havelund, K., Reger, G.: A tutorial on runtime verification. In: Broy, M., Peled, D. (eds.) Summer School Marktoberdorf 2012 - Engineering Dependable Software Systems. IOS Press, Amsterdam (2013)
73. Falcone, Y., Currea, S.: Weave droid: aspect-oriented programming on android devices: fully embedded or in the cloud. In: Goedicke, M., Menzies, T., Saeki, M. (eds.) IEEE/ACM International Conference on Automated Software Engineering, ASE 2012, Essen, Germany, 3–7 September 2012, pp. 350–353. ACM (2012)
74. Falcone, Y., Currea, S., Jaber, M.: Runtime verification and enforcement for Android applications with RV-Droid. In: Qadeer, S., Tasiran, S. (eds.) RV 2012. LNCS, vol. 7687, pp. 88–95. Springer, Heidelberg (2013). https://doi.org/10.1007/978-3-642-35632-2_11

75. Falcone, Y., Fernandez, J.-C., Mounier, L.: Runtime verification of safety-progress properties. In: Bensalem, S., Peled, D.A. (eds.) RV 2009. LNCS, vol. 5779, pp. 40–59. Springer, Heidelberg (2009). https://doi.org/10.1007/978-3-642-04694-0_4
76. Falcone, Y., Fernandez, J.-C., Mounier, L.: What can you verify and enforce at runtime? STTT **14**(3), 349–382 (2012)
77. Falcone, Y., Havelund, K., Reger, G.: A tutorial on runtime verification. In: Broy, M., Peled, D.A., Kalus, G. (eds.) Engineering Dependable Software Systems. NATO Science for Peace and Security Series, D: Information and Communication Security, vol. 34, pp. 141–175. IOS Press, Amsterdam (2013)
78. Falcone, Y., Jaber, M., Nguyen, T.-H., Bozga, M., Bensalem, S.: Runtime verification of component-based systems. In: Barthe, G., Pardo, A., Schneider, G. (eds.) SEFM 2011. LNCS, vol. 7041, pp. 204–220. Springer, Heidelberg (2011). https://doi.org/10.1007/978-3-642-24690-6_15
79. Falcone, Y., Jaber, M., Nguyen, T.-H., Bozga, M., Bensalem, S.: Runtime verification of component-based systems in the bip framework with formally-proved sound and complete instrumentation. Softw. Syst. Model. **14**(1), 173–199 (2015)
80. Falcone, Y., Mariani, L., Rollet, A., Saha, S.: Runtime failure prevention and reaction. In: Bartocci, E., Falcone, Y. (eds.) Lectures on Runtime Verification. LNCS, vol. 10457, pp. 103–134. Springer, Cham (2018)
81. Falcone, Y., Mounier, L., Fernandez, J.-C., Richier, J.-L.: Runtime enforcement monitors: composition, synthesis, and enforcement abilities. Form. Methods Syst. Des. **38**(3), 223–262 (2011)
82. Faymonville, P., Finkbeiner, B., Schirmer, S., Torfah, H.: A stream-based specification language for network monitoring. In: Falcone, Y., Sánchez, C. (eds.) RV 2016. LNCS, vol. 10012, pp. 152–168. Springer, Cham (2016). https://doi.org/10.1007/978-3-319-46982-9_10
83. Fei, L., Midkiff, S.P.: Artemis: practical runtime monitoring of applications for execution anomalies. In: Proceedings of the ACM SIGPLAN 2006: Conference on Programming Language Design and Implementation, pp. 84–95. ACM (2006)
84. Fischmeister, S., Lam, P.: On time-aware instrumentation of programs. In: Proceedings of the 2009 15th IEEE Symposium on Real-Time and Embedded Technology and Applications, RTAS 2009, pp. 305–314. IEEE Computer Society, Washington, DC (2009)
85. Foster, H.Q., Marschner, E., Wolfsthal, Y.: IEEE 1850 PSL: The Next Generation (2005)
86. Francalanza, A.: A theory of monitors. In: Jacobs, B., Löding, C. (eds.) FoSSaCS 2016. LNCS, vol. 9634, pp. 145–161. Springer, Heidelberg (2016). https://doi.org/10.1007/978-3-662-49630-5_9
87. Francalanza, A.: Consistently-detecting monitors. In: CONCUR. LIPIcs, vol. 85, pp. 8:1–8:19 (2017)
88. Francalanza, A., Aceto, L., Achilleos, A., Attard, D.P., Cassar, I., Della Monica, D., Ingólfsdóttir, A.: A foundation for runtime monitoring. In: Lahiri, S., Reger, G. (eds.) RV 2017. LNCS, vol. 10548, pp. 8–29. Springer, Cham (2017). https://doi.org/10.1007/978-3-319-67531-2_2
89. Francalanza, A., Aceto, L., Ingolfsdottir, A.: On verifying Hennessy-Milner logic with recursion at runtime. In: Bartocci, E., Majumdar, R. (eds.) RV 2015. LNCS, vol. 9333, pp. 71–86. Springer, Cham (2015). https://doi.org/10.1007/978-3-319-23820-3_5
90. Francalanza, A., Aceto, L., Ingólfsdóttir, A.: Monitorability for the Hennessy-Milner logic with recursion. J. Form. Methods Syst. Des. (FMSD) **51**(1), 87–116 (2017)

91. Francalanza, A., Gauci, A., Pace, G.J.: Distributed system contract monitoring. JLAP **82**(5–7), 186–215 (2013)

92. Francalanza, A., Perez, J.A., Sanchez, C.: Runtime verification for decentralized and distributed systems. In: Bartocci, E., Falcone, Y. (eds.) Lectures on Runtime Verification. LNCS, vol. 10457, pp. 176–210. Springer, Cham (2018)

93. Francalanza, A., Seychell, A.: Synthesising correct concurrent runtime monitors. FMSD **46**(3), 226–261 (2015)

94. Di Giusto, C., Perez, J.A.: Disciplined structured communications with disciplined runtime adaptation. Sci. Comput. Program. **97**(2), 235–265 (2015)

95. Goldberg, A., Havelund, K.: Automated runtime verification with Eagle. In: Modelling, Simulation, Verification and Validation of Enterprise Information Systems, Proceedings of the 3rd International Workshop on Modelling, Simulation, Verification and Validation of Enterprise Information Systems, MSVVEIS 2005, In Conjunction with ICEIS 2005, Miami, FL, USA, May 2005

96. Haghighi, I., Jones, A., Kong, Z., Bartocci, E., Grosu, R., Belta, C.:. SpaTeL: a novel spatial-temporal logic and its applications to networked systems. In: Proceedings of HSCC 2015: The 18th International Conference on Hybrid Systems: Computation and Control, pp. 189–198. IEEE (2015)

97. Hallé, S., Villemaire, R.: Runtime monitoring of message-based workflows with data. In: ECOC 2008, pp. 63–72. IEEE Computer Society (2008)

98. Hauswirth, M., Chilimbi, T.M.: Low-overhead memory leak detection using adaptive statistical profiling. In: Proceedings of ASPLOS: The 11th International Conference on Architectural Support for Programming Languages and Operating Systems, pp. 156–164. ACM (2004)

99. Havelund, K.: Rule-based runtime verification revisited. STTT **17**(2), 143–170 (2015)

100. Havelund, K., Goldberg, A.: Verify your runs. In: Meyer, B., Woodcock, J. (eds.) VSTTE 2005. LNCS, vol. 4171, pp. 374–383. Springer, Heidelberg (2008). https://doi.org/10.1007/978-3-540-69149-5_40

101. Havelund, K., Reger, G.: Runtime verification logics a language design perspective. In: Aceto, L., Bacci, G., Bacci, G., Ingólfsdóttir, A., Legay, A., Mardare, R. (eds.) Models, Algorithms, Logics and Tools: Essays Dedicated to Kim Guldstrand Larsen on the Occasion of His 60th Birthday. LNCS, vol. 10460, pp. 310–338. Springer, Cham (2017). https://doi.org/10.1007/978-3-319-63121-9_16

102. Havelund, K., Reger, G., Zalinescu, E., Thoma, D.: Monitoring events that carry data. In: Bartocci, E., Falcone, Y. (eds.) Lectures on Runtime Verification. LNCS, vol. 10457, pp. 61–102. Springer, Cham (2018)

103. Huang, X., Seyster, J., Callanan, S., Dixit, K., Grosu, R., Smolka, S.A., Stoller, S.D., Zadok, E.: Software monitoring with controllable overhead. STTT **14**(3), 327–347 (2012)

104. Jaksic, S., Bartocci, E., Grosu, R., Kloibhofer, R., Nguyen, T., Ničković, D.: From signal temporal logic to FPGA monitors. In: Proceedings of MEMOCODE 2015: The 13th ACM/IEEE International Conference on Formal Methods and Models for Codesign, pp. 218–227. IEEE (2015)

105. Jakšić, S., Bartocci, E., Grosu, R., Ničković, D.: Quantitative monitoring of STL with edit distance. In: Falcone, Y., Sánchez, C. (eds.) RV 2016. LNCS, vol. 10012, pp. 201–218. Springer, Cham (2016). https://doi.org/10.1007/978-3-319-46982-9_13

106. Kalajdzic, K., Bartocci, E., Smolka, S.A., Stoller, S.D., Grosu, R.: Runtime verification with particle filtering. In: Legay, A., Bensalem, S. (eds.) RV 2013. LNCS, vol. 8174, pp. 149–166. Springer, Heidelberg (2013). https://doi.org/10.1007/978-3-642-40787-1_9

107. Kiczales, G., Hilsdale, E., Hugunin, J., Kersten, M., Palm, J., Griswold, W.G.: An overview of AspectJ. In: Knudsen, J.L. (ed.) ECOOP 2001. LNCS, vol. 2072, pp. 327–354. Springer, Heidelberg (2001). https://doi.org/10.1007/3-540-45337-7_18

108. Kim, M., Kannan, S., Lee, I., Sokolsky, O., Viswanathan, M.: Computational analysis of run-time monitoring - fundamentals of Java-MaC. Electr. Notes Theor. Comput. Sci. **70**(4), 80–94 (2002)

109. Laurent, J., Goodloe, A., Pike, L.: Assuring the guardians. In: Bartocci, E., Majumdar, R. (eds.) RV 2015. LNCS, vol. 9333, pp. 87–101. Springer, Cham (2015). https://doi.org/10.1007/978-3-319-23820-3_6

110. Laurenzano, M., Tikir, M.M., Carrington, L., Snavely, A.: PEBIL: efficient static binary instrumentation for Linux. In: IEEE International Symposium on Performance Analysis of Systems and Software, ISPASS 2010, 28–30 March 2010, White Plains, NY, USA, pp. 175–183. IEEE Computer Society (2010)

111. Leucker, M., Sánchez, C.: Regular linear temporal logic. In: Jones, C.B., Liu, Z., Woodcock, J. (eds.) ICTAC 2007. LNCS, vol. 4711, pp. 291–305. Springer, Heidelberg (2007). https://doi.org/10.1007/978-3-540-75292-9_20

112. Leucker, M., Schallhart, C.: A brief account of runtime verification. J. Log. Algebr. Program. **78**(5), 293–303 (2009)

113. Libkin, L., Vrgoč, D.: Regular expressions for data words. In: Bjørner, N., Voronkov, A. (eds.) LPAR 2012. LNCS, vol. 7180, pp. 274–288. Springer, Heidelberg (2012). https://doi.org/10.1007/978-3-642-28717-6_22

114. Ligatti, J., Bauer, L., Walker, D.: Edit automata: enforcement mechanisms for run-time security policies. IJIS **4**(1–2), 2–16 (2005)

115. Lourenço, J., Fiedor, J., Krena, B., Vojnar, T.: Discovering concurrency errors. In: Bartocci, E., Falcone, Y. (eds.) Lectures on Runtime Verification. LNCS, vol. 10457, pp. 34–60. Springer, Cham (2018)

116. Luk, C.-K., Cohn, R.S., Muth, R., Patil, H., Klauser, A., Lowney, P.G., Wallace, S., Reddi, V.J., Hazelwood, K.M.: Pin: building customized program analysis tools with dynamic instrumentation. In: Proceedings of the ACM SIGPLAN 2005: The Conference on Programming Language Design and Implementation, pp. 190–200. ACM (2005)

117. Luo, Q., Roşu, G.: EnforceMOP: a runtime property enforcement system for multithreaded programs. In: ISSTA. ACM, New York (2013)

118. Majma, N., Babamir, S.M., Monadjemi, A.: Runtime verification of pacemaker using fuzzy logic and colored petri-nets. In: 2015 4th Iranian Joint Congress on Fuzzy and Intelligent Systems (CFIS), pp. 1–5, September 2015

119. Maler, O., Nickovic, D.: Monitoring temporal properties of continuous signals. In: Lakhnech, Y., Yovine, S. (eds.) FORMATS/FTRTFT 2004. LNCS, vol. 3253, pp. 152–166. Springer, Heidelberg (2004). https://doi.org/10.1007/978-3-540-30206-3_12

120. Meredith, P., Jin, D., Griffith, D., Chen, F., Roşu, G.: An overview of the MOP runtime verification framework. Int. J. Softw. Tools Technol. Transf. **14**(3), 249–289 (2012). https://doi.org/10.1007/s10009-011-0198-6

121. Nanda, S., Li, W., Lam, L.-C., Chiueh, T.: BIRD: binary interpretation using runtime disassembly. In: Proceedings of CGO 2006: The Fourth IEEE/ACM International Symposium on Code Generation and Optimization, pp. 358–370. IEEE Computer Society (2006)

122. Nazarpour, H., Falcone, Y., Bensalem, S., Bozga, M.: Concurrency-preserving and sound monitoring of multi-threaded component-based systems: theory, algorithms, implementation, and evaluation. Formal Asp. Comput. **29**(6), 951–986 (2017)

123. Nenzi, L., Bortolussi, L., Ciancia, V., Loreti, M., Massink, M.: Qualitative and quantitative monitoring of spatio-temporal properties. In: Bartocci, E., Majumdar, R. (eds.) RV 2015. LNCS, vol. 9333, pp. 21–37. Springer, Cham (2015). https://doi.org/10.1007/978-3-319-23820-3_2

124. Nethercote, N., Seward, J.: Valgrind: a framework for heavyweight dynamic binary instrumentation. In: Proceedings of the ACM SIGPLAN 2007 Conference on Programming Language Design and Implementation, pp. 89–100. ACM (2007)

125. Nguyen, T., Bartocci, E., Ničković, D., Grosu, R., Jaksic, S., Selyunin, K.: The HARMONIA project: hardware monitoring for automotive systems-of-systems. In: Margaria, T., Steffen, B. (eds.) ISoLA 2016. LNCS, vol. 9953, pp. 371–379. Springer, Cham (2016). https://doi.org/10.1007/978-3-319-47169-3_28

126. Pintér, G., Majzik, I.: Runtime verification of statechart implementations. In: de Lemos, R., Gacek, C., Romanovsky, A. (eds.) WADS -2004. LNCS, vol. 3549, pp. 148–172. Springer, Heidelberg (2005). https://doi.org/10.1007/11556169_7

127. Pnueli, A.: The temporal logic of programs. In: Proceedings of the 18th Annual Symposium on Foundations of Computer Science, SFCS 1977, pp. 46–57. IEEE Computer Society, Washington, DC (1977)

128. Pnueli, A., Zaks, A.: PSL model checking and run-time verification via testers. In: Misra, J., Nipkow, T., Sekerinski, E. (eds.) FM 2006. LNCS, vol. 4085, pp. 573–586. Springer, Heidelberg (2006). https://doi.org/10.1007/11813040_38

129. Reger, G., Havelund, K.: What is a trace? A runtime verification perspective. In: Margaria, T., Steffen, B. (eds.) ISoLA 2016, Part II. LNCS, vol. 9953, pp. 339–355. Springer, Cham (2016). https://doi.org/10.1007/978-3-319-47169-3_25

130. Reger, G., Rydeheard, D.: From first-order temporal logic to parametric trace slicing. In: Bartocci, E., Majumdar, R. (eds.) RV 2015. LNCS, vol. 9333, pp. 216–232. Springer, Cham (2015). https://doi.org/10.1007/978-3-319-23820-3_14

131. Roşu, G., Havelund, K.: Rewriting-based techniques for runtime verification. Autom. Softw. Eng. **12**(2), 151–197 (2005)

132. Roşu, G., Bensalem, S.: Allen linear (interval) temporal logic – translation to LTL and monitor synthesis. In: Ball, T., Jones, R.B. (eds.) CAV 2006. LNCS, vol. 4144, pp. 263–277. Springer, Heidelberg (2006). https://doi.org/10.1007/11817963_25

133. Saidi, S., Falcone, Y.: Dynamic detection and mitigation of DMA races in MPSoCs. In: 2015 Euromicro Conference on Digital System Design, DSD 2015, Madeira, Portugal, 26–28 August 2015, pp. 267–270. IEEE Computer Society (2015)

134. Schneider, F.B.: Enforceable security policies. ACM Trans. Inf. Syst. Secur. **3**(1), 30–50 (2000)

135. Selyunin, K., Jaksic, S., Nguyen, T., Reidl, C., Hafner, U., Bartocci, E., Nickovic, D., Grosu, R.: Runtime monitoring with recovery of the SENT communication protocol. In: Majumdar, R., Kunčak, V. (eds.) CAV 2017. LNCS, vol. 10426, pp. 336–355. Springer, Cham (2017). https://doi.org/10.1007/978-3-319-63387-9_17

136. Selyunin, K., Nguyen, T., Bartocci, E., Grosu, R.: Applying runtime monitoring for automotive electronic development. In: Falcone, Y., Sánchez, C. (eds.) RV 2016. LNCS, vol. 10012, pp. 462–469. Springer, Cham (2016). https://doi.org/10.1007/978-3-319-46982-9_30

137. Selyunin, K., Nguyen, T., Bartocci, E., Ničković, D., Grosu, R.: Monitoring of MTL specifications with IBM's spiking-neuron model. In: Proceedings of DATE 2016: The 2016 Design, Automation & Test in Europe Conference, pp. 924–929. IEEE (2016)

138. Sen, K., Vardhan, A., Agha, G., Roşu, G.: Efficient decentralized monitoring of safety in distributed systems. In: ICSE, pp. 418–427 (2004)

139. Seyster, J., Dixit, K., Huang, X., Grosu, R., Havelund, K., Smolka, S.A., Stoller, S.D., Zadok, E.: Interaspect: aspect-oriented instrumentation with GCC. Form. Methods Syst. Des. **41**(3), 295–320 (2012)

140. Sokolsky, O., Havelund, K., Lee, I.: Introduction to the special section on runtime verification. STTT **14**(3), 243–247 (2012)

141. Spinczyk, O., Lohmann, D.: The design and implementation of AspectC++. Know.-Based Syst. **20**(7), 636–651 (2007)

142. Stoller, S.D., Bartocci, E., Seyster, J., Grosu, R., Havelund, K., Smolka, S.A., Zadok, E.: Runtime verification with state estimation. In: Khurshid, S., Sen, K. (eds.) RV 2011. LNCS, vol. 7186, pp. 193–207. Springer, Heidelberg (2012). https://doi.org/10.1007/978-3-642-29860-8_15

143. Stollon, N.: On-Chip Instrumentation. Springer, New York (2011). https://doi.org/10.1007/978-1-4419-7563-8

144. Stolz, V.: Temporal assertions with parametrized propositions. J. Log. Comput. **20**(3), 743–757 (2010)

145. Thati, P., Roşu, G.: Monitoring algorithms for metric temporal logic specifications. Electron. Notes Theor. Comput. Sci. **113**, 145–162 (2005)

146. Winslett, M.: Bruce lindsay speaks out: on System R, benchmarking, life as an IBM fellow, the power of DBAs in the old days, why performance still matters, heisenbugs, why he still writes code, singing pigs, and more. SIGMOD Rec. **34**(2), 71–79 (2005)

147. Zhou, S., Zedan, H., Cau, A.: Run-time analysis of time-critical systems. J. Syst. Archit. **51**(5), 331–345 (2005)

Discovering Concurrency Errors

João M. Lourenço[1]([✉])(iD), Jan Fiedor[2], Bohuslav Křena[2](iD),
and Tomáš Vojnar[2](iD)

[1] NOVA LINCS, DI, FCT, NOVA University Lisbon, Lisbon, Portugal
`joao.lourenco@fct.unl.pt`
[2] Faculty of Information Technology, IT4Innovations Centre of Excellence,
Brno University of Technology, Brno, Czech Republic

Abstract. Lots of concurrent software is being developed for the now ubiquitous multicore processors. And concurrent programming is difficult because it is quite easy to introduce errors that are really hard to diagnose and fix. One of the main obstacles to concurrent programming is that threads are scheduled nondeterministically and their interactions may become hard to predict and to devise. This chapter addresses the nature of concurrent programming and some classes of concurrency errors. It discusses the application of dynamic program analysis techniques to detect, locate and diagnose some common concurrency errors like data races, atomicity violations and deadlocks. This chapter also mentions some techniques that can help with quality assurance of concurrent programs, regardless of any particular class of concurrency errors, like noise injection and systematic testing, and it is closed by some prospects of concurrent software development.

Keywords: Software correctness · Quality assurance
Nondeterminism · Concurrency errors · Atomicity violations
Data races · Deadlocks · Dynamic analysis · Noise injection

1 Introduction

The arrival of multi-core processors into computers, laptops, tablets, phones, and other devices demands the development of software products that make use of multi-threaded design to better use the available hardware resources. Modern programming languages allow programmers to easily create multi-threaded programs, at the expense of a significant increase in the number and variety of errors appearing in the code. The basic difficulty is introduced by the conflict between safety and efficiency. It is not easy to set up the appropriate synchronisation among threads ensuring safety and low overhead simultaneously. If the synchronisation is too strict, the performance of the application degrades as the computation power brought by the presence of several computational cores becomes underused. On the other hand, if the concurrent program is under-synchronised, some failures may occur, like wrong results and application crashes. As an example of what can be the impact of a concurrency error, we refer to the Northeastern

© Springer International Publishing AG, part of Springer Nature 2018
E. Bartocci and Y. Falcone (Eds.): Lectures on Runtime Verification, LNCS 10457, pp. 34–60, 2018.
https://doi.org/10.1007/978-3-319-75632-5_2

U.S. blackout in August 2003, where a race condition error was identified as one of the causes [59,60].

Creating concurrent programs is more demanding on programmers, since people usually think in a linear way. It is not easy to imagine the parallel execution and the possible interactions of dozens of threads, even if the programmer concentrates on it; on the contrary, programmers think most of the time about snippets of sequential code despite they may be executed in parallel. Moreover, errors in concurrency are not only easy to create, but also very difficult to detect and diagnose due to the nondeterministic nature of multi-threaded computation. For instance, the error from Northeastern blackout has been unmasked about eight weeks after the blackout [60]. Some concurrent errors may manifest rarely or under special circumstances, making it difficult to discover them by testing as well as to reproduce them while debugging.

This chapter is organised as follows. It starts with a discussion on the nature of concurrent computations and on the errors that can arise from the execution of concurrent programs, including a motivating example, in Sect. 2. Different concurrency errors are then presented and classified in Sect. 3. Section 4 describes various approaches for monitoring the execution of concurrent programs as monitoring allows one to obtain all the necessary information to perform an analysis and detect errors. Follows a discussion on the detection of common classes of concurrency errors, with Sect. 5 addressing errors related to atomicity violations, and Sect. 6 addressing deadlocks. The detection of less common concurrency errors is discussed in Sect. 7. Techniques that can help with quality assurance of concurrent programs, regardless of any particular class of concurrency errors, like noise injection and systematic testing, are discussed in Sect. 8. Section 9 sums up the chapter and provides some prospects for concurrent software development.

2   Errors in Concurrency

To understand errors in concurrency, one first needs to understand the nature of concurrent execution. The execution of a concurrent program is performed simultaneously by several processes (they can be called threads or nodes as well). All the processes have access to a shared memory that serves as a communication mean among them.[1] Additionally, each process has its own local memory that can be typically accessed much faster than the shared memory. Although memory in computers is usually organised in a hierarchy with several levels, each with different size, speed, and price per bit, simple differentiation between shared and local memory of processes is enough to show the basis of concurrent errors.

As the shared memory is usually much slower than the local memory, a typical scenario of the execution performed by a process is copying data from the shared memory to its local memory, performing the given computation using the local memory, and storing the result back to the shared memory. At the first sight,

---

[1] In this Chapter, we concentrate on the shared memory paradigm, leaving behind the distributed memory and message passing paradigms, which are covered elsewhere in this book.

there is no problem with this operation model, however, this is true only if a single process is working with that particular data in the shared memory. If two or more processes are operating concurrently over the same data in the shared memory (perceived by a programmer, for instance, as a shared variable), some problems may arise. We illustrate this with the help of a very simple concurrent system.

Let us have a shared variable x, initialised to zero, and two threads operating concurrently on x, one thread adding one to x and the other adding two to x.

$$x=0 . (x++ \parallel x+=2)$$

What will be the final value of the variable x after this computation ends? The most obvious answer would be 3. However, it is not necessarily the case if we take concurrency into account. First, it may happen that incrementing and adding are not implemented using single instructions. For instance, they can be implemented by a three steps procedure: (1) loading the value of a shared variable x from the shared memory to the local memory (e.g., to a processor register); (2) adding the intended value to the local copy of x; and (3) storing the new value of x back into the shared memory.

Here is an example in Java bytecode (no knowledge of Java neither of Java bytecode is required to understand the example):

```
Thread 1:        Thread 2:

load x           load x
inc              add 2
store x          store x
```

Nothing bad happens if the threads do not interfere with each other while executing. In the following, Thread 2 starts its work only after Thread 1 completes its whole execution. On the right-hand side we can see the evolution of the values of the shared variable x and of its local copies x_1 for Thread 1 and x_2 for Thread 2. The outcome of the execution is highlighted by a frame.

Thread 1:	Thread 2:	x	x_1	x_2
load x		0	0	
inc		0	1	
store x		1	1	
	load x	1		1
	add 2	1		3
	store x	[3]		3

The same outcome is achieved if Thread 1 starts its work after Thread 2 completes its executions. The problem occurs when the executions of these two threads are interleaved. For instance, the first thread starts executing as in the previous example, however, the second thread starts and loads the value of the shared variable x before the first thread stores its result back. Then, the result of Thread 1 is lost because it is overwritten by Thread 2 when it stores its own result back to x, as illustrated by the example below.

Thread 1:	Thread 2:	x	x_1	x_2
load x		0	0	
inc		0	1	
	load x	0	1	0
store x		1	1	0
	add 2	1		2
	store x	\boxed{2}		2

Yet another outcome can be seen if the result produced by Thread 2 is overwritten by Thread 1.

Thread 1:	Thread 2:	x	x_1	x_2
load x		0	0	
inc		0	1	
	load x	0	1	0
	add 2	1	1	2
	store x	2	1	2
store x		\boxed{1}	1	

In this example, we can highlight two issues related to concurrency. First, programmers usually write code in a more abstract level than what it is actually executed. When writing code, the programmer does not need to care (and sometimes does not even know) about the underlying implementation. Rather, it is quite natural to assume that adding a value to a variable is an atomic operation. Thus, the non-atomicity of some operations is actually hidden from the programmer and the concurrency errors are not easily visible in the source code.

It is commonly accepted that errors that are not realised by the programmer, because they are hidden in less frequent operations or branches of the source code, can frequently be uncovered by a proper testing activity. And this raises the second issue. When a code block contains a concurrency related error, frequently there is a huge number of different ways this erroneous code block can interact with the other code blocks of the program, and all but a few of them will trigger the error. Thus, even when involving the erroneous code block, the testing procedures most probably will not uncover the error, which will stay hidden. The error will be uncovered only if one of the low-probable erroneous interactions is exercised by the testing procedures. And this may happen very seldom or, in some cases, even never!

The execution order of particular instructions by some given threads is called *thread interleaving*. The set of all possible thread interleavings defines the semantics of a concurrent program. In the previous example, there are 20 possible thread interleavings from which most probably only two are common: one where thread 1 executes before thread 2 and another where thread 2 executes before thread 1. These two common interleavings have, moreover, special importance because they can also be achieved by a sequential execution. Interleavings which are equivalent to some sequential execution are called *serialisable*. If all the possible thread interleavings are serialisable, the multi-threaded program is correct (of course, provided that the sequential program is correct). This notion of correctness of multiprocess programs called *sequential consistency* has been introduced by Lamport in [42]. Obviously, our example is not sequentially consistent because it can produce results that cannot be obtained by a sequential execution of the given threads.

3   Classification of Concurrency Errors

In general, we can think of a concurrency error as a behaviour that does not respect the sequential consistency model, which, in a nutshell, means the behaviour/result could not be obtained by a sequential execution (i.e., it is *unserialisable*). For efficient handling of concurrency errors, however, one needs to use the divide-and-conquer strategy and concentrate and deal with only some particular kinds of such errors at a time.

To classify concurrency errors, we can adopt classification of general programming errors and distinguish between safety errors and liveness errors like we have done in [19]. Safety errors violate safety properties of a program, i.e., they cause something bad to happen. They always have a finite witness leading to an error state, so, they may be seen as easier to detect. Liveness errors are errors which violate liveness properties of a program, i.e., prevent something good from happening. To detect them one needs to find an infinite path showing that the intended behaviour cannot be achieved, and thus, it may be more complicated to detect liveness errors.

In the following, however, we present the classes of concurrency errors rather with respect to the underlying mechanism that leads to a failure. It allows us later to address the practical aspects of error detection, focusing on some particular errors that violate program safety, in the same way.

Atomicity Violation. The first group of concurrency errors we address in this book chapter is related to wrong atomicity, i.e., some operations unintentionally interfere with the execution of some other operations. We can define it more formally as follows.

Definition 1. Atomicity Violation—*A program execution violates atomicity iff it is not equivalent to any other execution in which all code blocks which are assumed to be atomic are executed serially.*

We have already seen an atomicity violation in our example above where the operations of incrementing and adding a value to a shared variable were not executed atomically. This kind of concurrency errors is, however, usually treated as a special subclass of atomicity violation called data race or race condition.

Definition 2. Data Race—*A program execution contains a data race iff it contains two unsynchronised accesses to a shared variable and at least one of them is a write access.*

Data races are one of the most common and most undesirable phenomena in concurrent programs. However, one should note that not all data races are harmful. Data races that cannot cause application failures are often referred to as *benign data races* and are sometimes intentionally left in concurrent programs. As an example of a benign data race consider two unsynchronised threads, one thread updating a shared integer variable with the percentage of the completed work, and another thread reading this shared variable and drawing a progress bar. Even in the absence of synchronisation between the threads, this program will behave as expected and, thus, we are facing a benign data race.

Similar to data races with respect to the behaviour scheme, but rather different regarding their origins, are the so-called *high-level data races* [4]. For instance, consider a complex number whose real and imaginary values are protected by two separate locks. Updating such complex number can never cause a data race as presented in Definition 2, because the accesses to both parts of the complex number are always protected by the corresponding lock. Nevertheless, when the complex number is updated concurrently by two threads, the complex number may, after both the updates, contain the real part from one of the updates and the imaginary part from the other. This inconsistency did not occur directly on the shared variables (the complex number real and imaginary parts) but on the complex number itself as a whole, which is at the higher level of abstraction and, therefore, it is called a high-level data race.

Deadlock. Deadlocks are another kind of safety concurrency errors. Actually, one may see them as a consequence of tackling atomicity violations—to avoid, for instance, data races, one should use locks to guard accesses to shared resources, e.g., shared variables. Using locks in a wrong way may, however, cause a deadlock, which is definitely undesirable because the application stops working.

Despite deadlocks being quite often studied in the literature, the understanding of deadlocks still varies, depending on the specific setting being considered. Here we stick to the meaning common in the classical literature on operating systems. To define deadlocks in a general way, we assume that given any state of a program: (1) one can identify threads that are blocked and waiting for some event to happen; and (2) for any waiting thread t, one can identify threads that could generate an event that would unblock t.

Definition 3. Deadlock—*A program state contains a set S of deadlocked threads iff each thread in S is blocked and waiting for some event that could unblock it, but such an event could only be generated by a thread also in S.*

Most works consider a special case of deadlocks, namely, the so-called *Coffman deadlock* [10]. A Coffman deadlock happens in a state in which four conditions are met: (1) Processes have an exclusive access to the resources granted to them, (2) processes hold some resources and are waiting for additional resources, (3) resources cannot be forcibly removed from the tasks holding them (no preemption on the resources), and (4) a circular chain of tasks exists in which each task holds one or more resources that are being requested by the next task in the chain. Such a definition perfectly fits deadlocks caused by blocking lock operations but does not cover deadlocks caused by message passing (e.g., a thread t_1 can wait for a message that could only be sent by a thread t_2, but t_2 is waiting for a message that could only be sent by t_1).

Order Violation. Order violations form a much less studied class of concurrency errors than atomicity violations and deadlocks. An order violation is a problem of a missing enforcement of some higher-level ordering requirements.[2] An order violation can be defined as follows.

Definition 4. Order Violation—*A program execution exhibits an order violation if some of its instructions are not executed in the expected order.*

Missed Signal. Missed signals are another less studied class of concurrency errors. The notion of missed signals assumes that it is known which signal is *intended* to be delivered to which thread or threads. A missed signal error can be defined as follows.

Definition 5. Missed Signal—*A program execution contains a missed signal iff there is a signal sent that is not delivered to the thread or threads for which it was intended.*

Since signals are often used to unblock waiting threads, a missed signal error typically leads to a thread or threads being blocked forever and can lead to a deadlock as well.

Starvation. Starvation is a behaviour that can cover several safety as well as liveness (or mixed[3]) errors, such as the already discussed deadlocks and missed signals, and the to be discussed livelocks and blocked threads. Starvation occurs when a thread is waiting for an event that never happens. If the probability of the event is very low but will eventually happen, the thread is not exhibiting a starvation, but in these cases the performance degradation imposed by the waiting for the event may become unacceptable and render the solution invalid as would a starvation situation.

Definition 6. Starvation—*A program execution exhibits starvation iff there exists a thread which waits (blocked or continually performing some computation) for an event that needs not to occur.*

---

[2] Some atomicity violations can be, actually, seen as a low-level violations of ordering expectations and deadlocks, in addition, are often caused by a wrong order of locking operations. Here, we do not consider atomicity violations and deadlocks as order violations.

[3] Mixed errors are errors that have both finite witnesses as well as infinite ones whose any finite prefix does not suffice as a witness.

Livelock and Non-progress Behaviour. There are various different definitions of a livelock in the literature. Often, the works consider some kind of a *progress* notion for expressing that a thread is making some useful work, i.e., doing something of what the programmer intended to be done. Then they see a livelock as a problem when a thread is not blocked but is not making any progress as well.

Definition 7. Livelock and Non-progress Behaviour—*An infinite program execution exhibits a non-progress behaviour iff there is a thread which is continually performing some computation, i.e., it is not blocked, but it is not making any progress either.*

Blocked Thread. We speak about a *blocked thread* appearing within some execution when a thread is blocked and waiting forever for some event which can unblock it. Like for a deadlock, one must be able to say what the blocking and unblocking operations are. The problem can then be defined as follows.

Definition 8. Blocked Thread—*A program execution contains a blocked thread iff the thread is waiting for some event to continue, and this event never occurs in the execution.*

The absence of some unblocking event may leave a thread blocked forever. There may be many reasons for leaving a thread blocked. A common reason is that a thread that was holding a lock ends unexpectedly, leaving another thread (or threads) waiting forever for that lock to be released. Another common reason are missed signals. Blocked threads may also be called *orphaned threads* [18].

4   Monitoring of Concurrent Program Execution

One of the strategies to find errors in concurrent programs makes use of dynamic program analysis that, in turn, requires to observe and monitor the execution of the program under analysis. To monitor the program execution, one needs to inject additional code into selected locations of the original program, which when executed will generate observation points for program analysis. There are several levels at which such additional code can be inserted, including the source code level, the level of the intermediate code, and the binary level.

From the three approaches above, inserting the monitoring code at the binary level has a big advantage of not requiring the source code of the program under analysis. This is particularly important when dealing with proprietary or legacy libraries whose source files are not available even for the developers of the program under analysis. Another advantage might be that this kind of instrumentation is more precise in that the monitoring code can be inserted exactly where necessary, and the placement is not affected by any optimisations possibly made by the compiler. Yet another advantage is getting access to some low-level information, such as register allocation, which might be important for some analyses.

All these advantages come at the expense of sometimes loosing access to various pieces of high-level information about the program (organisation of complex data objects, names of variables, etc.).

There exist several frameworks for binary instrumentation, which can be used to insert the execution-monitoring code into a program. They might be divided into two groups: static and dynamic binary instrumentation frameworks. *Static binary instrumentation frameworks*, e.g., PEBIL [44], insert monitoring code to a program by rewriting the object or executable code of the program before it is executed, thus generating a new modified version of the original program's binary file, which will be executed afterwards. *Dynamic binary instrumentation frameworks*, e.g., PIN [49] and Valgrind [55], insert execution-monitoring code to the program image in memory at runtime, leaving the program's binary file untouched.

An advantage of static binary instrumentation is that it does not suffer from the overhead of instrumenting the code of a program every time it is executed. On the other hand, it cannot handle constructions such as self-modifying and self-generating code, which is not known before the program actually executes. On the contrary, dynamic binary instrumentation is slower, but it can cover all the code that is executed by a program. Furthermore, since the binary file of the program is not modified in any way, the instrumentation is more transparent to the user who can run some (possibly lengthy) analysis on the program and, at the same time, use the program as usual. As the dynamic binary instrumentation changes the in-memory image of the program, it also allows to instrument and monitor shared libraries without requiring to generate and maintain two versions of the library, one normal and the other instrumented.

Regardless of which type of the instrumentation approaches is used, there are some issues that need to be dealt with when analysing multi-threaded programs at the binary level [21]. One of these problems is the monitoring of function calls/execution. This is because the monitoring code has to handle cases where the control is passed among several functions by jumps, and the return is from a different function than the one that was called. Another problem is that the monitoring code must properly trigger notifications for various special types of instructions such as atomic instructions, which access several memory locations at once but in an atomic way, and conditional and repeatable instructions, which might be executed more than once or not at all. Further, some pieces of information about the execution of instructions and functions (such as the memory locations accessed by them), which are crucial for various analyses, may be lost once the instruction or function finishes its execution, and it is necessary to explicitly preserve this information for later use. Finally, in order to support various multithreading libraries, the analysers must be abstracted from the particular library used.

Inserting additional code needed for monitoring at the intermediate code level is suitable for programming languages that use intermediate code like Java. It does not require the source code of the application while it stays at a level of abstraction that retains more information about the original program, making it easier to explain the errors found than if the monitoring code is inserted at the binary level. One may find useful tools, like RoadRunner [27], which provide an instrumentation facility and allows one to fully concentrate on the development of the analyser.

When the source code of the application is available, one may insert monitoring code directly into the application source code. Preparation of each such application for analysis, however, requires some manual work even when aspect-oriented programming is employed.

5   Detection of Atomicity Errors

In this section, we describe possible ways for detecting atomicity violations. We start with the detection of data races as a special and very important case of atomicity violations, and then we follow with the detection of general atomicity violations, detecting first single and then multiple variable atomicity violations.

5.1   Detection of Data Races

To recall Definition 2, a data race occurs if there are two unsynchronised accesses to a shared variable within the execution of a concurrent program and at least one of them is a write access. To be able to identify an occurrence of a data race, one thus needs to detect (1) which variables are shared by any two given threads, and (2) whether all pairs of accesses to a given shared variable are synchronised.

As data races are a well-studied concurrency problem, many different techniques have been proposed to tackle their detection. Dynamic techniques that analyse one particular execution of a program are usually based on computing the so-called locksets and/or happens-before relations along the witnessed execution. Static techniques often either look for particular code patterns that are likely to cause a data race, or compute locksets and/or happens-before relations over all executions considered feasible by a static analyser [16,39,50,54]. It is also possible to use type systems to detect and/or avoid data races by design [23,25,73]. One may also consider model checking approach [67]. However, we discuss dynamic techniques and their principles in the remainder of this section.

Lockset-Based Algorithms. The techniques based on *locksets* build on the idea that all accesses to a shared variable should be guarded by a lock. A lockset is defined as a set of locks that guard all accesses to a given variable. Detectors then use the assumption that, if the lockset associated with a certain shared variable is non-empty, i.e., all accesses to that variable are protected by at least one lock, then no data race is possible.

The first algorithm which used the idea of locksets was Eraser [64]. The algorithm maintains for each shared variable v a set $C(v)$ of candidate locks for v. When a new variable is initialised, its candidate set $C(v)$ contains all possible locks. Whenever a variable v is accessed, Eraser updates $C(v)$ by intersecting

$C(v)$ and the set $L(t)$ of locks held by the current thread at the moment. Eraser warns about a possible data race if $C(v)$ becomes empty for some shared variable v along the execution being analysed. In order to reduce the number of false alarms, Eraser introduces an internal state $s(v)$ used to identify the access pattern for each shared variable v: if the variable is used exclusively by one thread, if it is written by a single thread and read by multiple threads, or if it can be changed by multiple threads. The lockset $C(v)$ is then modified only if the variable is shared, and a data race is reported only if $C(v)$ becomes empty and $s(v)$ is in the state denoting the case where multiple threads can access v for writing.

The original Eraser algorithm designed for C programs has been modified for programs written in object-oriented languages, e.g., [7,8,63,76]. The main modification (usually called as the *ownership model*) is inspired by the common idiom used in object-oriented programs where the creator of an object is actually not the owner of the object. Then, one should take into account that the creator always accesses the object first and no explicit synchronisation with the owner is needed, because the synchronisation is implicitly taken care of by the Java virtual machine. This idea is reflected by adding a new internal state for the shared variables. The modification introduces a small possibility of having false negatives [41,63], but greatly reduces the number of false alarms caused by the object-oriented programming idiom.

Locksets-based techniques do not support other synchronisation mechanisms than locks and thus, if other mechanisms are also used, these techniques may produce too many false alarms.

Happens-before-based Algorithms. The happens-before-based techniques exploit the so-called *happens-before relation* [43] (denoted →), which is defined as the least strict partial order that includes every pair of causally ordered events. For instance, if an event x occurs before an event y in the same thread, then it is denoted as $x \rightarrow y$. Also, if x is an event creating some thread and y is an event in that thread, then $x \rightarrow y$. Similarly, if some synchronisation or communication means is used that requires an event x to precede an event y, then $x \rightarrow y$. All notions of synchronisation and communication, such as sending and receiving a message, unlocking and locking a lock, sending and receiving a notification, etc., are to be considered. Detectors build (or approximate) the happens-before relation among accesses to shared variables and check that no two accesses (out of which at least one is for writing) can happen simultaneously, i.e., without a happens-before relation between them.

Most happens-before-based algorithms use the so-called *vector clocks* introduced in [51]. The idea of vector clocks for a message passing system is as follows. Each thread t has a vector of clocks T_{vc} indexed by thread identifiers. One position in T_{vc} holds the value of the clock of t. The other entries in T_{vc} hold logical timestamps indicating the last event in a remote thread that is known to be in the happens-before relation with the current operation of t. Vector clocks are partially-ordered in a point-wise manner ($\sqsubseteq$) with an associated join operation

($\sqcup$) and the minimal element (0). The vector clocks of threads are managed as follows: (1) initially, all clocks are set to 0; (2) each time a thread t sends a message, it sends also its T_{vc} and then t increments its own logical clock in its T_{vc} by one; (3) each time a thread receives a message, it increments its own logical clock by one and further updates its T_{vc} according to the received vector T'_{vc} to $T_{vc} = T_{vc} \sqcup T'_{vc}$.

Algorithms [61,62] detect data races in systems with locks via maintaining a vector clock C_t for each thread t (corresponding to T_{vc} in the original terminology above), a vector clock L_m for each lock m, and two vector clocks for write and read operations for each shared variable x (denoted W_x and R_x, respectively). W_x and R_x simply maintain a copy of the C_t of the last thread that accessed x for writing or reading, respectively. A read from x by a thread is race-free if $W_x \sqsubseteq C_t$ (it happens after the last write of each thread). A write to x by a thread is race-free if $W_x \sqsubseteq C_t$ and $R_x \sqsubseteq C_t$ (it happens after all accesses to the variable).

Maintaining such a big number of vector clocks as above generates a considerable overhead. Therefore, in [26], the vector clocks from above that were associated with variables were mostly replaced by the so-called *epochs*. The epoch of a variable v is represented as a tuple $(t,c)_v$, where t identifies the thread that last accessed v and c represents the value of its clock. The idea behind this optimisation is that, in most cases, a data race occurs between two subsequent accesses to a variable. In such cases, epochs are sufficient to detect unsynchronised accesses. However, in cases where a write operation needs to be synchronised with multiple preceding read operations, epochs are not sufficient and the algorithm has to build an analogy of vector clocks for sequences of read operations.

A bit different detection approach has been introduced in TRaDe [9] where a *topological race detection* [31] is used. This technique is based on an exact identification of objects which are reachable from a thread. This is accomplished by observing manipulations with references which alter the interconnection graph of the objects used in a program—hence the name topological. Then, vector clocks are used to identify possibly concurrently executed segments of code, called *parallel segments*. If an object is reachable from two parallel segments, a race has been detected. A disadvantage of this solution is its considerable overhead.

Although the algorithms mentioned above exhibit good precision, their computational demands are sometimes prohibitive, which inspired researchers to come up with some combinations of happens-before-based and lockset-based algorithms. These combinations are often called *hybrid algorithms*.

Hybrid Algorithms. Hybrid algorithms such as [15,24,58,76] combine the two approaches described above.

In RaceTrack [76], the notion of a *threadset* was introduced. The threadset is maintained for each shared variable and contains information concerning the threads currently working with the variable. The method works as follows. Each time a thread performs a memory access on a variable, it forms a label consisting of the thread identifier and its current private clock value. The label is then added to the threadset of the variable. The thread also uses its vector clock to identify and remove from the threadset the labels that correspond to accesses that are ordered before the current access. Hence, the threadset contains solely the labels for accesses that are concurrent. At the same time, locksets are used to track locking of variables, which is not tracked by the used approximation of the happens-before relation. Intersections on locksets are applied if the approximated happens-before relation is not able to assure an ordered access to shared variables. If an ordered access to a shared variable is assured by the approximated happens-before relation, the lockset of the variable is reset to the lockset of the thread that is currently accessing it.

One of the most advanced lockset-based algorithms that also uses the happens-before relation is Goldilocks [15]. The main insight of this algorithm is that locksets can contain not only locks but also volatile variables (i.e., variables with atomic access that may also be used for synchronisation) and, most importantly, also threads. The appearance of a thread t in the lockset of a shared variable v means that t is properly synchronised for using the given variable. The information about threads synchronised for using certain variables is then used to maintain a transitive closure of the happens-before relation via the locksets. The advantage of Goldilocks is that it allows locksets to grow during the computation when the happens-before relation is established between operations over v. The basic Goldilocks algorithm is relatively expensive but can be optimised by *short circuiting the lockset computation* (three cheap checks are sufficient for ensuring race freedom between the last two accesses on a variable) and using *a lazy computation of the locksets* (locksets are computed only if the previous optimisation is not able to detect that some events are in the happens-before relation). The optimised algorithm has a considerably lower overhead, in some cases approaching the pure lockset-based algorithms.

A similar approach to Goldilocks but for the Java Path Finder model checker has been presented in [40]. This algorithm does not map variables to locksets containing threads and synchronisation elements (such as locks), but rather threads and synchronisation elements to sets of variables. This modification is motivated by the fact that the number of threads and locks is usually much lower than the number of shared variables. Such a modification is feasible because model checking allows the method to modify structures associated with different threads at once. Methods based on dynamic analysis cannot use this modification and locksets must be kept using the original relation.

5.2   Detection of Atomicity Violations

Taking into account the generic notion of atomicity, methods for detecting atomicity violations can be classified according to: (1) the way they obtain information about which code blocks should be expected to execute atomically; (2) the notion of equivalence of executions used (we will get to several commonly used equivalences in the following); and (3) the actual way in which an atomicity violation is detected (i.e., using static analysis, dynamic analysis, etc.).

As for the blocks to be assumed to execute atomically, some authors expect the programmers to annotate their code to delimit such code blocks [29]. Some other works come with predefined patterns of code which should typically execute atomically [32, 48, 66]. Yet other authors try to infer blocks to be executed atomically, e.g., by analysing data and control dependencies between program statements [72], where dependent program statements form a block which should be executed atomically, or by finding access correlations between shared variables [47], where a set of accesses to correlated shared variables should be executed atomically (together with all statements between them).

Below, we first discuss approaches for detecting atomicity violations when considering accesses to a single shared variable only and then those which consider accesses to several shared variables.

Atomicity Over One Variable. Most of the existing algorithms for detecting atomicity violations are only able to detect atomicity violations within accesses to a single shared variable. They mostly attempt to detect situations where two accesses to a shared variable should be executed atomically, but are interleaved by an access from another thread.

In [72], blocks of instructions which are assumed to execute atomically are approximated by the so-called *computational units* (CUs). CUs are inferred automatically from a single program trace by analysing data and control dependencies between instructions. First, a dependency graph is created which contains control and read-after-write dependencies between all instructions. Then, the algorithm partitions this dependency graph to obtain a set of distinct subgraphs which form the CUs. The partitioning works in such a way that each CU is the largest group of instructions where all instructions are control or read-after-write dependent, but no instructions which access shared variables are read-after-write dependent, i.e., no read-after-write dependencies are allowed between shared variables in the same computational unit. Since these conditions are not sufficient to partition the dependency graph to distinct subgraphs, additional heuristics are used. Atomicity violations are then detected by checking if the strict 2-phase locking (2PL) discipline [17] is violated in a program trace. Violating the strict 2PL discipline means that some CU has written or accessed a shared variable which another CU is currently reading from or writing to, respectively (i.e., some CU accessed a shared variable and before its execution is finished, another CU accesses this shared variable). If the strict 2PL discipline is violated, the program trace is not identical to any serial execution, and so seen as violating atomicity. Checking if the strict 2PL discipline is violated is done dynamically during a program execution in case of the online version of the algorithm, or on a previously recorded execution trace using the off-line version of the algorithm.

A much simpler approach of discovering atomicity violations was presented in [48]. Here, any two consecutive accesses from one thread to the same shared variable are considered an atomic section, i.e., a block which should be executed atomically. Such blocks can be categorised into four classes according to the types of the two accesses (read or write) to the shared variable. Serialisability is then defined based on analysis of what can happen when a block b of each of the possible classes is interleaved with some read or write access from another thread to the same shared variable which is accessed in b. Out of the eight total cases arising in this way, four (namely, r-w-r, w-w-r, w-r-w, r-w-w) are considered to lead to an unserialisable execution. However, the detection algorithm does not consider all the unserialisable executions as errors. Detection of atomicity violations is done dynamically in two steps. First, the algorithm analyses a set of correct (training) runs in which it tries to detect atomic sections which are never unserialisably interleaved. These atomic sections are called *access interleaving invariants* (AI invariants). Then, the algorithm checks if any of the obtained AI invariants is violated in a monitored run, i.e., if there is an AI invariant which is unserialisably interleaved by an access from another thread to a shared variable which the AI invariant (atomic section) accesses. While the second step of checking AI invariants violation is really simple and can be done in a quite efficient way, the training step to get the AI invariants can lead to a considerable slowdown of the monitored application and has to be repeated if the code base of the application changes (e.g., for a new version of the application).

A more complicated approach was introduced in [24, 69], where atomicity violations are sought using the Lipton's reduction theorem [46]. The approach is based on checking whether a given run can be transformed (reduced) to a serial one using commutativity of certain instructions (or, in other words, by moving certain instructions back or forward in the execution timeline). Both [24, 69] use procedures as atomic blocks by default, but users can annotate blocks of code which they assume to execute atomically to provide a more precise specification of atomic sections for the algorithm. For the reduction used to detect atomicity violations, all instructions are classified, according to their commutativity properties, into 4 groups: (1) *Left-mover* instructions L that may be swapped with the immediately preceding instruction; (2) *Right-mover* instructions R that may be swapped with the immediately succeeding instruction; (3) *Both-mover* instructions B that are simultaneously left and right mover, i.e., they may be swapped with both the immediately preceding and succeeding instructions; and (4) *Non-mover* instructions N that are not known to be left or right mover instructions.

Classification of instructions to these classes is based on their relation to synchronisation operations, e.g., lock acquire instructions are right-movers, lock release instructions are left-movers, and race free accesses to variables are both-movers (a lockset-based dynamic detection algorithm is used for checking race freeness). An execution is then serialisable if it is deadlock-free and each atomic section in this execution can be reduced to a form $R^* N^? L^*$ by moving the instructions in the execution in the allowed directions. Here, $N^?$ represents a single non-mover instruction and both-mover instructions B can be taken as either right-mover instructions R or left-mover instructions L. Algorithms in both [24, 69] use dynamic analysis to detect atomicity violations using the reduction algorithm described above.

Other approaches using the Lipton's reduction theorem [46] can be found in [28,68] where type systems based on this theorem are used to deal with atomicity violations.

Atomicity Over Multiple Variables. The above mentioned algorithms consider atomicity of multiple accesses to the same variable only. However, there are situations where we need to check atomicity over multiple variables, e.g., when a program modifies two or more interrelated variables in several atomic blocks (such variables can represent, for instance, a point in a three-dimensional space or the real and imaginary parts of a complex number). Even if we ensure that all the read and write accesses to these variables are executed atomically, the program can still have an unserializable execution. This happens when the boundaries of the atomic block guarding the access to these variables are misdefined, and what should be a single atomic block was split into two or more smaller atomic blocks. The interleaving of these smaller atomic blocks with other atomic blocks may violate the integrity of the data and expose states that would never be observed in a sequential execution. Nevertheless, the algorithms and the detectors discussed above cannot address these multiple-variable atomicity errors.

In [4], the problem of violation of atomicity of operations over multiple variables is referred to as a *high-level data race*. In the work, all synchronised blocks (i.e., blocks of code guarded by the `synchronized` statement) are considered to form atomic sections. The proposed detection of atomicity violations is based on checking the so-called *view consistency*. For each thread, a set of views is generated. A view is a set of fields (variables) which are accessed by a thread within a single synchronised block. From this set of views, a set of maximal views (maximal according to set inclusion) is computed for each thread. An execution is then serialisable if each thread only uses views that are compatible, i.e., form a chain according to set inclusion, with all maximal views of other threads. Hence, the detection algorithm uses a dynamic analysis to check whether all views are compatible within a given program trace. Since the algorithm has to operate over a high number of sets (each view is a set), it suffers from a big overhead. Dias et al. in [13] adapted this approach to apply static analysis techniques and extended it to reduce the number of false warnings.

A different approach is associated with the Velodrome detector [29]. Here, atomic sections (called transactions) are given as methods annotated by the user. Detection of atomicity violations is based on constructing a graph of the *transactional happens-before relation* (the happens-before relation among transactions). An execution is serialisable if the graph does not contain a cycle. The detection algorithm uses a dynamic analysis to create the graph from a program trace and then checks it for a cycle. If a cycle is found, the program contains an atomicity violation. Since creating the graph for the entire execution is inconvenient, nodes that cannot be involved in a cycle are garbage-collected or not created at all. Like the previous algorithm, Velodrome may suffer from a considerable overhead in some cases, too.

The simple idea of *AI invariants* described in [48] has been generalised for checking atomicity over pairs of variables in [32,66], where a number of problematic interleaving scenarios were identified. The user is assumed to provide the so-called *atomic sets* that are sets of variables which should be operated atomically. In [66] an algorithm to infer which procedure bodies should be the so-called *units of work* w.r.t. the given atomic sets is proposed. This is done statically using dataflow analysis. An execution is then considered serialisable if it does not correspond to any of the problematic interleavings of the detected units of work. An algorithm capable of checking unserialisability of execution of units of work (called atomic-set-serialisability violations) is described in [32]. It is based on a dynamic analysis of program traces. The algorithm introduces the so-called *race automata*, which are simple finite state automata used to detect the problematic interleaving scenarios.

There are also attempts to enhance well-known approaches for data race analysis to detect atomicity violations over multiple variables. One method can be found in [47], where data mining techniques are used to determine *access correlations* among an arbitrary number of variables. This information is then used in modified lockset-based and happens-before-based detectors. Since data race detectors do not directly work with the notion of atomicity, blocks of code accessing correlated variables are used to play the role of atomic sections. Access correlations are inferred statically using a correlation analysis. The correlation analysis is based on mining association rules [3] from frequent itemsets, where items in these sets are accesses to variables. The obtained association rules are then pruned to allow only the rules satisfying the minimal support and minimal confidence constraints. The resulting rules determine access correlations between various variables. Using this information, the two mentioned data race detector types can then be modified to detect atomicity violations over multiple variables as follows. Lockset-based algorithms must check if, for every pair of accesses to a shared variable, the shared variable and all variables correlated with this variable are protected by at least one common lock. Happens-before-based algorithms must compare the logical timestamps not only with accesses to the same variable, but also with accesses to the correlated variables. The detection can be done statically or dynamically, depending on the data race detector used.

6   Detection of Deadlocks

As deadlock is connected with circular dependency among threads and shared resources, the detection of deadlocks usually involves various graph algorithms. For instance, the algorithm introduced in [57] constructs a *thread-wait-for graph* dynamically and analyses it for a presence of cycles. Here, a thread-wait-for graph is an arc-labelled digraph $G = (V, E)$ where vertices V are threads and locks, and edges E represent waiting arcs, which are classified (labelled) according to the synchronisation mechanism used (join synchronisation, notification, finalisation, and waiting on a monitor). A cycle in this graph involving at least two threads represents a deadlock. A disadvantage of this algorithm is that it is able to detect only deadlocks that actually happen. The following works can detect also potential deadlocks that can happen but did not actually happen during the witnessed execution.

In [33], a different algorithm called GoodLock for detecting deadlocks was presented. The algorithm constructs the so-called *runtime lock trees* and uses a depth-first search to detect cycles in it. Here, a runtime lock tree $T_t = (V, E)$ for a thread t is a tree where vertices V are locks acquired by t and there is an edge from $v_1 \in V$ to $v_2 \in V$ when v_1 represents the most recently acquired lock that t holds when acquiring v_2. A path in such a tree represents a nested use of locks. When a program terminates, the algorithm analyses lock trees for each pair of threads. The algorithm issues a warning about a possible deadlock if the order of obtaining the same locks (i.e., their nesting) in two analysed trees differs and no "gate" lock guarding this inconsistency has been detected.

The original GoodLock algorithm is able to detect deadlocks between two threads only. Later works, e.g., [2,6] improve the algorithm to detect deadlocks among multiple threads. In [2], a support for semaphores and wait-notify synchronisation was added. A stack to handle the so-called *lock dependency relation* is used in [38] instead of lock trees. The algorithm computes the transitive closure of the lock dependency relation instead of performing a depth first search in a graph. The modified algorithm uses more memory but the computation is much faster.

Static approaches can be employed also for deadlock detection. A purely data-flow-based interprocedural static detector of deadlocks called RacerX has been presented in [16] while a bottom-up data-flow static analysis is used to detect deadlocks in [70]. Both algorithms produce many false alarms due to the approximations they use. A combination of symbolic execution, static analysis, and SMT solving is used in [11] to automatically derive the so-called *method contracts* guaranteeing deadlock-free executions.

7   Detection of Other Errors in Concurrency

So far, we have covered detection of data races, atomicity violations, and deadlocks that are the most common concurrency errors in practice. In this section, we briefly touch detection of other concurrency errors, such as order violations, missed signals, and non-progress behaviour.

For detecting order violations one needs to be able to decide if, for a given execution, the instructions were or were not executed in the right order. There are only a few detection techniques which are able to detect order violations. These techniques try to detect that some instructions are executed in a wrong order by searching for specific behavioural patterns [77] or by comparing the order of instructions in a testing run with the order witnessed in a series of preceding, correct program runs [74].

Similarly to order violations, there are just a few methods for detecting missed signals. Usually, the problem is studied as part of detecting other concurrency problems, e.g., deadlocks. There is also an approach that uses pattern-based static analysis to search for code patterns that may lead to missed signals [37].

It is also possible to use *contracts for concurrency* [65] to detect some of the errors mentioned above. A contract for concurrency allows one to enumerate sequences of public methods of a module that are required to be executed atomically. Even though such contracts were designed to primarily capture atomicity violations, they are capable of capturing order violations and missed signals as well. Contracts may be written by a developer or inferred automatically from the program (based on its typical usage patterns) [65].

There are two methods [12,20] for dynamically verifying that such contracts are respected at program runtime. In particular, the first method [20] belongs among the so-called *lockset-based* dynamic analyses, whose classic example is the Eraser algorithm for data race detection [64]. Their common feature is that they track sets of locks that are held by various threads and used for various synchronisation purposes. The tracked lock sets are used to extrapolate the synchronisation behaviour seen in the witnessed test runs, allowing one to warn about possible errors even when they do not directly appear in the witnessed test runs.

While the lockset-based method works well in many cases, it may produce both false positives and negatives. Some of these problems are caused by the method itself as lockset-based methods are imprecise in general. However, many of the problems are caused by the limitations of the (basic) contracts which do not allow one to precisely describe which situations are errors and which are not. To address this problem, the notion of contracts for concurrency was extended in [12] to allow them to reflect both the *data flow* between the methods (in that a sequence of method calls only needs to be atomic if they manipulate the same data) and the *contextual information* (in that a sequence of method calls needs not be atomic w.r.t. all other sequences of methods but only some of them). The paper then proposes a method for dynamic validation of contracts based on the *happens-before relation* which utilises *vector clocks* in a way optimised for contract validation. This method does not suffer from false alarms and supports the extended contracts.

One of the most common approaches for detecting non-progress behaviour in finite-state programs is to use model checking and search for non-progress cycles [35]. In case of infinite-state programs, a long enough path of non-progress actions in the state space is often sufficient for proving a non-progress behaviour [30]. A similar approach is also used in dynamic techniques where *dynamic monitoring* [34] of an execution is performed in order to find an execution where no progress action is reached for a long period of time.

8   Boosting Detection of Errors in Concurrency

In this section, we discuss techniques that can help with quality assurance of concurrent programs regardless of particular class of concurrency errors, namely, noise injection and systematic testing.

Noise injection. Noise injection inserts delays into the execution of selected threads aiming at promoting the occurrence of low-probable interleavings that otherwise would happen very seldom or even never. This approach allows to test time-sensitive synchronisation interleavings that could hide latent errors. Noise injection is also able to test legal interleavings of actions which are far away from each other in terms of execution time and in terms of the number of concurrency-relevant events [14] between those actions during average executions provided that the appropriate noise is injected into some of the threads. In a sense, the approach is similar to running the program inside a model checker such as JPF [67] with a random exploration algorithm enabled. However, making purely random scheduling decisions may be less efficient than using some of the noise heuristics which influence the scheduling at some carefully selected places important from the point of view of synchronisation only. The approach of noise injection is mature enough to be used for testing of real-life software, and it is supported by industrial-strength tools, such as IBM Java Concurrency Testing Tool (ConTest) [14] and the Microsoft Driver Verifier, where the technique is called delay fuzzing [1]. A recent tool supporting noise-based testing of concurrent C/C++ code on the binary level is ANaConDA [12,22].

Systematic testing. Systematic testing of concurrent programs [36,52,53,71] has become popular recently. The technique uses a deterministic control over the scheduling of threads. A deterministic scheduler is sometimes implemented using intense noise injection keeping all threads blocked except the one chosen for making a progress. Often, other threads which do not execute synchronisation-relevant instructions or which do not access shared memory are also allowed to make progress concurrently.

The systematic testing approach can be seen as execution-based model checking which systematically tests as many thread interleaving scenarios as possible. Before execution of each instruction which is considered as relevant from the point of view of detecting concurrency-related errors, the technique computes all possible scheduler decisions. The concrete set of instructions considered as concurrency-relevant depends on the particular implementation of the technique (often, shared memory accesses and synchronisation relevant instructions are considered as concurrency-relevant). Each such a decision point is considered a state in the state space of the system under test, and each possible decision is considered an enabled transition at that state. The decisions that are explored from each state are recorded in the form of a partially ordered happens-before graph [52], totally ordered list of synchronisation events [71], or simply in the form of a set of explored decisions [36]. During the next execution of the program, the recorded scheduling decisions can be enforced again when doing a replay or changed when testing with the aim of enforcing a new interleaving scenario.

As the number of possible scheduling decisions is high for complex programs, various optimisations and heuristics reducing the number of decisions to explore have been proposed. For example, the *locality hypothesis* [52] says that most concurrency-related errors can be exposed using a small number of preemptions. This hypothesis is exploited in the CHESS tool [52], which limits the number of context switches taking place in the execution (iteratively increasing the bound on the allowed number of context switches). Moreover, the tool also utilises a partial-order reduction algorithm blocking exploration of states equal to the already explored states (based on an equivalence defined on happens-before graphs). Some further heuristics are then mentioned below when discussing the related approach of coverage-driven testing.

However, despite a great impact of the various reductions, the number of thread interleavings to be explored remains huge for real-life programs, and therefore the approach provides great benefit mainly in the area of unit testing [36,52]. The systematic testing approach is not as expensive as full model checking, but it is still quite costly because one needs to track which scheduling scenarios of possibly very long runs have been witnessed and systematically force new ones. The approach makes it easy to replay an execution where an error was detected, but it has problems with handling various external sources of nondeterminism (e.g., input events).

Systematic testing offers several important benefits over noise injection. Its full control over the scheduler allows systematic testing to precisely navigate the execution of the program under test, to explore different interleavings in each run, and to also replay interesting runs (if other sources of nondeterminism, such as input values, are handled). It allows the user to get information about what fraction of (discovered) scheduling decisions has already been covered by the testing process. On the other hand, the approach suffers from various problems, such as handling external sources of nondeterminism (user actions in GUI, client requests) as well as with continuously running programs where its ability to reuse already collected information is limited. In all those problematic cases, noise injection can be successfully used. Moreover, the performance degradation introduced by noise injection is significantly lower.

Coverage-driven testing. An approach related to systematic testing is the approach of *coverage-driven testing* implemented in the Maple tool [75]. Maple attempts to influence the scheduling such that the obtained coverage of several important synchronisation idioms (called iRoots) is maximised. These idioms capture several important memory access patterns that are shown to be often related with error occurrences. Maple uses several heuristics to likely increase the coverage of iRoots. The technique provides lower guarantees of finding an error than systematic testing, but it is more scalable. The Maple tool [75] limits the number of context switches to two and additionally gets use of the *value-independence hypothesis* which states that exposing a concurrency error does not depend on data values. Moreover, the Maple tool does not consider interleavings where two related actions executed in different threads are too far away from each other. The distance of such actions is computed by counting actions in one of the threads, and the threshold is referred to as a *vulnerability window* [75]. The approach of Maple does not support some kinds of errors (e.g., value-dependent errors or some forms of deadlocks). Multiple of the heuristics that Maple uses are based on randomisation. Maple can thus be viewed as being in between of systematic testing and noise-based testing.

9   Conclusions

In this chapter, we have explained problems connected with concurrent execution of programs on modern multi-core devices, listed common errors that can arise from concurrency and described possibilities how particular kinds of concurrency errors can be detected. We have also mentioned noise injection and systematic testing that can support the discovery of concurrency errors.

Understanding the problems connected with concurrency is the first and inevitable step to produce high quality concurrent software. We, however, believe that detection of concurrency errors followed by their manual elimination by a programmer is not the only way to handle failures caused by concurrency. In contrast to many other kinds of software defects, concurrency errors have one admirable feature emerging from usually huge space of possible thread interleavings which provides us with redundancy that can be employed for automatic correction of the error. If we are able to automatically detect and localise the concurrency defect, we can propose a fix to a programmer or heal it fully automatically at runtime because the set of interleavings contains, besides interleavings leading to a failure, also interleavings that lead to a correct outcome. This is not possible for most of other programmers mistakes because the intended behaviour of the program cannot be inferred automatically.

For instance, if a data race over a shared variable is detected, it can be healed by introducing a new lock for guarding this shared variable. That means that a code acquiring the new lock is inserted before each access to the variable, while a code releasing the lock is inserted after the access. As a reader can guess, adding a lock without knowledge of other locking operations can introduce a deadlock which may be even worse problem than the original data race. Another approach of healing data races we have studied [41] exploits noise injection technique. As noise injection can be used for increasing probability of spotting a concurrency errors by changing probabilities of particular interleavings it can also be used in an opposite manner to significantly reduce probability of interleavings that lead to a fault. This approach cannot introduce a deadlock, however, it does not guarantee that the error is fully covered. Other types of concurrency problems such as deadlocks [56] and atomicity violations [45] can be covered automatically as well.

One may also expect that there will be available programming paradigms like transactional memory [5] in the future that reduce or eliminate chances of creating concurrency errors.

Acknowledgment. This work was partially supported by the ARVI EU COST ACTION IC1402. Further, the Czech authors were supported by the EU ECSEL project Aquas, the internal BUT FIT project FIT-S-17-4014, and the IT4IXS project: IT4Innovations Excellence in Science (LQ1602). The Portuguese author was also supported by the Portuguese Science Foundation and NOVA LINCS (ref. UID/CEC/04516/2013).

References

1. Power Framework Delay Fuzzing, April 2013. http://msdn.microsoft.com/en-us/library/hh454184(v=vs.85).aspx
2. Agarwal, R., Stoller, S.D.: Run-time detection of potential deadlocks for programs with locks, semaphores, and condition variables. In: Proceedings of PADTAD 2006, pp. 51–60. ACM, New York (2006)
3. Agrawal, R., Imieliński, T., Swami, A.: Mining association rules between sets of items in large databases. In: Proceedings of the 1993 ACM SIGMOD International Conference on Management of Data, SIGMOD 1993, pp. 207–216. ACM, New York (1993)
4. Artho, C., Havelund, K., Biere, A.: High-level data races. In: The First International Workshop on Verification and Validation of Enterprise Information Systems, VVEIS 2003, Angers, France (2003)
5. Ayguade, E., Cristal, A., Unsal, O.S., Gagliardi, F., Smith, B., Valero, M., Harris, T.: Transactional memory: An overview. IEEE Micro **27**, 8–29 (2007)
6. Bensalem, S., Havelund, K.: Dynamic deadlock analysis of multi-threaded programs. In: Ur, S., Bin, E., Wolfsthal, Y. (eds.) HVC 2005. LNCS, vol. 3875, pp. 208–223. Springer, Heidelberg (2006). https://doi.org/10.1007/11678779_15
7. Bodden, E., Havelund, K.: Racer: Effective race detection using aspectj. In: Proceedings of the 2008 International Symposium on Software Testing and Analysis, ISSTA 2008, pp. 155–166. ACM, New York (2008)
8. Choi, J.D., Lee, K., Loginov, A., O'Callahan, R., Sarkar, V., Sridharan, M.: Efficient and precise datarace detection for multithreaded object-oriented programs. In: Proceedings of the ACM SIGPLAN 2002 Conference on Programming Language Design and Implementation, PLDI 2002, pp. 258–269. ACM, New York (2002)
9. Christiaens, M., De Bosschere, K.: TRaDe: Data race detection for java. In: Alexandrov, V.N., Dongarra, J.J., Juliano, B.A., Renner, R.S., Tan, C.J.K. (eds.) ICCS 2001. LNCS, vol. 2074, pp. 761–770. Springer, Heidelberg (2001). https://doi.org/10.1007/3-540-45718-6_81
10. Coffman, E.G., Elphick, M., Shoshani, A.: System deadlocks. ACM Comput. Surv. **3**, 67–78 (1971)
11. Deshmukh, J., Emerson, E.A., Sankaranarayanan, S.: Symbolic deadlock analysis in concurrent libraries and their clients. In: Proceedings of the 2009 IEEE/ACM International Conference on Automated Software Engineering, ASE 2009, pp. 480–491. IEEE, Washington, DC (2009)
12. Dias, R.F., Ferreira, C., Fiedor, J., Lourenço, J.M., Smrčka, A., Sousa, D.G., Vojnar, T.: Verifying concurrent programs using contracts. In: Proceedings of ICST 2017. IEEE Computer Society, Washington, DC (2017)
13. Dias, R.J., Pessanha, V., Lourenço, J.M.: Precise detection of atomicity violations. In: Biere, A., Nahir, A., Vos, T. (eds.) HVC 2012. LNCS, vol. 7857, pp. 8–23. Springer, Heidelberg (2013). https://doi.org/10.1007/978-3-642-39611-3_8
14. Edelstein, O., Farchi, E., Goldin, E., Nir, Y., Ratsaby, G., Ur, S.: Framework for testing multi-threaded java programs. Concurrency Comput. Pract. Experience **15**(3–5), 485–499 (2003)
15. Elmas, T., Qadeer, S., Tasiran, S.: Goldilocks: a race and transaction-aware java runtime. In: Proceedings of PLDI 2007, pp. 245–255. ACM, New York (2007)
16. Engler, D., Ashcraft, K.: RacerX: Effective, static detection of race conditions and deadlocks. SIGOPS Oper. Syst. Rev. **37**(5), 237–252 (2003)

17. Eswaran, K.P., Gray, J.N., Lorie, R.A., Traiger, I.L.: The notions of consistency and predicate locks in a database system. Commun. ACM **19**, 624–633 (1976). http://doi.acm.org/10.1145/360363.360369

18. Farchi, E., Nir, Y., Ur, S.: Concurrent bug patterns and how to test them. In: Proceedings of the 17th International Symposium on Parallel and Distributed Processing, IPDPS 2003, p. 286.2. IEEE Computer Society, Washington, DC (2003)

19. Fiedor, J., Křena, B., Letko, Z., Vojnar, T.: A uniform classification of common concurrency errors. In: Moreno-Díaz, R., Pichler, F., Quesada-Arencibia, A. (eds.) EUROCAST 2011. LNCS, vol. 6927, pp. 519–526. Springer, Heidelberg (2012). https://doi.org/10.1007/978-3-642-27549-4_67

20. Fiedor, J., Letko, Z., Lourenço, J., Vojnar, T.: Dynamic validation of contracts in concurrent code. In: Moreno-Díaz, R., Pichler, F., Quesada-Arencibia, A. (eds.) EUROCAST 2015. LNCS, vol. 9520, pp. 555–564. Springer, Cham (2015). https://doi.org/10.1007/978-3-319-27340-2_69

21. Fiedor, J., Vojnar, T.: Noise-based testing and analysis of multi-threaded C/C++ programs on the binary level. In: PADTAD 2012, pp. 36–46. ACM (2012)

22. Fiedor, J., Vojnar, T.: ANaConDA: A framework for analysing multi-threaded C/C++ programs on the binary level. In: Qadeer, S., Tasiran, S. (eds.) RV 2012. LNCS, vol. 7687, pp. 35–41. Springer, Heidelberg (2013). https://doi.org/10.1007/978-3-642-35632-2_5

23. Flanagan, C., Freund, S.N.: Type-based race detection for java. In: Proceedings of the ACM SIGPLAN 2000 Conference on Programming Language Design and Implementation, PLDI 2000, pp. 219–232. ACM, New York (2000)

24. Flanagan, C., Freund, S.N.: Atomizer: A dynamic atomicity checker for multi-threaded programs. SIGPLAN Not. **39**(1), 256–267 (2004)

25. Flanagan, C., Freund, S.N.: Type inference against races. Sci. Comput. Program. **64**(1), 140–165 (2007)

26. Flanagan, C., Freund, S.N.: FastTrack: efficient and precise dynamic race detection. In: Proceedings of the 2009 ACM SIGPLAN Conference on Programming Language Design and Implementation, PLDI 2009, pp. 121–133. ACM, New York (2009)

27. Flanagan, C., Freund, S.N.: The roadrunner dynamic analysis framework for concurrent programs. In: Proceedings of the 9th ACM SIGPLAN-SIGSOFT Workshop on Program Analysis for Software Tools and Engineering, PASTE 2010, pp. 1–8. ACM, New York (2010). http://doi.acm.org/10.1145/1806672.1806674

28. Flanagan, C., Freund, S.N., Lifshin, M., Qadeer, S.: Types for atomicity: static checking and inference for java. ACM Trans. Program. Lang. Syst. **30**(4), 1–53 (2008)

29. Flanagan, C., Freund, S.N., Yi, J.: Velodrome: A sound and complete dynamic atomicity checker for multithreaded programs. SIGPLAN Not. **43**(6), 293–303 (2008)

30. Godefroid, P.: Software model checking: The verisoft approach. Form. Methods Syst. Des. **26**(2), 77–101 (2005)

31. Goubault, E.: Geometry and concurrency: a user's guide. Math. Struct. Comput. Sci. **10**(4), 411–425 (2000)

32. Hammer, C., Dolby, J., Vaziri, M., Tip, F.: Dynamic detection of atomic-set-serializability violations. In: Proceedings of the 30th International Conference on Software Engineering, ICSE 2008, pp. 231–240. ACM, New York (2008)

33. Havelund, K.: Using runtime analysis to guide model checking of java programs. In: Havelund, K., Penix, J., Visser, W. (eds.) SPIN 2000. LNCS, vol. 1885, pp. 245–264. Springer, Heidelberg (2000). https://doi.org/10.1007/10722468_15

34. Ho, A., Smith, S., Hand, S.: On deadlock, livelock, and forward progress. University of Cambridge, Technical report (2005)
35. Holzmann, G.: Spin Model Checker, The: Primer and Reference Manual. Addison-Wesley Professional, Reading (2003)
36. Hong, S., Ahn, J., Park, S., Kim, M., Harrold, M.J.: Testing concurrent programs to achieve high synchronization coverage. In: Proceedings of ISSTA 2012, pp. 210–220. ACM, New York (2012)
37. Hovemeyer, D., Pugh, W.: Finding concurrency bugs in java. In: 23rd Annual ACM SIGACTSIGOPS Symposium on Principles of Distributed Computing (PODC 2004) Workshop on Concurrency and Programs, July 2004
38. Joshi, P., Park, C.S., Sen, K., Naik, M.: A randomized dynamic program analysis technique for detecting real deadlocks. In: Proceedings of the 2009 ACM SIGPLAN Conference on Programming Language Design and Implementation, PLDI 2009, pp. 110–120. ACM, New York (2009)
39. Kahlon, V., Yang, Y., Sankaranarayanan, S., Gupta, A.: Fast and accurate static data-race detection for concurrent programs. In: Damm, W., Hermanns, H. (eds.) CAV 2007. LNCS, vol. 4590, pp. 226–239. Springer, Heidelberg (2007). https://doi.org/10.1007/978-3-540-73368-3_26
40. Kim, K., Yavuz-Kahveci, T., Sanders, B.A.: Precise data race detection in a relaxed memory model using heuristic-based model checking. In: ASE, pp. 495–499. IEEE (2009)
41. Křena, B., Letko, Z., Tzoref, R., Ur, S., Vojnar, T.: Healing data races on-the-fly. In: Proceedings of PADTAD 2007, pp. 54–64. ACM, New York (2007)
42. Lamport, L.: How to make a multiprocessor computer that correctly executes multiprocess programs. IEEE Trans. Comput. **28**(9), 690–691 (1979). https://doi.org/10.1109/TC.1979.1675439
43. Lamport, L.: Time, clocks, and the ordering of events in a distributed system. Commun. ACM **21**(7), 558–565 (1978)
44. Laurenzano, M., Tikir, M., Carrington, L., Snavely, A.: PEBIL: Efficient static binary instrumentation for linux. In: ISPASS 2010, pp. 175–183 (2010)
45. Letko, Z., Vojnar, T., Křena, B.: Atomrace: Data race and atomicity violation detector and healer. In: Proceedings of the 6th Workshop on Parallel and Distributed Systems: Testing, Analysis, and Debugging, PADTAD 2008, pp. 7:1–7:10. ACM, New York (2008). http://doi.acm.org/10.1145/1390841.1390848
46. Lipton, R.J.: Reduction: A method of proving properties of parallel programs. Commun. ACM **18**(12), 717–721 (1975)
47. Lu, S., Park, S., Hu, C., Ma, X., Jiang, W., Li, Z., Popa, R.A., Zhou, Y.: MUVI: Automatically inferring multi-variable access correlations and detecting related semantic and concurrency bugs. SIGOPS Oper. Syst. Rev. **41**(6), 103–116 (2007)
48. Lu, S., Tucek, J., Qin, F., Zhou, Y.: AVIO: Detecting atomicity violations via access interleaving invariants. In: Proceedings of ASPLOS 2006, pp. 37–48. ACM, New York (2006)
49. Luk, C.K., Cohn, R., Muth, R., Patil, H., Klauser, A., Lowney, G., Wallace, S., Reddi, V.J., Hazelwood, K.: Pin: building customized program analysis tools with dynamic instrumentation. In: Proceedings of PLDI 2005. ACM (2005)
50. Masticola, S.P., Ryder, B.G.: Non-concurrency analysis. In: Proceedings of the Fourth ACM SIGPLAN Symposium on Principles and Practice of Parallel Programming, PPOPP 1993, pp. 129–138. ACM, New York (1993)
51. Mattern, F.: Virtual time and global states of distributed systems. In: Proceedings of the International Workshop on Parallel and Distributed Algorithms. Elsevier Science Publishers (1988). http://citeseer.ist.psu.edu/mattern89virtual.html

52. Musuvathi, M., Qadeer, S., Ball, T.: CHESS: A Systematic Testing Tool for Concurrent Software. Technical report MSR-TR-2007-149, Microsoft Research (2007)
53. Musuvathi, M., Qadeer, S., Ball, T., Basler, G., Nainar, P.A., Neamtiu, I.: Finding and reproducing heisenbugs in concurrent programs. In: OSDI 2008, pp. 267–280. USENIX Association, Berkeley (2008). http://dl.acm.org/citation.cfm?id=1855741.1855760
54. Naik, M., Aiken, A., Whaley, J.: Effective static race detection for java. SIGPLAN Not. **41**(6), 308–319 (2006)
55. Nethercote, N., Seward, J.: Valgrind: a framework for heavyweight dynamic binary instrumentation. In: PLDI 2007, pp. 89–100. ACM, New York (2007). http://doi.acm.org/10.1145/1250734.1250746
56. Nir-Buchbinder, Y., Tzoref, R., Ur, S.: Deadlocks: from exhibiting to healing. In: Leucker, M. (ed.) RV 2008. LNCS, vol. 5289, pp. 104–118. Springer, Heidelberg (2008). https://doi.org/10.1007/978-3-540-89247-2_7
57. Nonaka, Y., Ushijima, K., Serizawa, H., Murata, S., Cheng, J.: A run-time deadlock detector for concurrent java programs. In: Proceedings of the Eighth Asia-Pacific on Software Engineering Conference, APSEC 2001, p. 45. IEEE, Washington, DC (2001)
58. O'Callahan, R., Choi, J.D.: Hybrid dynamic data race detection. In: Proceedings of the Ninth ACM SIGPLAN Symposium on Principles and Practice of Parallel Programming, PPoPP 2003, pp. 167–178. ACM, New York (2003)
59. Park, S., Vuduc, R.W., Harrold, M.J.: Falcon: Fault localization in concurrent programs. In: Proceedings of the 32nd ACM/IEEE International Conference on Software Engineering - Volume 1, ICSE 2010, pp. 245–254. ACM, New York (2010). http://doi.acm.org/10.1145/1806799.1806838
60. Poulsen, K.: Tracking the blackout bug (2004). http://www.securityfocus.com/news/8412
61. Pozniansky, E., Schuster, A.: Efficient on-the-fly data race detection in multi-threaded C++ programs. In: Proceedings of PPoPP 2003, pp. 179–190. ACM, New York (2003)
62. Pozniansky, E., Schuster, A.: MultiRace: efficient on-the-fly data race detection in multithreaded C++ programs: research articles. Concurr. Comput. Pract. Exper. **19**(3), 327–340 (2007)
63. von Praun, C., Gross, T.R.: Object race detection. In: Proceedings of OOPSLA 2001, pp. 70–82. ACM, New York (2001)
64. Savage, S., Burrows, M., Nelson, G., Sobalvarro, P., Anderson, T.: Eraser: a dynamic data race detector for multi-threaded programs. In: Proceedings of SOSP 1997, pp. 27–37. ACM, New York (1997)
65. Sousa, D.G., Dias, R.J., Ferreira, C., Lourenço, J.M.: Preventing atomicity violations with contracts, May 2015. arXiv preprint arXiv:1505.02951
66. Vaziri, M., Tip, F., Dolby, J.: Associating synchronization constraints with data in an object-oriented language. In: Conference Record of the 33rd ACM SIGPLAN-SIGACT Symposium on Principles of Programming Languages, POPL 2006, pp. 334–345. ACM, New York (2006)
67. Visser, W., Havelund, K., Brat, G., Park, S.: Model checking programs. In: Proceedings of ASE 2000, p. 3. IEEE Computer Society, Washington, DC (2000)
68. Wang, L., Stoller, S.D.: Static analysis of atomicity for programs with non-blocking synchronization. In: Proceedings of the Tenth ACM SIGPLAN Symposium on Principles and Practice of Parallel Programming, PPoPP 2005, pp. 61–71. ACM, New York (2005)

69. Wang, L., Stoller, S.D.: Runtime analysis of atomicity for multithreaded programs. IEEE Trans. Softw. Eng. **32**(2), 93–110 (2006)
70. Williams, A., Thies, W., Ernst, M.D.: Static deadlock detection for java libraries. In: Black, A.P. (ed.) ECOOP 2005. LNCS, vol. 3586, pp. 602–629. Springer, Heidelberg (2005). https://doi.org/10.1007/11531142_26
71. Wu, J., Tang, Y., Hu, G., Cui, H., Yang, J.: Sound and precise analysis of parallel programs through schedule specialization. In: Proceedings of PLDI 2012, pp. 205–216. ACM, New York (2012)
72. Xu, M., Bodík, R., Hill, M.D.: A serializability violation detector for shared-memory server programs. SIGPLAN Not. **40**(6), 1–14 (2005)
73. Yang, Y., Gringauze, A., Wu, D., Rohde, H.: Detecting Data Race and Atomicity Violation via Typestate-Guided Static Analysis. Technical report MSR-TR-2008-108, Microsoft Research (2008)
74. Yu, J., Narayanasamy, S.: A case for an interleaving constrained shared-memory multi-processor. SIGARCH Comput. Archit. News **37**(3), 325–336 (2009)
75. Yu, J., Narayanasamy, S., Pereira, C., Pokam, G.: Maple: A coverage-driven testing tool for multithreaded programs. In: Proceedings of OOPSLA 2012, pp. 485–502. ACM, New York (2012)
76. Yu, Y., Rodeheffer, T., Chen, W.: RaceTrack: efficient detection of data race conditions via adaptive tracking. SIGOPS Oper. Syst. Rev. **39**(5), 221–234 (2005)
77. Zhang, W., Sun, C., Lu, S.: ConMem: detecting severe concurrency bugs through an effect-oriented approach. In: Proceedings of the Fifteenth Edition of ASPLOS on Architectural Support for Programming Languages and Operating Systems, ASPLOS 2010, pp. 179–192. ACM, New York (2010)

Monitoring Events that Carry Data

Klaus Havelund[1], Giles Reger[2(✉)], Daniel Thoma[3], and Eugen Zălinescu[4]

[1] Jet Propulsion Laboratory, California Institute of Technology, Pasadena, USA
[2] University of Manchester, Manchester, UK
giles.reger@manchester.ac.uk
[3] Universität zu Lübeck, Lübeck, Germany
[4] Technische Universität München, Munich, Germany

Abstract. Very early runtime verification systems focused on monitoring what we can refer to as propositional events: just names of events. For this, finite state machines, standard regular expressions, or propositional temporal logics were sufficient formalisms for expressing properties. However, in practice there is a need for monitoring events that in addition carry data arguments. This adds complexity to both the property specification languages, and monitoring algorithms, which is reflected in the many alternative such approaches suggested in the literature. This chapter presents five different formalisms and monitoring approaches that support specifications with data, in order to illustrate the challenges and various solutions.

Keywords: Runtime verification · Data rich events · Temporal logic
State machines · Rule systems · Stream processing

1 Introduction

Runtime verification (RV) as a field is broadly defined as focusing on processing execution traces (output of an observed system) for verification and validation purposes, ignoring how the traces are generated, in contrast to testing, where test case (input to observed system) generation is in focus. Of particular interest is the problem of verifying that a sequence of events, a trace, satisfies a temporal property, formulated e.g. as a state machine or temporal logic formula. Applications cover such domains as security monitoring and safety monitoring.

We shall distinguish between two variants of this problem: *propositional* and *parameterised* runtime verification, according to the format of events. In the propositional case, events are atomic without structure, for example simple identifiers, such as *openGate* and *closeGate*. Here we assume a finite (and usually small) alphabet Σ of atomic identifiers. This case resembles the classic finite trace language membership of language theory [52], where properties are

K. Havelund—The research performed by this author was carried out at Jet Propulsion Laboratory, California Institute of Technology, under a contract with the National Aeronautics and Space Administration.

E. Bartocci and Y. Falcone (Eds.): Lectures on Runtime Verification, LNCS 10457, pp. 61–102, 2018.
https://doi.org/10.1007/978-3-319-75632-5_3

stated for example as finite state machines or regular expressions with atomic letters, as in the following regular expression: ($openGate$; $closeGate$)*. Similarly, the propositional verification problem has been studied in model checking [51], where properties for example are stated in Linear Temporal Logic (LTL), and where models are infinite traces of atomic propositions. Very early RV systems supported only this propositional case. Within recent years, however, emphasis within the research community has been on parameterised runtime verification, where events carry data. Here events are drawn from an alphabet $\Sigma \times D^*$ for some possibly infinite value domain D, which includes values occurring in monitored events, for example reals, strings, objects, etc. This chapter reviews five alternative approaches to parameterised runtime verification, covering extensions of temporal logic and automata with quantification, as well as rule-based and stream processing systems.

As an example consider the following (well studied) data parameterised property, which we shall name *UnsafeMapIterator*, and which will be formalised in the different approaches. The property concerns the use of Java collections, which are part of the Java library API. The property requires that if a collection is created from a java.util.Map object (i.e. the key set of the map), and then a java.util.Iterator object is created from that collection, and the original map thereafter is updated, then thereafter the next() method cannot be called on that iterator. Four events are relevant: create(m, c) records the creation of collection c from map m; iterator(c, i) records the creation of iterator i from collection c; update(m) records the update of m; and next(i) records the call of the next() method on iterator i. More complicated properties can easily be imagined, requiring computations to be performed, such as counting, etc. Due to lack of space we shall, however, limit ourselves to this property as a running example.

The chapter presents five formalisms and monitoring approaches, chosen to represent a broad view of the solution space wrt. logics and algorithms. FOTL [16, 17] is a first-order temporal logic, with a monitoring algorithm that has roots in approaches for checking temporal integrity constraints of databases [26]. MMT (Monitoring Modulo Theories) [34] is a generic framework that allows lifting monitor synthesis procedures for propositional temporal logics to a temporal logic over structures within some first-order theory using SMT solving. These first two approaches represent variations of first-order linear temporal logic, a very important class of candidate logics for runtime verification. The two systems also represent different interesting monitoring algorithms for this case. QEA (Quantified Event Automata) [10] are automata supporting quantification over data. The corresponding approach generalises the concept of trace slicing as found in earlier influential RV systems such as TRACEMATCHES [5] and MOP [25, 62]. Trace slicing likely provides the most efficient monitors among state-of-the-art systems. LOGFIRE [47] is a rule-based framework interpreting rules working on a collection of facts. It is implemented using an adaption of the RETE algorithm known from artificial intelligence. It is furthermore implemented as an internal DSL (an API in the Scala programming language). LOLA [29] is a stream-based specification language inspired by

Lustre and Esterel. The corresponding approach incrementally constructs output streams from input streams. This is a rather new approach to monitoring.

The chapter is organised as follows. Section 2 introduces preliminary notation. Sections 3 to 7 introduce the five different formalisms and monitoring approaches. Section 8 further discusses and compares the five approaches. Section 9 presents related work, while Sect. 10 concludes the chapter.

2   Preliminaries

Primitive Types. By $\mathbb{B}$ we denote the set of Boolean values $\{\mathsf{true}, \mathsf{false}\}$ together with the usual operators such as $\neg, \wedge, \vee, \rightarrow$. By $\mathbb{N}$ we denote the set of natural numbers $\{0, 1, 2, \ldots\}$ and by $\mathbb{R}$ the set of real numbers. We assume a set of event names $\mathcal{N}$, a set of variable names $\mathcal{V}$, and an infinite domain $\mathbb{D}$ of values (data occurring in events).

Non-primitive Types. A power set type is denoted by $\wp(T)$, denoting the set of all subsets of the type T. Tuple types are denoted by $T_1 \times T_2 \times \ldots \times T_n$, containing elements of the form $(v_1, ..., v_n)$ for $v_i \in T_i$.

By $S \rightarrow T$ we denote the set of total functions from S to T. By $S \nrightarrow T$ we denote the set of partial functions from S to T with a finite domain, also referred to as maps. A map can be explicitly constructed with the notation: $[x_1 \mapsto v_1, ..., x_n \mapsto v_n]$, with $[\,]$ denoting the empty map. A map is applied with the same notation as function application: $m(x_i)$ yielding v_i. The values for which a map m is defined is denoted by $\mathsf{dom}(m)$, resulting in the set $\{x_1, ..., x_n\}$. One map m_1 is overridden by another map m_2 with the notation $m_1 \dagger m_2$. That is, if $m = m_1 \dagger m_2$ then $m(x) = m_2(x)$ if $x \in \mathsf{dom}(m_2)$ else $m(x) = m_1(x)$. Maps are expected to be applied to values in their domain.

By T^* we denote the set of finite sequences over T where each sequence element is of type T. A sequence σ of length N is a function of type $\{n \in \mathbb{N} \mid n < N\} \rightarrow T$. The length of a sequence σ is denoted by $|\sigma|$. The element at position $i \in \mathbb{N}$ in sequence σ is denoted $\sigma(i)$ or σ_i. A sequence can be explicitly constructed using the notation: $\langle v_1, \ldots, v_n \rangle$, with $\langle\,\rangle$ denoting the empty sequence. A non-empty sequence $s = \langle v_1, v_2, \ldots, v_n \rangle$ of type T^* can be deconstructed with the functions $\mathsf{head} : T^* \rightarrow T$ and $\mathsf{tail} : T^* \rightarrow T^*$ as follows: $\mathsf{head}(s) = v_1$ and $\mathsf{tail}(s) = \langle v_2, \ldots, v_n \rangle$. We occasionally write $\bar{v}$ to represent a sequence $\langle v_1, \ldots, v_n \rangle$. Sequences are also referred to as lists.

First-Order Logic. A *signature* $S = (C, P, \mathsf{ar})$ consists of finite disjoint sets C and P of constant and respectively relation (or predicate) symbols, and a *arity* function $\mathsf{ar} : P \rightarrow \mathbb{N}$. A *term* is a constant $c \in C$ or a variable $x \in \mathcal{V}$.

First-order *formulas* over the signature $S = (C, P, \mathsf{ar})$ are given by the grammar

$$\varphi ::= p(t_1, \ldots, t_{\mathsf{ar}(p)}) \mid \neg\varphi \mid \varphi \vee \varphi \mid \exists x.\,\varphi,$$

where p ranges over P, the t_is range over terms, and x ranges over $\mathcal{V}$. As syntactic sugar, we use standard Boolean constants and connectives such as *true*, *false*, $\wedge$, $\rightarrow$, and the universal quantifier $\forall x$. The set of *free variables* of a formula φ, that is, those that are not in the scope of some quantifier in φ, is denoted by $fv(\varphi)$. A *sentence* is a formula without free variables.

A *structure* $\mathscr{S}$ over the signature S consists of a (finite or infinite) *domain* $D \neq \emptyset$ and *interpretations* $c^{\mathscr{S}} \in D$ and $p^{\mathscr{S}} \subseteq D^{\mathsf{ar}(r)}$, for each $c \in C$ and $p \in P$. Given a structure with domain D, a *valuation* is a mapping $\theta : \mathcal{V} \rightarrow D$. For a valuation θ, $\bar{x} = (x_1, \ldots, x_n) \in \mathcal{V}^n$, and $\bar{d} = (d_1, \ldots, d_n) \in D^n$, we write $\theta[\bar{x} \mapsto \bar{d}]$ for the valuation that maps x_i to d_i, for $1 \leq i \leq n$, and leaves the other variables' valuation unaltered. We abuse notation and apply a valuation θ also to constants, with $\theta(c) = c^{\mathscr{S}}$, for all $c \in C$. The semantics of first-order formulas is defined as usual. We write $(\mathscr{S}, \theta) \models \varphi$ if a formula φ is satisfied for some structure $\mathscr{S}$ and valuation θ.

Events and Traces. An *event* is a tuple $(id, \langle v_1, \ldots, v_n \rangle)$ consisting of a name $id \in \mathcal{N}$ and a sequence of values $v_i \in \mathbb{D}$. An event is typically written as $id(v_1, \ldots, v_n)$. The type of events is denoted by $\mathbb{E} = \mathcal{N} \times \mathbb{D}^*$. The type of (event) *traces* is denoted by $\mathbb{E}^*$.

The Monitoring Problem. We will focus on the following problem: given some specification language $\mathscr{L}$, find a procedure $M : \mathscr{L} \rightarrow (\mathbb{E}^* \rightarrow \mathit{Verdict})$, that for any specification $\varphi \in \mathscr{L}$ and any trace $\tau \in \mathbb{E}^*$, computes a verdict $M(\varphi)(\tau)$ indicating whether the trace τ satisfies the specification φ or not. Note, however, that *Verdict* generally can be any data domain, including the traditional case of Booleans or some extension of Booleans. Such a procedure normally processes the trace iteratively, event by event, keeping state between iterations. A verdict is consequently issued for each new event, and not just at the end of the trace. Thus, *Verdict* typically includes a special verdict with the meaning "unknown verdict" or "no definitive verdict (yet)." We refer to such a procedure as a *monitoring algorithm*.

3   Monitoring First-Order Temporal Properties

3.1   Overview

First-order temporal logics are natural specification languages for formalising requirements of hardware and software systems. In particular, the first-order aspect is well-suited to capture relations between data and quantify over data. While first-order temporal logics are not widely used in verification because of decidability issues [50], they do admit efficient monitoring.

In this section we present a monitoring approach for the past-only fragment of first-order temporal logic (FOTL). The presentation is a stripped-down version, due to limited space, of the approaches in [16,17], given for richer logics, which additionally include future temporal operators, quantitative temporal constraints to express deadlines, interpreted functions like arithmetic operators, rigid predicates like inequality, and SQL-like aggregation operators. In a nutshell, the monitoring algorithm is based on a translation of formulas in a fragment of FOTL into relational algebra expressions. The algorithm is implemented in the MonPoly tool [15].

To get a glimpse of the specification language, we formalise next the *Unsafe-MapIterator* property. To each event we associate a corresponding predicate symbol. Then the following FOTL formula represents a possible formalisation.

$$\Box \forall i. \Big(\mathsf{next}(i) \rightarrow \exists m, c. \big(\neg \mathsf{update}(m) \mathbin{\mathsf{S}} \big(\mathsf{iterator}(c,i) \wedge \blacklozenge \mathsf{create}(m,c) \big) \big) \Big)$$

The formula requires that always,[1] for any iterator i, if this iterator is used, then there are a map m and a collection c such that (a) at some previous time point the iterator i was created from collection c, (b) before that, the collection c was created from the map m, and (c) since the iterator's creation, the map m has not been updated.

3.2 Syntax and Semantics

FOTL *formulas* over the signature $S = (C, P, \mathsf{ar})$ are given by the grammar

$$\varphi ::= p(t_1, \ldots, t_{\mathsf{ar}(p)}) \mid \neg \varphi \mid \varphi \vee \varphi \mid \exists x. \, \varphi \mid \bullet \varphi \mid \varphi \mathbin{\mathsf{S}} \varphi$$

where p ranges over P, the t_is range over $C \cup \mathscr{V}$, and x ranges over $\mathscr{V}$. The symbols $\bullet$ and S denote the "previous" and the "since" temporal operators. Intuitively, the formula $\bullet \varphi$ states that φ holds at the previous time point, while the formula $\varphi \mathbin{\mathsf{S}} \psi$ states that there is a time point in the past where ψ holds and from the next time point and onwards the formula φ continuously holds. As syntactic sugar, besides the one for first-order logic, we use the temporal operator $\blacklozenge$ ("once") with $\blacklozenge \varphi := \mathit{true} \mathbin{\mathsf{S}} \varphi$.

A *temporal structure* over the signature S is a sequence $\overline{\mathscr{T}} = (\mathscr{T}_0, \mathscr{T}_1, \ldots)$ of structures over S such that

(1) all structures $\mathscr{T}_i$, with $i \geq 0$, have the same domain, denoted D, and
(2) constant symbols have rigid interpretation: $c^{\mathscr{T}_i} = c^{\mathscr{T}_0}$, for all $c \in C$ and $i > 0$.

We call the indices of the elements in the sequence $\overline{\mathscr{T}}$ *time points*. In a temporal structure, predicates may have different interpretations at different time points. As detailed later, predicates and their interpretations are used to represent events. Recall that there are no function symbols (beside constants) to be interpreted.

---

[1] Since we restrict ourselves to the past-only fragment of FOTL, the outermost temporal operator $\Box$ ("always") is not part of our definition of the logic given in Sect. 3.2. However, we include it in the formalisation to emphasise that the property must be fulfilled at all time points.

Definition 1. *Let $\overline{\mathscr{T}}$ be a temporal structure over the signature S, with $\overline{\mathscr{T}} = (\mathscr{T}_0, \mathscr{T}_1, \dots)$, φ a formula over S, θ a valuation, and $i \in \mathbb{N}$. We define the satisfaction relation $(\overline{\mathscr{T}}, \theta, i) \models \varphi$ inductively as follows:*

$$
\begin{aligned}
(\overline{\mathscr{T}}, \theta, i) &\models p(t_1, \dots, t_{\mathsf{ar}(p)}) & \textit{iff} \quad & \big(\theta(t_1), \dots, \theta(t_{\mathsf{ar}(p)})\big) \in p^{\mathscr{T}_i}, \\
(\overline{\mathscr{T}}, \theta, i) &\models \neg\psi & \textit{iff} \quad & (\overline{\mathscr{T}}, \theta, i) \not\models \psi, \\
(\overline{\mathscr{T}}, \theta, i) &\models \psi \vee \psi' & \textit{iff} \quad & (\overline{\mathscr{T}}, \theta, i) \models \psi \textit{ or } (\overline{\mathscr{T}}, \theta, i) \models \psi', \\
(\overline{\mathscr{T}}, \theta, i) &\models \exists x. \, \psi & \textit{iff} \quad & (\overline{\mathscr{T}}, \theta[x \mapsto d], i) \models \psi, \textit{ for some } d \in D, \\
(\overline{\mathscr{T}}, \theta, i) &\models \bullet\psi & \textit{iff} \quad & i > 0 \textit{ and } (\overline{\mathscr{T}}, \theta, i-1) \models \psi, \\
(\overline{\mathscr{T}}, \theta, i) &\models \psi \, \mathsf{S} \, \psi' & \textit{iff} \quad & \textit{for some } j \leq i, \ (\overline{\mathscr{T}}, \theta, j) \models \psi', \textit{ and} \\
& & & (\overline{\mathscr{T}}, \theta, k) \models \psi, \textit{ for all } k \textit{ with } j < k \leq i.
\end{aligned}
$$

For a temporal structure $\overline{\mathscr{T}}$, a time point $i \in \mathbb{N}$, and a formula φ with the vector $\bar{x}$ of free variables, let $\llbracket\varphi\rrbracket^{(\overline{\mathscr{T}}, i)} := \big\{\bar{d} \in D^{|fv(\varphi)|} \,\big|\, (\overline{\mathscr{T}}, \theta[\bar{x} \mapsto \bar{d}], i) \models \varphi\big\}$. The set $\llbracket\varphi\rrbracket^{(\overline{\mathscr{T}}, i)}$ consists of the satisfying elements of φ at time point i in $\overline{\mathscr{T}}$. Instead of $\llbracket\varphi\rrbracket^{(\overline{\mathscr{T}}, i)}$ we write $\llbracket\varphi\rrbracket^i$ when $\overline{\mathscr{T}}$ is clear from the context.

3.3   Monitoring Algorithm

Setup. We assume that property formalisations are of the form $\Box\forall\bar{x}. \, \varphi$, where φ is an FOTL formula and $\bar{x}$ is the sequence of φ's free variables. The property requires that $\forall\bar{x}. \, \varphi$ holds at every time point in the temporal structure $\overline{\mathscr{T}}$ representing the monitored system's behaviour. Moreover, we assume that $\overline{\mathscr{T}}$ has domain $\mathbb{D}$ and it is a *temporal database*, i.e. the relation $p^{\mathscr{T}_i}$ is finite, for any $p \in P$ and $i \in \mathbb{N}$.

The inputs of the monitoring algorithm are a formula ψ, which is logically equivalent to $\neg\varphi$, and a temporal database $\overline{\mathscr{T}}$, which is processed iteratively. That is, at each iteration $i \geq 0$, the monitor processes the structure $\mathscr{T}_i$. The algorithm outputs, again iteratively, the relation $\llbracket\psi\rrbracket^i$, for each $i \geq 0$. As ψ and $\neg\varphi$ are equivalent, the tuples in $\llbracket\psi\rrbracket^i$ represent the property violations at time point i. Note that we drop the topmost universal quantifier, since an instantiation of the free variables $\bar{x}$ that satisfies ψ provides additional information about the violation. Note that the property is satisfied if and only if the output at each iteration is the empty set.

Remark 1. Given an event trace τ, we build a temporal database as follows, assuming that all events with the same name have the same number of arguments. We also assume a signature (C, P, ar) with $\mathscr{N} \subseteq P$, and arities of predicate symbols matching those of the corresponding events names. The temporal database $\overline{\mathscr{T}}$ is built as follows: if at position i, with $0 \leq i < |\tau|$ the event $e(d_1, \dots, d_n)$ occurs then $e^{\mathscr{T}_i} = \{(d_1, \dots, d_n)\}$ and $p^{\mathscr{T}_i} = \emptyset$, for any $p \in P$ with $p \neq e$. For all $i \geq |\tau|$ we take $p^{\mathscr{T}_i} = \emptyset$, for all $p \in P$.

Note that, since we are considering here the past-only fragment of FOTL, structures at time points $j > i$ are irrelevant for the evaluation at time point i. Thus, when monitoring a trace τ, the algorithm is stopped after iteration $|\tau| - 1$[2].

Example 1. We illustrate this setup on the *UnsafeMapIterator* property. Consider the following event sequence:

$$\text{create}(m, c_1).\text{create}(m, c_2).\text{iterator}(c_1, i_1).\text{update}(m).\text{iterator}(c_2, i_2).\text{next}(i_1)$$

The corresponding temporal database contains the interpretations $\text{create}^{\mathcal{T}_0} = \{(m, c_1)\}$, $\text{create}^{\mathcal{T}_1} = \{(m, c_2)\}$, and $\text{create}^{\mathcal{T}_i} = \emptyset$, for $i \in \{2, 3, \dots\}$, etc.

Let φ be the formula from Sect. 3.1 formalising the *UnsafeMapIterator* property with the $\square$ operator and the $\forall$ quantifier stripped off. Furthermore let $\gamma(i)$ be the consequent of the implication in φ and let $\psi(i) := \text{next}(i) \wedge \neg\gamma(i)$. We thus have $\psi(i) \equiv \neg\varphi(i)$. One can check that $[\![\psi]\!]^i = \emptyset$, for $i \in \{0, \dots, 4\}$, and that $[\![\psi]\!]^5 = \{(i_1)\}$, meaning that there are no violations at time points 0 to 4, and there is a violation at time point 5, for iterator i_1.

Remark 2. Note that when encoding event traces as temporal databases, the interpretation of predicate symbols are always either empty or singleton relations. This need not be the case in arbitrary temporal databases. For instance, the relations at a time point could contain the tuples involved in a database transaction.

Monitorable Fragment. The computation of $[\![\psi]\!]^i$ is by recursion over ψ's formula structure, using relational algebra operators to compute the evaluation of a formula from the evaluation of its direct subformulas, possibly from previous time points. Not all formulas in FOTL are effectively monitorable, since unrestricted use of logic operators may require infinite relations to be built during evaluation. Thus the algorithm is only able to deal with formulas from the following *monitorable fragment* of FOTL, which consists of the formulas ψ that satisfy the following conditions:

1. $fv(\alpha) = fv(\beta)$, for any subformula of ψ of the form $\alpha \vee \beta$;
2. $fv(\alpha) \subseteq fv(\beta)$, for any subformula of ψ of the form $\beta \wedge \neg\alpha$,[3] $\alpha \, \mathsf{S} \, \beta$, and $\neg\alpha \, \mathsf{S} \, \beta$;
3. a subformula of the form $\neg\alpha$ can only appear as part of a subformula of the form $\beta \wedge \neg\alpha$ or $\neg\alpha \, \mathsf{S}_I \, \beta$.

---

[2] When considering specifications with a future dimension, see [17], we require that future operators are bounded: they only look boundedly far into the future; this corresponds to hard-time specifications, and can be specified with metric temporal constraints; that is in Metric FOTL [53]. Note that the approach thus handles a safety fragment of (Metric) FOTL. Then, to handle a finite trace, since it is assumed that time is observed by the monitoring algorithm only through event timestamps, a new dummy event with a sufficiently large timestamp is added at the end of the trace, and the algorithm is stopped after observing this last event.

[3] Note that here we treat the operator $\wedge$ as a primitive.

This set of syntactic restrictions on ψ ensure in particular that $[\![\psi]\!]^i$ is finite, for any $i \in \mathbb{N}$. Consider for instance the non-monitorable formula $\psi = p(x) \vee q(y)$. Given that $\mathbb{D}$ is infinite, there are infinitely many tuples $(a, b) \in \mathbb{D}^2$ that satisfy ψ, at any time point i, namely all tuples in $(p^{\mathscr{I}_i} \times \mathbb{D}) \cup (\mathbb{D} \times q^{\mathscr{I}_i})$. For example, if $p(a)$ holds at i (i.e. $a \in p^{\mathscr{I}_i}$), then, *for any* $b \in \mathbb{D}$, the formula $p(a) \vee q(b)$ holds at i, i.e. $(a, b) \in [\![\psi]\!]^i$.

The MONPOLY tool implements a set of heuristics to rewrite non-monitorable formulas into monitorable formulas. While these heuristics have proved to be effective in practice, they are often not necessary as it is usually easy to directly express a domain-independent[4] formula $\neg\varphi$ as an equivalent monitorable formula ψ. For instance, for $\varphi = p(x, y) \rightarrow \blacklozenge(q(x) \vee r(y))$, the non-monitorable formula $\psi = p(x, y) \wedge \neg\blacklozenge(q(x) \vee r(y))$ can be rewritten to the monitorable formula $(p(x, y) \wedge \neg\blacklozenge q(x)) \vee (p(x, y) \wedge \neg\blacklozenge r(y))$.

Algorithm. We start with some definitions. A *table* is a tuple $(R, \bar{x})$, written $R_{\bar{x}}$, where $R \subseteq \mathbb{D}^k$ is a relation and $\bar{x}$ is a sequence of k variables, for some $k \in \mathbb{N}$. Given tables A and B and variable sequence $\bar{x}$, we denote by $\sigma_C(A)$, $\pi_{\bar{x}}(A)$, $A \bowtie B$, $A \triangleright B$, and $A \cup B$, the relational algebra operators *selection, projection, (natural) join, antijoin,* and respectively *union* applied to tables A and B, where C is a set of constraints of the form $t = t'$, for $t, t' \in C \cup \mathscr{V}$. We refer to textbooks on databases, e.g. [4], for their definitions.

Example 2. Let $A_{\langle x, y \rangle}, B_{\langle y, z \rangle}, C_{\langle y \rangle}$ be tables with $A = \{(1, 2), (1, 4), (3, 4)\}$, $B = \{(2, 5), (2, 6)\}$, and $C = \{4\}$. We have $A_{\langle x, y \rangle} \bowtie B_{\langle y, z \rangle} = \{(1, 2, 5), (1, 2, 6)\}_{\langle x, y, z \rangle}$, $A_{\langle x, y \rangle} \triangleright C_{\langle y \rangle} = \{(1, 2)\}_{\langle x, y \rangle}$, $\sigma_{x=3}(A_{\langle x, y \rangle}) = \{(3, 4)\}_{\langle x, y \rangle}$, and $\pi_{\langle y \rangle}(A_{\langle x, y \rangle}) = \{2, 4\}_{\langle y \rangle}$.

Next, the free variables of a formula α are used as attributes of the relation $[\![\alpha]\!]^i$. We write $[\![\alpha]\!]^i_{\bar{x}}$ for the table $([\![\alpha]\!]^i)_{\bar{x}}$, where $\bar{x}$ is the vector of free variables of α. The following equalities express in our notation the standard correspondence, known as Codd's theorem, between first-order logic and relational algebra.

$$[\![\alpha \wedge \beta]\!]^i_{\bar{z}} = [\![\alpha]\!]^i_{\bar{x}} \bowtie [\![\beta]\!]^i_{\bar{y}} \qquad [\![\alpha \vee \beta]\!]^i_{\bar{x}} = [\![\alpha]\!]^i_{\bar{x}} \cup [\![\beta]\!]^i_{\bar{x}}$$
$$[\![\alpha \wedge \neg\beta]\!]^i_{\bar{z}} = [\![\alpha]\!]^i_{\bar{x}} \triangleright [\![\beta]\!]^i_{\bar{y}} \qquad [\![\exists y'. \alpha]\!]^i_{\bar{x}'} = \pi_{\bar{x}'}[\![\alpha]\!]^i_{\bar{x}}$$

where α and β are monitorable formulas with free variables $\bar{x}$ and respectively $\bar{y}$, $\bar{z}$ is the sequence $\bar{x}$ concatenated with the subsequence of $\bar{y}$ of variables not in $\bar{x}$, and $\bar{x}'$ is the subsequence of $\bar{x}$ without the variable y'. For instance, if $\alpha = p(x_1, x_2)$ and $\beta = q(x_2, x_3)$, then $\bar{x} = \langle x_1, x_2 \rangle$, $\bar{y} = \langle x_2, x_3 \rangle$, and $\bar{z} = \langle x_1, x_2, x_3 \rangle$. We have omitted the equation for predicates $p(\bar{t})$, which is straightforward but tedious, and uses the selection and projection operators. E.g., if x is a variable

---

[4] The notion of domain independence [4,17] intuitively requires that the satisfying valuations of a formula are independent of the domain of quantification. This semantic notion is laxer than the monitorability requirement, and also guarantees finiteness of $[\![\psi]\!]^i$, but is, however, undecidable.

and a is a constant, then $[\![p(x,a)]\!]^i_{\langle x\rangle} = \pi_{\langle x\rangle}(\sigma_{\{y=a\}}(p^{\mathcal{T}_i}_{\langle x,y\rangle}))$. Note also that when $\bar{x} = \bar{y}$, then the join (i.e. $\bowtie$) and antijoin (i.e. $\triangleright$) operations are identical to the set intersection (i.e. $\cap$) and respectively set difference (i.e. $\setminus$) operations.

We now consider the evaluation of formulas ψ that have temporal operators as their main connective. In contrast to the first-order connectives, their evaluation at a time point depends on the evaluation of their subformulas at previous time points. The evaluation of $[\![\psi]\!]^i$ for $i > 0$ is based on the following equalities:

$$[\![\bullet\alpha]\!]^i_{\bar{x}} = [\![\alpha]\!]^{i-1}_{\bar{x}} \qquad [\![\alpha\,\mathsf{S}\,\beta]\!]^i_{\bar{y}} = [\![\beta]\!]^i_{\bar{y}} \cup ([\![\alpha\,\mathsf{S}\,\beta]\!]^{i-1}_{\bar{y}} \bowtie [\![\alpha]\!]^i_{\bar{x}})$$

where α, β, $\bar{x}$, and $\bar{y}$ are as in the previous set of equations. For $i = 0$, we have $[\![\bullet\alpha]\!]^i_{\bar{x}} = \emptyset_{\bar{x}}$ and $[\![\alpha\,\mathsf{S}\,\beta]\!]^i_{\bar{y}} = [\![\beta]\!]^i_{\bar{y}}$. A similar equality is used for formulas of the form $\neg\alpha\,\mathsf{S}\,\beta$, replacing the join with the antijoin. To accelerate the computation of $[\![\psi]\!]^i$, the monitoring algorithm maintains state for each temporal subformula, storing previously computed intermediate results. Namely, the algorithm stores between the iterations $i-1$ and i, when $i > 0$, the relation $[\![\alpha]\!]^{i-1}$ and respectively $[\![\alpha\,\mathsf{S}\,\beta]\!]^{i-1}$. By storing these relations, the subformulas α and β need not be evaluated again at time points $j < i$ during the evaluation of ψ at time point i.

It is straightforward to translate the previous equalities into a bottom-up evaluation procedure of $[\![\varphi]\!]^i$, for $i \in \mathbb{N}$. We note that relational algebra operators have standard, efficient implementations [42], which can be used to evaluate the right-hand side relational algebra expressions.

Example 3. We present next a partial run of the algorithm for the property UnsafeMapIterator on the event sequence from Example 1. The formulas ψ and γ are as in Example 1. We also let the subformulas β, β', and γ' be as follows:

$$\psi(i) = \mathsf{next}(i) \wedge \neg\exists m, c.\ \underbrace{\Big(\neg\mathsf{update}(m)\,\mathsf{S}\,\big(\mathsf{iterator}(c,i) \wedge \underbrace{\blacklozenge\mathsf{create}(m,c)}_{\beta'(m,c)}\big)\Big)}_{\gamma'(m,c,i)}$$

$$\underbrace{\phantom{\mathsf{iterator}(c,i) \wedge \blacklozenge\mathsf{create}(m,c)}}_{\beta(c,i,m)}$$

That is, we have

$$\beta'(m,c) := \blacklozenge\mathsf{create}(m,c), \qquad\qquad \gamma(i) = \exists m, c.\ \gamma'(m,c,i),$$
$$\beta(c,i,m) := \mathsf{iterator}(c,i) \wedge \beta'(m,c), \qquad \psi(i) = \mathsf{next}(i) \wedge \neg\gamma(i).$$
$$\gamma'(m,c,i) := \neg\mathsf{update}(m)\,\mathsf{S}\,\beta(c,i,m),$$

The algorithm computes the set $[\![\psi]\!]^j$ of violations, for $j \in \mathbb{N}$, based on the following equalities:

$$[\![\beta']\!]^j_{\langle m,c\rangle} = \begin{cases} \mathsf{create}^{\mathcal{T}_j}_{\langle m,c\rangle} \cup [\![\beta']\!]^{j-1}_{\langle m,c\rangle} & \text{if } j > 0 \\ \mathsf{create}^{\mathcal{T}_j}_{\langle m,c\rangle} & \text{if } j = 0 \end{cases} \qquad \begin{aligned} [\![\gamma]\!]^j_{\langle i\rangle} &= \pi_{\langle i\rangle}([\![\gamma']\!]^j_{\langle c,i,m\rangle}) \\ [\![\psi]\!]^j_{\langle i\rangle} &= \mathsf{next}^{\mathcal{T}_j}_{\langle i\rangle} \triangleright [\![\gamma]\!]^j_{\langle i\rangle} \end{aligned}$$

$$[\![\beta]\!]^j_{\langle c,i,m\rangle} = \mathsf{iterator}^{\mathcal{T}_j}_{\langle c,i\rangle} \bowtie [\![\beta']\!]^j_{\langle m,c\rangle}$$

$$[\![\gamma']\!]^j_{\langle c,i,m\rangle} = \begin{cases} [\![\beta]\!]^j_{\langle c,i,m\rangle} \cup ([\![\gamma']\!]^{j-1}_{\langle c,i,m\rangle} \triangleright \mathsf{update}^{\mathcal{T}_j}_{\langle c,i\rangle}) & \text{if } j > 0 \\ [\![\beta]\!]^j_{\langle c,i,m\rangle} & \text{if } j = 0 \end{cases}$$

Table 1. Relations computed by the monitoring algorithm for a sample trace.

j	next$^{\mathcal{T}j}$	update$^{\mathcal{T}j}$	iterator$^{\mathcal{T}j}$	create$^{\mathcal{T}j}$	$[\![\beta']\!]^j$	$[\![\beta]\!]^j$	$[\![\gamma']\!]^j$	$[\![\gamma]\!]^j$	$[\![\psi]\!]^j$
0	$\emptyset$	$\emptyset$	$\emptyset$	$\{(m, c_1)\}$	$\{(m, c_1)\}$	$\emptyset$	$\emptyset$	$\emptyset$	$\emptyset$
1	$\emptyset$	$\emptyset$	$\emptyset$	$\{(m, c_2)\}$	B	$\emptyset$	$\emptyset$	$\emptyset$	$\emptyset$
2	$\emptyset$	$\emptyset$	$\{(c_1, i_1)\}$	$\emptyset$	B	$\{(c_1, i_1, m)\}$	$\{(c_1, i_1, m)\}$	$\{i_1\}$	$\emptyset$
3	$\emptyset$	$\{m\}$	$\emptyset$	$\emptyset$	B	$\emptyset$	$\emptyset$	$\emptyset$	$\emptyset$
4	$\emptyset$	$\emptyset$	$\{(c_2, i_2)\}$	$\emptyset$	B	$\{(c_2, i_2, m)\}$	$\emptyset$	$\emptyset$	$\emptyset$
5	$\{i_1\}$	$\emptyset$	$\emptyset$	$\emptyset$	B	$\emptyset$	$\emptyset$	$\emptyset$	$\{i_1\}$

Concretely, the algorithm computes the relations $[\![\alpha]\!]^j$, shown in Table 1, at iterations $j \in \{0, \ldots, 5\}$, for $\alpha \in \{\beta', \beta, \gamma', \gamma, \psi\}$, where $B = \{(m, c_1), (m, c_2)\}$. We recall that the relations $[\![\beta']\!]^j$ and $[\![\gamma']\!]^j$ are stored by the algorithm between iterations, while all other relations are discarded.

4   Monitoring Modulo Theories

4.1   Overview

For propositional temporal logics such as LTL or CaRet [6] monitoring has been studied extensively and appropriate semantics and monitor synthesis procedures have been developed [20–22,31,35]. Monitoring Modulo Theories (MMT) is a general framework for lifting any of these logics, their semantics and the corresponding synthesis algorithms from the propositional setting to the setting of data values and data constraints. To achieve this, it introduces a general notion of *temporal logic*, capturing many well known propositional temporal logics such as LTL, RLTL [54] or CaRet [6], and the notion of *data logic* based on first-order theories to express constraints over data without any temporal aspects. Next, it combines the two logics into one, *temporal data logic*, whose semantics clearly separates the time and data aspects. This separation gives rise to a monitoring procedure that combines classical monitoring of propositional temporal properties with SMT solving. In this section we present a simplified version of the framework, instantiated for a particular data logic, namely the logic of equality constraints. We refer to [33,34] for the general framework and for more details. We note that the restriction to equality constraints is a significant restriction and also means that a full SMT solver is not needed. The approach is implemented in the jUnit^{RV} tool [32].

For a brief illustration, consider the *UnsafeMapIterator* property. Its temporal aspect can be modelled naturally using LTL. Its data aspect can be modelled easily using equality constraints. Combining LTL as a temporal logic and the logic of equality constraints as a data logic results in a formalism that is well suited to model our example property, using for instance the following formula.

$$\forall c, m, i. \, \Box(\mathsf{create}(m, c) \to \bigcirc\Box(\mathsf{iterator}(c, i) \to \bigcirc\Box(\mathsf{update}(m) \to \bigcirc\Box\neg\mathsf{next}(i))))$$

Due to the simplicity of the data aspect in this example the formula does not contain any explicit first-order constraint. However, the first-order subformulas create(m, c), iterator(c, i), update(m), and next(i) are seen as atomic propositions for the temporal logic, and they give raise to equality constraints at run time. For instance, if the event next(i_1) occurs, then the constraint $i = i_1$ is generated.

4.2 Syntax and Semantics

We will define a *temporal data logic* (TDL) as the extension of a *temporal logic* (TL) from the propositional setting to the first-order setting. There are two main differences between TDL and FOTL from the previous section: first, TDL is parameterised by the propositional temporal logic, and second, it has a finite not an infinite trace semantics.

We assume that the temporal logic is given over some finite non-empty set AP of atomic propositions, its models are finite traces over $\Sigma := \wp(AP)$, and its truth values are elements of a complete lattice $(\mathbb{V}, \sqsubseteq)$ (that is, it does not necessarily have a Boolean semantics).[5] Thus, the semantics of a TL formula ψ is given as a function $[\![\psi]\!] : \Sigma^* \to \mathbb{V}$.

To define TDL in terms of TL, we fix a first-order signature S (see Sect. 2), a finite set $X \subseteq \mathcal{V}$ of variables, and a finite set $F := \{\chi_1, \ldots, \chi_n\}$ of first-order formulas over S with free variables from X. The set F constitutes TL's set AP of "atomic propositions." That is, TDL and TL view the same set differently: TDL considers its elements as formulas and TL views them as propositions i.e. it is agnostic to their structure.[6]

A TDL formula φ consists of a TL *core formula* ψ over AP and a sequence of preceding *global first-order quantifiers* binding free variables in ψ. Formally, the syntax of TDL formulas φ is defined according to the grammar

$$\varphi ::= \exists x.\varphi \mid \forall x.\varphi \mid \psi$$

where $x \in \mathcal{V}$ is a variable and ψ is a TL formula over F.

Example 4. We illustrate how the formula given in Sect. 4.1 can be seen as a TDL formula. We take $S = (\emptyset, \{\text{next}, \text{update}, \text{iterator}, \text{create}, =\}, \text{ar})$, with ar as expected, $X = \{m, c, i\}$, and $F = \{\text{cr}, \text{it}, \text{u}, \text{n}\}$, where cr $:=$ create(m, c), it $:=$ iterator(c, i), u $:=$ update(m), and n $:=$ next(i). Then $\varphi = \forall c, m, i. \psi$, with

$$\psi = \Box(\text{cr} \to \bigcirc\Box(\text{it} \to \bigcirc\Box(\text{u} \to \bigcirc\Box\neg\text{n})))$$

TDL formulas are interpreted over finite sequences of first-order structures[7] over the signature S, with the same domain $\mathbb{D}$, and with finite interpretations

---

[5] A complete lattice is a partial order $(M, \sqsubseteq)$ where every subset $N \subseteq M$ has a least upper bound $\sqcup N$ and a greatest lower bound $\sqcap N$.

[6] A one-to-one mapping from F to AP can be defined, but we refrain to do so, for simplicity.

[7] These relate directly to the notion of event, as in Sect. 3 (see Remark 1). E.g., the event create(m_1, c_1) would be represented as the structure interpreting create as the set $\{(m_1, c_1)\}$.

of predicate symbols. We also assume that S contains the equality predicate symbol $=$, interpreted rigidly, that is, all structures interpret equality in the same way, as expected. The original approach from [33] generalises this assumption and presents a setting where data constraints can be expressed in a so-called *data logic*, not only through equality, but through richer first-order theories; see [34] for details. We let Γ denote the set of all such first-order structures, which we call *observations*.

Finally, to define the TDL semantics, we also need a way to project a sequence of observations from Γ into a sequence of letters from Σ. To this end, we define next, for a valuation $\theta : \mathcal{V} \to \mathbb{D}$, the projection function $\pi_\theta : \Gamma \to \Sigma$ as follows.

$$\pi_\theta(\gamma) := \{\chi \in F \mid (\gamma, \theta) \models \chi\}$$

That is, the projection of a first-order structure γ is the set of formulas in F that are true in that structure for θ. Recall that such formulas can be viewed as propositional symbols in the temporal logic as there is a direct mapping between F and AP.

We define the semantics of a TDL formula φ as a mapping $[\![\varphi]\!]_\theta : \Gamma^* \to \mathbb{V}$, with respect to a valuation $\theta : \mathcal{V} \to \mathbb{D}$, as follows:

$$[\![\exists x.\varphi']\!]_\theta(\overline{\gamma}) := \bigsqcup_{d \in \mathbb{D}} [\![\varphi']\!]_{\theta[x \mapsto d]}(\overline{\gamma}), \qquad [\![\forall x.\varphi']\!]_\theta(\overline{\gamma}) := \bigsqcap_{d \in \mathbb{D}} [\![\varphi']\!]_{\theta[x \mapsto d]}(\overline{\gamma}),$$

$$[\![\psi]\!]_\theta(\overline{\gamma}) := [\![\psi]\!](\pi_\theta(\overline{\gamma}))$$

where ψ is a TL formula, $\sqcap$ and $\sqcup$ denote the meet and respectively the join of the lattice $(\mathbb{V}, \sqsubseteq)$, and π_θ is extended to sequences as expected: $\pi_\theta(\gamma_1 \ldots \gamma_n) = \pi_\theta(\gamma_1) \ldots \pi_\theta(\gamma_n)$. If φ is a *sentence*, that is, it does not contain any free variable, we omit to annotate a specific valuation θ and write $[\![\varphi]\!]$ for its semantics. This is well-defined since valuations of variables that do not occur freely in φ do not affect its semantics. Note also that the $[\![\cdot]\!]$ notation is overloaded; however, its meaning will be clear from the context.

In examples, we use LTL$_3$ [22] as a concrete TL. We recall it briefly: $[\![\psi]\!](\overline{\sigma}) = $ true, if $\overline{\sigma}\overline{\tau} \models \psi$ for any $\overline{\tau} \in \Sigma^\omega$, $[\![\psi]\!](\overline{\sigma}) = $ false, if $\overline{\sigma}\overline{\tau} \not\models \psi$ for any $\overline{\tau} \in \Sigma^\omega$, and $[\![\psi]\!](\overline{\sigma}) = ?$ otherwise, where $\overline{\tau} \models \psi$ denoted the standard, infinite trace LTL semantics and $\mathbb{V} = (\{\text{false}, \text{true}, ?\}, \sqsubseteq)$ with false $\sqsubseteq ? \sqsubseteq$ true. Other examples of TLs are RLTL [54], CaRet [6], and versions of LTL with finite trace semantics, see e.g. [37].

Example 5. We illustrate the TDL semantics on the formula from Example 4. To this end, we recall the trace from Example 1:

create(m_1, c_1).create(m_1, c_2).iterator(c_1, i_1).update(m_1).iterator(c_2, i_2).next(i_1)

The sequence $\overline{\gamma}$ of observations modelling this trace is obtained as in Sect. 3 (see Example 1). Table 2 presents the projections $\overline{\sigma}$ of $\overline{\gamma}$ obtained for some valuations θ, and the corresponding verdicts for ψ on $\overline{\sigma}$, where m', c', and i' denote arbitrary values from $\mathbb{D}$ different from m_1, from c_1 and c_2, and from i_1 and i_2, respectively. As expected, we have $[\![\varphi]\!](\overline{\gamma}) = $ false, by taking the meet of all the values $[\![\psi]\!](\overline{\sigma})$.

Table 2. Evaluation of a TL core formula over a trace for various valuations.

θ	$\bar{\sigma} := \pi_\theta(\bar{\gamma})$	$[\![\psi]\!](\bar{\sigma})$
$[m \mapsto \mathsf{m}_1, c \mapsto \mathsf{c}_1, i \mapsto \mathsf{i}_1]$	$\{\mathsf{cr}\}.\emptyset.\{\mathsf{it}\}.\{\mathsf{u}\}.\emptyset.\{\mathsf{n}\}$	false
$[m \mapsto \mathsf{m}_1, c \mapsto \mathsf{c}_1, i \mapsto \mathsf{i}_2]$	$\{\mathsf{cr}\}.\emptyset.\emptyset.\{\mathsf{u}\}.\emptyset.\{\mathsf{n}\}$	?
$[m \mapsto \mathsf{m}_1, c \mapsto \mathsf{c}_1, i \mapsto \mathsf{i}']$	$\{\mathsf{cr}\}.\emptyset.\emptyset.\emptyset.\emptyset.\emptyset.$	?
$\ldots$		
$[m \mapsto \mathsf{m}'_1, c \mapsto \mathsf{c}', i \mapsto \mathsf{i}']$	$\emptyset.\emptyset.\emptyset.\emptyset.\emptyset.\emptyset$	?

4.3 Monitoring Algorithm

Preliminaries. A *symbolic monitor* $\mathcal{M} = (Q, \Sigma, \delta, q_0, \lambda, \mathbb{V})$ is a state machine with output, where Q is a finite set of states, Σ and $\mathbb{V}$ are as defined in Sect. 4.2, $\delta : Q \times \Sigma \to Q$ is a transition function, $q_0 \in Q$ is the initial state, and $\lambda : Q \to \mathbb{V}$ is a labelling function mapping states to verdicts from $\mathbb{V}$. It is assumed that for a given TL, there is a monitor generation procedure which, for any TL formula ψ builds a monitor $\mathcal{M}$ such that $\lambda(\delta(q_0, \bar{\sigma})) = [\![\psi]\!](\bar{\sigma})$, for any $\bar{\sigma} \in \Sigma^*$.

A *constraint* is a quantifier-free first-order formula over a signature that contains no predicate symbol except equality.[8] For instance, $x = a \wedge y \neq b$ is a constraint. Note that such a constraint ρ describes the set Θ_ρ of valuations θ such that $\rho\theta$ holds in the theory of equality. It is easy to see that for any observation (i.e. first-order structure) γ and a first-order formula χ, there exists a constraint, denoted $\hat{\gamma}(\chi)$, such that $(\gamma, \theta) \models \chi$ iff $\hat{\gamma}(\chi)\theta$ holds, for any valuation θ. For instance, if γ is the observation corresponding to the event $\mathsf{iterator}(\mathsf{c}_1, \mathsf{i}_1)$, then $\hat{\gamma}(\chi)$ is $c = \mathsf{c}_1 \wedge i = \mathsf{i}_1$ for $\chi = \mathsf{iterator}(c, i)$, while $\hat{\gamma}(\chi)$ is false for $\chi = \mathsf{next}(i)$. Note that $\Theta_{\hat{\gamma}(\chi)} = \{\theta \mid (\gamma, \theta) \models \chi\}$ and thus $\hat{\gamma}(\chi)$ can be used to represent the set $\{\theta \mid (\gamma, \theta) \models \chi\}$. This property that will be used in the monitoring algorithm. We also assume a procedure SAT that takes as input a constraint and outputs whether the constraint is satisfiable or not. We recall that the general framework [34] considers arbitrary theories, not only that of equality, as presented here. In general, the SAT procedure is implemented by invoking an SMT solver for the considered theory.

A *constraint tree* t is a finite, non-empty, full binary tree having constraints as inner nodes and monitor states as leafs. A tree is denoted either by $\mathsf{Inner}(\rho, t_1, t_2)$ where ρ is a constraint, and t_1 and t_2 are the root's left and right subtrees respectively, or by $\mathsf{Leaf}(q)$ where $q \in Q$. Each node v in a tree t induces a constraint $\rho(v)$ defined as the conjunction of the constraints on the path from the root to the node v.

Algorithm. The monitoring algorithm incrementally processes a sequence $\bar{\gamma}$ of observations in order to compute the semantics of some given TDL formula φ. Let ψ be φ's TL core formula. The algorithm uses the symbolic monitor $\mathcal{M}$ for ψ.

---

[8] In the more general framework constraints must contain interpreted predicates only.

Algorithm 1. The monitoring algorithm.

---

proc step(t, γ) = traverse(γ, t, true)

proc traverse(γ, t, ρ)
    case t = Inner(ρ', t_1, t_2): Inner(ρ', traverse(γ, t_1, $\rho \wedge \rho'$), traverse(γ, t_2, $\rho \wedge \neg\rho'$))
    case t = Leaf(q): split(γ, q, F, ρ, $\emptyset$)

proc split(γ, q, P, ρ, a)
  if $P = \emptyset$ **then** Leaf($\delta(q, a)$)
  else
    χ, P' := choose(P)
    t_1 := **if** SAT($\rho \wedge \hat{\gamma}(\chi)$) **then** split($\gamma$, q, P', $\rho \wedge \hat{\gamma}(\chi)$, $a \cup \{\chi\}$) **else** Empty
    t_2 := **if** SAT($\rho \wedge \neg\hat{\gamma}(\chi)$) **then** split($\gamma$, q, P', $\rho \wedge \neg\hat{\gamma}(\chi)$, a) **else** Empty
    if t_1 = Empty **then** t_2 **else if** t_2 = Empty **then** t_1 **else** Inner($\hat{\gamma}(\chi)$, t_1, t_2)

Intuitively, the algorithm executes one instance of $\mathcal{M}$ for each projection $\pi_\theta(\bar{\gamma})$, with $\theta : \mathscr{V} \to \mathbb{D}$ some valuation. As there are finitely many projections, they partition the set of valuations into a finite number of equivalence classes. The algorithm maintains a mapping from representatives θ of these classes to states q of $\mathcal{M}$, where $q = \delta(q_0, \pi_\theta(\bar{\gamma}))$. The property that $[\![\psi]\!](\pi_\theta(\bar{\gamma})) = \lambda(q)$ allows the algorithm to compute the verdict associated with the current sequence $\bar{\gamma}$ of observations, by iterating through the verdicts $\lambda(q)$, for q in the image of the mentioned mapping. Indeed, in case all global quantifiers in φ are universal, the verdict is the meet over all verdicts $\lambda(q)$. In general, when existential quantifiers are also present, the computation of the verdict is more involved; see [34].

The mapping from equivalence classes of valuations to states q is represented algorithmically by a constraint tree. Namely, for each leaf node v with state q, the constraint $\rho = \rho(v)$ describes the set Θ_ρ of valuations. By construction, these sets of valuations are the equivalence classes mentioned previously. We briefly describe how the algorithm maintains the constraint tree. The initial constraint tree is Leaf(q_0). For a new observation $\gamma \in \Gamma$ and a monitor instance at v, if all valuations in Θ_ρ project γ to the same letter $a \in \Sigma$, then the monitor instance changes its state from q to $\delta(q, a)$. Otherwise, if γ is mapped to different letters for different valuations in Θ_ρ, then Θ_ρ is split and new monitor instances are created. More precisely, if for some $\chi \in F$ both $\rho \wedge \hat{\gamma}(\chi)$ and $\rho \wedge \neg\hat{\gamma}(\chi)$ are satisfiable, then there are two valuations $\theta, \theta' \in \Theta_\rho$ such that $(\gamma, \theta) \models \chi$ and $(\gamma, \theta') \not\models \chi$. It follows that $\chi \in \pi_\theta(\gamma)$ while $\chi \notin \pi_{\theta'}(\gamma)$, and thus the projections are different. In this case, a new inner node with constraint $\hat{\gamma}(\chi)$ is created. This procedure is performed for each $\chi \in F$. For each new path to a leaf, the state at the leaf node is updated to $\delta(q, a)$, where a is the projection corresponding to that path. The pseudo-code of the procedure that updates the constraint tree is given in Listing 1.

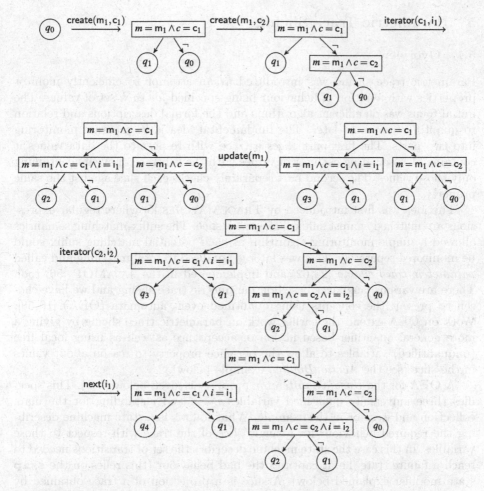

Fig. 1. Constraint trees built by the monitoring algorithm for a sample trace.

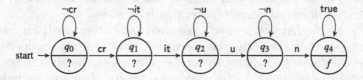

Fig. 2. Symbolic monitor for the formula $\Box(cr \rightarrow \bigcirc\Box(it \rightarrow \bigcirc\Box(u \rightarrow \bigcirc\Box\neg n)))$.

Example 6. Figure 1 shows a run of the algorithm for the *UnsafeMapIterator* property on the event sequence from Example 5, using the symbolic monitor given in Fig. 2.

5   Parametric Trace Slicing

5.1   Overview

Parametric trace slicing was introduced as an attempt to efficiently monitor properties with a notion of behaviour being specified *for each* set of values. The initial focus was on efficient algorithms and the formal descriptions and relation to quantification came later. The fundamental idea is to separate monitoring into two parts. The first part *slices* a trace with respect to the data values it contains by associating each set of values with the subtrace of events containing only those values. The second part separately checks each slice against the same property.

The idea was first introduced by TRACEMATCHES [5] where regular expressions are matched against suffixes of a trace slice. The suffix-matching semantics allowed a simple monitoring algorithm as each potential matching suffix could be monitored separately. This was later generalised to total matching and called *parametric trace slicing* [25,62] and implemented in the JAVAMOP [56] tool. There are various languages based on parametric trace slicing and we have chosen to present the concepts using quantified event automata (QEA) [10,58]. Work on QEA extend the earlier work on parametric trace slicing by giving a more general quantifier-based notion of acceptance as well as using local free (unquantified) variables to allow the per-slice property to reason about values in the slice (see the *AuctionBidding* example below).

A QEA for the *UnsafeMapIterator* property is given below (left). This specifies three universally quantified variables m, c, and i standing for the map, collection and iterator in the example. What follows is a state machine describing the required behaviour for a single *slice* of the trace with respect to those variables. In this case the state machine describes the set of transitions needed to reach a failure state, i.e. it captures the bad behaviour (this relies on the **skip** state modifier explained below). A slice is a projection of a trace obtained by keeping only events that are relevant to a given instantiation of the quantified variables. Acceptance is defined in terms of which slices are accepted by the state machine i.e. for universal quantification this is all slices.

The *UnsafeMapIterator* property is suited (and often used) for parametric trace slicing as, once the slicing has occurred, the underlying property can be treated propositionally. To demonstrate a case where the slice is not treated propositionally consider an *AuctionBidding* property of an auction bidding site where items are listed with a reserve price and bids are strictly increasing. This is captured by the second QEA below where transitions are extended with optional *guards* and *assignments*. Notice how variables r and a are not quantified, these are used to store the reserve price and current bid amount respectively. As these values are used to evaluate the property they must be preserved in the trace so this can no longer be treated propositionally. Lastly, this second QEA does not use an explicit **failure** state but relies on *state closure* (see later), i.e. it captures good behaviour.

```
qea(UnsafeMapIterator) {                qea(AuctionBidding) {
  forall(m, c, i)                         forall(i)
  accept skip(start){                     accept next(start){
    create(m, c) → createdC}                list(i, r) do c := 0 → listed}
  accept skip(createdC){                  accept next(listed){
    iterator(c, i) → createdI}              bid(i, a) if a > c do c := a → listed
  accept skip(createdI){                    sell(i) if c > r → sold
    update(m) → updated}                  }
  accept skip(updated){                   accept next(sold){}
    next(i) → failure}                  }
}
```

5.2   Syntax and Semantics

In Roşu and Chen's parametric trace slicing theory [25,62] there is a strong separation between the notion of quantification (although they did not call it quantification) which defines what the slices are, and per-slice acceptance (by so-called *plugin* languages) which decides whether a slice is accepted. We repeat this presentation here with event automata describing the plugin language.

Basic Definitions. An *event pattern* is an ordered pair of an event name and a list of parameters where a parameter is a variable in $\mathcal{V}$ or value in $\mathbb{D}$. That is, an event pattern is a tuple $(id, \bar{p}) \in \mathcal{N} \times (\mathcal{V} \cup \mathbb{D})^*$, written $id(\bar{p})$. When an event pattern only contains values in $\mathbb{D}$ it coincides with the notion of an event as defined in Sect. 2. We write $\mathcal{N}(X)$ for any *event alphabet* that contains event patterns using names in $\mathcal{N}$, variables in $X \subseteq \mathcal{V}$, and values in $\mathbb{D}$. Note that $\mathcal{N}(X)$ does not contain all such event patterns but the ones relevant to the monitored property. For instance, for the *UnsafeMapIterator* property we have $\mathcal{N}(\{m, c, i\}) = \{\mathsf{create}(m, c), \mathsf{iterator}(c, i), \mathsf{update}(m), \mathsf{next}(i)\}$.

A *valuation* $\theta \in Env = \mathcal{V} \rightharpoonup \mathbb{D}$ is a map from variables to values. By abusing valuations to treat them as total functions (by implicit extension with the identify function) we can apply valuations to event patterns as follows: given an event pattern $id(p_1, \ldots, p_n)$ let $\theta(id(p_1, \ldots, p_n)) = id(\theta(p_1), \ldots, \theta(p_n))$. An event e and an event pattern ep match if there exists a valuation θ such that $\theta(ep) = e$. Let $\mathsf{matches}(e, ep)$ hold iff e and ep match and let $\mathsf{match}(e, ep)$ be the smallest (wrt $\sqsubseteq$) valuation that matches them (and undefined if they do not match). Two valuations θ and θ' are consistent, written $\mathsf{consistent}(\theta, \theta')$, if for every x in $\mathsf{dom}(\theta) \cap \mathsf{dom}(\theta')$ we have $\theta(x) = \theta'(x)$. We also write $\theta_1 \sqsubseteq \theta_2$ iff $\mathsf{dom}(\theta) \subseteq \mathsf{dom}(\theta')$ and θ_1 and θ_2 are consistent.

A *guard* $g \in Guard = Env \rightarrow \mathbb{B}$ is a predicate on valuations and an *assignment* $\gamma \in Assign = Env \rightarrow Env$ is a function from valuations to valuations. We do not fix a guard or assignment language, but use programming language notation in examples.

Trace Slicing. Slicing a trace means projecting it to a subtrace, called a slice, with respect to a valuation, which identifies the relevant events in the trace. An event e is *relevant* to a valuation θ and event alphabet $\mathcal{N}(Z)$ if there is an event pattern in $\mathcal{N}(Z)$ that matches e with respect to θ, i.e.

$$\text{relevant}(e, \theta, \mathcal{N}(Z)) \quad \textit{iff} \quad \exists ep \in \mathcal{N}(Z) : \text{matches}(e, \theta(ep))$$

Trace slicing is then defined as follows. Giving a valuation θ, the θ-slice of trace τ with respect to event alphabet $\mathcal{N}(Z)$ is the trace $\tau \downarrow_\theta^{\mathcal{N}(Z)}$, defined as follows:

$$\langle \rangle \downarrow_\theta^{\mathcal{N}(Z)} = \langle \rangle \qquad e.\tau \downarrow_\theta^{\mathcal{N}(Z)} = \begin{cases} e.(\tau \downarrow_\theta^{\mathcal{N}(Z)}) & \text{if relevant}(e, \theta, \mathcal{N}(Z)), \\ \tau \downarrow_\theta^{\mathcal{N}(Z)} & \text{otherwise.} \end{cases}$$

Example 7. Consider the AuctionBidding QEA from Sect. 5.1 and the trace

$$\tau = \text{list}(b, 5).\text{bid}(b, 1).\text{list}(d, 2).\text{bid}(b, 2).\text{bid}(d, 1).\text{sell}(d).\text{bid}(b, 2)$$

we compute (for $\mathcal{N}(Z) = \{\text{list}(i, r), \text{bid}(i, a), \text{sell}(i)\}$) the trace slices

$$\tau \downarrow_{[i \mapsto b]}^{\mathcal{N}(Z)} = \text{list}(b, 5).\text{bid}(b, 1).\text{bid}(b, 2).\text{bid}(b, 2)$$
$$\tau \downarrow_{[i \mapsto d]}^{\mathcal{N}(Z)} = \text{list}(d, 2).\text{bid}(d, 1).\text{sell}(d)$$

Event Automata. An event automaton $\mathcal{E}$ over the event alphabet $\mathcal{N}(Z)$ is a tuple $(\mathcal{N}(Z), Q, q_0, \delta, F)$ where Q is a finite set of states with $q_0 \in Q$ an initial state and $F \subseteq Q$ a set of final states, and $\delta \subseteq Q \times \mathcal{N}(Z) \times Guard \times Assign \times Q$ is a finite set of transitions between states labelled with an event pattern, a guard, and an assignment. Furthermore, there are exactly two states that have no outgoing transitions: **success** $\in F$ and **failure** $\notin F$.

A *configuration* is a tuple $(q, \theta) \in Q \times Env$. A trace τ is in the language of the event automaton $\mathcal{E}$, written $\tau \in \mathcal{L}(\mathcal{E})$, if there exists a state $q \in F$ such that $(q_0, [\,]) \xrightarrow{\tau} (q, \theta)$ for some valuation θ, where $\xrightarrow{\tau}$ is the transitive lifting of $\xrightarrow{e}$ defined by

$$(q, \theta) \xrightarrow{e} \begin{cases} (q', \gamma(\theta')) & \textit{if} \quad \begin{aligned} \exists (q, ep, g, \gamma, q') \in \delta : \text{matches}(e, ep) \wedge \\ \theta' = \theta \dagger \text{match}(e, ep) \wedge g(\theta') \end{aligned} \\ (q, \theta) & \textit{otherwise} \end{cases}$$

Quantified Event Automata. A *quantified event automaton* (QEA) over the event alphabet $\mathcal{N}(X \cup Y)$ is a tuple $(\Lambda, \mathcal{E})$ where $\Lambda \in (\{\forall, \exists\} \times X)^*$ is a sequence of quantifications and $\mathcal{E}$ is an event automata over the same alphabet, with X and Y disjoint sets of *quantified* and *free* variables respectively. The QEA is well-formed if Λ mentions each of the variables in X exactly once.

The domain of a (quantified) variable is derived form a trace τ by matching against event patterns in the alphabet as follows:

$$\text{dom}_\tau(x) := \{\text{match}(e, ep)(x) \mid e \in \tau \wedge ep \in \mathcal{N}(X \cup Y) \wedge \text{matches}(e, ep) \wedge$$
$$x \text{ is a parameter of } ep\}.$$

A trace τ is accepted by the QEA if $\tau \models_{[\ ]} \Lambda.\mathscr{E}$ where $\models_\theta$ is defined as

$$\tau \models_\theta (\forall x)\Lambda'.\mathscr{E} \quad \text{iff} \quad \text{for all } d \text{ in } \mathrm{dom}_\tau(x) \text{ we have } \tau \models_{\theta\dagger[x\mapsto d]} \Lambda'.\mathscr{E}$$
$$\tau \models_\theta (\exists x)\Lambda'.\mathscr{E} \quad \text{iff} \quad \text{for some } d \text{ in } \mathrm{dom}_\tau(x) \text{ we have } \tau \models_{\theta\dagger[x\mapsto d]} \Lambda'.\mathscr{E}$$
$$\tau \models_\theta \langle\ \rangle.\mathscr{E} \qquad \text{iff} \quad \tau \downarrow_\theta^{\mathcal{N}(X\cup Y)} \in \mathscr{L}(\mathscr{E}(\theta))$$

where $\mathscr{E}(\theta)$ denotes the instantiation of the event automaton as expected i.e. by replacing variables by values in event patterns, guards and assignments. Informally, checking acceptance using this definition consists of building valuations θ of quantified variables, slicing the trace with respect to θ, checking per-slice acceptance, and finally combining the results to produce a verdict.

To describe QEA textually we rely on the (not formally defined) language used earlier where a state and its transitions may be written as

```
[accept] [next/skip](state){
    id(p_1,...,p_n) if [guard] do [assign] → state list
}
```

The optional **accept** modifier captures if the state is in F. The **next/skip** modifiers refer to the implicit closure of the state, i.e. what should happen when a transition for an event does not exist; **next** closes to a failure state and **skip** introduces self-looping transitions. The above semantics assumed **skip**. Each transition starting at the state is given with (optional) guards and assignments.

Example 8. We can now complete the example given in Example 7 by computing the configurations reached by each slice to obtain the following runs:

$$(\texttt{start}, [\ ]) \xrightarrow{\text{list}(b,5)} (\texttt{listed}, [r \mapsto 5, c \mapsto 0]) \xrightarrow{\text{bid}(b,1)}$$
$$(\texttt{listed}, [r \mapsto 5, a \mapsto 1, c \mapsto 1]) \xrightarrow{\text{bid}(b,2)} (\texttt{listed}, [r \mapsto 5, a \mapsto 2, c \mapsto 2])$$
$$\xrightarrow{\text{bid}(b,2)} (\textbf{failure}, [r \mapsto 5, a \mapsto 2, c \mapsto 2])$$

and

$$(\texttt{start}, [\ ]) \xrightarrow{\text{list}(d,2)} (\texttt{listed}, [r \mapsto 2, c \mapsto 2]) \xrightarrow{\text{bid}(d,1)}$$
$$(\texttt{listed}, [r \mapsto 2, a \mapsto 1, c \mapsto 2]) \xrightarrow{\text{sell}(d)} (\textbf{failure}, [r \mapsto 2, a \mapsto 1, c \mapsto 2]).$$

As $\mathrm{dom}_\tau(i) = \{b, d\}$ and both runs reach the **failure** state, we conclude that $\tau \not\models \forall i.\,\text{AuctionBidding}$. The two runs fail as we cannot satisfy the guard needed to take a transition and as the state modifier is **next** this leads to implicit failure (not directly captured in the above semantics).

5.3   Monitoring Algorithm

The semantics introduced previously is non-incremental; it is necessary to first extract the domains of quantified variables before slicing and checking the trace. To address this we introduce an incremental algorithm and discuss optimisations.

Algorithm 2. A basic monitoring algorithm for QEA.

1: $M \leftarrow [[\ ] \mapsto \{(q_0, [\ ])\}]$
2: **for** event $e \in \tau$ **do**
3:     $New \leftarrow \{\theta \mid \forall (x_i \mapsto v_i) \in \theta : \exists ep \in \mathcal{N}(X \cup Y) : (x_i \mapsto v_i) \in \mathsf{match}(e, ep) \wedge x_i \in X\}$
4:     **for** $\theta \in \mathrm{dom}(M)$ sorted from largest to smallest **do**
5:         $Extensions \leftarrow \{\theta \dagger \theta' \mid \theta' \in New \wedge \mathsf{consistent}(\theta, \theta') \wedge \mathsf{relevant}(e, \theta \dagger \theta', \mathcal{N}(X \cup Y))\}$
6:         **for** $\theta_{Ext} \in Extensions$ **do**
7:             **if** $\theta = \theta_{Ext}$ or $\theta_{Ext} \notin \mathrm{dom}(M)$ **then**
8:                 $C \leftarrow \{(q, \theta_{free}) \mid \exists c \in M(\theta) : c \xrightarrow{e}_{\mathscr{E}(\theta_{Ext})} (q, \theta_{free}) \wedge \mathrm{dom}(\theta_{free}) \cap X = \emptyset\}$
9:                 $M \leftarrow M \dagger [\theta_{Ext} \mapsto C]$

A Basic Incremental Algorithm. Algorithm 2 presents a basic incremental algorithm for monitoring QEA. This assumes a QEA described using the notation discussed previously. The algorithm maintains a mapping M from valuations (of quantified variables) to sets of configurations. The valuations may be *partial* with respect to quantified variables in X as the events building a full valuation may appear incrementally. The algorithm does not show how M can be used to determine a verdict but this follows the definition of acceptance above; in the case of pure universal quantification all configuration sets must contain a final state. This gives a verdict for the current trace prefix, which can be lifted to a four-valued domain providing anticipatory results [10].

For each event, the algorithm first computes any potentially new values for variables in X. Then, for each existing valuation θ in M, it tries to extend θ with this new information and update M accordingly. Key to this approach is the way in which M is iterated over; from the largest valuations to the smallest (wrt $\sqsubseteq$). This ensures that when a new valuation is added it extends the largest existing consistent valuation; this is the principle of *maximality*. Maximality is ensured by the check on line 7 i.e. if this check fails then θ_{Ext} has already been added, possibly earlier in this iteration by extending a larger valuation.

The set C computed on line 8 is the set of new configurations for θ_{Ext}. This uses $\rightarrow_{\mathscr{E}(\theta)}$ i.e. the transition relation for the instantiated event automaton $\mathscr{E}(\theta)$. Importantly, a transition cannot be taken if it captures quantified variables; this may be possible as θ_{Ext} can be partial with respect to X.

Event	Updates to M	Using $\theta \in \mathrm{dom}(M)$
$\mathsf{create}(\mathsf{m}_1, \mathsf{c}_1)$	$([m \mapsto \mathsf{m}_1, c \mapsto \mathsf{c}_1] \mapsto \mathsf{createdC})$	$[\ ]$
$\mathsf{create}(\mathsf{m}_1, \mathsf{c}_2)$	$([m \mapsto \mathsf{m}_1, c \mapsto \mathsf{c}_2] \mapsto \mathsf{createdC})$	$[\ ]$
$\mathsf{iterator}(\mathsf{c}_1, \mathsf{i}_1)$	$([m \mapsto \mathsf{m}_1, c \mapsto \mathsf{c}_1, i \mapsto \mathsf{i}_1] \mapsto \mathsf{createdI})$	$[m \mapsto \mathsf{m}_1, c \mapsto \mathsf{c}_1]$
$\mathsf{update}(\mathsf{m}_1)$	$([m \mapsto \mathsf{m}_1, c \mapsto \mathsf{c}_1] \mapsto \mathsf{createdC})$	$[m \mapsto \mathsf{m}_1, c \mapsto \mathsf{c}_1]$
	$([m \mapsto \mathsf{m}_1, c \mapsto \mathsf{c}_2] \mapsto \mathsf{createdC})$	$[m \mapsto \mathsf{m}_1, c \mapsto \mathsf{c}_2]$
	$([m \mapsto \mathsf{m}_1, c \mapsto \mathsf{c}_1, i \mapsto \mathsf{i}_1] \mapsto \mathsf{updated})$	$[m \mapsto \mathsf{m}_1, c \mapsto \mathsf{c}_1, i \mapsto \mathsf{i}_1]$
$\mathsf{iterator}(\mathsf{c}_2, \mathsf{i}_2)$	$([m \mapsto \mathsf{m}_1, c \mapsto \mathsf{c}_2, i \mapsto \mathsf{i}_2] \mapsto \mathsf{createdI})$	$[m \mapsto \mathsf{m}_1, c \mapsto \mathsf{c}_2]$
$\mathsf{next}(\mathsf{i}_1)$	$([m \mapsto \mathsf{m}_1, c \mapsto \mathsf{c}_1, i \mapsto \mathsf{i}_1] \mapsto \mathbf{failure})$	$[m \mapsto \mathsf{m}_1, c \mapsto \mathsf{c}_1, i \mapsto \mathsf{i}_1]$

Fig. 3. Illustrating the updates to M for the *UnsafeMapIterator* example.

Example 9. Figure 3 considers the `UnsafeMapIterator` QEA from Sect. 5.1 which has the alphabet $\mathcal{N}(X \cup Y) = \{\text{create}(m,c), \text{iterator}(c,i), \text{update}(m),$ $\text{next}(i)\}$ for $X = \{m,c,i\}$ and $Y = \emptyset$. We use the running trace from Sect. 3.3 and use single states to represent configurations as the property is deterministic without free variables. The table gives the valuation $\theta \in \text{dom}(M)$ used to make the update; note that new valuations follow the previously described notion of maximality. The final event produces a valuation in the **failure** state, meaning that the trace is rejected.

Indexing Approaches. This basic algorithm is still not efficient enough for effective monitoring as it requires a linear search of M for every event and M can grow very large. One solution is to use an *index* to identify the relevant valuations in M. In the following we describe the *value-based* indexing approach as, whilst other approaches exist [57, 59], this is the most prominent approach in the literature and in use in tools. These alternative approaches also make heavy use of indexing on values and therefore the approach described here is also the most relevant in general.

Value-based indexing was introduced in the JAVAMOP tool [56] and uses the values in an event to lookup the valuations in M that the current event is *relevant* to. As motivation consider some examples. When considering valuations possibly occurring at runtime, the event $\text{update}(c_1)$ is only relevant to valuations that already bind c_1, which could be found via direct lookup. However, to find valuations relevant to $\text{iterator}(c_1, i_1)$ we must, e.g., find $[m \mapsto m_1, c \mapsto c_1]$ which does not refer to i_1 but refers to more than c_1. Therefore, looking up the valuation or its subparts directly will not suffice.

To implement the necessary lookup a map $U : Env \nrightarrow \wp(Env)$ is maintained such that valuations in M are mapped to by their sub-valuations of interest. It can be complex to compute which sub-valuations are required and in the worst case all sub-valuations can be used. Algorithm 2 can be updated to use U by firstly ensuring U is

1. *sub-valuation-closed*: for any $\theta \in \text{dom}(M)$, we have $\theta' \in \text{dom}(U)$ if $\theta' \sqsubset \theta$,
2. *relevance-closed*: for any $\theta' \in \text{dom}(U)$ and $\theta \in \text{dom}(M)$, if $\theta' \sqsubseteq \theta$ then $\theta \in U(\theta')$.

These two conditions ensure that U can be used to find θ given any sub-valuation of θ. Secondly one must ensure that M is

3. *union-closed*: if two consistent valuations are in $\text{dom}(M)$, their union is in $\text{dom}(M)$.

This last condition is already ensured by Algorithm 2. If these properties are maintained (see e.g. [56], Algorithm C) then it is sufficient to update the configurations for valuations in $\{\theta\} \cup U(\theta)$ for each $\theta \in New$ i.e. line 4 of Algorithm 2 becomes

for $\theta \in New \cup \bigcup_{\theta' \in New} U(\theta')$ sorted from largest to smallest **do**

The amount of work needed to process each event is now bounded by the size of θ and $U(\theta)$, which are related to the size of X and density of values in τ (a pathological case could lead to $U(\theta)$ being proportional to the size of τ). This is a significant improvement; in certain cases a previously linear complexity becomes constant i.e. where there is a single quantified variable.

Example 10. After the third event ($\mathsf{iterator}(\mathsf{c_1}, \mathsf{i_1})$) in the above example, U would contain the following mappings:

$$
\begin{aligned}
[\,] &\mapsto \{[m \mapsto \mathsf{m_1}, c \mapsto \mathsf{c_1}], [m \mapsto \mathsf{m_1}, c \mapsto \mathsf{c_2}], [m \mapsto \mathsf{m_1}, c \mapsto \mathsf{c_1}, i \mapsto \mathsf{i_1}]\} \\
[m \mapsto \mathsf{m_1}] &\mapsto \{[m \mapsto \mathsf{m_1}, c \mapsto \mathsf{c_1}], [m \mapsto \mathsf{m_1}, c \mapsto \mathsf{c_2}], [m \mapsto \mathsf{m_1}, c \mapsto \mathsf{c_1}, i \mapsto \mathsf{i_1}]\} \\
[i \mapsto \mathsf{i_1}] &\mapsto \{[m \mapsto \mathsf{m_1}, c \mapsto \mathsf{c_1}, i \mapsto \mathsf{i_1}]\} \\
[c \mapsto \mathsf{c_1}] &\mapsto \{[m \mapsto \mathsf{m_1}, c \mapsto \mathsf{c_1}], [m \mapsto \mathsf{m_1}, c \mapsto \mathsf{c_1}, i \mapsto \mathsf{i_1}]\} \\
[c \mapsto \mathsf{c_2}] &\mapsto \{[m \mapsto \mathsf{m_1}, c \mapsto \mathsf{c_2}]\} \\
[m \mapsto \mathsf{m_1}, c \mapsto \mathsf{c_1}] &\mapsto \{[m \mapsto \mathsf{m_1}, c \mapsto \mathsf{c_1}, i \mapsto \mathsf{i_1}]\} \\
[m \mapsto \mathsf{m_1}, i \mapsto \mathsf{i_1}] &\mapsto \{[m \mapsto \mathsf{m_1}, c \mapsto \mathsf{c_1}, i \mapsto \mathsf{i_1}]\} \\
[c \mapsto \mathsf{c_1}, i \mapsto \mathsf{i_1}] &\mapsto \{[m \mapsto \mathsf{m_1}, c \mapsto \mathsf{c_1}, i \mapsto \mathsf{i_1}]\}
\end{aligned}
$$

On event $\mathsf{update}(\mathsf{m_1})$, $New = \{[m \mapsto \mathsf{m_1}]\}$, and $U([m \mapsto \mathsf{m_1}])$ gives the relevant valuations to update. Then on event $\mathsf{iterator}(\mathsf{c_2}, \mathsf{i_2})$, $New = \{[c \mapsto \mathsf{c_2}, i \mapsto \mathsf{i_2}]\}$ and we add the required $[m \mapsto \mathsf{m_1}, c \mapsto \mathsf{c_2}, i \mapsto \mathsf{i_2}]$ to M using $[m \mapsto \mathsf{m_1}, c \mapsto \mathsf{c_2}] \in U([c \mapsto \mathsf{c_2}])$ as we did before but without searching M.

As a final note, it is possible to statically (from $\mathcal{N}(X \cup Y)$) detect which entries in U may be used e.g. in this example we know we will never query using m and i together. This information can be used to optimise the entries stored in U.

6   Rule-Based Monitoring

6.1   Overview

Rule systems have been extensively studied within the artificial intelligence community, and used for example in expert systems. It turns out that with slight modifications these systems are applicable to runtime verification. A rule system can abstractly be seen as a collection of *rules*, each of the form: $c_1, \ldots, c_n \Rightarrow a$, consisting of a list of conditions c_i and an action a. A rule system executes on a rule state, referred to here as the *database*, which abstractly can be considered as a set of *facts* (named data records). A condition can for example be a fact pattern or the negation thereof. A rule will *fire* if each pattern on the left-hand side matches a fact in the database (in the case of negation: no matching fact exists), in which case the rule right-hand side executes. Multiple occurrences of a variable on the left-hand side must match the same value. In the case that all conditions on a rule's left-hand side match, producing an environment of bound variables, the right-hand side action is executed, adding and/or deleting facts to and from the database. A special fact is the *error* fact.

We here present LogFire [47], a rule-based monitoring framework implemented as an internal DSL, essentially an API/library, in the Scala programming language. The *UnsafeMapIterator* property can be formulated as follows:[9]

---

[9] The syntax has been modified slightly from Scala to a more mathematical notation.

```
class UnsafeMapIterator extends Monitor {
  val create, iterator, update, next = event
  val createdC, createdI, updated = fact

  r₁: create(m,c) ⇒ createdC(m,c)
  r₂: createdC(m,c), iterator(c,i) ⇒ createdI(m,i)
  r₃: createdI(m,i), update(m) ⇒ updated(i)
  r₄: updated(i), next(i) ⇒ error
}
```

The property is expressed as a SCALA class that extends a pre-defined class
Monitor, which provides all the LOGFIRE features. The UnsafeMapIterator
class defines four rules, named r_1, ..., r_4. Each rule name is followed by the
symbol ':' followed by a list of conditions on the left of the '⇒' symbol, and
an action on the right. The monitored events are create, iterator, update, and
next. An event will only be present in the database long enough to evaluate all
the left-hand sides of rules to determine which can fire, followed by the removal
of the event, and execution of the right-hand sides. Three facts are generated:
createdC(m, c) representing that the collection c has been extracted from the
map m, createdI(m, i) representing that the iterator i has been extracted from
the collection of the map m, and updated(i) representing that the iterator i no
longer is safe to iterate over since the corresponding map has been updated.

Rule r_1 states that upon observation of a create(m, c) event, a createdC(m, c)
fact is generated. Here m and c are free variables that get bound when the pattern
create(m, c) matches a fact (in this case an event) in the database. These bindings
will be passed to createdC(m, c). Rule r_2 states that upon observation of an
iterator(c, i) event in the presence of a createdC(m, c) fact, a createdI(m, i) fact
is generated. Similarly for the two remaining rules, noting that error denotes
the error fact. Note that left-hand sides of rules do not need to refer to events,
and can be purely fact-triggered, although this is not the case for the rules
r_1, ..., r_4. LOGFIRE furthermore allows to mix rule-based programming and
general purpose programming by allowing variables and methods to be declared
and used in monitor classes, and by allowing any SCALA code in conditions
and in actions. In the following, however, focus will be on the pure rule-based
fragment of this language.

6.2   Syntax and Semantics

We present the syntax and semantics of an idealised simple rule-based language
named LF illustrating the rule-based capabilities of LOGFIRE[10]. The syntax of
LF is defined by the following grammar, where id ranges over event and fact
names in $\mathcal{N}$ (fact names are assumed included in $\mathcal{N}$), x over variable names
in $\mathcal{V}$, v over values in $\mathbb{D}$, and exp over expressions (not defined further):

$$rs ::= \overline{\pi} \qquad\qquad\qquad fp ::= id(\overline{p})$$
$$\pi ::= id : \overline{c} \Rightarrow \overline{\alpha} \qquad\qquad p ::= x \mid v$$
$$c ::= fp \mid \textbf{not}(fp) \mid \textbf{when}(exp) \qquad \alpha ::= \textbf{insert}(id(\overline{exp})) \mid \textbf{remove}(id) \mid \textbf{error}$$

---

[10] Providing a full definition of LOGFIRE would be too space consuming for this presentation.

The above definition uses meta-variables ranging over types as follows: $rs \in \mathsf{RS}$ (Rule Systems), $\pi \in \mathsf{R}$ (Rules), $c \in \mathsf{C}$ (Conditions), $fp \in \mathsf{FP}$ (Fact Patterns), $p \in \mathsf{P}$ (Parameters), $\alpha \in \mathsf{A}$ (Actions), and $exp \in \mathsf{Exp}$ (Expressions). A rule system rs consists of a list of rules. A rule π consists of a name, followed by a non-empty list of conditions, forming the left-hand side of the rule, followed on the right-hand side by a non-empty list of actions. A condition c can be a fact pattern fp, corresponding to a fact that must be present in the database; or the negation $\mathbf{not}(fp)$ of a fact pattern, requiring that no matching fact exists; or a filter expression $\mathbf{when}(exp)$, which has to evaluate to true on the names bound so far in the conditions occurring earlier in the rule. A fact pattern fp consists of a fact name, and a list of parameter patterns. A parameter pattern p can either be a variable x or a literal value v, such as for example an integer or a string (not further specified). Finally, an action α can be a fact insertion $\mathbf{insert}(id(\overline{exp}))$, where the identifier is the name of the fact and the expression list (an expression can for example represent a computation, such as $x + 1$) evaluates to a list of fact arguments; or a fact removal $\mathbf{remove}(id)$, where the identifier is the name of a fact occurring on the rule left-hand side; or an $\mathbf{error}$ action adding the error fact.

A fact is a tuple $(id, \langle v_1, \ldots, v_n \rangle)$ consisting of a name $id \in \mathcal{N}$ and a sequence of values $v_i \in \mathbb{D}$. A fact is typically written as $id(v_1, \ldots, v_n)$. The type of facts is denoted by $\mathbb{F} = \mathcal{N} \times \mathbb{D}^*$. A database is a set of facts of type $\mathbb{DB} = \wp(\mathbb{F})$. Monitored events are just facts. In order to show intent in later definitions, however, we introduce the type $\mathbb{E} = \mathbb{F}$ to represent events. As mentioned above, a rule is evaluated by first evaluating the left-hand side, resulting in an environment binding free variables occurring in event and fact patterns to values in the actual event and in actual facts. An environment is a map of type $Env = \mathcal{V} \nrightarrow \mathbb{D}$. Finally, when executing a rule, the result is a change request (D, A) of type $\mathbb{CH} = \mathbb{DB} \times \mathbb{DB}$, consisting of a set of facts D to be deleted and a set of facts A to be added. We will encounter semantic definitions which produce sets of change requests. For this we need a function $\mathsf{merge} : \wp(\mathbb{CH}) \rightarrow \mathbb{CH}$, which merges the deleted facts respectively added facts, with the simple definition:

$$\mathsf{merge}(ch) = \left(\bigcup \{D \mid (D, A) \in ch\}, \bigcup \{A \mid (D, A) \in ch\} \right)$$

Definition 2. *Let $\tau \in \mathbb{E}^*$ be a trace and $rs \in \mathsf{RS}$ be a rule system. The relation $\tau \models rs$ (τ satisfies rs) is defined as: $\tau \models rs$ iff $\mathsf{error} \notin T[\![rs]\!](\emptyset)(\tau)$; where the function $T[\![\_]\!] : \mathsf{RS} \rightarrow \mathbb{DB} \rightarrow \mathbb{E}^* \rightarrow \mathbb{DB}$, here applied to the rule system, an initial empty set of facts, and the trace, is defined in Fig. 4.*

Function T (Fig. 4) is curried, and is applied to a rule system, a database, and a trace, returning a database with facts deleted and added. Function E evaluates the rule system against a single event. The special bottom value $\bot$ denotes an "error value". Given a type T, the type $T_\bot$ denotes $T \cup \{\bot\}$. Function X evaluates one step of the rule system against a database, which is assumed to contain the event just submitted. Function $Xrec$ evaluates the rule system against a database, executing (after the event has been removed) recursively

$T[\![\_]\!] : \mathrm{RS} \to \mathbb{DB} \to \mathbb{E}^* \to \mathbb{DB}$
$T[\![rs]\!](db)(\tau) =$
  if $\tau = \langle \, \rangle$ then db else
    let $db' = E[\![rs]\!](db)(\mathrm{head}(\tau))$ in
    if error $\in db'$ then db' else
      $T[\![rs]\!](db')(\mathrm{tail}(\tau))$

$E[\![\_]\!] : \mathrm{RS} \to \mathbb{DB} \to \mathbb{E} \to \mathbb{DB}$
$E[\![rs]\!](db)(e) =$
  let $db' = X[\![rs]\!](db \cup \{e\})$ in
  if $db' = \bot$ then db else
    $Xrec[\![rs]\!](db' \setminus \{e\})$

$X[\![\_]\!] : \mathrm{RS} \to \mathbb{DB} \to \mathbb{DB}_\bot$
$X[\![rs]\!](db) =$
  let $(D, A) =$
    $\mathrm{merge}(\{R[\![\pi]\!](db) \mid \pi \in rs\})$
  in
  if $D \cup A = \emptyset$ then $\bot$ else
    $(db \setminus D) \cup A$

$Xrec[\![\_]\!] : \mathrm{RS} \to \mathbb{DB} \to \mathbb{DB}$
$Xrec[\![rs]\!](db) =$
  let $db' = X[\![rs]\!](db)$ in
  if $db' = \bot$ then db else
    $Xrec[\![rs]\!](db')$

$R[\![\_]\!] : \mathrm{R} \to \mathbb{DB} \to \mathbb{CH}$
$R[\![id : \bar{c} \Rightarrow \bar{\alpha}]\!](db) =$
  let $\Theta = LHS[\![\bar{c}]\!](db)([\,])$ in
  $\mathrm{merge}(\{RHS[\![\bar{\alpha}]\!](\theta) \mid \theta \in \Theta\})$

$LHS[\![\_]\!] : \mathrm{C}^* \to \mathbb{DB} \to Env \to \wp(Env)$
$LHS[\![c_1,\ldots,c_n]\!](db)(\theta) =$
  if $n = 0$ then $\{\theta\}$ else
    let $\Theta = C[\![c_1]\!](db)(\theta)$ in
    $\bigcup\{LHS[\![c_2,\ldots,c_n]\!](db)(\theta') \mid \theta' \in \Theta\}$

$C[\![\_]\!] : \mathrm{C} \to \mathbb{DB} \to Env \to \wp(Env)$
$C[\![fp]\!](db)(\theta) = Fdb[\![fp]\!](db)(\theta)$

$C[\![\mathbf{not}(fp)]\!](db)(\theta) =$
  let $\Theta = Fdb[\![fp]\!](db)(\theta)$ in
  if $\Theta = \emptyset$ then $\{\theta\}$ else $\emptyset$

$C[\![\mathbf{when}(exp)]\!](db)(\theta) =$
  if $Exp[\![exp]\!](\theta)$ then $\{\theta\}$ else $\emptyset$

$Fdb[\![\_]\!] : \mathrm{FP} \to \mathbb{DB} \to Env \to \wp(Env)$
$Fdb[\![id(p_1,\ldots,p_n)]\!](db)(\theta) =$
  $\bigcup\{$
    let $\theta' = Ffact[\![id(p_1,\ldots,p_n)]\!](\kappa)(\theta)$ in
    if $\theta' = \bot$ then $\emptyset$ else
      $\{\theta' \dagger [id \mapsto \kappa]\}$
  $\mid$
  $\kappa \in db$
  $\}$

$Ffact[\![\_]\!] : \mathrm{FP} \to \mathbb{F} \to Env \to Env_\bot$
$Ffact[\![id_1(p_1,\ldots,p_n)]\!](id_2(v_1,\ldots,v_n))(\theta) =$
  if $id_1 \neq id_2$ then $\bot$ else
    $Args[\![p_1,\ldots,p_n]\!](v_1,\ldots,v_n)(\theta)$

$Args[\![\_]\!] : \mathrm{P}^* \to \mathbb{D}^* \to Env \to Env_\bot$
$Args[\![p_1,\ldots,p_n]\!](v_1,\ldots,v_n)(\theta) =$
  if $n = 0$ then θ else
    let $\theta' = Arg[\![p_1]\!](v_1)(\theta)$ in
    if $\theta' = \bot$ then $\bot$ else
      $Args[\![p_2,\ldots,p_n]\!](v_2,\ldots,v_n)(\theta \dagger \theta')$

$Arg[\![\_]\!] : \mathrm{P} \to \mathbb{D} \to Env \to Env_\bot$
$Arg[\![p]\!](v)(\theta) =$
  if $p \in \mathscr{V}$ then
    if $p \in \mathrm{dom}(\theta)$ then
      if $\theta(p) = v$ then θ else $\bot$
    else
      $\theta \dagger [p \mapsto v]$
  else
    if $p = v$ then θ else $\bot$

$RHS[\![\_]\!] : \mathrm{A}^* \to Env \to \mathbb{CH}$
$RHS[\![\bar{\alpha}]\!](\theta) =$
  $\mathrm{merge}(\{A[\![\alpha]\!](\theta) \mid \alpha \in \bar{\alpha}\})$

$A[\![\_]\!] : \mathrm{A} \to Env \to \mathbb{CH}$
$A[\![\mathbf{insert}(id(exp_1,\ldots,exp_n))]\!](\theta) =$
  $(\emptyset, \{id(Exp[\![exp_1]\!](\theta),\ldots,Exp[\![exp_n]\!](\theta))\})$

$A[\![\mathbf{remove}(id)]\!](\theta) =$
  $(\{\theta(id)\}, \emptyset)$

$A[\![\mathbf{error}]\!](\theta) =$
  $(\emptyset, \{\mathrm{error}\})$

$Exp[\![\_]\!] : \mathrm{Exp} \to Env \to \mathbb{D}$
  $\ldots$

Fig. 4. Semantics of LF.

until no rules can fire ($\perp$ returned from a call of X). Function R evaluates a single rule against a database. Function LHS evaluates the rule's conditions against a database and the environment obtained so-far by evaluating previous conditions of the rule. Function C evaluates a single condition against a database and an environment. Function Fdb evaluates a fact pattern against a database by matching the pattern against each fact in the database. A binding $id \mapsto \kappa$ is introduced, and later used in the semantics of remove actions of the form: **remove**(id) (it is assumed that $\mathbb{D}$ contains facts). Function $Ffact$ evaluates a fact pattern against a fact. Function $Args$ evaluates a list of fact pattern parameters against a list of actual arguments to a fact. Function Arg evaluates a single fact pattern parameter against a single fact argument. Function RHS evaluates the right-hand side of a rule, a list of actions, in an environment generated by evaluating the left-hand side. Function A evaluates a single action in an environment, returning a change request. Function Exp (not further defined) evaluates an expression in an environment, resulting in a value.

6.3   Monitoring Algorithm

In principle, the semantics shown in Sect. 6.2 is sufficient for execution[11]. However, it is inefficient in that for each event, we process in function X each rule (rule overhead), in LHS each condition (condition overhead), and in Fdb each database fact (fact overhead). In the typical RV case the number of rules and conditions are small and fixed but the facts grow, resulting in the fact overhead potentially becoming the main source of inefficiency. These inefficiencies are addressed by the RETE algorithm (although only to some degree in the case of fact overhead), developed by Charles L. Forgy in the 1970s [40], and explained in careful detail in [36]. The name *Rete* means *network* in Latin, and reflects the way rules are represented and facts stored by the algorithm. In order to illustrate the algorithm we shall consider the *UnsafeMapIterator* example. For illustration purposes, we shall add a new rule r_5 to the rule system, in addition to rule r_4, to reflect that it is also an error to observe a call of hasNext() on an unsafe iterator:

```
r₄: updated(i), next(i) ⇒ error
r₅: updated(i), hasNext(i) ⇒ error
```

The two rules share the prefix updated(i). They (ignoring here the other rules) are translated into the RETE network shown in Fig. 5 (top). This data structure represents the full structure of the rules, and in addition stores all received events and generated facts during monitoring. In general, a RETE network consists of four kinds of nodes:

- *alpha memories*: white rectangular nodes. There is an alpha memory for each kind of event and fact. When a new event is received or fact generated, it is inserted into the corresponding alpha memory, which can be viewed as a set of events/facts.

---

[11] A Scala version of this semantics has been developed.

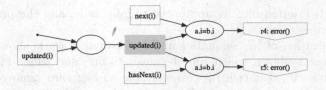

Event	Rule	Added facts
create(m_1,c_1)	r_1	createdC(m_1,c_1)
create(m_1,c_2)	r_1	createdC(m_1,c_2)
iterator(c_1,i_1)	r_2	createdI(m_1,i_1)
update(m_1)	r_3	updated(i_1)
iterator(c_2,i_2)	r_2	createdI(m_1,i_2)
next(i_1)	r_4	error

Fig. 5. Top: RETE network for UnsafeMapIterator rules r_4 and r_5. Bottom: result of applying algorithm to example trace.

- *beta memories*: grey rectangular nodes, containing so-called *tokens*. A token (an alternative representation of what we called an environment in the semantics) is a list of events/facts matching a prefix of one or more rules. The leftmost •-node symbolises an initial beta memory (a singular set containing an empty token). This is introduced to make the behaviour of join nodes (see below) uniform.
- *join nodes*: round processing nodes, each connected to an alpha memory and a beta memory, the input nodes, and an output node: a beta memory or an action node. When a fact or token arrives in a connected input alpha or beta memory: the other (beta or alpha) memory is searched for matches. The join node contains the fact pattern of a condition occurring in one or more rules. A match occurs in this example when the alpha node's i parameter equals the beta node's i parameter (in the graph expressed as $a.i = b.i$). Each match results in a new token created from the old token by appending the event/fact from the alpha memory. The new token is sent to the child beta memory or action node.
- *action nodes*: downwards arrow shaped nodes deleting and/or adding facts.

Let's summarise how the algorithm works. When an event is received, it is added to the appropriate alpha memory. This again triggers the connected child join node to execute a search in its connected input beta memory for a matching token, each of which is a list of previous matching facts to a rule prefix. For each such match a new token is generated by appending the event to the input token. The new extended token is then sent to the child beta node or action. If the child node is an action it will execute, and add/remove facts. If the child node is another beta node, then that will again trigger its connected child join node to search its connected input alpha node for matches, etc. Likewise when a fact is added, it is inserted into its appropriate alpha node, and the process is the same as just described.

The application of the semantics in Fig. 4 to our trace is shown in Fig. 5. For each event is shown which rule it causes to fire, and which fact is added to the database by that rule (in this example no facts are removed). We can illustrate the algorithm using the RETE network as well. Since the network in Fig. 5 is partial and only reflects two rules, the illustration will be partial as well. When the updated(i_1) fact is generated in the 4th step (in Fig. 5), it is inserted in the left-most alpha memory. This triggers the connected child join node to search its connected input beta memory for matches. This is the initial beta memory containing an empty token matching everything, and the updated(i_1) fact is thus propagated to the child beta node as the token $\langle$updated(i_1)$\rangle$ (a list containing that fact). The 6th next(i_1) event is inserted in the top-most alpha node, which again causes its child join node to search for matches in its input beta memory, which now contains the $\langle$updated(i_1)$\rangle$ token. This is a match, and the token $\langle$updated(i_1), next(i_1)$\rangle$ is sent to the r_4 action node, causing an error to be generated.

The RETE algorithm reduces overhead by adding a fact to only the relevant alpha memory, thereby restricting evaluation to that corresponding condition, restricting evaluation to only rules connected to that alpha memory, and restricting evaluation to only that fact. The RETE algorithm optimises situations where two or more rules have a common condition prefix, sharing conditions. The RETE algorithm needs a couple of modifications for runtime verification, however, as described in [47]. First of all, for each update to an alpha or beta memory, the other memory is searched sequentially for matches. This is inefficient in the case of large data volumes in these memories. An indexing approach can address this problem. Second, events need to be handled differently than facts: they should only be around long enough to trigger rules to execute, but should be deleted as soon as this objective is reached. This corresponds to the removal of the event e in the semantic function E in Sect. 6.2.

7   Stream Processing

7.1   Overview

Runtime verification can be seen as a special case of stream processing, in which the observable system behaviour is represented by a set of input streams, and the monitored property is represented by a (Boolean) output stream of verdicts. The LOLA framework [29] was the first to explicitly cast runtime verification as stream computation. Inspired by functional stream computation languages like Lustre [45] and Esterel [23], LOLA proposed a minimalistic language in which output streams are specified using expressions over the same or other streams. These expressions establish dependencies between the current value of an output stream with values of the same or other streams at the current, past, or future positions. Evaluation is synchronous, i.e. there is a global index into all streams representing the current progress of evaluation. Output streams are not restricted to contain Boolean values and thus the framework goes beyond property checking and allows for quantitative analyses to be carried over, such as computing statistics over the observed system behaviour. In this rest of this section, we present the LOLA framework,[12] mainly following the presentation in [24].

We start by formalising in LOLA the *UnsafeMapIterator* property. This property is somehow unnatural for stream processing, as it considers *event streams* and not *data streams* (i.e. sequences of data values). There are several approaches to encode events as stream elements, and we use one which allows for fewer intermediary streams. Namely, we assume that a stream element is a set of tuples of data values. For input streams, these sets are always singletons, as one element encodes one event. For instance, if at some position j of the monitored trace the event create(m_1, c_1) occurs, then, at position j, the input stream create contains the element $\{(m_1, c_1)\}$, otherwise (if a different event type occurs at j) it contains the empty set. Note that we assume here four input streams, one for each event type. The following stream equations specify the property.

$$\text{createdC} = \text{create} \cup \text{createdC}[-1|\emptyset]$$
$$\text{createdI} = (\text{iterator} \bowtie \text{createdC}) \cup \text{createdI}[-1|\emptyset]$$
$$\text{updated} = (\text{update} \bowtie \text{createdI}) \cup \text{updated}[-1|\emptyset]$$
$$\text{ok} = \text{next} \not\subseteq \pi_{\langle i \rangle}(\text{updated})$$

The formalisation uses three intermediary streams, and one output stream, namely ok. Each stream equation represents an equality between the element at the (implicit) position j in the stream on the left hand side of the equation and the elements of the streams occurring on the right hand side of the equation, at positions j' obtained from j by an offset, for any position j in the input streams. The first equation relates, recursively, the jth element of createdC with the jth element of create and the $(j-1)$th element of createdC (unless $j = 0$, see below). In general, the expression s refers to the value of the stream s at the current position j, and the expression $s[-1|v]$ refers to the value of s at the position with offset -1 with respect to the current position, that is, $j - 1$, if $j > 0$, and otherwise it refers to the value v, i.e. a default value given after the $|$ symbol. LOLA allows for any computable function to be used for obtaining output stream elements from input stream elements. In this example we use relational algebra operators (see also Sect. 3.3).[13] Thus, the stream createdC contains the tuples (m, c) of collections c created so far from maps m. Similarly, the streams createdI and updated contain the tuples (c, i, m) of iterators i created so far from collections c, in turn created from maps m; with m referring to updated maps in case of the stream updated. Finally, the stream ok is the Boolean stream representing whether the property is satisfied at the current position, is computed by checking whether the iterator i (if any) is among those for which the

---

[12] An implementation can be found at https://www.react.uni-saarland.de/tools/lola/.

[13] We abuse notation and apply them on unnamed relations, as their attributes are as expected, e.g. $\langle m, c \rangle$ for createdC, and $\langle c, i, m \rangle$ for createdI and updated.

corresponding map was updated. We end this section by noting the similarity between this formalisation and the ones QEA and LOGFIRE have used.

7.2   Syntax and Semantics

We assume a finite set of interpreted, typed function symbols f, where f denotes a computable function of some type $T_1 \times \cdots \times T_k \to T$. By abuse of notation, we identify function symbols with their interpretation. Note that 0-ary function symbols, that is, constants, are associated with individual values of some type. We also assume a set of typed *stream variables*.

A *stream of type T* is a finite sequence over T. A stream is *Boolean* if its type is $\mathbb{B}$. For a finite set Z of stream variables, a *stream valuation over Z* is a partial function θ over stream variables assigning to each variable $z \in Z$, a stream $\theta(z)$ such that the streams associated with the different variables in Z have the same length n for some $n \geq 0$. We also say that n is the length of θ, which is denoted by $|\theta|$.

Stream Expressions. Given a finite set Z of stream variables, the set of *stream expressions exp of type T over Z* is inductively defined by the following syntax:

$$exp := z \mid z[\ell|c] \mid f(exp_1, \ldots, exp_k)$$

where $z \in Z$ is a variable of type T, $\ell \neq 0$ is a non-zero integer, c is a constant of type T, $k \geq 0$ is a positive integer, $f \in F$ is a function symbol of some type $T_1 \times \cdots \times T_k \to T$, and $exp_1, \ldots, exp_k$ are stream expression of type $T_1, \ldots, T_k$, respectively. Informally, $z[\ell|c]$ refers to the value of e at the position obtained from the current position offset by ℓ, and the constant c is the default value assigned to positions from which the offset is after the end or before the beginning of the stream.

Stream expressions e of type T over Z are interpreted over stream valuations θ of type T over Z. The valuation of exp with respect to θ, written $[\![exp]\!](\theta)$, is the stream of type T and length $|\theta|$ inductively defined as follows for all $0 \leq i < |\theta|$:

- $[\![z]\!](\theta)(i) = \theta(z)(i)$, for all $z \in Z$,
- $[\![z[\ell|c]]\!](\theta)(i) = \begin{cases} [\![z]\!](\theta)(i+\ell) & \text{if } 0 \leq i+\ell < |\theta|, \\ c & \text{otherwise,} \end{cases}$
- $[\![f(exp_1, \ldots, exp_k)]\!](\theta)(i) = f([\![exp_1]\!](\theta)(i), \ldots, [\![exp_k]\!](\theta)(i))$.

Example 11. Consider the Boolean stream expression $exp := x \lor x[1|\text{true}]$ over $\{x\}$. For every stream valuation θ over $\{x\}$ such that $\theta(x) \in (\text{false true})^+$, i.e. alternating false and true, the valuation of exp with respect to θ is the Boolean stream $\text{true}^{|\theta|}$, that is, the sequence of length $|\theta|$ where each element is true.

Specification Language. Given a finite set X of stream variables and a set $Y = \{y_1, \ldots, y_n\}$, with $n \geq 1$, of stream variables of type $T_1, \ldots, T_n$ respectively, with $X \cap Y = \emptyset$, a LOLA *specification E over (input variables) X and (output variables) Y* is a set of equations

$$\{y_1 = exp_1, \ldots, y_n = exp_n\}$$

where $exp_1, \ldots, exp_n$ are stream expressions over $X \cup Y$ of type $T_1, \ldots, T_n$ respectively. Note that there is exactly one equation for each output variable.

A *stream valuation of E* is a stream valuation over $X \cup Y$. An *input* (resp. *output*) of E is a stream valuation over X (resp. Y). The LOLA specification E describes a relation, written $[\![E]\!]$, between inputs θ_X of E and outputs θ_Y of E, defined as follows: $(\theta_X, \theta_Y) \in [\![E]\!]$ iff $|\theta_X| = |\theta_Y|$ and for each equation $y = exp$ of E,

$$[\![y]\!](\theta) = [\![exp]\!](\theta)$$

where $\theta = \theta_X \cup \theta_Y$, defined as expected. The stream valuation $\theta_X \cup \theta_Y$ is a *valuation model* of E (associated with the input θ_X) if $(\theta_X, \theta_Y) \in [\![E]\!]$. Note that in general, for a given input θ_X, there may be zero, one, or multiple valuation models associated with θ_X. A LOLA specification E is *well-defined* iff for each input θ_X, there is exactly one valuation model of E associated with θ_X.

A distinction can be made between streams that are meant to represent the output corresponding to some input and intermediate streams that only facilitate the computation of the intended output. Such a distinction is not essential here.

Example 12. We present next an alternative formalisation of the *UnsafeMap-Iterator* property. We assume the same input streams as in Sect. 7.1, namely create, iterator, update, and next.[14] Note that their type is of the form $\wp(T_1 \times \ldots \times T_k)$, with $T_1 \ldots, T_k$ among *Map, Collection, Iterator*. The following stream equations specify the property.

$$\text{created} = \text{create} \cup \text{created}[-1|\emptyset]$$
$$\text{notupdated} = ((\text{iterator} \bowtie \text{created}) \cup \text{notupdated}[-1|\emptyset]) \rhd \text{update}$$
$$\text{ok} = \text{next} \subseteq \pi_{\langle i \rangle}(\text{notupdated})$$

The stream ok is the Boolean stream representing the satisfaction or the violation of the property at each position in the event sequence, i.e. $\text{ok}(j) = \text{false}$ iff there is a violation at position j. The auxiliary stream created of type $\wp(Map \times Collection)$ stores at position j all tuples (m, c) that have appeared in the input stream create up to (and including) position j. The auxiliary stream notupdated of type $\wp(Map \times Collection \times Iterator)$ stores at position j all tuples (c, i, m) such that (a) at some previous position j', the tuples (c, i) and (m, c) appeared in the stream iterator and respectively the stream created, and (b) between position j' and j the tuple (m) has not appeared in the stream update. In other words, notupdated stores those iterators that are safe to call next() on (along with the related map and collection objects).

---

[14] In examples we do not make a distinction between stream variables and their denoted streams, that is, we identify x and $\theta(x)$.

We note the similarity of this LOLA specification with the computation performed by the FOTL-based monitoring algorithm for the corresponding FOTL specification (see Example 3). Namely, there is a direct correspondence between how the streams created, notupdated, and ok are computed and how the satisfying elements of the formulas β', γ', and respectively φ are computed. In particular, given the trace from Example 1, the output streams notupdated and created are given by the columns $[\![\beta']\!]^j$ and respectively $[\![\gamma']\!]^j$ of Table 1, while for ok we have ok(i) = true for $i \in \{0, \ldots, 4\}$ and ok(5) = false.

Well-Formed Specifications. Note that well-definedness is a semantic restriction on LOLA specifications. To detect ill-defined specifications, like $y = y$ or $y = \neg y$, we present next a syntactic restriction that guarantees well-definedness.

Let E be a LOLA specification over X and Y. A *dependency graph* for E is a weighted and directed multi-graph with vertex set $X \cup Y$. There is an edge (z, z', w) from z to z' with weight w iff the expression *exp* contains $z'[w|c]$ as a subexpression of *exp*, where *exp* is z's expression in E, i.e. $(z = exp) \in E$. Intuitively, the edge records that the value of (the stream denoted by) z at a particular position depends on the value of z', offset by w positions. Note that there can be multiple edges between z and z' with different weights on each edge. Vertices $x \in X$ have no outgoing edges.

A *walk* of a graph is a sequence $v_1, e_1, v_2, \ldots, v_k, e_k, v_{k+1}$ of vertices and edges, for $k \geq 1$, such that $e_i = (v_i, v_{i+1}, w_i)$, for all i with $1 \leq i \leq k$. The walk is *closed* iff $v_1 = v_{k+1}$. The weight of a walk is the sum of weights of its edges.

A LOLA specification is *well-formed* if there is no closed walk with total weight zero in its dependency graph. Every well-formed LOLA specification is well-defined [29]. The converse is not true. For instance, the specification $y = y \wedge \neg y$ is well-defined, but not well-formed.

7.3   Monitoring Algorithm

The monitoring algorithm takes as input a LOLA specification E over X and Y, with E assumed to be well-formed, and an input valuation θ_X of E, which is processed iteratively. That is, at the $(i+1)$st iteration, the monitor receives the values of all input streams at position i, namely $\theta_X(x)(i)$, for $x \in X$. The goal of the monitoring algorithm is to incrementally compute the output valuation θ_Y. Concretely, the monitor outputs at each iteration the newly computed values $\theta_Y(y)(j)$, where $y \in Y$ and $j \in \{0, \ldots, |\theta_X| - 1\}$.

Before presenting the algorithm, we introduce some additional notation. Let $\mathscr{X}_Z$ be the set of variables $\{z_j \mid z \in Z, 0 \leq j \leq |\theta_X|\}$, for $Z \in \{X, Y\}$, and let $\mathscr{X} := \mathscr{X}_X \cup \mathscr{X}_Y$. Given a stream expression *exp* and a position $j \in \{0, \ldots, |\theta_X| - 1\}$, we denote by $t_j(exp)$ the following term over $\mathscr{X}$ defined inductively over the structure of *exp*: if $exp = z$ then $t_j(exp) = z_j$, if $exp = f(exp_1, \ldots, exp_k)$ then $t_j(exp) = f(t_j(exp_1), \ldots, t_j(exp_k))$, and if $exp = z[\ell|c]$ then $t_j(exp) = z_{j+\ell}$ if $0 \leq j + \ell < |\theta_X|$ and $t_j(exp) = c$ otherwise.

The monitoring algorithm maintains two sets of equations:

– A set R of *resolved equations* $z_i = c$, where $z_i \in \mathscr{X}$ and c is a constant.
– A set U of *unresolved equations* $y_i = t$, where $y_i \in \mathscr{X}_Y$ and t is a non-ground term over $\mathscr{X}$.

Initially both stores are empty. At the $(i+1)$st iteration, the values $\theta_X(x)(i)$ for $x \in X$ become available and the monitor carries out the following steps:

1. The equation $x_i = \theta_X(x)(i)$ is added to R, for each $x \in X$.
2. The equation $y_i = t_i(exp)$ is added to U, for each equation $(y = exp) \in E$.
3. The equations in U are simplified as much as possible, using the following rules:
   – Partial evaluation rules for function applications, such as $0 + a \rightarrow a$.
   – If $(y_j = c) \in R$, then every occurrence of y_j in (the terms in) U is substituted by c and possibly simplified further.
   If an equation becomes of the form $y_j = c$, it is removed from U and added to R; furthermore, $\theta_Y(y)(j)$ is set to c.
4. Equations $z_{i-k} = c$ are removed from R, where

$$k := \max(\{0\} \cup \{\ell \mid \ell > 0 \text{ and } z[-\ell|c] \text{ is a subexpression in } E\})$$

Concerning the last step, we have that, for any position j, the position $j+k$ is the latest future position for which the monitor requires the value of $(\theta_X \cup \theta_Y)(z)(j)$. Thus the equation $z_{i-k} = c$ can be safely removed from R at position i. This is important as it places a bound on the amount of history that needs to be stored. Also, note that the well-formedness condition ensures that each equation in U is eventually resolved.

Example 13. To illustrate the last point, consider the specification $y = y[-3|0] + x$. The value of k for y is 3 and for x is 0. This indicates that for any input stream σ, the equation $x_j = \sigma(j)$ can be removed from R at position j itself. Similarly, $y_j = \tau(j)$ can be removed from R at (or after) position $j + 3$, where τ is the output stream.

If in a specification all offsets are negative, that is, the stream expressions only refer to current or previous stream positions, then at the end of each iteration all equations are resolved, i.e. $U = \emptyset$, because all new terms in U can be evaluated and simplified to constants. The specifications from Sect. 7.1 and Example 12 fall in this category. We therefore illustrate next the algorithm on a specification which contains positive offsets.

Example 14. Consider the specification $y = x' \lor (x \land y[1|\mathsf{false}])$ over $\{x, x'\}$ and $\{y\}$, corresponding to the LTL specification $x \, \mathsf{W} \, x'$ over finite traces, where W denotes the "weak until" operator. That is, y_j stores the satisfaction of $x \, \mathsf{W} \, x'$ on the word encoding the suffixes of the streams x and x' starting at position j. The associated equations are:

$$y_j = \begin{cases} x'_j \lor (x_j \land y_{j+1}) & \text{if } j < n - 1, \\ x'_j & \text{otherwise (that is, } j = n - 1) \end{cases}$$

Table 3. Sample execution of the monitoring algorithm.

Position	R	U
0	$x_0 = \text{false}, x_0' = \text{true}$	$y_0 = x_0' \vee (x_0 \wedge y_1)$
	$y_0 = \text{true}$	–
1	$x_1 = \text{false}, x_1' = \text{false}$	$y_1 = x_1' \vee (x_1 \wedge y_2)$
	$y_1 = \text{false}$	–
2	$x_2 = \text{true}, x_2' = \text{false}$	$y_2 = x_2' \vee (x_2 \wedge y_3)$
	–	$y_2 = y_3$
6	$x_6 = \text{true}, x_6' = \text{false}$	$y_2 = y_3, y_3 = y_4, y_4 = y_5, y_5 = y_6, y_6 = x_6'$
	$y_2 = \text{false}, y_3 = \text{false}, y_4 = \text{false},$ $y_5 = \text{false}, y_6 = \text{false}$	–

for $0 \le j < n$, with n the input streams' length. Let x, x' be the following input streams.

x	false	false	true	true	true	true	true
x'	true	false	false	false	false	false	false

Table 3 lists the contents of the sets R and U at various stream positions j. For each position j there are two rows in the table; the first row lists the contents of R and U after executing steps 1 and 2 of the algorithm, while the second row does the same after executing steps 3 and 4. At position 0, we add $x_0 = x(0)$, i.e. $x_0 = \text{false}$, and $x_0' = x'(0)$, i.e. $x_0' = \text{true}$, to R, and $y_0 = x_0' \vee (x_0 \wedge y_1)$ to U. The equation for y_0 simplifies to $y_0 = \text{true}$, and is thus moved to R. At position 1, we have $x_1 = \text{false}$ and $x_1' = \text{false}$ in R and thus we can set $y_1 = \text{false}$, which is also added to R. From $j = 2$ until $j = 5$, we have $x_j = \text{true}$ and $x_j' = \text{false}$. At each of these positions the equations $y_j = y_{j+1}$ are added to U. The set U now contains the equations $y_2 = y_3, y_3 = y_4, \ldots, y_5 = y_6$. At position 6, we have $x_6 = \text{true}$ and $x_6' = \text{false}$ with the added information that the trace has ended, i.e. $y_6 = x_6'$. Thus we set $y_6 = \text{false}$ and add it to R. This lets us resolve the equations in U and set $y_j = \text{false}$, for all the positions j from 2 to 6.

We end this section by noting that a run of the algorithm on the *Unsafe-MapIterator* property can be easily simulated by the reader; see the remark from Example 12.

8   Discussion

In this section we briefly discuss and compare the five different approaches outlined. It is common to compare approaches on *expressiveness* of the specification languages, their *elegance*, and *efficiency* of monitoring algorithms. However, due to lack of available complete results, our comparison is inherently subjective, rather than objective based on concrete data. Hopefully future research and future editions of the runtime verification competition (CRV) [14,38,60] will improve on this situation. Some first steps in this direction have been taken in [61]. We also compare the approaches in terms of the type of data structure used to store data values and of the type of produced output.

Expressiveness. The FOTL-based approach supports extensions to real-time constraints and aggregation operators, which allow for a wide range of practically relevant properties to be specified in a convenient manner. FOTL specifications are furthermore compatible with an interpretation over infinite traces, which means that specifications can be used for model checking purposes as well as for monitoring purposes. MMT provides a generic framework that allows to use a variety of data algebras with existing monitoring approaches for temporal logics. This genericity allows for a wide range of specifications to be expressed. Furthermore, the MMT approach can monitor any FOTL formula that can be put in prenex normal form – a different kind of restriction than that imposed by the FOTL-based approach. The expressiveness of QEA, LF, and LOLA depend on their guard, assignment, expression, and function languages. Assuming rich such languages, these systems are Turing complete, and therefore more expressive than temporal logics such as FOTL and TDL. However, it is unclear that full Turing completeness is required for a practically useful RV specification language. The extended state machines of QEA allow fundamentally to write programs, assuming a general guard and assignment language. The rule-based LOGFIRE allows a form of programming where arbitrary data can be passed as arguments to facts, thereby simulating a program state. Added to that is that LOGFIRE is an internal DSL (an API) allowing full fledged programming in SCALA. The LOLA framework phrases runtime verification as a stream processing problem. The framework goes beyond property checking and generally supports computation of any data from traces (quantitative analysis). FOTL, QEA, and LOGFIRE also support such quantitative analysis. Finally, we note that in LOLA much of the performed stream computations are not specified within the approach, but instead through interpreted functions.

Elegance. First-order temporal logics such as FOTL and TDL are quite standard, and allow for very elegant specifications, compared to the other approaches described here. Although this should not be a surprise, it is quite a commonly stated opinion (folklore) that temporal logics are hard to use by practitioners. However, as discussed in [48], we believe that in many cases a temporal logic specification is the most convenient form of formalisation, and that temporal logics certainly deserve to be taken seriously for runtime verification purposes, preferably augmented with other constructs such as sequencing, scopes, etc. Specifications in the other formalisms are less elegant in the average case due to the fact that they operate at a lower level of operational abstraction. For example, in QEA states in state machines have to explicitly named. This issue could be alleviated by extending the approach to multiple plugins, as is done in the JAVAMOP work which QEA builds on. Similarly, in LOGFIRE, intermediate facts have to be named, created, and deleted. One way to look at QEA, LOGFIRE, and LOLA, is as low-level formalisms to be targets of translations from higher-level logics. For instance, a translation from FOTL's monitorable fragment to LOLA seems straightforward.

Efficiency. The analysis of the complexity of monitoring algorithms for specifications with data has not received much attention so far. Of the presented approaches, we know that the FOTL-based algorithm has polynomial time and space complexity in the number of data values in the trace (see [17] for details), while LOLA's algorithm uses time and space that is linear in the length of the trace under the assumption that interpreted functions execute in linear time [29].[15] We note that under the anticipation requirement [55] (which asks that a verdict should be output as soon as every extension of the current trace leads to the same verdict), the monitoring problem often becomes a hard one because it requires to solve the satisfiability problem for the considered specification language, which is usually a hard problem for expressive languages (e.g., for FOTL it is undecidable). Anticipation is partially supported among the systems presented here by MMT and QEA. Finally, part of the reason for the scarcity of worst-case complexity analyses is that such results often offer little insight into the efficiency of the tools implementing the monitoring algorithms, an aspect that we consider next.

Each of the monitoring approaches presented here has been implemented. There is not enough data to make thorough comparisons between the performance of these tools. However, based on the results of the runtime verification competitions, and experimental evaluation sections in various papers, we can still formulate some observations. The most efficient tools so far explored in the literature appear to be those based on the slicing approach, which was introduced in systems such as TRACEMATCHES and MOP, and carried further in MARQ [59]. The key advantage of parametric trace slicing is that it admits efficient indexing approaches that have a significant impact on monitoring overhead. The generic nature of MMT, which allows to combine any data algebra with temporal logic, and the use of an SMT solver to check, for each incoming event, the generated constraints, makes performance an issue. Performance can be improved significantly by using a dedicated decision procedure instead of a generic solver. Furthermore, on a particular class of properties, namely LTL over tree-ordered ids (and a particular theory, namely that of equality), the MMT algorithm lent itself to a highly effective optimisation [30], implemented in the MUFIN tool. LOGFIRE's implementation, which uses the RETE algorithm, is rather complex, and does not seem to yield the same efficient solution for runtime verification as trace slicing. As documented in [47], however, LOGFIRE performs well compared to other rule systems.

Data Structures. We focus here on the general nature of the data structures used for representing the observed history in the trace at any point during monitoring. With this perspective three different approaches emerge. Both the FOTL and the LOGFIRE algorithms store observed data explicitly as data records, that is, tuples of data values. The FOTL-based algorithm operates with relations (sets of such tuples), which can also be seen as database tables, while LOGFIRE operates with individual tuples, stored as facts in a network. The QEA-based algorithm stores a mapping from valuations to automata states. Valuations can

---

[15] This assumption is not satisfied for our formalisations of the *UnsafeMapIterator* property.

also be seen as data records. Valuations are indexed such that the relevant ones can be found efficiently. The MMT and LOLA systems approach the problem differently by storing constraints between variables and data values; their denotation are the data records stored in the other approaches. As such the five different algorithms use three main approaches to storage of data during monitoring: data record collections, indexed mappings, and constraints.

Monitor Output. The systems presented yield different forms of output. FOTL outputs sets of tuples, representing violations. MMT yields a verdict from an arbitrary truth-value lattice, which can include values like "unknown". QEA yields a verdict from a 4-valued Boolean logic.[16] LOGFIRE by default only outputs a result (an error trace) if the specification is violated, but for each event it offers access to the set of all facts generated so far. LOLA produces a data value at each step during monitoring as part of an output stream. QEA, LOGFIRE, and to some extent FOTL, also can produce any form of output from a trace, although these systems were not created for this purpose.

9   Related Work

In the following we discuss some related work, grouping it by the five presented approaches. As with the FOTL and MMT approaches, a number of other runtime verification approaches also use formalisms based on extensions of (linear) temporal logics with variables modeling event parameters. All these (linear) temporal logic extensions thus exhibit variable quantification, either implicitly or explicitly. In most extensions [12, 18, 19, 44, 46, 63, 64], the domain of a quantifier is restricted to the data appearing at the current position in the trace. When a single event can occur at a position in the trace, as in this chapter and in [12, 44], the domain thus consists of at most one value and quantification has the flavor of the so-called freeze quantification [7]. In all these works, quantification is handled algorithmically by encoding (at runtime) quantifiers with a finite number of conjunctions (∀) and disjunctions (∃), one for each variable instantiation encountered during runtime. The monitoring algorithms are either based on a translation from the underlying propositional formulas to automata, as in [19, 63], or on a syntax-oriented tableaux-like procedure, as in [12, 18, 46]. In contrast to the above, in the FOTL and MMT approaches quantification is over the whole data domain as it is in classic first-order logic. This is also the case with [27], which presents a similar monitoring algorithm to that in [17].

The presented FOTL monitoring approach shares similarities with algorithms for checking temporal integrity constraints of databases and for specifying temporal database triggers, and in particular with [26], which the approach in [17] extends. The MMT framework takes an indirect approach for monitoring first-order temporal logics, by providing a way to lift propositional monitors to the setting of data values. Thus, in its aim to achieve a temporal logic

---

[16] Assuming a guard and assignment language such that checking QEA emptiness is decidable.

independent solution, the MMT approach presents similarities with the MOP framework [25,56].

Trace slicing was introduced in [5] with a suffix-matching semantics and then extended to total-matching (which is non-trivial) in the JAVAMOP work [56]. The latter work also introduces different notions of *matching* which are difficult to capture in the quantification framework introduced earlier, for example, on non-total and connected[17] bindings. The JAVAMOP language, however, introduces an unnecessary restriction on expressiveness by enforcing a unique mapping from event names to parameter names, disallowing an event name to be used with different parameters in a specification. This prevents, for example, a property like *"a lock acquired by a thread t cannot be acquired by another thread t' until first released by t"* as here the lock action refers to two different variables. On the other hand, JAVAMOP supports infinite-state specifications as context-free grammars (CFGs), which are not supported directly by any of the other formalisms. CFG properties can be only expressed indirectly, and much less elegantly, in other formalisms (including QEA and LOGFIRE) by simulating push-down automata. The work of [8] extends the parametric trace slicing approach with constraints, similar to the combination of free variables and guards in QEA. The work in [30] introduces more efficient monitoring algorithm by restricting specifications to those with hierarchical relationships between quantified variables. Other parametric monitoring approaches, that like QEA are automata-based, include LARVA [28] and ORCHIDS [43].

The RETE-based LOGFIRE is inspired by the RULER rule system [9,13] (not based on RETE), which again was influenced by the EAGLE system [11] (a linear μ-calculus supporting parametric monitoring with past time, future time, and sequencing operators). Several RETE-based external rule DSLs exist, such as DROOLS [2] and CLIPS [1]. HAMMURABI [41] (actor-based) and ROOSCALOO [3] (RETE based) are two other internal SCALA rule DSLs. Unlike LOGFIRE, none of these rule systems treat events specially. A RETE-based system for aspect-oriented programming with history pointcuts is described in [49].

The stream-based approach of LOLA resembles synchronous programming languages such as Lustre [45] and Esterel [23]. The approach was extended in LOLA 2.0 [39] with two new language features, namely template stream expressions and dynamic stream generation, which support a notion of slicing similar to that found in QEA.

10   Conclusion

We have described five different formalisms for parameterised runtime verification. The field of runtime verification is still young and there is no clear agreement on what constitutes a good specification formalism. This is in contrast to the field of e.g. model checking, where LTL and CTL have become de facto standards. Part of the reason is possibly data parameterisation, which opens up new doors as to what a specification language can look like, as this chapter illustrates.

---

[17] Bindings whose values are explicitly connected by events in the trace.

References

1. Clips website. http://clipsrules.sourceforge.net
2. Drools website. http://www.jboss.org/drools
3. Rooscaloo website. https://github.com/daveray/rooscaloo
4. Abiteboul, S., Hull, R., Vianu, V.: Foundations of Databases: The Logical Level. Addison Wesley, Boston (1994)
5. Allan, C., Avgustinov, P., Christensen, A.S., Hendren, L., Kuzins, S., Lhoták, O., de Moor, O., Sereni, D., Sittampalam, G., Tibble, J.: Adding trace matching with free variables to AspectJ. SIGPLAN Not. **40**, 345–364 (2005)
6. Alur, R., Etessami, K., Madhusudan, P.: A temporal logic of nested calls and returns. In: Jensen, K., Podelski, A. (eds.) TACAS 2004. LNCS, vol. 2988, pp. 467–481. Springer, Heidelberg (2004). https://doi.org/10.1007/978-3-540-24730-2_35
7. Alur, R., Henzinger, T.A.: A really temporal logic. J. ACM **41**(1), 181–204 (1994)
8. Ballarin, C.: Two generalisations of Roşu and Chen's trace slicing algorithm A. In: Bonakdarpour, B., Smolka, S.A. (eds.) RV 2014. LNCS, vol. 8734, pp. 15–30. Springer, Cham (2014). https://doi.org/10.1007/978-3-319-11164-3_3
9. Barringer, H., Rydeheard, D., Havelund, K.: Rule systems for run-time monitoring: from Eagle to Ruler. In: Sokolsky, O., Taşıran, S. (eds.) RV 2007. LNCS, vol. 4839, pp. 111–125. Springer, Heidelberg (2007). https://doi.org/10.1007/978-3-540-77395-5_10
10. Barringer, H., Falcone, Y., Havelund, K., Reger, G., Rydeheard, D.: Quantified event automata: towards expressive and efficient runtime monitors. In: Giannakopoulou, D., Méry, D. (eds.) FM 2012. LNCS, vol. 7436, pp. 68–84. Springer, Heidelberg (2012). https://doi.org/10.1007/978-3-642-32759-9_9
11. Barringer, H., Goldberg, A., Havelund, K., Sen, K.: Rule-based runtime verification. In: Steffen, B., Levi, G. (eds.) VMCAI 2004. LNCS, vol. 2937, pp. 44–57. Springer, Heidelberg (2004). https://doi.org/10.1007/978-3-540-24622-0_5
12. Barringer, H., Havelund, K.: TraceContract: a Scala DSL for trace analysis. In: Butler, M., Schulte, W. (eds.) FM 2011. LNCS, vol. 6664, pp. 57–72. Springer, Heidelberg (2011). https://doi.org/10.1007/978-3-642-21437-0_7
13. Barringer, H., Rydeheard, D.E., Havelund, K.: Rule systems for run-time monitoring: from Eagle to RuleR. J. Log. Comput. **20**(3), 675–706 (2010)
14. Bartocci, E., Falcone, Y., Bonakdarpour, B., Colombo, C., Decker, N., Havelund, K., Joshi, Y., Klaedtke, F., Milewicz, R., Reger, G., Rosu, G., Signoles, J., Thoma, D., Zalinescu, E., Zhang, Y.: First international competition on runtime verification: rules, benchmarks, tools, and final results of CRV 2014. Int. J. Softw. Tools Technol. Trans. 1–40 (2017)
15. Basin, D., Harvan, M., Klaedtke, F., Zălinescu, E.: MONPOLY: monitoring usage-control policies. In: Khurshid, S., Sen, K. (eds.) RV 2011. LNCS, vol. 7186, pp. 360–364. Springer, Heidelberg (2012). https://doi.org/10.1007/978-3-642-29860-8_27
16. Basin, D.A., Klaedtke, F., Marinovic, S., Zălinescu, E.: Monitoring of temporal first-order properties with aggregations. Form. Method. Syst. Des. **46**(3), 262–285 (2015)
17. Basin, D.A., Klaedtke, F., Müller, S., Zălinescu, E.: Monitoring metric first-order temporal properties. J. ACM **62**(2), 15 (2015)

18. Bauer, A., Goré, R., Tiu, A.: A first-order policy language for history-based trans-action monitoring. In: Leucker, M., Morgan, C. (eds.) ICTAC 2009. LNCS, vol. 5684, pp. 96–111. Springer, Heidelberg (2009). https://doi.org/10.1007/978-3-642-03466-4_6

19. Bauer, A., Küster, J., Vegliach, G.: The ins and outs of first-order runtime verification. Form. Method. Syst. Des. **46**(3), 286–316 (2015)

20. Bauer, A., Leucker, M., Schallhart, C.: Monitoring of real-time properties. In: Arun-Kumar, S., Garg, N. (eds.) FSTTCS 2006. LNCS, vol. 4337, pp. 260–272. Springer, Heidelberg (2006). https://doi.org/10.1007/11944836_25

21. Bauer, A., Leucker, M., Schallhart, C.: The good, the bad, and the ugly, but how ugly is ugly? In: Sokolsky, O., Taşıran, S. (eds.) RV 2007. LNCS, vol. 4839, pp. 126–138. Springer, Heidelberg (2007). https://doi.org/10.1007/978-3-540-77395-5_11

22. Bauer, A., Leucker, M., Schallhart, C.: Runtime verification for LTL and TLTL. ACM Trans. Softw. Eng. Methodol. **20**(4), 1–64 (2011)

23. Berry, G.: The foundations of Esterel. In: Plotkin, G., Stirling, C., Tofte, M. (eds.) Proof, Language, and Interaction, pp. 425–454. MIT Press, Cambridge (2000)

24. Bozzelli, L., Sánchez, C.: Foundations of Boolean stream runtime verification. Theoret. Comput. Sci. **631**, 118–138 (2016)

25. Chen, F., Roşu, G.: Parametric trace slicing and monitoring. In: Kowalewski, S., Philippou, A. (eds.) TACAS 2009. LNCS, vol. 5505, pp. 246–261. Springer, Heidelberg (2009). https://doi.org/10.1007/978-3-642-00768-2_23

26. Chomicki, J.: Efficient checking of temporal integrity constraints using bounded history encoding. ACM Trans. Database Syst. **20**(2), 149–186 (1995)

27. Chowdhury, O., Jia, L., Garg, D., Datta, A.: Temporal mode-checking for runtime monitoring of privacy policies. In: Biere, A., Bloem, R. (eds.) CAV 2014. LNCS, vol. 8559, pp. 131–149. Springer, Cham (2014). https://doi.org/10.1007/978-3-319-08867-9_9

28. Colombo, C., Pace, G.J., Schneider, G.: LARVA — safer monitoring of real-time Java programs (tool paper). In: Proceedings of the 7th IEEE International Conference on Software Engineering and Formal Methods, SEFM 2009, pp. 33–37. IEEE Computer Society (2009)

29. D'Angelo, B., Sankaranarayanan, S., Sánchez, C., Robinson, W., Finkbeiner, B., Sipma, H.B., Mehrotra, S., Manna, Z.: LOLA: runtime monitoring of synchronous systems. In: Proceedings of the 12th International Symposium on Temporal Representation and Reasoning, pp. 166–174. IEEE Computer Society (2005)

30. Decker, N., Harder, J., Scheffel, T., Schmitz, M., Thoma, D.: Runtime monitoring with union-find structures. In: Chechik, M., Raskin, J.-F. (eds.) TACAS 2016. LNCS, vol. 9636, pp. 868–884. Springer, Heidelberg (2016). https://doi.org/10.1007/978-3-662-49674-9_54

31. Decker, N., Leucker, M., Thoma, D.: Impartiality and anticipation for monitoring of visibly context-free properties. In: Legay, A., Bensalem, S. (eds.) RV 2013. LNCS, vol. 8174, pp. 183–200. Springer, Heidelberg (2013). https://doi.org/10.1007/978-3-642-40787-1_11

32. Decker, N., Leucker, M., Thoma, D.: jUnit^{RV}–adding runtime verification to jUnit. In: Brat, G., Rungta, N., Venet, A. (eds.) NFM 2013. LNCS, vol. 7871, pp. 459–464. Springer, Heidelberg (2013). https://doi.org/10.1007/978-3-642-38088-4_34

33. Decker, N., Leucker, M., Thoma, D.: Monitoring modulo theories. In: Ábrahám, E., Havelund, K. (eds.) TACAS 2014. LNCS, vol. 8413, pp. 341–356. Springer, Heidelberg (2014). https://doi.org/10.1007/978-3-642-54862-8_23

34. Decker, N., Leucker, M., Thoma, D.: Monitoring modulo theories. Int. J. Softw. Tools Technol. Trans. **18**(2), 205–225 (2016)
35. Dong, W., Leucker, M., Schallhart, C.: Impartial anticipation in runtime-verification. In: Cha, S.S., Choi, J.-Y., Kim, M., Lee, I., Viswanathan, M. (eds.) ATVA 2008. LNCS, vol. 5311, pp. 386–396. Springer, Heidelberg (2008). https://doi.org/10.1007/978-3-540-88387-6_33
36. Doorenbos, R.B.: Production matching for large learning systems. Ph.D. thesis, Carnegie Mellon University, Pittsburgh, PA (1995)
37. Eisner, C., Fisman, D., Havlicek, J., Lustig, Y., McIsaac, A., Van Campenhout, D.: Reasoning with temporal logic on truncated paths. In: Hunt, W.A., Somenzi, F. (eds.) CAV 2003. LNCS, vol. 2725, pp. 27–39. Springer, Heidelberg (2003). https://doi.org/10.1007/978-3-540-45069-6_3
38. Falcone, Y., Ničković, D., Reger, G., Thoma, D.: Second international competition on runtime verification. In: Bartocci, E., Majumdar, R. (eds.) RV 2015. LNCS, vol. 9333, pp. 405–422. Springer, Cham (2015). https://doi.org/10.1007/978-3-319-23820-3_27
39. Faymonville, P., Finkbeiner, B., Schirmer, S., Torfah, H.: A stream-based specification language for network monitoring. In: Falcone, Y., Sánchez, C. (eds.) RV 2016. LNCS, vol. 10012, pp. 152–168. Springer, Cham (2016). https://doi.org/10.1007/978-3-319-46982-9_10
40. Forgy, C.: Rete: a fast algorithm for the many pattern/many object pattern match problem. Artif. Intell. **19**, 17–37 (1982)
41. Fusco, M.: Hammurabi - a Scala rule engine. In: Scala Days 2011, Stanford University, California (2011)
42. Garcia-Molina, H., Ullman, J.D., Widom, J.: Database Systems: The Complete Book. Pearson Education, Upper Saddle River (2009)
43. Goubault-Larrecq, J., Olivain, J.: A smell of ORCHIDS. In: Leucker, M. (ed.) RV 2008. LNCS, vol. 5289, pp. 1–20. Springer, Heidelberg (2008). https://doi.org/10.1007/978-3-540-89247-2_1
44. Håkansson, J., Jonsson, B., Lundqvist, O.: Generating online test oracles from temporal logic specifications. Int. J. Softw. Tools Technol. Trans. **4**(4), 456–471 (2003)
45. Halbwachs, N., Caspi, P., Raymond, P., Pilaud, D.: The synchronous dataflow programming language Lustre. Proc. IEEE **79**(9), 1305–1320 (1991)
46. Hallé, S., Villemaire, R.: Runtime enforcement of web service message contracts with data. IEEE Trans. Servic. Comput. **5**(2), 192–206 (2012)
47. Havelund, K.: Rule-based runtime verification revisited. Int. J. Softw. Tools Technol. Trans. **17**(2), 143–170 (2015)
48. Havelund, K., Reger, G.: Runtime verification logics - a language design perspective. In: Aceto, L., Bacci, G., Bacci, G., Ingólfsdóttir, A., Legay, A., Mardare, R. (eds.) Models, Algorithms, Logics and Tools: Essays Dedicated to Kim Guldstrand Larsen on the Occasion of His 60th Birthday. LNCS, vol. 10460, pp. 310–338. Springer, Cham (2017). https://doi.org/10.1007/978-3-319-63121-9_16
49. Herzeel, C., Gybels, K., Costanza, P.: Escaping with future variables in HALO. In: Sokolsky, O., Taşıran, S. (eds.) RV 2007. LNCS, vol. 4839, pp. 51–62. Springer, Heidelberg (2007). https://doi.org/10.1007/978-3-540-77395-5_5
50. Hodkinson, I.M., Wolter, F., Zakharyaschev, M.: Decidable fragment of first-order temporal logics. Ann. Pure Appl. Log. **106**(1–3), 85–134 (2000)
51. Holzmann, G.J.: The Spin Model Checker - Primer and Reference Manual. Addison-Wesley, Boston (2004)

52. Hopcroft, J.E., Motwani, R., Ullman, J.D.: Introduction to Automata Theory, Languages, and Computation, 3rd edn. (2007)
53. Koymans, R.: Specifying real-time properties with metric temporal logic. Real-Time Syst. **2**(4), 255–299 (1990)
54. Leucker, M., Sánchez, C.: Regular linear temporal logic. In: Jones, C.B., Liu, Z., Woodcock, J. (eds.) ICTAC 2007. LNCS, vol. 4711, pp. 291–305. Springer, Heidelberg (2007). https://doi.org/10.1007/978-3-540-75292-9_20
55. Leucker, M., Schallhart, C.: A brief account of runtime verification. J. Log. Algebr. Program. **78**(5), 293–303 (2009)
56. Meredith, P.O., Jin, D., Griffith, D., Chen, F., Roşu, G.: An overview of the MOP runtime verification framework. Int. J. Softw. Tools Technol. Trans. **14**(3), 249–289 (2012)
57. Purandare, R., Dwyer, M.B., Elbaum, S.: Monitoring finite state properties: algorithmic approaches and their relative strengths. In: Khurshid, S., Sen, K. (eds.) RV 2011. LNCS, vol. 7186, pp. 381–395. Springer, Heidelberg (2012). https://doi.org/10.1007/978-3-642-29860-8_31
58. Reger, G.: Automata based monitoring and mining of execution traces. Ph.D. thesis, University of Manchester (2014)
59. Reger, G., Cruz, H.C., Rydeheard, D.: MarQ: monitoring at runtime with QEA. In: Baier, C., Tinelli, C. (eds.) TACAS 2015. LNCS, vol. 9035, pp. 596–610. Springer, Heidelberg (2015). https://doi.org/10.1007/978-3-662-46681-0_55
60. Reger, G., Hallé, S., Falcone, Y.: Third international competition on runtime verification. In: Falcone, Y., Sánchez, C. (eds.) RV 2016. LNCS, vol. 10012, pp. 21–37. Springer, Cham (2016). https://doi.org/10.1007/978-3-319-46982-9_3
61. Reger, G., Rydeheard, D.: From first-order temporal logic to parametric trace slicing. In: Bartocci, E., Majumdar, R. (eds.) RV 2015. LNCS, vol. 9333, pp. 216–232. Springer, Cham (2015). https://doi.org/10.1007/978-3-319-23820-3_14
62. Roşu, G., Chen, F.: Semantics and algorithms for parametric monitoring. Log. Methods Comput. Sci. **8**(1), 1–47 (2012)
63. Stolz, V.: Temporal assertions with parameterized propositions. J. Logic Comput. **20**(3), 743–757 (2010)
64. Stolz, V., Bodden, E.: Temporal assertions using AspectJ. In: Proceeding of the 5th International Workshop on Runtime Verification (RV 2005). ENTCS, vol. 144(4), pp. 109–124. Elsevier (2006)

Runtime Failure Prevention and Reaction

Yliès Falcone[1]([envelope]) [iD], Leonardo Mariani[2] [iD], Antoine Rollet[3], and Saikat Saha[2]

[1] Univ. Grenoble Alpes, CNRS, Inria, Grenoble INP, LIG, 38000 Grenoble, France
ylies.falcone@univ-grenoble-alpes.fr
[2] University of Milano Bicocca, 20126 Milan, Italy
{mariani,saha}@disco.unimib.it
[3] LaBRI, Bordeaux INP, University of Bordeaux, Bordeaux, France
antoine.rollet@labri.fr

Abstract. This chapter describes how to use in-the-field runtime techniques to improve the dependability of software systems. In particular, we first present an overall vision of the problem of ensuring highly-dependable behaviours at runtime based on the concept of autonomic monitor, and then we present the two families of relevant approaches for this purpose. First, we present techniques related to *runtime enforcement* that can prevent the system producing bad behaviours. Second, we describe *healing* techniques that can detect if the system has produced a bad behaviour and react to the situation accordingly (e.g., moving the system back to a correct state).

Keywords: Runtime enforcement · Prevention of failures
Reaction to failures · Self-healing · Autonomic computing

1 Introduction

Fully assessing the quality of software systems in-house is infeasible for several well-known reasons. For instance, the space of the behaviours and the configurations that must be validated in-house and their combination might be intractable; many real usage scenarios might be impossible to reproduce and validate in-house; and the context of execution of a system might be only partially known, such as for the many software applications that can be extended directly by their end-users through the installation of plug-ins, which makes the problem of verifying software in-house extremely hard.

To improve the dependability of software systems, the software running in the field can be equipped with solutions to prevent, detect, and react to failures. These solutions attempt to handle the faults that have not been revealed in-house directly in the field, once they produce observable effects. The range of solutions to cope with failures at runtime is quite broad. It spans from fault tolerance techniques, which exploit various forms of redundancy to overcome the impact of failures, to self-healing approaches, which can automatically heal executions before they produce an observable effect.

© Springer International Publishing AG, part of Springer Nature 2018
E. Bartocci and Y. Falcone (Eds.): Lectures on Runtime Verification, LNCS 10457, pp. 103–134, 2018.
https://doi.org/10.1007/978-3-319-75632-5_4

In this chapter, we discuss approaches concerning two complementary, although related, aspects: *runtime enforcement* techniques, which can prevent a monitored program from misbehaviouring by enforcing the program to run according to its specification, and *healing* techniques, which can react to misbehaviours and failures to restore the normal execution of the monitored program, possibly completely masking any observed failure.

Runtime enforcement and healing techniques look at the same problem from the opposite sides. The former affects executions with the objective of preventing failures, for instance preventing that a wrong result is ultimately generated by a program. The latter affects executions with the objective of restoring normal executions once a failure has been observed, possibly masking the failure to any external observer (e.g., the users of a system).

Runtime enforcement typically requires a specification of a system, for instance the specification of a property that must be satisfied by an application, to properly steer executions. When such a specification is available, it can be extremely effective in preventing failures. However, its effectiveness is limited by the scope and availability of the specifications. On the other hand, healing techniques often exploit source of information alternative to ad-hoc specifications (e.g., program versions, redundancy, and failure patterns) to be able to remedy to the observed problems. The two classes of solutions together represent a relevant range of options to deal with failures at runtime.

Of course, the boundaries between enforcement and healing are not always sharp, and some approaches in one category may have some characteristics present also in the approaches in the other category, and vice versa. In this chapter, we do not aim to exhaustively discuss the approaches in the two areas or claim that the distinction between enforcement and healing is effective in all the cases, but rather we aim to give a general and coherent vision of these techniques and to provide an initial set of references for the readers interested in more details. The discussion is mostly informal, and specific details are provided only when needed.

The chapter is organised as follows. Section 2 presents the concept of autonomic monitoring, which is exploited to discuss as part of the same conceptual framework both runtime enforcement and healing techniques. Section 3 discusses techniques to prevent failures by enforcing the correct behaviours. Section 4 presents techniques to react to failures by restoring the correct behaviour. Section 5 discusses some open challenges, and finally Sect. 6 provides final remarks.

2   Autonomic Monitors

Runtime enforcement and healing techniques have to deal with faults, anomalous behaviours and failures. In this chapter, a *failure* is the inability of a system or component to perform its required functions within previously specified limits, a *fault* is an incorrect step, process or data definition, and an *anomalous behaviour* (or a *bad behaviour*) is anything observed in the operation of software that deviates from expectations based on previously verified software products, reference documents, or other sources of indicative behaviour [53]. A fault present in a software may cause anomalous behaviours and even worse failures.

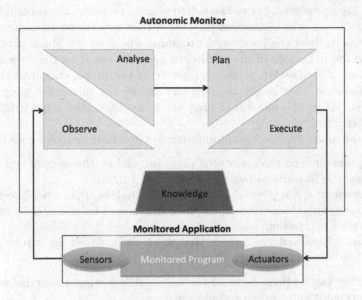

Fig. 1. General architecture for enforcement and healing at runtime.

We present solutions for runtime enforcement and healing referring to the same high-level software architecture. Since both runtime enforcement and healing represent specific cases of autonomic computing technologies, we adapt the architecture of a general autonomic manager proposed by IBM [56] to the case of an *Autonomic Monitor* that can perform enforcement and healing at runtime. The resulting architecture is shown in Fig. 1.

The two main components of the architecture are the *Monitored Program* and the *Autonomic Monitor*. The Monitored Program is coupled with the Autonomic Monitor, which adds behaviour enforcement and healing capabilities to the monitored program. The interaction between these two components is possible through *Sensors*, which are probes or gauges that collect information about the monitored program, and *Effectors*, which are handles that can be used to change the behaviour of the monitored program according to the decisions taken by the Autonomic Monitor. We consider here the *Monitored Program* in a general sense, meaning that for instance its configuration or its environment is included in this definition.

The behaviour of the Autonomic Monitor is determined by a feedback loop that comprises four phases: *Observe*, *Analyse*, *Plan*, and *Execute*. These four phases exploit some *Knowledge* about the monitored program to work effectively. In particular, the *Observe* phase collects information and data from the monitored program using sensors, and filters the collected data until events that need to be analysed are generated and passed to the analysis phase. The Observe phase can also update the Knowledge based on the collected information. The Analyse phase performs data analysis depending on the knowledge and the events that have been produced. Should an action need to be taken, the control is passed to the Plan phase, which identifies the appropriate procedures to enforce a given behaviour or to heal the monitored program. The Execute phase actuates the changes to the behaviour of the monitored program based on the decision taken by the Plan. The Execute phase also performs the preparation tasks, such as locking resources, that might be necessary before the monitored program can be affected. When the monitored program is modified, the Knowledge can be updated accordingly.

In this chapter, we describe the enforcement and healing techniques based on:

- the *requirements* on the monitored program, and on the sensors and effectors that must be introduced into the monitored program;
- the *behaviour of the four phases* Observe, Analyse, Plan and Execute that characterise an autonomic monitor, note that some phases might be extremely simple for some techniques;
- the *knowledge* about the system that must be provided and updated to let the autonomic monitor work properly.

The following two sections organise the approaches distinguishing between *runtime enforcement* and *healing* techniques.

3   Enforce the Correct Behaviour

We overview some of the research efforts in the domain of *runtime enforcement* [35,59]. Runtime enforcement is a "branch" of runtime verification focusing on preventing and reacting to misbehaviours and failures. While runtime verification generally focuses on the oracle problem, namely assigning verdicts to a system execution, runtime enforcement focuses on ensuring the correctness of the sequence of events by possibly modifying the system execution.

Structure of this section. The rest of this section is organised as follows. Section 3.1 introduces runtime enforcement and presents how it contributes to the runtime quality assurance and fits into the general software architecture presented in Sect. 2. Section 3.2 overviews the main existing models of enforcement mechanisms. Section 3.3 focuses on the notion of enforceability of a specification, namely the conditions under which a specification can be enforced. Section 3.4 presents work related to the synthesis of enforcement mechanisms. Section 3.5 discusses some implementation issues and solutions, and presents some tool implementations of runtime enforcement frameworks.

3.1   Introduction and Definitions

Research efforts in runtime enforcement generally abstract away from implementation details and more precisely on how the specification is effectively enforced

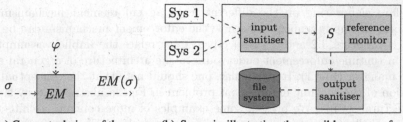

(a) Conceptual view of the runtime enforcement problem

(b) Scenario illustrating the possible usages of an
enforcement mechanism

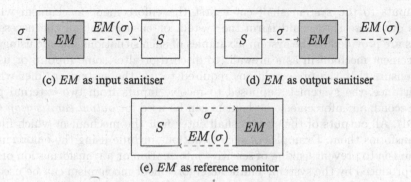

(c) *EM* as input sanitiser

(d) *EM* as output sanitiser

(e) *EM* as reference monitor

Fig. 2. Illustration of the runtime enforcement problem: an enforcement mechanism
EM transforms an input σ to an output $EM(\sigma)$ according to property φ and for a
system S.

on the system. That is, in regard of Fig. 1, one generally assumes that sensors
and effectors are available by means of instrumentation and one focuses on the
Analyse and Plan phases instead of the Observe and Execute ones. Moreover,
runtime enforcement problems revolve mainly on defining *input-output relationships* on sequences of events (see Fig. 2a). That is, the actual execution, made
available through the Observe module, is abstracted into a sequence of events of
interest (according to the specification). More precisely, a runtime enforcement
framework shall describe how to transform a (possibly incorrect according to
the specification) input sequence of events into an output sequence of events by
means of a so-called *enforcement mechanism*.[1] The transformation is performed
according to the given specification which is used to synthesise the enforcement
mechanism.

---

[1] We follow the terminology of [40] which generalises previous terminologies used in
runtime enforcement. We use the term enforcement mechanism to encompass definitions of mechanisms dedicated to enforcement described at different abstraction
levels. Moreover, using the term enforcement mechanism allows us to abstract away
the architecture of the autonomic monitor and its placement w.r.t. the monitored
system.

Before elaborating on the different ways an enforcement mechanism can transform the input sequence and how the enforcement mechanism can be synthesised (in Sects. 3.2 and 3.4 respectively), we relate the implicit assumptions made in runtime enforcement endeavours to the architecture of a general autonomic manager (Fig. 1). In particular, one should note that the conceptual presentation of the runtime enforcement problem in Fig. 2a abstracts away several architectural setups. We present some examples of more concrete architectural setups and illustrate them on a scenario in Example 1. First, an enforcement mechanism can be used for *input sanitisation* (see Fig. 2c). In such a case, the mechanism is used to "protect" the system from its (untrusted) environment. All inputs to the system shall enter first the enforcement mechanism which filters out those that could harm the system or ensure that all the necessary inputs are provided to the system. Examples of such situations include using the enforcement mechanism as a firewall (to discard or alter some inputs) or using it to ensure that the pre-conditions required to use the system are met when, for instance, the system is supposed to receive inputs from two external parties. Second, an enforcement mechanism can be used for *output sanitisation* (see Fig. 2d). All outputs of the system shall enter first the mechanism which filters or transforms them. Examples of such situations include using the enforcement mechanism to prevent leaking of sensitive information or a transformation of the trace produced by the system. Third, an enforcement mechanism can be used as *reference monitor* (see Fig. 2e). This architecture is close to the one of the autonomic monitor presented in Fig. 1. There is a closed loop between the system and the enforcement mechanism. All actions of interest or relevant state changes are first submitted to the enforcement mechanism which then grants, denies or alters state changes. Examples of such situations include using the enforcement mechanism to grant access to sensitive primitives or system operations.

Example 1 (Using enforcement mechanisms). Consider the example system S depicted in Fig. 2b where enforcement mechanisms are used to enforce the correct behaviour and ensure quality at runtime. Let us assume that S is purposed to realise some behaviour based on services provided by external systems Sys1 and Sys2. Actions of S are driven by some users (not depicted in Fig. 2b) and the actions should be logged to a file system. The input sanitiser is used to forward to S information only when both Sys1 and Sys2 provide the expected service, possibly discard or reformat some information from the users. The reference monitor is used to monitor the important actions of S by for instance rescheduling the actions or not letting S execute some actions when these are not allowed. The output sanitiser is used to ensure that actions are logged properly by enforcing a pre-defined log format, anonymising user sensitive information, or discarding irrelevant information.

The input-output relationship realised by the enforcement mechanism should fulfill the following constraints.

Table 1. Summary of existing models of enforcement mechanisms with the specification formalism from which they can be synthesised.

References	Models of enforcement mechanisms	Specification formalisms used for synthesis
[88]	Security automata	Büchi automata
[62]	Edit-automata	Deterministic finite-state automata
[37]	Generalised enforcement monitors	Streett automata
[20]	Edit automata	Rabin automata
[76]	Delayers	Timed automata
[40]	Delayers with suppression	Timed automata
[65]	Security automata	μ-calculus formulae
[42]	Generalised enforcement monitors	Labelled transition systems
[39]	Enforcement mechanisms with rollback	Finite-state automata
[15]	Safety shields	Safety automata
[92]	Shields for burst errors	Temporal logic (safety)
[13]	Iteration suppression automata	Deterministic finite-state automata

- *Soundness:* the output sequence should be correct w.r.t. the specification.
- *Transparency:* a correct input sequence should not be modified, if possible.[2]

Remark 1 (Runtime enforcement vs supervisory control theory). Runtime enforcement share the same objectives with supervisory control theory, which was introduced by Ramadge and Wonham [81,82]. In supervisory control theory, one uses an automaton modelling the system to synthesise a *supervisor* and a list of forbidden states. Events of the system are partitioned into the so-called controllable and non-controllable events. Intuitively, the supervisor is composed with an automaton model of the system (synchronous product) and ensures the most permissive behaviour of the initial system while preventing bad behaviour (rejected by the automaton). Should the system try to execute an action that could lead the system to exhibit a bad behaviour, the supervisor disables this action which then cannot execute on the system anymore.

3.2 Models of Enforcement Mechanisms/Monitors

The first model of enforcement mechanism was *security automata* (SA) [88]. An SA is a finite-state machine that executes in parallel with the monitored

---

[2] This is the notion of transparency adopted in a majority of papers on runtime enforcement. Some research efforts notice that this notion of transparency only constrains correct execution sequences; and they advocate that constraints should be placed on how an enforcement mechanism transforms incorrect execution sequences [11,12,58].

program. Whenever the target programs want to execute an action in the scope of the enforced property, two cases arise. Either the transition is defined and then the SA lets the target system execute the action, otherwise the target system is halted. We note the follow up work [50] which corrects and extends the results in [88] related to the enforcement abilities of security automata (see Sect. 3.3).

Ligatti et al. later extended the work of Schneider et al. by noticing that security automata are (only) sequence recognisers. They propose the model of *edit-automata* (EA) [62] which are sequence transformers. In addition of halting the target system, edit-automata can insert and suppress actions (originating from the target system or not). For instance, an EA can suppress and memorise an action of the target system for later replay. In an EA, the memorisation of actions is realised using the state-space. Several variants of edit-automata have been proposed [11].

Falcone et al. generalised edit automata with the so-called *generalised enforcement monitors* (GEMs) [43]. Contrarily to EAs, a GEM clearly separates sequence recognition from sequence transformation: GEMs are based on finite-state machines extended with generic enforcement operations that act on an internal memory. Separating sequence recognition from action memorisation has several advantages. First, GEMs are more amenable to implementation. Second, one can define easily formal composition operations on GEMs by computing the product state space and composing memory operations.

Bielova and Massacci proposed Iterative Suppression Automata (ISAs) [13], as a variant of EAs. They noticed that the usual requirements of soundness and transparency (and their implementation with EAs) do not distinguish what should happen when the input execution does not satisfy the specification. The underlying motivation is to be able to compare EAs in the manners they intervene on incorrect executions.

As noticed in [37], EAs and GEMs suffer from a practical limitation. Both of these models assume being able to freeze an unbounded number of actions to be replayed later. This amounts to assuming that an enforcement mechanism is able to predict the result of any action. To address this issue, Dolzhenko et al. introduce Mandatory Results Automata (MRAs) [30,64]. Upon the observation of any action, an MRA should return a result to the target application before seeing the next action. An MRA is placed between the untrusted target application and the executing system, and enforces the actions executed by the target as well as the results returned. Then, an MRA has to consider input and output events on traces.

In [24,39], Charafeddine et al. propose enforcement mechanism with k-step *roll-back* abilities. Such enforcement mechanism allows the system to deviate from the desired property up to k observable execution steps. Should the system not return to a correct state after k steps, the enforcement mechanism rolls the (non-deterministic) system back to the last correct state and forces it to explore alternative executions. An instantiation with 1 step of such general definition enforcement mechanisms is then implemented and integrated in component-based systems (cf. [6]).

Similar to the above models are the so-called *safety shields* [15] for reactive hardware systems, i.e. systems with Boolean signals as inputs and outputs. A shield is a Mealy machine which ensures soundness and minimum interference according to a notion of distance measuring the deviation between the output and the input of the shield. When a state where a property violation becomes unavoidable is reached, the shield enters in a *recovery* period, called *k-stabilisation*, and is allowed to deviate from its input for at most k consecutive steps. Bloem et al. assume here that the violation should be a rare event, and then the monitor keeps track of all possibilities assuming that it was an isolated error. If another violation arises during this recovery period, the shield enters in a *fail-safe* mode, where correctness is still ensured, but no minimal deviation. Note, a shield cannot buffer events. Wu et al. extends shields and propose enforcement mechanisms that respond immediately to violations and guarantees the safety under burst errors [92]. Similar to the model in [24], k-stabilising shields (which recover the system in a finite time) and admissible shields (which collaborate with the system) are introduced in [52].

Models with memory constraints. Most of the above models of enforcement mechanisms are endowed with an infinite memory as they allow the possible memorisation of an unbounded number of events. Several models have been proposed to account for practical memory limitations and bound the memory needed by enforcement mechanisms. Fong proposed Shallow History Automata (SHAs) [44] as security automata that do not keep track of the order of event arrival. Fong generalised SHA as α-SA which are SA endowed with a morphism α abstracting the current input sequence. Talhi et al. introduced Bounded Security Automata (BSAs) and Bounded Edit-Automata (BEAs) [91]. BSAs and BEAs are SAs and EAs with a bounded memory to memorise the input sequence respectively. The previous models bound the size of the memory of the enforcement mechanism (with an integer). Beauquier et al. introduced finite EAs and deterministic context-free EAs, that is EAs with a finite set of states [10]. They prove that finite EAs are strictly less expressive than EAs and study the conditions under which a property can be enforced by a finite EA.

Models with real-time enforcement primitives. The previously described models of enforcement mechanisms feature untimed sequence recognition mechanisms and enforcement primitives. In particular, when they do not account for the time that elapses between the occurrence of two received events. Moreover, the amount of time during which an event remains in the memory of the enforcement mechanism is not taken into account. Models for enforcing timed properties have been defined as *delayers* in [76, 77] to enforce timed properties. Such models account for the physical time elapsing during the reception of actions, storing and releasing actions in real-time. Later, the model of delayers has been extended into *delayers with suppression* [40] where actions are discarded from the memory when releasing such events would irremediably make the underlying property violated. Since physical time has consequences on the implementability of enforcement mechanisms, soundness and transparency need to be redefined and additional constraints such as optimality are required on how such enforcement mechanisms release actions.

Models supporting uncontrollable events. Closer to controllers in supervisory-control theory (see Remark 1), enforcement mechanisms accounting for uncontrollable actions (i.e., actions that cannot be affected by the enforcement mechanism) have been defined [57,85]. In addition to the current satisfaction of the output execution, such models take into account the possible reception of uncontrollable events. Uncontrollable actions as clock ticks were first introduced by Basin et al. in [5]. Unrestricted uncontrollable actions were later introduced in extensions of GEMs in [84–86] and of EAs in [57].

Predictive enforcement mechanisms. Inspired by the predictive semantics of runtime verification monitors [94], predictive enforcement mechanisms were proposed in [78,79]. Predictive enforcement mechanisms leverage some apriori knowledge of the system to output some events faster, instead of delaying them until more events are observed (or permanently).

3.3 Enforceable Specifications

We now turn our attention to the existing characterisations of the so-called *enforceable* specifications, i.e., specifications that can be enforced. Before elaborating on the existing characterisation, we first narrow down the term specification. As suggested by Schneider [88], one can distinguish properties from policies when specifying systems. A property (can be seen as a predicate that) partitions individual executions, while a policy (can be seen as a predicate that) partitions sets of executions. Hence, not all policies are properties. When observing a system execution, it is possible to determine the membership to a property; while determining membership to a policy generally requires observing additional executions.[3] Examples of properties include deadlock and starvation freedom, fairness, access control constraints, formalised requirements over executions. The classical example of policy (which is not a property, i.e., it can not be expressed with predicates over single execution) is information-flow because it requires checking for potential correlation between executions.

Enforceability of a property depends on several factors:

– the formalism used to specify the property, and more particularly whether the formalism describes finite or infinite executions;[4]
– the enforcement primitives endowed to the monitors and how these enforcement primitives are mapped to actual system effectors;
– constraints stemming from the system in which enforcement monitors are to be integrated.

---

[3] We note that some ongoing research efforts study *hyper-properties* [26], which resemble policies. We also note ongoing work advocating monitoring hyper-properties [16].

[4] As was the case in runtime verification, early work on runtime enforcement considered infinite executions.

In the pioneering work of Schneider on security automata, safety properties were characterised as enforceable [88]. Since a security automaton can only either (1) let a system action execute or (2) halt permanently the system, its decisions are irremediable. Concurrently, Kim et al. noticed that any monitoring mechanism (evaluating the execution of a system against a property) should be able to determine if the current execution is outside the set of allowed executions [60]. Thus, properties should be also *co-recursively enumerable*, that is, the non-membership test should be computable. We note that the results in [88] were later refined in [50][5], with the insights given in [60].

Ligatti et al. proved that, compared to security automata, using the additional enforcement primitives, edit-automata can enforce the so called *renewal* properties [8,62,63]. In the safety-liveness classification of properties [71], renewal properties form a superset of safety properties which contains some liveness properties. Intuitively, a property is a renewal if (a) any infinite execution sequence in the property contains infinitely many prefixes in the property, and (b) any infinite execution sequence not in the property contains only finitely many prefixes in the property. Falcone et al. proved that Generalised Enforcement Monitors instantiated with the *store* and *dump* operations, which respectively memorise and release events, can enforce the so-called *response* properties [38] in the Safety-Progress hierarchy of properties [21]. Response properties are properties for which some expected good behaviour should happen infinitely often. They can be intuitively understood as repeated transactions.

Moreover, we note that on finite sequences all properties are renewals. This observation is in line with the fact that (pure) response properties coincide with renewal properties, as noticed in [38].

Ligatti et al. proved that the MRA approach permits the enforcement of a new variant of properties, named *result-sanitization* or *monitor-centric* policies which are simpler and more expressive than usual definitions (*target-centric* ones). They also provide a hierarchical characterisation of the policies enforceable or not with MRAs. For instance, they show that MRAs precisely enforce a strict subset of safety properties, whereas Non-deterministic MRAs (NMRAs) precisely enforce a strict superset of safety properties. Depending on the definition chosen for non-safety properties or with additional assumptions, MRAs can also enforce some non-safety properties.

---

[5] Hamlen et al. [50] additionally introduce the notion of *RW-enforceable* policies (policies enforceable by enforcement mechanisms with Program Rewriting abilities), and use it to define a more precise characterisation of enforceable security policies. They model the untrusted programs as Türing machines with deterministic transition relations with three infinite-length tapes. They divide enforcement mechanisms into three categories: static analysers, reference monitors, and program rewriters. Static analysers operate strictly prior to running the untrusted program. Reference monitors intercept events or actions the program under scrutiny and intervene before occurrence of an event violating the policy, by terminating it or applying some other corrective action. Program rewriters modify in a finite time the program under scrutiny prior to execution.

Falcone and Jaber [24,39] showed that stutter-free safety properties are enforceable on component-based systems with monitors that can roll the system back by one observable execution step. Stutter-invariance is required on properties because of constraints stemming from the nature of synchronisation of components. A hierarchy of enforceable properties according to the number of steps the enforcement mechanism can roll the system back (the so-called k-step enforceability) is defined [39]. While 1-step enforceable properties are characterised, a general characterisation of k-step enforceable properties is left open.

Basin et al. extend the characterisation given in [50,88] of enforceable properties by additionally considering a universe of possible (input) traces and a set of controllable actions [5]. A property is enforceable if it is a safety and is such that violations are not caused by uncontrollable actions, and the set of prefixes of sequences in the universe and the property is decidable.

3.4 Synthesising Enforcement Mechanisms

We now report on some of the existing techniques used to synthesise enforcement mechanisms from properties described in several specification languages/formalisms (Table 1, gives the specification formalism from which each type of enforcement mechanisms can be synthesised). Schneider et al. synthesise SAs from Büchi automata [88]. Ligatti et al. synthesise EAs from deterministic finite-state automata describing renewal properties [62]. Falcone et al. synthesise GEMs from Streett automata [37]. Chabot et al. synthesise EAs from Rabin automata [20]. Pinisetty et al. synthesise delayers in [73,74,76] and Falcone et al. synthesise delayers with suppression in [40], from timed automata. Using partial model-checking techniques, Mateucci and Martinelli synthesise SAs from μ-calculus formulae [65]. Enforcement mechanisms are described as algebraic operators driven by controller programs. Falcone and Marchand synthesise GEMs from labelled transition system marked with secret states to enforce opacity properties [42]. Charafedine et al. transforms deterministic finite-state automata into enforcement mechanisms with 1-step roll-back abilities and integrate them into a component-based system [24,39]. Bloem et al. synthesise safety shields from safety automata by solving 2-player safety games [15]. Wu et al. synthesise shields that handle burst errors using a game-based algorithm [92]. Bielova and Masacci adapt the construction of EAs to synthesise a variant called iteration suppression automata for iterative properties described by deterministic finite-state automata. Iterative properties are such that the good executions are formed of "iterations" that can repeat an arbitrary number of times.

3.5 Implementations and Applications

The principles of runtime enforcement have been implemented and applied to several domains. Most of these approaches are based on either SAs, EAs, or GEMs.

Tool implementations. While there is a plethora of tools for runtime verification [4], there are only a few tool implementations for the runtime enforcement of properties on systems: Polymer [9], Mobile [49], TiPeX [75], and more recently GREP [83,86]. Polymer is a language and system for the definition and composition of enforcement mechanisms for Java applications. Mobile is a language-support for verified enforcement on .NET. Whenever a Mobile program type-checks with respect to a security policy, it is guaranteed that the program respects the policy. TiPEX implements algorithms for enforcing timed properties described as timed automata. TiPEX enforcement mechanisms correct input sequences by delaying actions. GREP also implements algorithms for enforcing timed properties described as timed automata with the ability to handle uncontrollable events. These algorithms are based on game theory.

We note that runtime verification tools can perform for free basic form of runtime enforcement as in security automata by halting the target system whenever a violation of the property occurs. Java-MOP [25] is a tool for runtime verification which arguably provides some support for ad-hoc runtime enforcement. Java-MOP provides self-recovery mechanisms in case of violation in the form of *handlers*. Handlers are code snippets that can be integrated in the target program in order to handle the violation (or validation) of a property using contextual execution information retrieved using aspect-oriented programming.

Application domains. One of the first domains of application is the security domain; and enforcement mechanisms were initially defined as security devices. Runtime enforcement was applied to enforce security policies [34], availability requirements in [28], privacy policies [54,61], opacity properties in [41,42], role-based access control security policies in [72], usage-control policies [66], the confidentiality of artifacts in [47]. There is also a body of work applying runtime enforcement principles on mobile devices such as Android-based mobile phones [1,31,36,67–69].

Limitations of enforcement. Even if a system is equipped with an enforcement mechanism, it may reach a failing situation. This is due to several reasons. Firstly, the enforcement mechanism considers only the described property and then acts according to this latter only. Any other (maybe unexpected) event not taken into account by the property may lead to a failure. Moreover, an enforcement mechanism has a restricted enforcing power since it follows a specific set of rules. If the necessary correcting action is not included in this set, then a failure may arise. As shown by [85], there are some situations in case of uncontrollable events where it is not possible to avoid an incorrect situation. Finally, there may be a gap between the abstract description of the enforcement mechanism and its real implementation. In this case, this is more a problem of instrumentation of the approach.

4   Healing Failures

In this section, we discuss techniques that can be used to heal executions after the failure has been observed by the autonomic monitor. In this context, a failure is defined as an execution that deviates from the intended semantics of the monitored program.

In order to automatically react to failures, it is first necessary to detect them. We can distinguish between domain independent failures, that is, failures that do not depend on the specific semantics of an application (e.g., crashes, uncaught exceptions, and deadlocks) and domain-dependent failures, that is, failures that depend on the specific semantics of the system (e.g., the generation of a wrong output).

Domain-independent failures can be trivially detected with an implicit oracle, that is, an oracle that can simply recognise the event that represents the failure (e.g., the application that quits abruptly, an exception reported in a log file, and the application that stops responding). Domain-dependent failures can be detected with program-specific oracles, that is, oracles obtained from a definition of the semantics of the program. These oracles detect failures by comparing the observed behaviour to the behaviour defined in the specification, for instance, an oracle might be obtained from a logical specification of the input/output behaviour of the system to detect incorrect outputs [3].

Detecting failures is a responsibility shared between the Observer and the Analyser components of the Autonomic Monitor architecture introduced in Sect. 2. The Observer is responsible for collecting events that can be processed by the Analyser to establish if the monitored program has failed. In the case of domain independent failures, the Observer has to simply detect the events that characterise failures and notify them to the Analyser, which reacts by triggering the healing process. In the case of domain dependent failures, the Observer collects the events relevant to the classes of failures that can be recognised, while the Analyser processes these events based on its Knowledge of the expected behaviour of the system. If a mismatch between the expected behaviour and the actual behaviour of the monitored program is observed, the Analyser triggers the healing process.

The healing process is driven by the Planner that activates appropriate mechanisms, based on its knowledge of the system and the available strategies, as described in the rest of this chapter. The Executor concretely actuates the plan elaborated by the Planner.

Since techniques that react to failures can affect a monitored program only after a failure has been observed, they need to incorporate mechanisms to either *rollback* the execution to a safe point before the failure happened, to successively influence the execution preventing any failure, or to *compensate* the effect of an observed failure moving the monitored system to the same state that would be observed if the failure has never happened.

Techniques for reacting to failures rely to one of the following three main sources of information: knowledge about the *redundant* elements of a system that can be exploited to workaround a failure, knowledge about the *actions* that

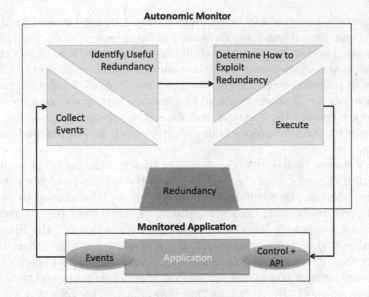

Fig. 3. General architecture for reacting to failures exploiting redundancy

can be taken to react to some *specific types of failures*, and knowledge about the *actions* that can be taken to explore program and configuration variants in response to an *unknown type of failure*.

The rest of this section presents the techniques for reacting to failures organised according to the knowledge that is exploited for the reaction: Sect. 4.1 presents techniques that exploit the knowledge of the redundant elements, Sect. 4.2 presents techniques that exploit the knowledge of specific failure types, and Sect. 4.3 presents techniques that exploit the knowledge of the existing program variants.

4.1   Techniques that Exploit Redundancy

We say that two processing units (e.g., two components or two code fragments) are functionally redundant if they produce the same outputs for the same inputs. Note that redundant units are allowed to show behavioural differences, for instance in their internal structure, or in their non-functional characteristics, such as performance and usability. A monitored program may include functionally redundant units, either introduced intentionally or incidentally. Techniques relying on redundancy may exploit both forms of redundancy.

Techniques based on *explicit redundancy* exploit the redundant elements intentionally introduced into the monitored system, such as the multiple redundant copies of a same fault-tolerant component, to workaround failures, while the techniques based on *intrinsic redundancy* exploit the redundant elements incidentally present in the monitored system to workaround failures. An example of incidentally redundant elements is the case of two different functionalities that, although not designed to be redundant, might be used to achieve the same result in specific situations (e.g., for some specific inputs).

The general architecture of the techniques exploiting redundancy is shown in Fig. 3. The sensor sends *events* from the monitored application to the Observer. The types of collected events might change depending on the specific technique and application, for instance they could be method invocations or http requests. The Observer *collects* these events, maintains the relevant parts of the history of the execution and intercepts failure signals, such as crashes and uncaught exceptions.

When a failure is detected, the Analyser matches the collected sequence of events with its knowledge of the *redundancy* of the system to *identify the useful redundancy*, that is, the redundant units that might be exploited to avoid the failure. If some useful redundancy is present in the system (e.g., a redundant copy of a component or a functionality involved in the failure), the Planner has to *determine how to specifically exploit the redundancy* in the system to avoid the failure. For instance, the Planner may decide to transfer the execution to another component or to rollback the execution to a safe point and then execute a redundant copy of the operation that has failed. The Executor concretely *executes* the plan, exploiting its knowledge of the implementation of the system. The Effectors are the elements that support the execution of the plan within the target application, that is, the Executor interacts with them to run the plan. They usually consist of the *API* of the monitored system, sometime suitably extended with mechanisms to *control* the execution, for instance to transfer the execution across components or to rollback executions.

In the rest of this section we discuss some techniques exploiting these two forms of redundancy.

Explicit Redundancy. A well-known way to tolerate failures is through the deployment of multiple redundant components into the same system. The general intuition is that if a component fails, the failure might be worked around by transferring the execution to a redundant copy of the same component. This solution has been extensively investigated in the context of fault-tolerant systems, especially in N-version programming [2].

In addition to classic fault-tolerance, there are other ways of taking advantage of the redundancy explicitly introduced into a monitored program. In particular, recent approaches investigate scenarios that might be less effort-demanding than N-version programming, which requires the independent implementation of multiple copies of the same component. An interesting approach is the one investigated by Hosek and Cadar [51], who exploited the multiple versions available for the same program to automatically react to failures caused by faulty software updates.

The key idea is to maintain alive both versions of a software system after an update. The two versions are then executed side by side and when a failure is experienced in one version, the other one is exploited to overcome the failure. To achieve this capability, the execution of the two versions must be monitored and synchronised. The monitor collects and compares the system calls performed by the monitored programs. When a diverging behaviour is observed, appropriate actions are taken. The execution is also synchronised, that is one version cannot proceed with the execution until the other version has produced the same system call. In this way, the execution might be timely switched from one version to the other.

A divergent behaviour might produce different reactions depending on the kind of divergence. If the two versions produce different system calls, the result produced by one version is simply preferred to the other, for instance the new version of the system might be preferred to the old one. If one program crashes, the approach performs a lightweight rollback to the last system call, executes the code in the other version until the next system call is produced, and then continues with the execution of the version that produced the failure. This strategy de facto reuses the code in the other version to avoid failures, and it might be effective to overcome bugs introduced with faulty upgrades. Note that this explicit form of redundancy does not require special effort to be generated because it is naturally introduced with the evolution of a software system.

Intrinsic Redundancy. Since intrinsic redundancy is not documented explicitly, discovering the intrinsically redundant operations might be hard and expensive, indeed it is undecidable in general. The effort required to discover these elements is compensated by the possibility to augment systems that have not been designed to react to failures with the capability to handle them.

Intrinsic redundancy can be extracted in various ways, for instance using testing and analysis techniques [45], and can be suitably integrated with mechanisms to either rollback executions or compensate the effect of failures to obtain systems with high reliability. When integrated with *rollback* mechanisms, failures can be handled by first bringing the execution back to a safe point and then running an intrinsically-redundant alternative operation with the one that has failed [18]. When integrated with *compensation mechanisms*, failures can be handled by first compensating their effects, if any, and then again executing an alternative operation intrinsically redundant with the one that has failed [19].

The knowledge of the intrinsically redundant operations can be encoded using rewriting rules, which associate a sequence of operations to another sequence of operations that has the same observable behaviour of the original sequence. As discussed in [19], examples of intrinsically redundant operations typically present in container classes are:

```
addAll(a,b) → add(a); add(b)
add(a) → addAll(a,b); remove(b)
```

The first rule indicates that adding the elements a and b using the `addAll` method produces the same effect as adding first a and then b using the `add` method. Alternatively, the second rule indicates that adding element a with the `add` method produces the same effect as adding the element a and an element b using the `addAll` method and then removing b.

When a failure is detected, the sequence of the operations performed by the monitored program is analysed, checking if any rewriting rule can be exploited to change the failing sequence into an alternative sequence. The intuition for exploiting intrinsically redundant operations is that a failing execution might be worked around by replaying the execution using some alternative but equivalent operations. For instance, if a failure has been observed when running the sequence of operations

```
newList(); addAll(a,b)
```

the sequence might be automatically replaced with the alternative sequence

```
newList(); add(a); add(b)
```

using the first rewriting rule.

Note that the rewriting rules above allow substituting a sequence of operations with alternative, but equivalent, sequences of operations that do not share any operation with the original sequence. Avoiding to reuse operations executed during the failure intuitively increases the probability to produce a new sequence that does not fail.

If the opportunity to workaround the failure is detected, the planner elaborates a suitable strategy, which could be based either on rollback or on compensation mechanisms. If multiple rules could be exploited, the plan may attempt to execute a sequence of rollback/compensation operations followed by the execution of a rewritten sequence until the failure is overcame or no more options are available. The order of application of the rules might be based on historical information, giving precedence to the rules that have been most successful in the past.

The choice of using rollback or compensation before executing a rewritten sequence of operations depends on the nature of the system that must react to errors. For instance, rollback has been used to overcome failures in container classes [18], while compensation has been exploited with Web applications where it is often sufficient to reload a Web page to cancel the effect of a failure [19].

In general, not all the systems can be addressed with rollback or compensation mechanisms. For instance, the state of a system might be too large, complex and difficult to observe and control to be rolled back. Similarly, the impact of a failure may have consequences that cannot be cancelled by any other system operation. However, when at least one of the two approaches can be feasibly applied to a software system, the system could be potentially extended with healing capabilities.

4.2   Failure-Specific Techniques

Failure-specific techniques exploit the knowledge about some specific classes of failures to effectively recognise and react to them. These techniques have a narrow applicability compared to techniques addressing broader classes of failures, such as the ones based on redundancy (see Sect. 4.1) and the ones exploring variants (see Sect. 4.3). However, when an observed failure is in their scope, they can be dramatically effective.

The general architecture of failure-specific techniques is shown in Fig. 4. The sensor sends *events* from the monitored application to the Observer, which *collect*s these events, maintains the relevant parts of the history of the execution, and intercepts failure signals, such as crashes and uncaught exceptions. When a

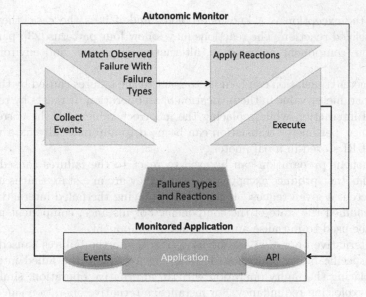

Fig. 4. General architecture for reacting to specific failures types

failure is detected, the Analyser matches the failure and the collected sequence of events with the known failure types. If the observed failure matches with some known failure types, the corresponding reactions are retrieved. The Planner is then responsible for defining a strategy to apply the selected reactions, contextualising them to the monitored program, if needed, and defining their order of application. The Executor concretely *executes* the plan, exploiting its knowledge of the implementation of the system. The Effectors are the elements that support the execution of the plan, that is, the Executor interacts with the Effectors when running the plan. In this case, the Effectors usually consist of the *API* of the monitored system whose operations are invoked while applying a selected reaction.

In the following, we present two failure-specific techniques, one addressing a pre-defined set of failure types, and another that can dynamically learn how to react to failures based on a set of samples.

Pre-defined Failure Types. Techniques addressing pre-defined failure types are techniques designed to handle specific situations in specific systems. A notable example is the case of healing connectors [22, 23], which are connectors that can be deployed on a component-based system to react to failures caused by incorrect interactions between components.

Healing connectors implement reaction mechanisms that are activated when a component throws exceptions that should not be raised. To react correctly and efficiently, they exploit the *knowledge* of how the interaction between components may fail due to some specific classes of integration problems that may result in some exceptions. When an exception is caught, healing connectors check if the cause of the exception is a known problem, and if it is the case, they apply the pre-defined reaction. The reactions may follow four patterns [23]: parameter translation, component preparation, alternative operation, and environmental changes.

Parameter translation can be used to react to the failures caused by the use of a wrong parameter value in the invocation of an operation. It reacts by replaying the failed interaction while replacing the incorrect value with the correct one. For instance, parameter translation can be used to automatically fix a wrongly encoded URI stored in a parameter.

Component preparation can be used to react to the failures caused by the components that produce exceptions because they are in a state that is not suitable to accept a given request. It reacts by replaying the failed interaction after having modified the state of the component. For instance, component preparation can be used to initialise an uninitialised component.

An alternative operation can be used to react to the failures caused by the use of a specific faulty operation. It reacts by replaying the failed interaction while replacing the faulty operation with an alternative operation, similarly to methods exploiting redundancy. For instance, alternative operation can be used to replace the invocation of a deprecated method with the invocation of an up-to-date method.

Finally, an environmental change can be performed to react to the failures caused by problems in the environment. It works by replaying the failed interaction after having modified the environment in a way that may prevent the failure from occurring again. For instance, an environmental change can be used to create the missing folders that cause an application to fail.

When an uncaught exception is raised, multiple healing patterns might be eligible to react to the failure. The Planner is responsible for organising the applicable patterns in a pipeline. Healing connectors do not require special effectors, but they simply take advantage of the API of the monitored program. If necessary, depending on the failure, they may incorporate actions to compensate the effect of a failure so that the failed interaction can be safely re-executed.

Sample-Based Approaches. Sample-based approaches exploit the *knowledge* of how failures have been (manually) handled in the past to automatically react to new occurrences of the same failures [29]. They thus rely on the assumption that a repository of failures and corresponding countermeasures is available.

Sample-based approaches are failure-specific because they can only address the failures that have been observed in the past. However, the set of supported failures is changed every time by simply providing a different set of samples to learn from, potentially increasing the generality of the technique.

Comparing actual failures to sample failures is challenging because failures caused by the same problem are never exactly the same. The same failures may occur in many different circumstances, such as different states of the system, different inputs, and in different environment conditions. To match a pair of failures, sample-based approaches distill a signature that characterises a failure

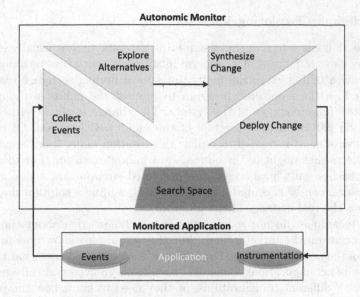

Fig. 5. General architecture for reacting to failures by exploring variants

regardless of the specific circumstances in which it occurred. In their work, Ding et al. [29] apply concept and contrast analysis to the log files collected during failures to produce signatures that characterise failures in terms of the key events reported in the log files.

Signatures are derived for both the sample failures and the newly observed failures. When an observed failure has a signature matching the signature of a failure in the repository, an appropriate reaction can be automatically extracted from the repository and executed.

Reactions that have been taken in the past necessarily refer to a specific situation. For instance, they may concern rebooting specific machines and changing specific configurations. When the same failure is observed, it might occur in slightly different circumstances, which may require slightly different reactions. For instance, if in the past machine hostA has been rebooted because it stopped responding, and in the actual execution the machine that is not responding is machine hostB, the reboot operation should be executed on hostB and not on hostA. The approach described in [29] can achieve this capability by executing an operation called contextualisation of the reaction. Contextualisation extracts the parameters used in the sample reaction (e.g., the name of the machine), matches the observed failure with the sample failure in the repository identifying the actual value for all the extracted parameters (e.g., the actual name of the machine that is not responding), and executes the reaction replacing parameters with actual values.

This strategy has been mostly experienced with large service-based systems to turn the manual reactions executed in the past by the operators into automatic reactions, reducing maintenance cost and increasing system reliability.

4.3   Techniques Exploring Variants

Techniques that react to failures by exploring variants are not usually explicitly tied to any class of failures. The general intuition is that these techniques may try to replay a failing execution many times until finding a change that might be operated on the monitored program to prevent the failure without breaking the other functionalities of the system. The change might be either on the configuration [90] or in the code [46] of the monitored program. Of course, a suitable environment is needed to replay an execution many times regardless of the side-effects that might be introduced by a failing execution. For this reason, these approaches must have access to a protected environment where a copy of the application can be executed many times until finding a solution that can be deployed on the real instance of the program.

These techniques do not require any specific knowledge about the failures that may occur on the target system, but they require to know how to explore the space of the possible variants. For instance, they need to know what the space of the possible configurations looks like, to be able to systematically execute a program with different configurations, or they need to know how the code of a program can be modified, to explore the space of the code changes that might fix a faulty program.

The general architecture of techniques reacting to failures by looking for variants is shown in Fig. 5. The sensor sends *events* from the monitored application to the Observer. The collected events usually consist of the inputs received by the monitored program and failure signals. When a failure is detected, the control is transferred to the Analyser that exploits the knowledge of the *search space* to *explore alternatives* that might prevent the occurrence of the failure. Each alternative is checked by replaying the observed failure.

Alternatives might consist of different configurations of the monitored applications or even program variants. When a suitable alternative is identified, the Planner *synthesises a change* that the Executor can *deploy* on the monitored program. The Effectors consist of mechanisms that allow the modification of either the program or its environment.

In the following, we present two techniques, one that reacts to failures by exploring alternative configurations and the other that reacts to failures by synthesising code changes.

Alternative Configurations. The assumption made by approaches exploring the space of the possible configurations of a program is that there may exist a configuration under which a failed functionality may run correctly. The strategy to find a workaround consists of transferring the control to a separate instance of the monitored program running in a sandboxed environment to replay the failed execution several times for many different configurations, until finding a configuration that makes the program pass. In order to apply this process, the knowledge of the autonomic monitor has to incorporate information about the shape of the space of all the legal configurations. Such a space must be sampled efficiently to quickly find a solution to an observed problem.

REFRACT implements this strategy using a feature model as representation of the configuration space [90]. In practice, when a failure is observed, REFRACT replays the failed execution in a separate environment and samples the configuration space described by the feature model according to three possible strategies: n-hops sampling, random sampling, and covering array sampling.

The n-hops sampling strategy systematically investigates all the configurations that can be obtained from the configuration of the monitored program by changing n options. The random sampling generates a completely random configuration. Covering array sampling considers a set of configurations that include every possible combination of values for up to t configuration options. If a configuration that prevents the failure is detected, the configuration is further modified using the delta-debugging algorithm [93] to minimise the set of changes that must be operated on the current configuration to workaround the failure.

The new configuration can then be deployed to the monitored program. If the execution in the monitored program could be suspended while waiting for a better configuration, the monitored program may immediately benefit from the new configuration, otherwise only future occurrences of the failure will be prevented by the deployment of the updated configuration.

Alternative Implementations. When a failure is observed, alternative implementations that may include a fix to the problem that caused the failure can be generated using automatic program repair techniques. While these techniques have been originally designed to assist developers when fixing programs, they can also be exploited to automatically react to failures, as proposed in Gen-Prog [46]. The idea is that automatic program repair can be used to generate many tentative program fixes that are deployed and tested in a separate instance of the monitored program. The separate instance runs in a sandboxed environment to prevent the generation of any harmful side-effect. If a fix can be found, it is deployed on the original instance of the monitored program to prevent future occurrences of the same failure. If the execution in the original instance can be suspended, the fix can also be exploited to turn the currently failing execution into a correct one.

To synthesise fixes automatically, the knowledge must include information on how to change a monitored program and how to verify the correctness of the tentative fixes. In GenProg, the synthesis of the fixes is driven by a genetic programming algorithm that modifies the program exploiting single-point crossover and three mutation operators. The mutation operators can change a program by deleting a statement, adding a statement copied elsewhere from the program, and replacing a statement with another statement copied elsewhere from the program. The locations where the mutant operators should be applied to are identified using spectrum-based fault localisation [55], which can automatically assign to each statement a score representing its likelihood to be faulty. To increase the probability to produce mutations that can affect the faults in a program, the probability to mutate a statement is proportional to its suspiciousness, so that the statements that are more likely to be faulty are more likely to be modified. The verification strategy simply runs the available test suite to check the correctness of a fix, that is, a fix that passes all the available test cases is assumed to be correct.

GenProg has been exploited to react to failures produced by programs that respond to http requests (e.g., a Web server) [46]. The idea is that the monitored system can be extended with anomaly detection techniques to detect if an untrusted input causing a suspicious execution has been received. When an anomalous execution is detected, the program is suspended and the control is transferred to GenProg, which runs an automatic repair process in a separate machine. If GenProg can find a fix, that is, a change in the program that prevents the anomalous execution without causing the failure of any of the available test cases, the fix is deployed on the original program and the execution resumed. This strategy may prevent the immediate failure of the program, but also prevent any similar failure in the future.

5   Open Challenges

There are still several open challenges to achieve effective failure prevention and reaction. In this section, we discuss some of the main open challenges. We note that some of these challenges apply more broadly to runtime verification.

Gap Between Models and Software. Enforcement models might be difficult to implement into the corresponding autonomic monitors because they may require a strong adaptation and instrumentation effort resulting from the gap between the abstraction used in the model and the concrete behaviour of the software. Solutions that can reduce this gap to make monitors easier to implement and reuse are necessary to make runtime enforcement more practical.

Property Specification. Usually the languages proposed by the tools are rather simple and do not permit to describe complex properties. Effort should be done in designing formalism in order to describe and manage more complex properties in an intuitive way.

Distributed and Multi-threaded Systems. Nowadays, many systems are distributed and need to be observed and controlled in several points. The generation of distributed enforcement mechanisms, communicating together in a minimal way, in order to ensure a global property is still an open challenge. A similar challenge is present in the case of multi-threaded programs, where the effect of the monitors on multiple partially-independent threads must be coordinated and controlled. In both cases, it will require means to decentralise enforcement mechanisms. For this purpose, one can inspire from the decentralisation of runtime verification monitors [7,27], the monitoring of decentralised specifications [32,33] and the decentralised enforcement of document lifecyles [48].

The Oracle Problem. In order to react to a failure, it is necessary to recognise that a failure has happened. While some failures are trivial to detect (e.g., crashes), other failures (e.g., wrong results) require a thorough and detailed knowledge of the system to be recognised. Unfortunately this knowledge is seldom available, and when it is available it is typically expensive to encode in a machine-processable form. Researchers have investigated how to automatically extract this knowledge from software artefacts produced for other purposes, but despite these early attempts, how to systematically extract and exploit such knowledge to detect non-trivial failures is still an open challenge.

Specific vs General Solutions. Techniques for reacting to failures might be defined to be either general, that is, to be able to potentially address a large family of failures, or specific, that is, to be able to address a restricted family of software failures. While general approaches might be frequently useful, since they cover a broad range of situations, their effectiveness is intrinsically limited by their generality. In practice, general approaches can hardly react to a failure in an optimal way because their strategies are designed to be broadly useful. On the other hand, failure-specific approaches are useful in a limited number of cases, but they can be extremely effective when applicable. Finding a good compromise between generality and specificity in designing techniques that may optimally address an extensive number of cases is still a challenge.

Non-intrusiveness. Both techniques for preventing and reacting to failures work in the field directly in the end-user environment. Any operation that is performed in the field in the attempt to prevent or react to a failure may potentially cause even more serious consequences than the failure itself to the user data and processes. Although there are several environments providing a degree of isolation (e.g., virtual machines and containers), how to employ them in a resource-constrained environment for preventing and reacting to failures is still an open challenge. More in general, it is hard to design techniques that can prevent and react to failures providing the guarantee of not affecting the user.

Provably-Correct Monitoring. To ensure a better confidence in enforcement mechanisms, or more generally, in the mechanisms protecting the system from faults, it is desirable to ensure that the monitoring code conforms to the property or security policy at hand. This check can then be performed (using a proof checker) by a third-party who does not necessarily trust the monitoring process. Preliminary work has been carried out on this topic in [89] to verify the soundness and transparency of SAs, in [14] to check the transition function of monitors generated from regular expressions, and in [87] to verify the lack of interference between enforcers.

6   Conclusions

Society demands for highly-dependable, large and dynamic systems that can serve citizens in their daily operations. Such systems are increasingly difficult to verify in-house due to their size, complexity and dynamic nature. Runtime techniques, in particular enforcement and healing solutions, can be exploited in the field to compensate the validation and verification activities performed in-house. The joint collaboration of enforcement techniques, which can prevent failures, and healing techniques, which can overcome an observed failure, can significantly increase the dependability of software systems.

This chapter discusses some of the achievements in these related areas, providing an overview of the available solutions. The material presented in this chapter can represent a valuable starting point for researchers interested in enforcement and healing solutions.

Acknowledgment. The authors would like to thank Antoine El-Hokayem, Raphaël Khoury, and Srinivas Pinisetty for commenting on the section related to runtime enforcement. The authors warmly thank the reviewers for their comments on a preliminary version of this chapter.

References

1. Arzt, S., Rasthofer, S., Fritz, C., Bodden, E., Bartel, A., Klein, J., Traon, Y.L., Octeau, D., McDaniel, P.D.: FlowDroid: precise context, flow, field, object-sensitive and lifecycle-aware taint analysis for android apps. In: O'Boyle, M.F.P., Pingali, K. (eds.) ACM SIGPLAN Conference on Programming Language Design and Implementation, PLDI 2014, Edinburgh, UK, 9–11 June 2014, pp. 259–269. ACM (2014)
2. Avizienis, A.: The N-version approach to fault-tolerant software. IEEE Trans. Softw. Eng. (TSE) **11**(12), 1491–1501 (1985)
3. Barr, E.T., Harman, M., McMinn, P., Shahbaz, M., Shin, Y.: The Oracle problem in software testing: a survey. IEEE Trans. Softw. Eng. (TSE) **41**(5), 507–525 (2015)
4. Bartocci, E., Falcone, Y., Bonakdarpour, B., Colombo, C., Decker, N., Havelund, K., Joshi, Y., Klaedtke, F., Milewicz, R., Reger, G., Rosu, G., Signoles, J., Thoma, D., Zalinescu, E., Zhang, Y.: First international competition on runtime verification: rules, benchmarks, tools, and final results of CRV 2014. Int. J. Softw. Tools Technol. Transf. 1–40 (2017). https://doi.org/10.1007/s10009-017-0454-5
5. Basin, D., Jugé, V., Klaedtke, F., Zălinescu, E.: Enforceable security policies revisited. ACM Trans. Inf. Syst. Secur. **16**(1), 3:1–3:26 (2013). http://doi.acm.org/10.1145/2487222.2487225
6. Basu, A., Bensalem, S., Bozga, M., Combaz, J., Jaber, M., Nguyen, T., Sifakis, J.: Rigorous component-based system design using the BIP framework. IEEE Softw. **28**(3), 41–48 (2011)
7. Bauer, A., Falcone, Y.: Decentralised LTL monitoring. Formal Meth. Syst. Des. **48**(1–2), 46–93 (2016)
8. Bauer, L., Ligatti, J., Walker, D.: More enforceable security policies. In: Proceedings of the Workshop on Foundations of Computer Security (FCS 2002), Copenhagen, Denmark (2002)

9. Bauer, L., Ligatti, J., Walker, D.: Composing security policies with polymer. In: Sarkar, V., Hall, M.W. (eds.) Proceedings of the ACM SIGPLAN 2005 Conference on Programming Language Design and Implementation, Chicago, IL, USA, 12–15 June 2005, pp. 305–314. ACM (2005)

10. Beauquier, D., Cohen, J., Lanotte, R.: Security policies enforcement using finite and pushdown edit automata. Int. J. Inf. Sec. **12**(4), 319–336 (2013). https://doi.org/10.1007/s10207-013-0195-8

11. Bielova, N., Massacci, F.: Do you really mean what you actually enforced? - edited automata revisited. Int. J. Inf. Sec. **10**(4), 239–254 (2011)

12. Bielova, N., Massacci, F.: Predictability of enforcement. In: Erlingsson, Ú., Wieringa, R., Zannone, N. (eds.) ESSoS 2011. LNCS, vol. 6542, pp. 73–86. Springer, Heidelberg (2011). https://doi.org/10.1007/978-3-642-19125-1_6

13. Bielova, N., Massacci, F.: Iterative enforcement by suppression: towards practical enforcement theories. J. Comput. Secur. **20**(1), 51–79 (2012)

14. Blech, J.O., Falcone, Y., Becker, K.: Towards certified runtime verification. In: Aoki, T., Taguchi, K. (eds.) ICFEM 2012. LNCS, vol. 7635, pp. 494–509. Springer, Heidelberg (2012). https://doi.org/10.1007/978-3-642-34281-3_34

15. Bloem, R., Könighofer, B., Könighofer, R., Wang, C.: Shield synthesis: - runtime enforcement for reactive systems. In: Tools and Algorithms for the Construction and Analysis of Systems - 21st International Conference, TACAS 2015, Held as Part of the European Joint Conferences on Theory and Practice of Software, ETAPS 2015, London, UK, 11–18 April 2015, Proceedings, pp. 533–548 (2015)

16. Bonakdarpour, B., Finkbeiner, B.: Runtime verification for HyperLTL. In: Falcone, Y., Sánchez, C. (eds.) RV 2016. LNCS, vol. 10012, pp. 41–45. Springer, Cham (2016). https://doi.org/10.1007/978-3-319-46982-9_4

17. Bultan, T., Sen, K. (eds.): Proceedings of the 26th ACM SIGSOFT International Symposium on Software Testing and Analysis, Santa Barbara, CA, USA, 10–14 July 2017. ACM (2017)

18. Carzaniga, A., Gorla, A., Mattavelli, A., Perino, N., Pezzè, M.: Automatic recovery from runtime failures. In: Proceedings of the International Conference on Software Engineering (ICSE), pp. 782–791. IEEE Press (2013)

19. Carzaniga, A., Gorla, A., Perino, N., Pezzè, M.: Automatic workarounds: exploiting the intrinsic redundancy of web applications. ACM Trans. Softw. Eng. Methodol. (TOSEM) **24**(3), 16 (2015)

20. Chabot, H., Khoury, R., Tawbi, N.: Generating in-line monitors for Rabin automata. In: Jøsang, A., Maseng, T., Knapskog, S.J. (eds.) NordSec 2009. LNCS, vol. 5838, pp. 287–301. Springer, Heidelberg (2009). https://doi.org/10.1007/978-3-642-04766-4_20

21. Chang, E., Manna, Z., Pnueli, A.: The safety-progress classification. Technical report, Stanford University, Department of Computer Science (1992)

22. Chang, H., Mariani, L., Pezzè, M.: In-field healing of integration problems with COTS components. In: Proceedings of the International Conference on Software Engineering (ICSE) (2009)

23. Chang, H., Mariani, L., Pezzè, M.: Exception handlers for healing component-based systems. ACM Trans. Softw. Eng. Methodol. (TOSEM) **22**(4), 30 (2013)

24. Charafeddine, H., El-Harake, K., Falcone, Y., Jaber, M.: Runtime enforcement for component-based systems. In: Wainwright, R.L., Corchado, J.M., Bechini, A., Hong, J. (eds.) Proceedings of the 30th Annual ACM Symposium on Applied Computing, Salamanca, Spain, 13–17 April 2015, pp. 1789–1796. ACM (2015)

25. Chen, F., d'Amorim, M., Roşu, G.: Checking and correcting behaviors of Java programs at runtime with Java-MOP. Electron. Notes Theor. Comput. Sci. **144**(4), 3–20 (2006)
26. Clarkson, M.R., Schneider, F.B.: Hyperproperties. In: Proceedings of the 21st IEEE Computer Security Foundations Symposium, CSF 2008, Pittsburgh, Pennsylvania, 23–25 June 2008, pp. 51–65. IEEE Computer Society (2008)
27. Colombo, C., Falcone, Y.: Organising LTL monitors over distributed systems with a global clock. Formal Meth. Syst. Des. **49**(1–2), 109–158 (2016). https://doi.org/10.1007/s10703-016-0251-x
28. Cuppens, F., Cuppens-Boulahia, N., Ramard, T.: Availability enforcement by obligations and aspects identification. In: The First International Conference on Availability, Reliability and Security, ARES 2006, 10 pp. IEEE (2006)
29. Ding, R., Fu, Q., Lou, J.G., Lin, Q., Zhang, D., Shen, J., Xie, T.: Healing online service systems via mining historical issue repositories. In: Proceedings of the IEEE/ACM International Conference on Automated Software Engineering (ASE), pp. 318–321. IEEE (2012)
30. Dolzhenko, E., Ligatti, J., Reddy, S.: Modeling runtime enforcement with mandatory results automata. Int. J. Inf. Secur. **14**(1), 47–60 (2015)
31. El-Harake, K., Falcone, Y., Jerad, W., Langet, M., Mamlouk, M.: Blocking advertisements on android devices using monitoring techniques. In: Margaria, T., Steffen, B. (eds.) ISoLA 2014. LNCS, vol. 8803, pp. 239–253. Springer, Heidelberg (2014). https://doi.org/10.1007/978-3-662-45231-8_17
32. El-Hokayem, A., Falcone, Y.: Monitoring decentralized specifications. In: Bultan and Sen [17], pp. 125–135
33. El-Hokayem, A., Falcone, Y.: THEMIS: a tool for decentralized monitoring algorithms. In: Bultan and Sen [17], pp. 372–375
34. Erlingsson, Ú., Schneider, F.B.: SASI enforcement of security policies: a retrospective. In: Kienzle, D.M., Zurko, M.E., Greenwald, S.J., Serbau, C. (eds.) Proceedings of the 1999 Workshop on New Security Paradigms, Caledon Hills, ON, Canada, 22–24 September 1999, pp. 87–95. ACM (1999)
35. Falcone, Y.: You should better enforce than verify. In: Barringer, H., Falcone, Y., Finkbeiner, B., Havelund, K., Lee, I., Pace, G., Roşu, G., Sokolsky, O., Tillmann, N. (eds.) RV 2010. LNCS, vol. 6418, pp. 89–105. Springer, Heidelberg (2010). https://doi.org/10.1007/978-3-642-16612-9_9
36. Falcone, Y., Currea, S., Jaber, M.: Runtime verification and enforcement for Android applications with RV-Droid. In: Qadeer and Tasiran [80], pp. 88–95
37. Falcone, Y., Fernandez, J.-C., Mounier, L.: Synthesizing enforcement monitors wrt. the safety-progress classification of properties. In: Sekar, R., Pujari, A.K. (eds.) ICISS 2008. LNCS, vol. 5352, pp. 41–55. Springer, Heidelberg (2008). https://doi.org/10.1007/978-3-540-89862-7_3
38. Falcone, Y., Fernandez, J.C., Mounier, L.: What can you verify and enforce at runtime? Int. J. Softw. Tools Technol. Transfer **14**(3), 349–382 (2012)
39. Falcone, Y., Jaber, M.: Fully automated runtime enforcement of component-based systems with formal and sound recovery. Int. J. Softw. Tools Technol. Transf. **19**(3), 1–25 (2016)
40. Falcone, Y., Jéron, T., Marchand, H., Pinisetty, S.: Runtime enforcement of regular timed properties by suppressing and delaying events. Syst. Control Lett. **123**, 2–41 (2016)
41. Falcone, Y., Marchand, H.: Runtime enforcement of K-step opacity. In: Proceedings of the 52nd IEEE Conference on Decision and Control, CDC 2013, 10–13 December 2013, Firenze, Italy, pp. 7271–7278. IEEE (2013)

42. Falcone, Y., Marchand, H.: Enforcement and validation (at runtime) of various notions of opacity. Discrete Event Dyn. Syst. **25**(4), 531–570 (2015). http://dx.doi.org/10.1007/s10626-014-0196-4

43. Falcone, Y., Mounier, L., Fernandez, J., Richier, J.: Runtime enforcement monitors: composition, synthesis, and enforcement abilities. Formal Meth. Syst. Des. **38**(3), 223–262 (2011)

44. Fong, P.W.L.: Access control by tracking shallow execution history. In: 2004 IEEE Symposium on Security and Privacy (S&P 2004), 9–12 May 2004, Berkeley, CA, USA, pp. 43–55. IEEE Computer Society (2004)

45. Goffi, A., Gorla, A., Mattavelli, A., Pezzè, M., Tonella, P.: Search-based synthesis of equivalent method sequences. In: Proceedings of the ACM SIGSOFT International Symposium on Foundations of Software Engineering (FSE) (2014)

46. Goues, C.L., Nguyen, T., Forrest, S., Weimer, W.: GenProg: a generic method for automatic software repair. IEEE Trans. Softw. Eng. (TSE) **38**(1), 54–72 (2012)

47. Hallé, S., Khoury, R., El-Hokayem, A., Falcone, Y.: Decentralized enforcement of artifact lifecycles. In: Matthes, F., Mendling, J., Rinderle-Ma, S. (eds.) 20th IEEE International Enterprise Distributed Object Computing Conference, EDOC 2016, Vienna, Austria, 5–9 September 2016, pp. 1–10. IEEE Computer Society (2016)

48. Hallé, S., Khoury, R., Betti, Q., El-Hokayem, A., Falcone, Y.: Decentralized enforcement of document lifecycle constraints. Information Systems (2017)

49. Hamlen, K.W., Morrisett, G., Schneider, F.B.: Certified in-lined reference monitoring on .net. In: Sreedhar, V.C., Zdancewic, S. (eds.) Proceedings of the 2006 Workshop on Programming Languages and Analysis for Security, PLAS 2006, Ottawa, Ontario, Canada, 10 June 2006, pp. 7–16. ACM (2006)

50. Hamlen, K.W., Morrisett, G., Schneider, F.B.: Computability classes for enforcement mechanisms. ACM Trans. Program. Lang. Syst. (TOPLAS) **28**(1), 175–205 (2006)

51. Hosek, P., Cadar, C.: Safe software updates via multi-version execution. In: Proceedings of the International Conference on Software Engineering (ICSE) (2013)

52. Humphrey, L., Könighofer, B., Könighofer, R., Topcu, U.: Synthesis of admissible shields. In: Bloem, R., Arbel, E. (eds.) HVC 2016. LNCS, vol. 10028, pp. 134–151. Springer, Cham (2016). https://doi.org/10.1007/978-3-319-49052-6_9

53. IEEE: systems and software engineering - vocabulary. Technical report, ISO/IEC/IEEE 24765. IEEE International Standard (2010)

54. Johansen, H.D., Birrell, E., van Renesse, R., Schneider, F.B., Stenhaug, M., Johansen, D.: Enforcing privacy policies with meta-code. In: Kono, K., Shinagawa, T. (eds.) Proceedings of the 6th Asia-Pacific Workshop on Systems, APSys 2015, Tokyo, Japan, 27–28 July 2015, pp. 16:1–16:7. ACM (2015)

55. Jones, J.A., Harrold, M.J.: Empirical evaluation of the tarantula automatic fault-localization technique. In: Proceedings of the International Conference on Automated Software Engineering (ASE) (2005)

56. Kephart, J.O., Chess, D.M.: The vision of autonomic computing. Computer **36**(1), 41–50 (2003)

57. Khoury, R., Hallé, S.: Runtime enforcement with partial control. In: Garcia-Alfaro, J., Kranakis, E., Bonfante, G. (eds.) FPS 2015. LNCS, vol. 9482, pp. 102–116. Springer, Cham (2016). https://doi.org/10.1007/978-3-319-30303-1_7

58. Khoury, R., Tawbi, N.: Corrective enforcement: a new paradigm of security policy enforcement by monitors. ACM Trans. Inf. Syst. Secur. **15**(2), 10:1–10:27 (2012)

59. Khoury, R., Tawbi, N.: Which security policies are enforceable by runtime monitors? A survey. Comput. Sci. Rev. **6**(1), 27–45 (2012)

60. Kim, M., Kannan, S., Lee, I., Sokolsky, O., Viswanathan, M.: Computational analysis of run-time monitoring - fundamentals of Java-MAC. Electr. Notes Theor. Comput. Sci. **70**(4), 80–94 (2002)
61. Kumar, A., Ligatti, J., Tu, Y.-C.: Query monitoring and analysis for database privacy - a security automata model approach. In: Wang, J., Cellary, W., Wang, D., Wang, H., Chen, S.-C., Li, T., Zhang, Y. (eds.) WISE 2015. LNCS, vol. 9419, pp. 458–472. Springer, Cham (2015). https://doi.org/10.1007/978-3-319-26187-4_42
62. Ligatti, J., Bauer, L., Walker, D.: Enforcing non-safety security policies with program monitors. In: di Vimercati, S.C., Syverson, P., Gollmann, D. (eds.) ESORICS 2005. LNCS, vol. 3679, pp. 355–373. Springer, Heidelberg (2005). https://doi.org/10.1007/11555827_21
63. Ligatti, J., Bauer, L., Walker, D.: Run-time enforcement of nonsafety policies. ACM Trans. Inf. Syst. Secur. **12**(3), 19:1–19:41 (2009)
64. Ligatti, J., Reddy, S.: A theory of runtime enforcement, with results. In: Gritzalis, D., Preneel, B., Theoharidou, M. (eds.) ESORICS 2010. LNCS, vol. 6345, pp. 87–100. Springer, Heidelberg (2010). https://doi.org/10.1007/978-3-642-15497-3_6
65. Martinelli, F., Matteucci, I.: Through modeling to synthesis of security automata. Electr. Notes Theor. Comput. Sci. **179**, 31–46 (2007). http://dx.doi.org/10.1016/j.entcs.2006.08.029
66. Martinelli, F., Matteucci, I., Mori, P., Saracino, A.: Enforcement of U-XACML history-based usage control policy. In: Barthe, G., Markatos, E., Samarati, P. (eds.) STM 2016. LNCS, vol. 9871, pp. 64–81. Springer, Cham (2016). https://doi.org/10.1007/978-3-319-46598-2_5
67. Martinelli, F., Matteucci, I., Saracino, A., Sgandurra, D.: Remote policy enforcement for trusted application execution in mobile environments. In: Bloem, R., Lipp, P. (eds.) INTRUST 2013. LNCS, vol. 8292, pp. 70–84. Springer, Cham (2013). https://doi.org/10.1007/978-3-319-03491-1_5
68. Martinelli, F., Matteucci, I., Saracino, A., Sgandurra, D.: Enforcing mobile application security through probabilistic contracts. In: Joosen, W., Martinelli, F., Heyman, T. (eds.) Proceedings of the 2014 ESSoS Doctoral Symposium Co-located with the International Symposium on Engineering Secure Software and Systems (ESSoS 2014), Munich, Germany, 26 February 2014. CEUR Workshop Proceedings, vol. 1298. CEUR-WS.org (2014)
69. Martinelli, F., Mori, P., Saracino, A.: Enhancing android permission through usage control: a BYOD use-case. In: Ossowski [70], pp. 2049–2056
70. Ossowski, S. (ed.): Proceedings of the 31st Annual ACM Symposium on Applied Computing, Pisa, Italy, 4–8 April 2016. ACM (2016)
71. Owicki, S., Lamport, L.: Proving liveness properties of concurrent programs. ACM Trans. Program. Lang. Syst. **4**(3), 455–495 (1982)
72. Pavlich-Mariscal, J., Michel, L., Demurjian, S.: A formal enforcement framework for role-based access control using aspect-oriented programming. In: Briand, L., Williams, C. (eds.) MODELS 2005. LNCS, vol. 3713, pp. 537–552. Springer, Heidelberg (2005). https://doi.org/10.1007/11557432_41
73. Pinisetty, S., Falcone, Y., Jéron, T., Marchand, H.: Runtime enforcement of parametric timed properties with practical applications. In: Lesage, J., Faure, J., Cury, J.E.R., Lennartson, B. (eds.) 12th International Workshop on Discrete Event Systems, WODES 2014, Cachan, France, 14–16 May 2014, pp. 420–427. International Federation of Automatic Control (2014)

74. Pinisetty, S., Falcone, Y., Jéron, T., Marchand, H.: Runtime enforcement of regular timed properties. In: Cho, Y., Shin, S.Y., Kim, S., Hung, C., Hong, J. (eds.) Symposium on Applied Computing, SAC 2014, Gyeongju, Republic of Korea, 24–28 March 2014, pp. 1279–1286. ACM (2014)

75. Pinisetty, S., Falcone, Y., Jéron, T., Marchand, H.: TiPEX: a tool chain for timed property enforcement during execution. In: Bartocci, E., Majumdar, R. (eds.) RV 2015. LNCS, vol. 9333, pp. 306–320. Springer, Cham (2015). https://doi.org/10. 1007/978-3-319-23820-3_22

76. Pinisetty, S., Falcone, Y., Jéron, T., Marchand, H., Rollet, A., Nguena-Timo, O.: Runtime enforcement of timed properties revisited. Formal Meth. Syst. Des. **45**(3), 381–422 (2014)

77. Pinisetty, S., Falcone, Y., Jéron, T., Marchand, H., Rollet, A., Nguena-Timo, O.L.: Runtime enforcement of timed properties. In: Qadeer and Tasiran [80], pp. 229–244

78. Pinisetty, S., Preoteasa, V., Tripakis, S., Jéron, T., Falcone, Y., Marchand, H.: Predictive runtime enforcement. In: Ossowski [70], pp. 1628–1633

79. Pinisetty, S., Preoteasa, V., Tripakis, S., Jéron, T., Falcone, Y., Marchand, H.: Predictive runtime enforcement. Formal Meth. Syst. Des. **51**(1), 1–46 (2017)

80. Qadeer, S., Tasiran, S. (eds.): RV 2012. LNCS, vol. 7687. Springer, Heidelberg (2013). https://doi.org/10.1007/978-3-642-35632-2

81. Ramadge, P.J., Wonham, W.M.: Supervisory control of a class of discrete event processes. SIAM J. Control Optim. **25**(1), 206–230 (1987)

82. Ramadge, P.J., Wonham, W.M.: The control of discrete event systems. Proc. IEEE **77**(1), 81–98 (1989)

83. Renard, M.: GREP (2017). https://github.com/matthieurenard/GREP

84. Renard, M., Falcone, Y., Rollet, A., Jéron, T., Marchand, H.: Optimal enforcement of (timed) properties with uncontrollable events. In: Mathematical Structures in Computer Science, pp. 1–46 (2017)

85. Renard, M., Falcone, Y., Rollet, A., Pinisetty, S., Jéron, T., Marchand, H.: Enforcement of (timed) properties with uncontrollable events. In: Leucker, M., Rueda, C., Valencia, F.D. (eds.) ICTAC 2015. LNCS, vol. 9399, pp. 542–560. Springer, Cham (2015). https://doi.org/10.1007/978-3-319-25150-9_31

86. Renard, M., Rollet, A., Falcone, Y.: Runtime enforcement using Büchi games. In: Proceedings of Model Checking Software - 24th International Symposium, SPIN 2017, Co-located with ISSTA 2017, Santa Barbara, USA, pp. 70–79. ACM, July 2017

87. Riganelli, O., Micucci, D., Mariani, L., Falcone, Y.: Verifying policy enforcers. In: Proceedings of the International Conference on Runtime Verification (RV) (2017)

88. Schneider, F.B.: Enforceable security policies. ACM Trans. Inf. Syst. Secur. **3**(1), 30–50 (2000)

89. Sridhar, M., Hamlen, K.W.: Flexible in-lined reference monitor certification: challenges and future directions. In: Proceedings of the 5th ACM Workshop on Programming Languages Meets Program Verification, PLPV 2011, pp. 55–60 (2011)

90. Swanson, J., Cohen, M.B., Dwyer, M.B., Garvin, B.J., Firestone, J.: Beyond the rainbow: self-adaptive failure avoidance in configurable systems. In: Proceedings of the ACM SIGSOFT International Symposium on Foundations of Software Engineering (FSE) (2014)

91. Talhi, C., Tawbi, N., Debbabi, M.: Execution monitoring enforcement under memory-limitation constraints. Inf. Comput. **206**(2–4), 158–184 (2008). https:// doi.org/10.1016/j.ic.2007.07.009

92. Wu, M., Zeng, H., Wang, C.: Synthesizing runtime enforcer of safety properties under burst error. In: Rayadurgam, S., Tkachuk, O. (eds.) NFM 2016. LNCS, vol. 9690, pp. 65–81. Springer, Cham (2016). https://doi.org/10.1007/978-3-319-40648-0_6
93. Zeller, A., Hildebrandt, R.: Simplifying and isolating failure-inducing input. IEEE Trans. Softw. Eng. (TSE) 28(2), 183–200 (2002)
94. Zhang, X., Leucker, M., Dong, W.: Runtime verification with predictive semantics. In: Goodloe, A.E., Person, S. (eds.) NFM 2012. LNCS, vol. 7226, pp. 418–432. Springer, Heidelberg (2012). https://doi.org/10.1007/978-3-642-28891-3_37

Specification-Based Monitoring of Cyber-Physical Systems: A Survey on Theory, Tools and Applications

Ezio Bartocci[1(✉)], Jyotirmoy Deshmukh[2], Alexandre Donzé[3],
Georgios Fainekos[4], Oded Maler[5], Dejan Ničković[6],
and Sriram Sankaranarayanan[7]

[1] Technische Universität Wien, Vienna, Austria
ezio.bartocci@tuwien.ac.at
[2] University of Southern California, Los Angeles, USA
[3] University of California at Berkeley, Berkeley, USA
[4] Arizona State University, Tempe, USA
[5] VERIMAG, CNRS and University of Grenoble-Alpes (UGA),
Saint Martin d'Hères, France
[6] AIT Austrian Institute of Technology GmbH, Vienna, Austria
[7] University of Colorado, Boulder, USA

Abstract. The term Cyber-Physical Systems (CPS) typically refers to engineered, physical and biological systems monitored and/or controlled by an embedded computational core. The behaviour of a CPS over time is generally characterised by the evolution of physical quantities, and discrete software and hardware states. In general, these can be mathematically modelled by the evolution of continuous state variables for the physical components interleaved with discrete events. Despite large effort and progress in the exhaustive verification of such hybrid systems, the complexity of CPS models limits formal verification of safety of their behaviour only to small instances. An alternative approach, closer to the practice of simulation and testing, is to monitor and to predict CPS behaviours at simulation-time or at runtime. In this chapter, we summarise the state-of-the-art techniques for qualitative and quantitative monitoring of CPS behaviours. We present an overview of some of the important applications and, finally, we describe the tools supporting CPS monitoring and compare their main features.

1 Introduction

Dynamic Behaviours and Their Evaluation. The world around us is in a constant flux with "things" changing dynamically. Planets move, temperatures rise and fall, rivers flow, rocks break down. In addition to these physical dynamics, a large part of the changing world is due to the activities of living systems and in particular humans, their social constructs and the artefacts they build. Houses are illuminated and air-conditioned, power is generated, distributed and consumed, cars drive on roads and highways, plants manufacture

© Springer International Publishing AG, part of Springer Nature 2018
E. Bartocci and Y. Falcone (Eds.): Lectures on Runtime Verification, LNCS 10457, pp. 135–175, 2018.
https://doi.org/10.1007/978-3-319-75632-5_5

materials and objects, commercial transactions are made and recorded in information systems. Airplanes fly, continuously changing location and velocity while their controllers deal, via sensors and actuators, with various state variables in the engine and wings. Conceptually those processes can be viewed as temporal behaviours, waveforms or signals or time series or sequences, where continuous and discrete variables change their values over time and various types of events occur along the time axis.

The systems that generate these behaviours are evaluated to some extent as good or bad, efficient or worthless, excellent or catastrophic. Such an evaluation can apply to the system in question as a whole, to some of its components or to a particular period of operation. We use *monitoring* to denote the act of observing and evaluating such temporal behaviours. Behaviours can be very long, spanning over a large stretches of time, densely populated with observations. They can also be very wide, recording many variables and event types. As such they carry too much information by themselves to be easily and directly evaluated. What should be distilled out of these behaviours should somehow be expressed and specified. The mathematical objects that do this job are functions that map complex and information-rich behaviours into low dimensional vectors of bits and/or numbers that indicate satisfaction of logical requirements and the values of various performance indices, see Fig. 1.

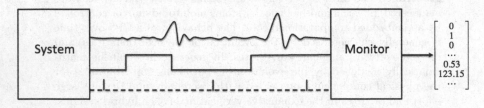

Fig. 1. Monitoring as reducing complex temporal behaviours into low-dimensional vectors of bits and numbers. The first of three behaviours is continuous and the two others are at the timed level of abstraction, state-based (signal) and event-based.

The evaluation can be based on a gross abstraction of the behaviour, for example the event of an airplane crash corresponds to a zero location on the z dimension and a large downward velocity at some point in time. Likewise the death of a patient can be specified by the stabilisation of his or her heart beat signal to a constant value. More often than not, those global catastrophic events may be related to (and preceded by) more detailed temporal behaviours that involve intermediate steps and variables, for example, some rise in the engine temperature which is not followed by certain actions such as turning on a cooling system. In less safety-critical contexts, systems are evaluated for performance, for example the time a client spends in a queue between requesting and being granted, or the energy consumption of a computer or a chemical plant along some segment of time.

Monitoring Real Systems and Monitoring Simulated Models. Before going further, let us distinguish between two major contexts in which the monitoring of dynamic behaviours can take place (see a more elaborate discussion in [95]). The first is the monitoring of real systems during their execution via online measurements. Here the role of monitoring is to alert in *real time* in order to trigger corrective actions, either by a human operator or by a supervisory layer of control. A primitive form of this type of monitoring exists in many domains: indicators on the control panel of a car, airplane or electronic device, monitors for physiological conditions of patients in a hospital and SCADA (Supervisory Control and Data Acquisition) systems for controlling complex large-scale systems such as airports, railways or industrial plants. In fact, any information system can be viewed as performing some kind of a monitoring activity.

The other context is during model-based system design and development where all or some of the system components do not exist yet in flesh and blood and their models, as well as the model of the environment they are supposed to interact with, exist as virtual objects of mathematical and computational nature. The design process of such systems is typically accompanied by an extensive simulation and verification campaign where the response of the system to numerous scenarios is simulated and evaluated. Most of the work described in this chapter originates from the design-time monitoring context, where simulation traces constitute the input of the monitoring process. Many techniques and considerations are shared, nevertheless, with the monitoring of real systems.

The activity of simulating a system and checking its behaviour is part of the verification and validation process whose goal is to ensure, as much as possible, that the system behaves as expected and to avoid unpleasant surprises after its deployment. In some restricted contexts of simple programs or digital circuits, this process can be made exhaustive and "formal" in the sense that all possible classes of scenarios are covered. When dealing with cyber-physical systems, whose existence and interaction scope are not confined to the world inside a computer for which practically exact models exist, complete formal verification is impossible, if not meaningless. In this domain, simulation-based lightweight verification is the common practice, accompanied by the hope of providing a good finite coverage of the infinite space of behaviours.

Rigorous Specification Formalisms. Part of the runtime verification movement is coming from formal verification circles, attempting to export to the simulation-based verification domain another ingredient of formal verification, namely, the rigorous specification of the system requirements. In the context of discrete systems, software or digital hardware, formalisms such as *temporal logic* or *regular expressions* are commonly used. They can specify in a declarative manner which system behaviours, that is, sequences of states and events, conform with the intention of the designer in terms of system functionality, and which of these behaviours do not. Such specifications can be effectively translated into monitoring programs that observe behaviours and check whether the requirements are satisfied. As such they can replace or complement tedious manual inspection of simulation traces or ad hoc programming of property testers.

Let us give some intuitive illustrations of the nature of these formalisms. Linear-time temporal logic (LTL) provides a compact language for speaking of sequences and the relations between their values at different points in time. The semantics of an LTL formula φ is time dependent with $(w, t) \models \varphi$ indicating that formula φ holds for sequence w at position t. The simplest formulas are state formulas which are satisfied at t according to the value of the sequence at t. That is, writing p for the truth value of a logical variable, or $x > 0$ for a numerical variable, is interpreted at each t as $p[t]$ and $x[t] > 0$, respectively.

More complex formulas are built using Boolean and temporal operators. The latter are divided into two types, future and past operators. The satisfaction of a future operator at position t depends on the values of the sequence at some or all the positions from t onward, that is, the suffix of w from t to $|w|$. For example $\Box p$ (*always* p) is true at any t such that p holds at every $t' \geq t$. The analogous past formula $\boxminus p$ (*historically* p) holds at t if p holds at any position $t' \leq t$, in other words, along the prefix of w from 0 to t. The satisfaction of a future formula by the whole sequence w is defined as its satisfaction at position 0 while that of a past formula, by its satisfaction at $|w|$. Past formulas have some advantages such as causality, while future LTL is more commonly used and is considered by some to be more intuitive.

The formula $\Box p$ quantifies universally over all time instances. The dual formula $\Diamond p$ (*eventually* p) quantifies existentially. It holds at t if p holds at *some* t' in the future. The weakness of such a property from a practical standpoint is that there is no bound on the distance between t and t', a fact that may upset some impatient clients waiting for a response during their lifetime. We should note that in verification, formulas are often interpreted over *infinite* sequences generated by automata, while in monitoring we deal with finite sequences and if p never becomes true until the end of w, formula $\Diamond p$ is falsified.

A more quantitative alternative to $\Diamond$ can be expressed in discrete time using the *next* operator. Formula $\bigcirc p$ (*next* p) holds at t if p holds at $t+1$. Thus, the requirement that each p is followed by q within 2 to 3 time steps is captured by the formula

$$\Box (p \to (\bigcirc (\bigcirc q)) \vee (\bigcirc (\bigcirc (\bigcirc q)))).$$

This formulation may become cumbersome for large delay constants and by extending the syntax we can write this formula as

$$\Box (p \to \Diamond_{[2,3]} q)$$

with $\Diamond_{[a,b]} p$ being satisfied at t if p is satisfied at some $t' \in [t+a, t+b]$. In discrete time, this can be viewed as a syntactic sugar, but in dense time where *next* is anyway meaningless, this construct allows events to occur anywhere in an interval, not necessarily at sampling points or clock ticks.

Sequential composition is realised in future LTL using the *until* operator. The formula $p \mathcal{U} q$ (*p until q*) is satisfied at t if q occurs at some later point in time while p holds continuously until then. Using this operator, for which

◇ and □ are degenerate cases, one can require that some process should not start as long as another process has not terminated. The semantics of *until* is defined below.[1]

$$(w, t) \models \varphi_1 \mathcal{U} \varphi_2 \quad \text{iff} \quad \exists t' \geq t \, ((w, t') \models \varphi_2 \wedge \forall t'' \in [t, t'] \, (w, t'') \models \varphi_1) \quad (1)$$

The past counter-part of *until* is the *since* operator with $q \mathcal{S} p$ (q *since* p) meaning that p occurred in the past and q has been holding continuously since then. The semantics of *since* is given below.

$$(w, t) \models \varphi_2 \mathcal{S} \varphi_1 \quad \text{iff} \quad \exists t' \leq t \, ((w, t') \models \varphi_1 \wedge \forall t'' \in [t', t] \, (w, t'') \models \varphi_2) \quad (2)$$

It is interesting to compare these operators with the *concatenation* operation used in regular expressions.

Regular expressions constitute a fundamental and popular formalism in computer science, conceived initially to express the dynamic behaviour of neural networks, and later applied to lexical and grammatical analysis. Traditionally, such expressions are defined over a monolithic alphabet of symbols but in order to present them in the same style as LTL, we will use product alphabets such as $\{0, 1\}^n$, defined and accessed via variables. Thus an expression p in our approach would be interpreted in the traditional approach as the set of all Boolean vectors in a global alphabet in which the entry corresponding to p is 1.

In discrete time, p is satisfied by any sequence of length one in which p holds. Sequential composition is realised by the concatenation operation where $\varphi_1 \cdot \varphi_2$ is satisfied by any sequence w that admits a factorisation $w = w_1 \cdot w_2$ such that w_1 satisfies φ_1 and w_2 satisfies φ_2. This is best illustrated by defining the semantics using the satisfaction relation $(w, t, t') \models \varphi$ which holds whenever the subsequence of w starting at t and ending in t' satisfies expression φ:

$$(w, t, t') \models \varphi_1 \cdot \varphi_2 \quad \text{iff} \quad \exists t'' \in [t, t'] \, (w, t, t'') \models \varphi_1 \wedge (w, t'', t') \models \varphi_2 \quad (3)$$

The Kleene star allows to repeat concatenation for an indefinite but finite number times, with φ^* being satisfied by any sequence that admits a finite factorisation in which all factors satisfy φ. As an example, expression $(\neg p)^* \cdot q \cdot p$ specifies sequences in which a finite (possibly empty) time segment where p does not hold is followed by the occurrence of q followed by p.

Note that unlike LTL, regular expressions are more symmetric with respect to the arrow of time, as can be seen by the difference between their respective semantics definitions. The definitions of $\models$ in (1) and (2) go recursively from t to the future or the past, respectively. When they come up from the recursion they do it in the opposite direction: for future LTL, satisfaction is computed backwards and that of past LTL is computed forward. For concatenation, in contrast, the semantics of $\models$ in (3) is defined by a double recursion which takes the whole sequence and splits it into two parts which are the arguments for the two recursive calls. The semantics is collected from both ends while coming up from the recursion.

---

[1] Variants of *until* may differ on whether φ_2 is required to occur or whether φ_1 can cease to hold at the moment φ_2 starts or only after that.

Going Cyber-Physical. The exportation of these formalisms and their monitoring algorithms to the cyber-physical world has to cope with the hybrid nature of such systems. The dynamics of digital systems is captured by discrete event systems such as automata, generating discrete sequences of logical states and events. Physical systems are modelled using formalisms such as differential equations, producing behaviours viewed as continuous signals and trajectories. Specification formalisms and monitoring algorithms should then be extended so as to express and check temporal properties of such behaviours. This topic is the focus of the present chapter, centred around *Signal Temporal Logic* (STL), first presented in [96], along with a monitoring algorithm, further elaborated in the thesis [107] and explained from first principles in [98].

STL is a straightforward extension of (propositional) LTL along two orthogonal dimensions, namely, moving from discrete to dense time and using predicates on numerical values in addition to basic (atomic) propositions. The first feature is present in real-time variants of temporal logic such as MTL/MITL while the second has been explored in various first-order extensions of discrete-time LTL. We believe that some of the popularity of STL comes from the smooth and simple integration of these two features. This popularity, as attested by numerous publications that apply it to application domains ranging from analog circuits, via robotics, control systems and engineering education, down to biomedical and biochemical domains, justifies the role STL plays in this chapter, although in principle other variants of logic could do the job as well.

In order to be relevant to real applications, we should keep in mind that continuous dynamical systems are the object of study of various branches of mathematics and engineering, in particular, control and signal processing. These domains have developed over the years a variety of ways to measure and evaluate such systems and their behaviours, which are appropriate to their physical and mathematical nature. There is a variety of mathematical norms that reduce such behaviours into single numbers. There are transformations like Fourier's that extract the spectral properties of signals for the purpose of classification or noise removal. There are many statistical ways to assess signals and time series and detect occurring patterns. The challenge in monitoring cyber-physical systems is to integrate these traditional performance measures with those provided by the newly developed verification-inspired formalisms which are more suitable for capturing sequential aspects of behaviours.

2   Specification Languages

In this section, we present Signal Temporal Logic (STL) [96] as the specification language that we use in this document for expressing properties of CPS. We introduce the syntax of the formalism, together with its qualitative and quantitative semantics.

2.1 Signal Temporal Logic

STL [96] extends the continuous-time Metric Temporal Logic (MTL) [87] with numerical predicates over real-valued variables. In particular, STL enables reasoning about real-time properties at the interface between components that exhibit both discrete and continuous dynamics.

We denote by X and P finite sets of *real* and *propositional* variables. We let $w : \mathbb{T} \to \mathbb{R}^m \times \mathbb{B}^n$ be a multi-dimensional *signal*, where $\mathbb{T} = [0, d) \subseteq \mathbb{R}$, $m = |X|$ and $n = |P|$. Given a variable $v \in X \cup P$ we denote by $\pi_v(w)$ the *projection* of w on its component v.

We now define the variant of STL that contains both *past* and *future* temporal operators. The syntax of an STL formula φ over $X \cup P$ is defined by the grammar

$$\varphi := p \mid x \sim c \mid \neg\varphi \mid \varphi_1 \vee \varphi_2 \mid \varphi_1 \mathcal{U}_I \varphi_2 \mid \varphi_1 \mathcal{S}_I \varphi_2$$

where $p \in P$, $x \in X$, $\sim \; \in \{<, \leq\}$, $c \in \mathbb{Q}$, and $I \subseteq \mathbb{R}^+$ is an interval. We define the semantics of STL as the *satisfiability relation* $(w, t) \models \varphi$, indicating that the signal w satisfies φ at the time point t, according to the following definition. Given that we interpret the logic only over the finite traces, we let the satisfaction relation to be defined only for $t \in \mathbb{T}$.

$$
\begin{aligned}
(w, t) &\models p &&\leftrightarrow \pi_p(w)[t] = \mathsf{true} \\
(w, t) &\models x \sim c &&\leftrightarrow \pi_x(w)[t] \sim c \\
(w, t) &\models \neg\varphi &&\leftrightarrow (w, t) \not\models \varphi \\
(w, t) &\models \varphi_1 \vee \varphi_2 &&\leftrightarrow (w, t) \models \varphi_1 \text{ or } (w, t) \models \varphi_2 \\
(w, t) &\models \varphi_1 \mathcal{U}_I \varphi_2 &&\leftrightarrow \exists t' \in (t + I) \cap \mathbb{T} : (w, t') \models \varphi_2 \text{ and } \forall t'' \in (t, t')(w, t''), \models \varphi_1 \\
(w, t) &\models \varphi_1 \mathcal{S}_I \varphi_2 &&\leftrightarrow \exists t' \in (t - I) \cap \mathbb{T} : (w, t') \models \varphi_2 \text{ and } \forall t'' \in (t', t), (w, t'') \models \varphi_1
\end{aligned}
$$

We say that a signal w *satisfies* a STL formula φ, denoted by $w \models \varphi$, iff $(w, 0) \models \varphi$. In the remainder of this section, we discuss several specific aspects of the STL syntax and semantics.

Finitary interpretation. Specification formalisms with future temporal operators are typically defined over *infinite* behaviours. In particular, we can have a specification that is satisfied at time t iff a future obligation is fulfilled at some future time instant $t' > t$. Consequently, observing a finite prefix of a behaviour may not be sufficient to determine the satisfaction or the violation of a temporal specification according to its standard semantics. The finitary interpretation of future temporal logics is a well-studied problem in the monitoring research field. In order to tackle this issue, we adapt the semantics of $\mathcal{U}$ and restrict the existential quantification of time to the (possibly bounded) signal domain. This altered semantics provides a natural interpretation of STL over finite signals. In particular, the *eventually* operator has a so-called *strong* interpretation – $\diamondsuit \varphi$ is satisfied iff φ holds at any time before the signals ends. Similarly, the *always* operator has a *weak* interpretation under this semantics – $\square \varphi$ is satisfied iff φ is not violated during the signal duration.

The problem of interpreting temporal logic over finite or truncated behaviours was extensively studied in [57], where *weak*, *strong* and *neutral* views of the finitary semantics for LTL are proposed. In [56], the authors provide a topological characterisation of weak and strong temporal operators. An extensive discussion about different interpretations of temporal logics over finite traces is presented in [98]. Finally, we also mention the real-time monitoring framework from [29], where 3-valued {true, false, inconclusive} semantics are used to provide a finitary interpretation of a real-time temporal logic.

Strict interpretation of temporal operators. We adopt the *strict* semantics of until and since as originally proposed in [8]. The strict interpretation of $\varphi \mathcal{U} \psi$ evaluated at time t requires that both ψ is satisfied at some t' *strictly greater* than t and that φ continuously holds in the interval (t, t') that *excludes* t. In other words, the satisfaction of $\varphi \mathcal{U} \psi$ at t depends only on the evaluation of φ and ψ at some times in the future of t. This is in contrast to the classical non-strict semantics of *until* and *since* in the discrete-time LTL [110], where $\varphi \mathcal{U} \psi$ is satisfied if ψ holds at t. Let us first denote by $\bar{\mathcal{U}}$ the non-strict until operator, and by $\mathcal{U}$ its strict counterpart[2]. We also recall that LTL contains the *next* operator $\bigcirc$ in addition to $\bar{\mathcal{U}}$. We can show that in discrete time, a temporal logic with $\bar{\mathcal{U}}$ and $\bigcirc$ such as LTL is equivalent to the logic that has $\mathcal{U}$ only, by using the following rules.

$$\varphi_1 \mathcal{U} \varphi_2 \equiv \bigcirc (\varphi_1 \bar{\mathcal{U}} \varphi_2)$$
$$\bigcirc \varphi \equiv \text{false } \mathcal{U} \varphi$$
$$\varphi_1 \bar{\mathcal{U}} \varphi_2 \equiv \varphi_2 \vee (\varphi_1 \wedge (\varphi_1 \mathcal{U} \varphi_2))$$

In contrast to LTL, continuous-time temporal logics such as STL do not have the next operator. It turns out that the strict interpretation of the temporal operators strictly increases the expressiveness of the underlying logic in dense time, as it enables "forcing" the time to advance. The main practical consequence of strict interpretation of $\mathcal{U}$ and $\mathcal{S}$ is that it allows specification of instantaneous events in continuous time.

Derived operators. The syntactic definition of STL is minimal and includes only basic operators. We can derive other standard operators as follows:

True constant:	true	$\equiv p \vee \neg p$
False constant:	false	$\equiv \neg\text{true}$
Conjunction:	$\varphi_1 \wedge \varphi_2$	$\equiv \neg(\neg\varphi_1 \vee \neg\varphi_2)$
Implication:	$\varphi_1 \rightarrow \varphi_2$	$\equiv \neg\varphi_1 \vee \varphi_2$
Eventually:	$\Diamond_I \varphi$	$\equiv \text{true } \mathcal{U}_I \varphi$
Once:	$\Diamond_I \varphi$	$\equiv \text{true } \mathcal{S}_I \varphi$
Always:	$\Box_I \varphi$	$\equiv \neg\Diamond_I \neg\varphi$
Historically:	$\boxminus_I \varphi$	$\equiv \neg\Diamond_I \neg\varphi$

---

[2] We restrict our argument to the future operators for the sake of simplicity – the same reasoning can be applied to the past operators.

In addition to these derived operators, we can also define instantaneous *events* that have zero duration. Such events enable specification of *rising* and *falling* *edges* in boolean signals.

$$\text{Rising edge: } \uparrow \varphi \equiv (\varphi \wedge (\neg \varphi \, \mathcal{S} \text{ true})) \vee (\neg \varphi \wedge (\varphi \, \mathcal{U} \text{ true}))$$
$$\text{Falling edge: } \downarrow \varphi \equiv (\neg \varphi \wedge (\varphi \, \mathcal{S} \text{ true})) \vee (\varphi \wedge (\neg \varphi \, \mathcal{U} \text{ true}))$$

2.2 Signal Temporal Logic with Quantitative Semantics

In Sect. 2.1, we introduced STL with *qualitative* semantics. This classical definition of STL enables to determine the *correctness* of a signal with respect to a specification. Specifically, it gives a binary pass/fail answer to the monitoring problem. When reasoning about hybrid systems that involve both discrete and continuous dynamics, the qualitative verdict may not be informative enough. After all, systems with continuous dynamics are usually expected to admit some degree of tolerance with respect to initial conditions, system parameters and environmental perturbations. Consequently, a quantitative degree of satisfaction/violation would be preferable to a simple yes/no output given by the qualitative interpretation of STL.

Fages and Rizk [113] and Fainekos and Pappas [61] proposed to tackle this issue by equipping the temporal logic with *quantitative* semantics. This extension replaces the binary satisfaction relation with the quantitative *robustness degree* function, while preserving the original syntax of the specification language. In essence, the robustness degree function gives a real value that indicates how far is a signal from satisfying or violating a specification. We illustrate the concept of the robustness degree function with a simple example on numerical predicates. Let $x < c$ be a numerical predicate. This predicate partitions the $\mathbb{R}$ domain into the set of all real values that are strictly smaller than c and those that are greater or equal to c. Picking a concrete value for x, the robustness degree gives the relative position of x to c, instead of only indicating whether x is above or below the threshold. This idea is naturally extended to the logical and temporal operators that we now formalise.

Let φ be an STL formula, w a signal and t a time instant in $\mathbb{T}$. We then define the robustness degree function $\rho(\varphi, w, t)$ as follows.

$$\rho(p, w, t) = \begin{cases} \infty & \text{if } \pi_p(w)[t] = \text{true} \\ -\infty & \text{otherwise} \end{cases}$$
$$\rho(x \sim c, w, t) = c - \pi_x(w)[t]$$
$$\rho(\neg \varphi, w, t) = -\rho(\varphi, w, t)$$
$$\rho(\varphi_1 \vee \varphi_2, w, t) = \max\{\rho(\varphi_1, w, t), \rho(\varphi_2, w, t)\}$$
$$\rho(\varphi_1 \, \mathcal{U}_I \varphi_2, w, t) = \sup_{t' \in (t+I) \cap \mathbb{T}} \min\{\rho(\varphi_2, w, t'), \inf_{t'' \in (t, t')} \rho(\varphi_1, w, t'')\}$$
$$\rho(\varphi_1 \, \mathcal{S}_I \varphi_2, w, t) = \sup_{t' \in (t-I) \cap \mathbb{T}} \min\{\rho(\varphi_2, w, t'), \inf_{t'' \in (t', t)} \rho(\varphi_1, w, t'')\}$$

We note that for a fixed formula φ and a given signal w, the quantity $\rho(\varphi, w, t)$ is a function of time, and can thus be treated as a signal. We refer to it as the robust satisfaction signal or robustness signal.

There is a couple of fundamental properties that relate the STL quantitative semantics to its qualitative counterpart. Consider an arbitrary STL formula φ, a signal w and time $t \in \mathbb{T}$. The first property says that for any $\rho(\varphi, w, t) \neq 0$, its sign determines whether $(w, t) \models \varphi$. The second property states that if $(w, t) \models \varphi$, then for any signal w' whose pointwise distance from w is smaller than $\rho(\varphi, w, t)$ we also have $(w', t) \models \varphi$.

We illustrate the difference between the qualitative and the quantitative semantics in Fig. 2. We can also observe the relation between the two semantics as stated in the previous paragraph.

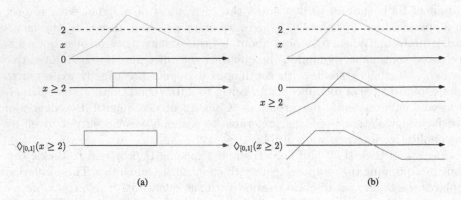

(a)   (b)

Fig. 2. Example for STL formula evaluation: (a) qualitative and (b) quantitative semantics.

Alternative quantitative semantics. In this section, we presented a quantitative semantics that allows measuring *spatial* robustness of STL specifications. This definition takes into account the spatial variations of signals when compared to STL specifications. Developing alternative notions of robustness degree for STL has been an active area of research in the recent years. In [51], the authors extend the quantitative semantics of STL by combining spatial with *time* robustness, thus also allowing to quantify temporal perturbations in signals. The idea of the combined space-time robustness for STL is further enhanced in [7] with *averaged* temporal operators. In [114], the authors identify that the bounded eventually $\Diamond_{[a,b]}$ operator behaves like the *convolution* operator commonly used in filtering and digital signal processing. Following this surprising observation, one can develop various quantitative semantics for temporal logic, by defining the appropriate kernel window used for evaluating the formula. These additional operators enable reasoning not only about the worst-case but also the average-case behaviours. The Skorokhod metric provides an alternative way to measure mismatches between continuous signals in both space and time. An effective procedure for computing the Skorokhod distance between two behaviours is developed and presented in [42,93]. This method is extended to estimate the Skorokhod distance between *reachpipes* in [94]. Nevertheless, there are no available methods yet to compute the Skorokhod distance between a signal and an STL formula.

3   Monitoring Algorithms

In this section, we present algorithms answering the following *monitoring* question: what is the qualitative and/or quantitative satisfaction of a formula φ by a signal w? This problem is much easier than *model-checking*, i.e., proving that a system satisfies a formula, which is undecidable for STL even for simple classes of systems. Yet, it is desirable that efficient algorithms exist for monitoring, as this task can typically be repeated on large numbers of instances, or on signals of long durations. We consider two different settings: offline and online. In the offline setting, we assume that w is known before computing the satisfaction of φ. In the online setting, we assume only a partial knowledge of w, and compute successive estimates of φ satisfaction as new samples of w become available.

3.1   Offline Monitoring

For simplicity we restrict the presentation to the case of STL with future operators, and piecewise constant signals, i.e., we assume that w is completely defined by a sequence of time instants $t_0 < t_1 < \ldots < t_i < \ldots$ and values $w_0, w_1, \ldots, w_i, \ldots$ such that

$$\forall t \in [t_i, t_{i+1}), w[t] = w_i[t].$$

Here, we assume that the sequence of (time, value) pairs is finite, i.e., $i \leq N$. Moreover, we assume that the signal w holds its final value indefinitely, i.e., for all $t > t_N$, $w[t] = w[t_N]$. We present briefly an algorithm computing quantitative satisfaction of φ by w, adapted in a simpler form from [49]. For a purely Boolean monitoring algorithm, see [108]. Computing the quantitative satisfaction is not more complex than computing the Boolean, as both can be achieved in linear complexity in the size of signals.

The algorithm work by induction on the structure of the formula following the generic scheme presented in Algorithm 1.

Algorithm 1. Monitor(φ, w)

---

  switch (φ)
  case p:
    return ComputeSatisfaction(p, w)
  case $x \sim c$:
    return ComputeSatisfaction$(x \sim c, w)$
  case $* \varphi$, where $* \in \{\neg, \Diamond_I, \Box_I\}$:
    $w' :=$ Monitor(φ, w)
    return ComputeSatisfaction$(*, w')$
  case $\varphi * \psi$, where $* \in \{\vee, \mathcal{U}_I\}$:
    $w' :=$ Monitor(φ, w)
    $w'' :=$ Monitor(ψ, w)
    return ComputeSatisfaction$(*, w', w'')$
  end switch

Table 1. ComputeSatisfaction for atomic predicate and Boolean operators. y is the signal returned, either Boolean or Real valued.

	Boolean	Quantitative
(p, w)	$y[t] = p$	if $p ==$ true, $y[t] = +\infty$, else $y[t] = -\infty$
$(x \sim c, w)$	$y[t] = (\pi_x(w)[t] \sim c)$	$y[t] = \pi_x(w)[t] - c$
$(\neg, w')$	$y[t] = \neg w[t]$	$y[t] = -w[t]$
$(\vee, w', w'')$	$y[t] = w'[t] \vee w''[t]$	$y[t] = \max(w'[t], w''[t])$

To implement Algorithm 1, we need to provide an implementation of the function ComputeSatisfaction for each instance of the switch statement. Instances which do not involve any temporal operator are straightforward and presented in Table 1. As can be expected, the only non-trivial case is with temporal operators.

In theory, we only need to handle the until operator ($\mathcal{U}_I$), as other temporal operators such as globally ($\square_I$) and eventually ($\Diamond_I$) are derived from $\mathcal{U}_I$ and Boolean operations. However, in practice, it is more efficient to deal with these operators separately. Also as we will see, $\mathcal{U}_I$ is handled by combining specific algorithms for $\square_I$ and $\Diamond_I$ and $\mathcal{U}_I$ with $I = [0, \infty)$ (unbounded until). It turns out that for offline monitoring, unbounded operators are easier to handle than bounded time ones. Hence, we will present implementations for the unbounded cases before the bounded cases. In the following, we explain how to implement the ComputeSatisfaction function for unbounded eventually, timed eventually. The bounded globally case can be deduced from eventually using the equivalence $\square_I \varphi \Leftrightarrow \neg \Diamond_I \neg \varphi$. Then we describe the algorithm for unbounded until and finally timed until operators.

$ComputeSatisfaction(\Diamond_{[0,\infty)}, w)$ *(Unbounded Eventually)*. From the quantitative semantics, recall that

$$\rho(\Diamond_I(\varphi, w, t) = \sup_I \rho(\varphi, w, t).$$

If $I = [0, \infty)$, that means that

$$y[t] = \sup_{t' \geq t}\{w[t]\} = \max_{t_i \geq t} w[t_i]$$

It is easy to see that y is defined by a finite sequence satisfying the (backward) recurrence relation:

$$\begin{cases} y_N = w_N \\ y_k = \max(w_k, y_{k+1}) \end{cases}$$

Note that in the case of $I = [a, \infty)$, the result is obtained by shifting time by $-a$.

$ComputeSatisfaction(\Diamond_{[a,b)}, w)$ *(Bounded Eventually)*. From the quantitative semantics, we have that:

$$\rho(\Diamond_{[a,b)}(\varphi, w, t) = \sup_{[a,b)} \rho(\varphi, w, t)$$

so that

$$y[t] = \max_{t_i \in [t+a, t+b)} \{w[t_i]\}.$$

In other words, the signal $t \to y[t]$ stores the sequence of maximums of signal w over a sliding finite window of size $b - a$. In [49], the authors observed that such a sliding window could be computed using an algorithm due to Daniel Lemire with linear complexity in the size of signal w [90]. We refer the reader to [49, 90] for details about this algorithm.

$ComputeSatisfaction(\diamondsuit_{[0,\infty)}, w)$ *(Untimed Until)*. To compute the satisfaction of untimed until, we are given two signals: w' and w'' and need to compute y. Since w' and w'' are of finite length N, y is also of finite length N. The computation goes backward starting from (y_N, t_N). The time sequence $t_0, t_1, \ldots, t_{N-1}$ is obtained by merging and sorting the sequences t'_i and t''_i so that to simplify the notations, we assume that the sequences w'_i and w''_i are defined on the same time sequence, i.c., $w'_i = w'[t_i]$ and $w''_i = w''[t_i]$ for all i. Using standard $\min - \max$ manipulations, we can show that the following recurrence is true:

$$\begin{cases} y_{N-1} = \min(w'_{N-1}, w''_{N-1}) \\ y_k = \max(\min(w'_k, w''_k), \min(w'_k, y_{k+1})), k \in \{0, \ldots, N-2\} \end{cases}$$

Implementing this recurrence yields an algorithm with complexity in $O(2N)$.

$ComputeSatisfaction((\mathcal{U}_{[a,b)}, w', w''))$ *(Bounded Until)*. To compute satisfaction signals for formulas involving timed operators, we make use of the following result:

Lemma 1. *For two STL formulas* φ, ψ,

$$\varphi \mathcal{U}_{[a,b)} \psi \Leftrightarrow \diamondsuit_{[a,b)} \psi \wedge \varphi \mathcal{U}_{[a,+\infty)} \psi \tag{4}$$

$$\varphi \mathcal{U}_{[a,+\infty)} \psi \Leftrightarrow \square_{[0,a)} (\varphi \mathcal{U} \psi) \tag{5}$$

Using this lemma, ComputeSatisfaction($\mathcal{U}_{[a,b)}, w', w''$) can be obtained by a sequence of intermediate computations using the algorithms above, as detailed in Algorithm 2. Note that all ComputeSatisfaction algorithm presented before run in linear time w.r.t. the number of samples in their input signals, so that for any STL formula, the computation of the robust satisfaction signal is also linear w.r.t. the size of the signals involved.

Algorithm 2. ComputeSatisfaction($\mathcal{U}_{[a,b)}, w', w''$) with $a < b < +\infty$

$w_1 := $ ComputeSatisfaction($\mathcal{U}_{[0,+\infty)}, w', w''$)
$w_2 := $ ComputeSatisfaction($\square_{[0,a)}, w_1$)   // w_2 *is the right hand side of* (5)
$w_3 := $ ComputeSatisfaction($\diamondsuit_{[a,b)}, w''$)
return ComputeSatisfaction($\wedge, w_2, w_3$)

3.2   Online Monitoring

Offline algorithms assume that the entire trace is available to the monitoring procedure, and then run on the trace to produce either a Boolean satisfaction value or a quantitative (robust) satisfaction value. There are a number of situations where offline monitoring is unsuitable. Consider the case where the monitor is to be deployed in an actual system to detect erroneous behaviour. As embedded software is typically resource constrained, offline monitoring – which requires storing the entire observed trace – is impractical. Also, when a monitor is used in a simulation-based validation tool, a single simulation may run for several minutes or even hours. If we wish to monitor a safety property over the simulation, a better use of resources is to abort the simulation whenever a violation (or satisfaction) is conclusive from the observed trace prefix. Such situations demand an *online monitoring algorithm*, which has markedly different requirements. In particular, a good online monitoring algorithm must: (1) be able to generate intermediate estimates of property satisfaction based on *partial signals*, (2) use minimal amount of data storage, and (3) be able to run fast enough in a real-time setting.

A basic online algorithm returns a *true* or *false* satisfaction value when the satisfaction or violation of the property being monitored can be concluded by observing the finite trace prefix. In many cases, the information in the trace prefix is insufficient to produce a conclusive answer. Thus, several kinds of semantics have been proposed to interpret MTL or STL formulae over truncated traces. These semantics typically extend the satisfaction in a Boolean sense as used by offline monitoring algorithms to a richer satisfaction domain, typically having three or four values.

A typical three-valued semantics, for instance, assigns the satisfaction value of *true* if given the truncated signal, it can be decided that the signal will definitely satisfy the property. For example, if the value of the signal w at time 2 is 5, then any trace prefix inclusive of this time-point definitely satisfies the formula $\Diamond_{[0,10]}(w > 0)$. Dually, it assigns the satisfaction value of *false* when the trace prefix is enough to establish that the signal definitely violates a given formula. If neither determination can be made, then the semantics assigns a satisfaction value of *unknown* [29]. Four-valued semantics that introduce *presumably true* and *presumably false* in addition to *true* and *false* for signal traces that are likely to respectively satisfy or violate the property have been proposed in [30].

In what follows, we first discuss qualitative monitoring algorithms; these algorithms, given an MTL or STL property, decide from a given prefix of a signal, if the entire signal would satisfy or violate the given property. An orthogonal, but relevant issue for online monitoring is the semantics of the MTL/STL property to be monitored on partial signal traces. We recall that following the tradition of the semantics for LTL on truncated traces [57], there are different notions of satisfaction that can be used to reason over prefixes of signals. We say that a signal-prefix *strongly* satisfies a given property if for *any* suffix the resulting signal would satisfy the property. In other words, the signal-prefix is sufficient to decide the satisfaction of the given property. We say that a signal-prefix *weakly* satisfies a given property if there is *some* suffix such that the resulting signal would satisfy the property. A third notion of satisfaction is *neutral satisfaction*, which is if the given signal-prefix satisfies the property where the temporal operators are restricted to quantify only over the length of the signal-prefix. Some algorithms for qualitative monitoring make use of such richer notions of satisfaction.

Qualitative Online Monitoring. There are two main flavours of qualitative online monitoring. The first, based on work in [97], uses a modification of an algorithm similar to Algorithm 1. This procedure called *incremental marking*, essentially treats the signal as being available in chunks. The algorithm computes the robustness signal in a bottom-up fashion, starting from the leaves (i.e., atomic formulas) appearing in the STL formula and then for each super-formula, combining the robust satisfaction signals for its subformulae. The algorithm maintains the robust satisfaction signal partitioned as the concatenation of two signals: the first segment containing values that have already been propagated to the super-formula (by virtue of having sufficient information to allow deciding the satisfaction of the super-formula), and the second segment containing values that have not yet been propagated, as they may influence the satisfaction of the super-formula because of a part of the signal not yet available.

The second flavour of qualitative online monitoring makes use of automata-based monitors [71] and the richer notions of strong and weak satisfaction of MTL properties by signal-prefixes. In this approach, the given MTL formula (with future and past modalities) is first rewritten so that all temporal operators bound by finite time intervals appear in the scope of zero or more temporal operators that are unbounded. Essentially, each bounded temporal formula defines a finite time-window into the signal, where signal values would have to be available to evaluate the subformula. The algorithm maintains a time-window for each such bounded temporal subformula as a tableau and updates it using dynamic programming methods. This effectively allows treating bounded temporal subformulae as atomic propositions. The outer unbounded operators are monitored using two-way alternating Büchi automata that accept *informative prefixes* of the signal. An informative prefix is a signal-prefix that allows deciding the satisfaction or violation of the given unbounded temporal formula. The procedure has space-bounds that are linear in the variability of the given signal, and length of the formula, and requires constructing automata that are doubly exponential in the size of the given MTL formula.

Quantitative Online Monitoring. Qualitative monitoring algorithms by their nature are unable to quantify the degree to which the signal corresponding to the given signal-prefix may satisfy or violate the property of interest. Online algorithms for computing robust satisfaction semantics seek to address this gap. We discuss three algorithms below. The operating assumption of each algorithm is the same: given a trace prefix, return a quantitative value that captures a notion of robust satisfaction over the incomplete trace. However, none of the algorithms are probabilistic in nature. The first and the third algorithms provide a quantitative value based only on the trace prefix observed (and possibly a forecast suffix). The second algorithm, given a formula φ, processes a trace prefix and returns a robust satisfaction interval that always contains the robust satisfaction value w.r.t. φ of any trace with this prefix.

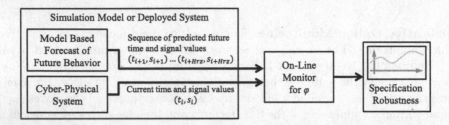

Fig. 3. The online temporal logic monitoring framework for bounded future and unbounded past formulas proposed in [44]. In case the monitored system contains a model which can be used for forecasting future behaviours up to a horizon Hrz, then these behaviours can be used to compute the robustness estimate of the specification φ. If a forecasting mechanism is not available, then it is preferable to monitor past formulas.

Quantitative monitoring of STL with past operators and predictors.
The first algorithm we discuss is for online monitoring of STL formulas with bounded future and unbounded past formulas [44]. For a given STL formula φ, the algorithm computes the horizon, or the number of look-ahead steps that would be required to evaluate the bounded future component of a formula, and the history or the number of samples in the past that would be needed to evaluate a given bounded past formula. The algorithm then maintains a tableau that is updated every time a new signal value becomes available using a dynamic programming based approach. For unbounded past operators, the algorithm exploits the fact that an unbounded past formula can be rewritten such that the computation over an unbounded history can be stored as a *summary* in a variable that is updated each time a new signal value becomes available. For the unobserved parts of the signal, which would be required to compute the satisfaction of a bounded future temporal subformula, the algorithm requires the use of a predictor in order to compute a robustness estimate (see Fig. 3).

In more detail, the algorithm monitors invariants expressed as STL formulas φ. That is, the assumption is that φ should be satisfied at all times of the system execution or model simulation. As an example, consider the specification

$$\varphi \equiv \neg(x \geq 0.5) \rightarrow \Diamond_{[0,1]} \Box_{[0,1]} (x \geq 0.5) \tag{6}$$

which states that if the value of the signal x decreases below 0.5, then within 1 s in the past it should have been higher than 0.5 for at least 1 s. In Fig. 4, we present a simple example of a signal x and the corresponding robustness value $\rho(\varphi, x, t)$ computed online for Eq. (6). Notice that the signal x decreases below the threshold 0.5 (i.e., the antecedent $\neg(x \geq 0.5)$ is now satisfied) at two points in time, at 5.5 s and at 12.25 s. In the first case, no violation of the requirement occurs (barely), while in the second case a violation occurs (the robustness drops below zero). In either case, the robustness of Eq. (6) starts decreasing at time 6 and at time 13, respectively, when the subformula $\Diamond_{[0,1]} \square_{[0,1]}(x \geq 0.5)$ starts changing robustness value. On the other hand, the robustness increases afterwards because the value of the signal x approaches the threshold 0.5 and, therefore, the antecedent comes closer again to being falsified. The fact that the specification robustness starts decreasing can be used as a warning that the system may be soon violating its requirement; and, thus, remedial action may be required.

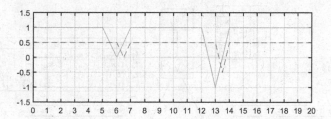

Fig. 4. A signal x (*solid blue line*) and the corresponding robustness value $\rho(\varphi, x, t)$ (*dashed red line*) computed for the formula in Eq. (6). (Color figure online)

Quantitative monitoring of robust satisfaction interval for bounded future STL formulas. The second algorithm computes *robust interval semantics* for STL formulas with bounded future formulas [40]. A robust satisfaction interval (ℓ, u) for a given signal-prefix is defined such that ℓ (respectively, u) is the infimum (respectively, supremum) over the robust satisfaction values of the given property for all signals that have the given partial signal as the prefix. For example, consider a constant signal-prefix with magnitude 1, defined over time $t \in [0, 5)$. The robust satisfaction interval for the formula $\square_{[0,10]}(x > 0)$ over this signal-prefix is $(-\infty, 1]$, while the robust satisfaction interval for the formula $\Diamond_{[0,10]}(x > 0)$ is $[1, \infty)$. The interval semantics generalises the notion of strong and weak semantics. A signal-prefix strongly satisfies (resp. violates) a property if the lower-bound of the robust satisfaction interval is positive (resp. upper-bound of the robust satisfaction interval is negative). A signal-prefix weakly satisfies a property if the upper bound of the robust satisfaction interval is positive.

In lieu of a detailed exposition of the algorithm, we demonstrate it with an example in Fig. 6 for the formula in Eq. (7).

$$\varphi \equiv \square_{[0,a]}\left(\neg(y > 0) \vee \Diamond_{[b,c]}(x > 0)\right) \tag{7}$$

We assume that the algorithm starts in a state where it has processed the partial signal till time t_2, and show the effect of receiving data at time-points t_3, t_4 and t_5. The algorithm maintains lists of robust satisfaction intervals at each node in the syntax tree of φ, and updates these lists when new time-points in the trace become available. Each row in the table adjacent to a node shows the

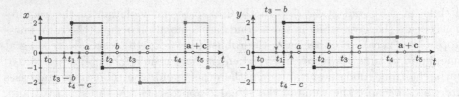

Fig. 5. These plots show the signals $x(t)$ and $y(t)$. Each signal begins at time $t_0 = 0$, and we consider three partial signals: till time t_3 (black + blue), and till time t_4 (black + blue + green), and till time t_5 (black + blue + green + red) (Color figure online)

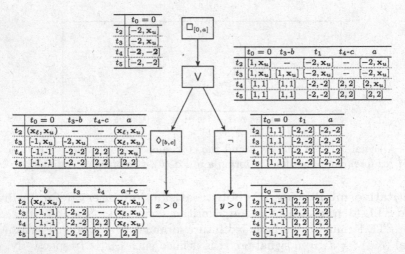

Fig. 6. We show a snapshot of the list at each node in the syntax tree of formula given in Eq. (7) maintained by the algorithm for four different (incremental) partial traces of the signals $x(t)$ and $y(t)$ shown in Fig. 5. Each row indicates the state of each list at the time indicated in the first column. An entry marked -- indicates that the corresponding element did not exist in the list at that time. Each colored entry indicates that the entry was affected by availability of a signal fragment of the corresponding color. (Color figure online)

state of the list after the algorithm processes the value at the time indicated in the first column.

The first row of the table shows the snapshot of the lists at time t_2. Observe that in the lists for the subformula $y > 0$, $\neg y > 0$, because $a < b$, the data required to compute the interval at t_0, t_1 and the time a, is available, and hence each of the intervals is singular. On the other hand, for the subformula $x > 0$, the time horizon is $[b, a + c]$, and no signal value is available at any time in this interval. Thus, at time t_2, all elements of the list at the node corresponding to $x > 0$ are $(\mathbf{x}_\ell, \mathbf{x}_u)$ corresponding to the user-provided greatest lower bound and lowest upper bound on the signal $\mathbf{x} = (x, y)$.

To compute the values of $\Diamond_{[b,c]}(x > 0)$ at any time t, we take the supremum over values from times $t + b$ to $t + c$. As the time horizon for the node corresponding to $\Diamond_{[b,c]}(x > 0)$ is $[0, a]$, t ranges over $[0, a]$. In other words, we wish to perform the sliding maximum over the interval $[0 + b, a + c]$, with a window of length $c - b$. We can use the algorithm for computing the sliding window maximum as discussed in the earlier section on offline monitoring. One caveat is that we need to store separate monotonic edges for the upper and lower bounds of the robust satisfaction intervals. The algorithm then proceeds upward on the syntax tree, only updating the list of a node only when there is an update to the lists of its children.

The second row in each table is the effect of obtaining a new time point (at time t_3) for both signals. Note that this does not affect the lists at the node $y > 0$ or the node $\neg y > 0$, as the robust satisfaction intervals are already singular, but does update the intervals for the node $x > 0$. The algorithm then invokes the sliding window computation on the list for $x > 0$ to update the list for $\Diamond_{[b,c]}(x > 0)$. Finally, we remark that the run of this algorithm shows that at time t_4, the interval for the formula φ is $[-2, -2]$, which yields a negative upper bound, showing that the formula is not satisfied irrespective of the suffixes of x and y. In other words, the satisfaction of φ is known before we have all the data required to fully determine the robust satisfaction value for the formula.

Quantitative monitoring for unbounded horizon STL formulas. Robust satisfaction intervals are meaningless for STL formulas with unbounded future operators. Hence, for such formulas, nominal quantitative semantics have been proposed in [41]. These semantics essentially compute the robust satisfaction value of the formula restricted to the trace prefix that is available. However, a key challenge is to avoid storing the entire signal or performing repeated computation whenever a new time-point becomes available. This can be circumvented by storing the *summary* of computation of the robust satisfaction value and then incrementally updating the summary variables. The number of summary variables required is finite and independent of the trace length, although exponential in the length of the formula. Nominal quantitative satisfaction values for arbitrary unbounded horizon STL formula can be monitored in this fashion. The rules for rewriting the nominal robustness computation of an unbounded horizon STL formula in terms of summary variables is involved, and we omit the details for brevity. Interested readers can find them in [41].

4   Extensions

It is out of doubt that STL has gained in the last decade an increased popularity among engineers for its conciseness and expressive power enabling to specify complex behavioural properties related to the order and the temporal distance among discrete *events* such as the satisfaction of predicates (e.g., threshold crossing) over the real variables.

However, the pure time-domain nature of this specification language sometimes has revealed to be a technical impediment to overcome for an immediate applicability to cyber-physical systems. In particular, abnormal signal behaviours such as undesirable oscillations and complex topological requirements (i.e., the spatial distribution of the entities generating signals) are very challenging to capture using only the time-domain.

For this reason, in the last decade STL has inspired a number of extensions that have been successfully applied in many applications ranging from identifying oscillatory behaviours in analog circuits [104], biological systems [32] and music melodies [52] to specifying spatiotemporal requirements in reaction-diffusion systems [12,13,16,102], smart grids [69] and mobile ad-hoc sensor networks [15]. In the following we aim to provide an overview of some of the STL extensions recently proposed.

4.1   Monitoring Complex Oscillatory Properties

The dynamical behaviour of a physical system often exhibits complex oscillatory patterns representing an infinite periodically behaviour. Real-life analog signals are characterised by omnipresent noise, i.e., random perturbations of the desired signal. Damped oscillations or oscillations with increasing amplitude are peculiar aspects in many biological systems [21,22,32]. Abnormal oscillations due to the presence of *spikes* or *hunting* oscillations [104] are considered undesired behaviours in analog circuit design. Signal-processing tasks such as *peak* detection [5,19,34] is common in many medical cyber-physical systems whose correctness impacts the performance and the sensitivity of the computational devices involved. Providing a concise formal specification language expressive

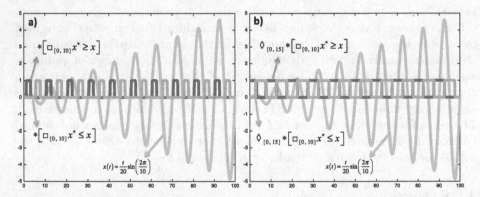

Fig. 7. The freezing operator of STL-∗ enables in (a) the specification of the notions of local maxima ($*[\Box_{[0,10]}x^* \geq x]$) and local minima ($*[\Box_{[0,10]}x^* \leq x]$) by comparing the value x with all the *frozen* values (represented by the expression x^*) within a time interval $[0,10]$. This feature is suitable to capture oscillatory behaviours without knowing a-priori specific signal thresholds. In (b) freezing operators are nested within the classical *eventually* STL operators to detect the possible occurrence of a local maxima and a local minima within $[0,15]$ time units.

enough to characterise such patterns and to efficiently monitor them is a very challenging task.

For example, the classic STL is not expressive enough to distinguish classes of oscillatory patterns such as damped oscillations or oscillations with increasing amplitude, because it is not able to globally reference and compare local properties (i.e., local minima/maxima) of a signal. Motivated by this necessity the authors in [32] have proposed an extension of STL (named STL-∗), augmenting STL with a freezing operator that allows to record the signal values during the evaluation of a sub-property, and to reuse it for comparison in the other parts of the formula. This operator increases the expressive power of STL and for instance it enables to express and to capture various dynamic aspects of oscillations (see Fig. 7). A quantitative semantics for STL-∗ is also proposed in [33]. However, the price to pay for this enhanced expressiveness is an higher computational complexity for the monitoring procedure. In [32] the authors show that the monitoring algorithm for STL with nesting freeze quantifiers is polynomial in the number of intervals on which the signals is defined and the size of the syntactic tree of the formula, but it is exponential in the number of the nested freeze operators in the formula.

Although STL-∗ is more expressive than STL, its analysis is still limited to the time-domain representation of a signal. However, oscillatory patterns (i.e., chirp signals, hunting behaviours, noise filtering) are in general very challenging and tedious to investigate using only time and a time-frequency analysis is essential sometime to efficiently detect them. Time-frequency analysis is an important branch of *signal processing* and it is based on the study of the *spectrogram* (see Fig. 8), a representation of the frequencies' magnitude in a signal as they vary with time. Spectrograms can be calculated from digitally sampled data in the time-domain representation of the signal using extensions of the classic Fourier transforms such as the Short Time Fourier Transform (STFT) or Wavelet Transforms (WTs). Although a preliminary work on combining time and frequency domain specifications for periodic signals is reported in [37], the first attempt to provide a unified formalism to express time-frequency properties of a signal is the *time-frequency logic* (TFL) introduced in [52]. TFL extends STL with predicates evaluating the magnitude of a particular frequency range in a point in time. The semantics of TFL operates over a spectrogram generated using STFT. In [52] TFL was applied to detect musical patterns, but it can be easily used in other application domains. More recently, TFL was extended in [104] to operate over spectrograms generated using WTs. These spectrograms generally provide a better trade-off between the resolution in the time domain and the resolution in the frequency domain w.r.t. STFT.

4.2   Monitoring Spatio-Temporal Behaviours

The components in CPS are generally distributed across space and connected via a communication infrastructure. The complex behaviour of each individual component due to a fully-integrated hybridisation of computational (logical) and physical action and the interactions between these components via the network

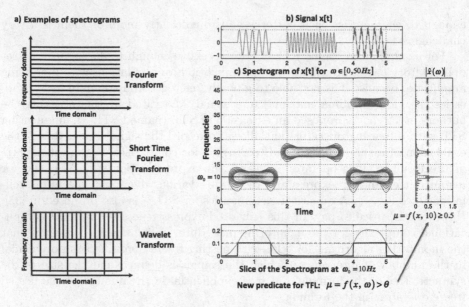

Fig. 8. In (a) we show three different examples of spectrogram obtained using different time to frequency domain signal transformations: Fourier Transform (FT), Short Time Fourier Transform (STFT) and Wavelet Transform (WT). FT provides the average magnitude of a signal for a certain interval of frequencies along the entire duration of the signal. FT are indeed not suitable to localise the time when a change of frequencies occurs. STFT consists instead in dividing a longer time signal into shorter segments of the same length and in computing the FT for each of these segments. This provides a better time resolution than FT. However, STFT has a fixed resolution that depends on the time length chosen for the shorter segments. A wide window gives better frequency resolution but poor time resolution and vice-versa. WT generally provides the best combination of good time resolution for high-frequency events and good frequency resolution for low-frequency events. In (b) we show an example of a signal with in (c) its STFT spectrogram for the frequencies in the range 0–50 Hz. On the right of the spectrogram we provide the projection of the magnitude associated with each frequency, while on the bottom we show a slice of the spectrogram for the frequency 10 Hz. TFL provides a special predicate that enables to compute such slicing and to compare the magnitude w.r.t. a user-defined threshold.

enable them to produce very rich and complicated emergent spatiotemporal behaviours, often impossible to predict at design time. Examples include smart grids, robotics teams or collections of genetically engineered living cells. In such examples, temporal logics may be not sufficient to capture also topological spatial requirements. For example, the notion of being *surrounded* or *spatial superpositioning* (averaging resources in a space) are not available in the standard STL and encoding them with specific functions may result cumbersome.

Recently, three different spatiotemporal extensions of STL, *Spatial-Temporal Logic* (SpaTeL) [69], the *Signal Spatio-Temporal Logic* (SSTL) [16,102] and the *Spatio-Temporal Reach and Escape Logic* (STREL) [15] have been proposed to accommodate the growing need of expressing not just temporal but also spatiotemporal requirements in CPS.

SpaTeL [69] is the unification of STL and Tree-Spatial-Superposition-Logic (TSSL) introduced in [12,13] to classify and detect spatial patterns. TSSL reasons over quadtrees, spatial data structures that are constructed by recursively partitioning the space into uniform quadrants. TSSL uses the notion of spatial superposition (introduced in [68]) that provides a way to describe statistically the distribution of discrete states in a particular partition of the space and that enable to specify self-similar and fractal-like structures that generally characterise the patterns emerging in nature. SpaTeL is equipped with both a qualitative and a quantitative semantics that provide a measure or robustness of how much the property is satisfied or violated. In [69] this measure of robustness is used as a fitness function to guide the parameter synthesis process for the neighbourhood prices in a demand-side management system model of a smart grid using particle swarm optimisation (PSO) algorithms.

SSTL [16,102] instead extends STL with three spatial modalities *somewhere*, *everywhere* and *surround*, which can be nested arbitrarily with the original STL temporal operator. SSTL is interpreted over a discrete model of space represented as a finite undirected graph. Each edge of the graph is labeled with a positive weight that can be used to represent the distance between two nodes. This provides a metric structure to the space, in terms of shortest path distances. However, the weight can be used to encode also other kind of information (i.e., the average travelling time between two cities). In [102], the authors provide a qualitative and quantitative semantics of SSTL and efficient monitoring algorithms for both semantics.

STREL [15] generalises SSTL by introducing two new spatial operators: *reach* and *escape*. These operators enable to express the same spatial modalities in SSTL and to compute the monitoring procedure locally at each location using the information of its neighbours. While SSTL can operate only on static spatial-temporal models (the position of the locations remains always fixed), STREL can handle also dynamic/mobile networks. Moreover, in [15] the authors show that for a certain class of models (called *euclidean spatial models*), all the spatial properties expressed in STREL that satisfy a model will also satisfy all the model transformations using rotation, translation and reflection.

4.3 Matching and Measuring Temporal Patterns over CPS Behaviours

In the introduction of this document, we mentioned that declarative specification languages are typically based on temporal logics or regular expressions. Both formalisms have their merits and weaknesses. Temporal logic are often good for describing global behaviours and the expected relations between the events and the states that evolve over time. In contrast, regular expressions are convenient for expressing local temporal patterns (consecutive sequences of events at states) that happen in a behaviour. In the digital hardware community, it has been observed that the necessary expressiveness and succinctness of the specification language is truly achieved when temporal logic is combined with regular expressions. In fact, both IEEE formal specification language standards, SystemVerilog Assertions (SVA) [126] and Property Specification Language (PSL) [55] adopt this combined approach.

In the context of continuous-time applications, Timed Regular Expressions (TRE) were proposed in [11] as a real-time extension of regular expressions. For a long time, this formalism was subject to theoretical studies, but without any real practical relevance. More recently, a novel algorithm for matching and extracting TRE patterns from hybrid behaviours was developed in [124]. The original offline pattern matching procedure was extended with an online version in [125]. These results on TRE pattern matching enabled the combination of STL with regular expressions also in the continuous-time setting, as it was shown in [64]. Finally, automated extractions of quantitative measurements from CPS behaviours based on TRE patterns was proposed in [65].

5   Applications to Cyber-Physical Systems (CPS)

In this section, we provide an overview of the important applications of temporal logic-based monitoring techniques presented thus far and conclude with a presentation of the practical challenges that need to be addressed through future research.

5.1   Practical Considerations for CPS Monitoring

CPS integrate computation and control of physical processes to enable safety critical applications in many domains including medical devices, automotive systems, avionics and power systems [88]. The problem of monitoring CPS has been a productive area for the runtime verification community as a whole, leading to many important considerations such as monitoring timed properties, quantitative semantics, simulation-guided falsification and online monitoring challenges.

Both offline and online monitoring setups present unique challenges for CPS applications. As described in Sect. 3, the offline monitoring setup analyses trace data collected from running a system, after the execution has terminated. A key challenge includes that of monitoring large volumes of data efficiently [26]. At the same time, richer specification languages with higher computational worst-case complexities can be accommodated in an offline monitoring setup, exacerbating the challenge of efficient offline monitoring.

Online monitoring, on the other hand, is constrained by the limited ability to store the trace as the system being monitored executes and the hard real time demands on the computation time. Furthermore, in practice, monitoring is often restricted to perform a single pass through the trace in the forward direction. This naturally restricts us to specification languages that can be monitored efficiently in an online fashion. For instance, the presence of unbounded until operators in the specification can potentially require a large lookahead to resolve the truth of the formula appropriately [39, 66, 70]. Finally, if the monitoring shares the same platform as the deployed system, it should be *non-intrusive* as much as possible: in other words, its consumption of resources such as CPU time, memory and I/O must not interfere with that of the running application [127]. The latter concern is especially acute for CPS, wherein instrumentation can potentially interfere with critical timing properties of the system being observed.

Finally, physical measurements are well known to be noisy and they require specialised sensors. As a result, the problem of monitoring under incomplete and noisy measurements is especially relevant for CPS applications [24,83].

Another important classification, especially for CPS applications, involves the problem of modelling the physical environment surrounding the closed loop being monitored [79]. Herein, different monitoring setups are distinguished by the complexity and fidelity of the physical plant models and the software runtime setup used [84]. Software-in-the-loop monitors properties using the control system being designed and a mathematical model of the plant. Hardware-in-the-Loop monitoring (also known as Processor in the Loop) executes the controller on the runtime platform used during deployment, while using a mathematical model of the plant [120]. The monitoring challenges include the problem of mapping the "simulation time" of the plant model to the real-time elapsed for the real-time software. Model-based development environments such as Matlab™, Simulink/Stateflow™, Modelica™, Scade™ and DSpace™ support software/hardware in the loop testing and runtime monitoring for complex CPS [76].

Real-time Monitoring of CPS. Monitoring of real systems in real time during their execution requires adapting the techniques and the algorithms presented so far in this document. In the case of real-time monitoring, the property observers are implemented on a physical device that is connected to the system-under-test (SUT) [105,118,119]. Several considerations must be taken into account - the real-time sensing of the SUT signals and the environment, the frequency of the monitor operation that must be at least as high as the frequency at which the SUT works, the limited availability of resources that are available on the monitor device, etc. When considering real-time monitors implemented in embedded software or hardware, it is often the case that both the computations are done at the periodic intervals over the quantised input signals. In that case, STL is interpreted over signals that are defined in discrete time and over finite domains. While in this setting, STL is not more expressive than LTL, keeping explicit real-time operators and numerical inputs allows efficient implementation of monitors and allows giving them both qualitative and quantitative semantics. A translation of STL specifications into real-time monitors implemented in FPGA is proposed in [77]. A quantitative semantics for such STL properties based on the *weighted edit distance*, together with the algorithms for computing the robustness degree of a trace with respect to a property are developed in [78].

5.2   Property Falsification and Parameter Synthesis

In this section, we summarise work on the application of specification robustness of traces (Sect. 2.2) to two very related problems: property falsification and parameter synthesis.

Falsification techniques attempt to find a counterexample to a given property and to a given model of a system (or even to the actual system). Falsification is a rather valuable approach, generalising manual testing to an automatic search for violating counterexamples. However, the core challenge in falsification is the question of where to search for violations. This is a very challenging problem for CPS due to the continuous nature of the input space which consists of initial conditions and input signals to the model.

The problem of parameter synthesis for property satisfaction can be thought of as a dual problem to the falsification problem. In the case of parameter synthesis, the search is typically not over the space of initial conditions and inputs to the model, but over the model's parameters. In addition, the goal is not to find a falsifying behaviour, but rather either a set of satisfying behaviours for a range of parameters, or a parameter which induces a model which robustly satisfies the property.

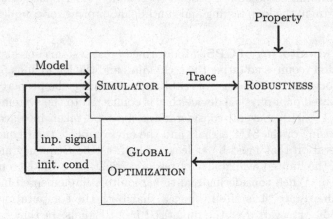

Fig. 9. Setup for the falsification of properties using robustness metrics.

To automate the search, we may use specification robustness to provide guidance on what to search for. Figure 9 illustrates the overall setup for falsification and/or parameter synthesis. As pointed out in [103] and in [2], robustness is a natural measure of a distance between a signal and a property. A tool that tries to minimise robustness by searching over inputs and initial conditions is in essence a tool for finding counterexamples. Similarly, a tool that attempts to maximise robustness by searching over a range of parameters is a parameter synthesis tool. To this end, a global optimisation engine is used to systematically guide the search for inputs (parameters) that minimise (maximise) the over-all robustness. The approach does not need to find the globally minimum (maximum) robustness. Rather, it stops whenever the specification robustness crosses a given threshold. For falsification methods, this threshold is typically the value zero indicating a change from positive robustness values (correct behaviour) to negative robustness values (incorrect behaviour). Also, in the case of counterexample search, even if a falsification is not obtained, then the minimum robustness obtained can serve as useful information to provide the engineer.

The idea of minimising robustness to search for falsification or maximising robustness for parameter synthesis has been implemented in tools such as Breach [46] and S-Taliro [10]. However, the challenges in these problems lie in the choice of a global optimisation solver that can efficiently (quickly) converge to local optima. In theory, any such solver will have to fundamentally grapple with the underlying undecidability of finding falsifying inputs for programs, in general. On the other hand, approaches such as Nelder-Meade algorithm [101], Simulated Annealing [103], Ant-Colony Optimization [9], Gaussian Process Optimization with Upper Confidence Bound [18], and the Cross-Entropy method [115] have been used to report success on large examples. Path-planning based methods like RRTs (rapidly exploring random trees) combined with online monitoring of STL robustness have shown promise in systems with hybrid dynamics [53].

As the model fidelity and complexity increases, so does the model simulation time. Long computation times are acceptable in optimal design applications, e.g., [58], since the system must be designed once; however, they can be problematic in system testing applications. Typically, the developers may be willing to wait overnight for test results, but most probably they will not be willing to wait for a week, for example. To improve the performance of stochastic optimisation methods, e.g., [9,18,103,115], in [1,6] they proposed hybrid techniques where robustness descent directions are analytically computed and interleaved with stochastic optimization methods. Such a process guarantees fast convergence to local optimiser points. On the other hand, it requires a white-box model, i.e., the mathematical model must be known to the falsification algorithm. Recently, the aforementioned restriction was relaxed in [130] where it was shown that the descent directions can be approximated as long as the system simulator can provide linearizations of the model along the simulation trace of the system. Finally, we should remark that some of the techniques which were used in [6] for falsification were initially used in [50] for parameter synthesis using simulations for computing reachable sets.

Automotive Systems. Automotive systems present an important application for many aspects of runtime monitoring and property falsification, discussed thus far. As automobiles become ever more autonomous, it is important to check the functional correctness of their core components.

The work in [62] describes the application of S-Taliro to automotive system models. Therein, they show the presence of unexpected behaviours in an automatic transmission model that were not revealed by previous testing approaches.

Falsification methods for stochastic systems were applied to stochastic models of automotive systems in [3]. The presented framework for robustness guided falsification in this section is also used as an intermediate step in specification mining methods [74,129]. The methods presented in [74,129] are primarily applied to automotive applications. In [131], the authors applied Breach as part of a compositional verification scheme for complex automotive system with many sub-modules. The Breach requirement mining feature was used at the system level to induce pre-conditions for sub-modules, making it easier to apply successfully model-checking analysis at the module level. The contribution in [85] formulated a library of control-theoretic specifications that can be expressed in STL and showed its application to an automotive powertrain control benchmark. Both STL and TRE have been recently used to specify, monitor and measure hybrid properties of the DSI3 standard [65,106].

CPS Engineering Education. STL monitoring was used in the context of a MOOC[3] (Massively Open Online Class) teaching basic concepts of CPS design [82]. A key assignment was for the student to design, simulate and execute on real hardware a control algorithm driving a robot in an environment with obstacles. In order to evaluate hundreds of students contributions, a simulator was designed and equipped with STL monitoring capabilities. Grading was then done by evaluating a set of test cases and STL properties implementing fault monitors, i.e., each STL property evaluated to true would indicate a specific type of fault. The system would then return either some feedback if the user were a student or a partial grade if the user were an instructor.

Systems and Synthetic Biology. The growing need of computational models and methods [25] to investigate and to design complex biological systems with a predictable behaviour has also benefited greatly from the use of the aforementioned monitoring techniques. STL has become popular also among bioscientists to specify in a concise and unambiguous way the behaviour of several cellular and molecular mechanisms. The quantitative semantics of STL and its extensions has triggered the development of several *parameter synthesis* techniques and invaluable tools [12,17,18,47,69] to automatically characterise the parameter region of a biological model responsible for a behaviour of interest. Similarly to falsification analysis, parameter synthesis leverages an optimisation process using a particular heuristic. The only difference is that the objective function is to maximise (instead of minimising) the robustness with respect to an STL requirement. This approach has been successfully employed to study several biological case studies. Examples include the study of the onset of new blood vessel sprouting [48], the programmed cell death (apoptosis) [123], the effect of iron metabolism on blood cell specialisation [100] and the logical characterisation of an oscillator of the circadian clock in the Ostreococcus Tauri [19].

---

[3] https://www.edx.org/course/cyber-physical-systems-uc-berkeleyx-eecs149-1x.

Medical Devices. The growing area of closed-loop medical devices has led to devices such as implantable pacemakers and artificial pancreas that provide life sustaining treatments in real-time. As a result, the problem of monitoring and verifying their operation takes on great significance. The broader area of closed loop medical devices has received a lot of recent interest from the formal verification community. This started with work on pacemakers and implantable cardiac defibrillators (ICDs) that includes hybrid automata models for excitable cells in the heart [20,67], leading to approaches that employ these models to test closed loop systems [80,81,109].

Other examples of safety critical medical devices include the ones used in intensive care. In [34], the authors propose a method to automatically detect ineffective breathing efforts in patients in intensive care subject to assisted ventilation. Their approach is based on learning and monitoring STL specification discriminating between normal and ineffective breaths.

More recently, also the artificial pancreas concept has emerged as an important approach to treat type-1 diabetes, approaching a *de facto* cure [86].

Artificial Pancreas Control Systems. The artificial pancreas concept refers to a series of increasingly sophisticated devices (see Fig. 10) that automate the delivery of insulin to patients with type-1 diabetes in a closed loop, automatically responding to changes in the patient's blood glucose levels and activities such as meals and exercise [38,72,86]. However, such systems can pose risks to the patient arising from defects and malfunctions. Short-term risks include extremely low blood glucose levels called *hypoglycemia*, that can lead to seizures, loss of consciousness, coma or even death in extreme cases.

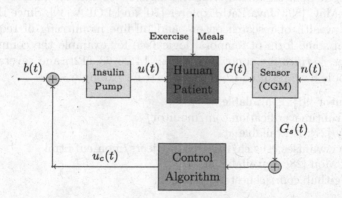

Fig. 10. Overview of the key components of an artificial pancreas control system. $b(t)$: external user commanded insulin, $u(t)$: insulin infused to patient, $G(t)$: blood glucose level of the patient, $n(t)$: sensor measurement error (noise), $G_s(t)$: glucose level estimated/reported by sensor, $u_c(t)$: insulin infusion commanded by the algorithm.

Cameron et al. use robustness-guided falsification techniques for checking properties of closed loop control systems for the artificial pancreas [36]. Their work investigates a PID controller proposed in [121, 122, 128] based on published descriptions of the control system available. The simulation environment incorporates this controller in a closed loop with models of the patient [99], the sensors and actuators. Their work formulated nearly six different temporal properties of the closed loop and obtained falsification for three of them. However, they could not falsify the remaining three properties that governed the absence of prolonged hypoglycemia and hyperglycemia in the patient.

Another recent study [116] was performed to test a predictive pump shutoff controller designed in [35] that has undergone outpatient clinical trials [92]. This study involved the entire controller software *as is*, without any modifications. At the same time, the closed loop simulation permits us to pose a rich set of questions that compare the closed loop performance with a corresponding open loop under the same meal inputs and physiological model conditions. The falsification discovered adverse noise patterns in the CGM sensor that could trick the Kalman filter into predicting inaccurate forecasts for the future glucose value, and thus prevent appropriate pump shutoff/resumption. At the same time, critical properties such as not commanding excess insulin when the patient is in hypoglycemia could not be violated. The study concluded the need to investigate these violations under more realistic patterns of CGM noise.

6   Tools

Due to relatively low computational complexity of the online and offline monitoring algorithms, many software tools have been developed over the last two decades. Among the first tools that were developed for monitoring (a subset or superset) of Boolean-valued temporal logic specifications were the Temporal Rover [54], MaC [89], Java PathExplorer [70] and LOLA [39]. Since then, there has been a wealth of research on on- and off-line monitoring of requirements expressed in some form of temporal logic (see for example the competition at the *Runtime Verification* conference series [14, 23, 63, 112]) and several publicly available tools have resulted from this effort, for example:

1. RV-Monitor [91]: is available at
   https://runtimeverification.com/monitor/
2. MonPoly [27]: is available at
   http://www.infsec.ethz.ch/research/projects/mon_enf.html
3. LTLFO2Mon [28] is available at
   https://github.com/jckuester/ltlfo2mon

The review in this section focuses only on tools that can reason about real-time properties of traces (output signals) since this is a necessity for testing and monitoring for Embedded and Cyber-Physical Systems. In addition, the focus is on publicly available software tools for off- and on-line monitoring that can be readily downloaded and utilized in testing and monitoring applications. Some of these tools are open source with licenses that allow extensions and redistribution. In the following, we group the software tools survey into two main broader categories: Boolean semantics and multi-valued semantics.

6.1   Software Tools for Boolean Semantics

In the first category, i.e., Boolean semantics, the tool AMT [108] available at:

http://www-verimag.imag.fr/DIST-TOOLS/TEMPO/AMT/content.html

analyzes STL properties over analog system output signals. In particular, the properties analyzed by AMT are an extension of the industrial specification language PSL with STL requirements. The software tool AMT is a stand alone executable with a graphical interface where the user provides the STL/PSL properties, the signals and whether the analysis is going to be offline or incremental. In return, the tool plots the Boolean satisfaction of each property over time.

6.2   Software Tools for Quantitative Semantics

When considering software tools for evaluating quantitative semantics of STL over signals, there are several options. The following tools are publicly available and they can monitor both real valued and Boolean signals:

1. Breach [46]: available at
   https://github.com/decyphir/breach
2. S-Taliro [10]: available at
   https://sites.google.com/a/asu.edu/s-taliro/
3. U-Check [31]: available at
   https://github.com/dmilios/U-check

Breach and S-Taliro are add-on toolboxes for the Matlab environment while U-Check is a stand-alone program written in Java. Breach and S-Taliro provide analysis tools for black box testing of models and hardware-in-the-loop systems while U-Check deals with stochastic models (Continuous-Time Markov Chains).

The efficient evaluation of STL requirements over real-valued and Boolean signals gave raise to a number of semi-formal verification methods from testing based verification [59] to parameter mining [129,132] to falsification [2] to

Table 2. Tools for reasoning with multi-valued temporal logics and their functionality.

Analysis	Functionality	Breach	S-Taliro	U-Check
Signal	Offline testing	[46,49]	[60–62]	
	Online monitoring	[40]	[43]	
System (best éffort)	Falsification	[46]	[2]	[31]
	Coverage testing		[45]	
	Requirement mining	[129]	[74,132]	
	Parameter synthesis	[46]	[117]	
	Conformance		[4]	
Specification	Visual specifications		[73,75]	
	Debugging		[44]	

synthesis [111]. As reviewed in Sect. 5, the aforementioned methods have been applied to a wide range of practical applications. Table 2 provides an overview with references of the various analysis methods that each tool supports.

7   Conclusion

Cyber-Physical Systems (CPS) combine heterogeneous and networked computational entities with physical components interacting with them through sensors and actuators. Continuous and hybrid behaviours naturally arise from such dynamical systems. Here, we have provided an in-depth overview of the state-of-the-art techniques for CPS monitoring.

The common denominator of all these methods is the possibility to express in a very powerful, concise and unambiguous way the properties of interest using a formal specification language. In this work, we have mainly focused our attention on Signal Temporal Logic (STL), a formalism enabling the designer to reason about real-time properties over real-valued signals. In the recent years, there has been a great effort to provide efficient algorithms to support online and offline monitoring of STL formulas over (system output) signals.

The introduction of novel quantitative semantics has considerably widened the spectrum of applications from just monitoring qualitatively real-time signals to providing novel falsification analysis and parameter synthesis techniques in model-based testing as well as hardware-in-the-loop testing. As a consequence, the application domains have also grown dramatically, ranging now from automotive systems to synthetic biology and medical devices.

We believe that these techniques will play more and more a key role in industry in the design and engineering safe and resilient CPS and/or to equip them with real-time hardware-based monitors enabling CPS self-awareness and adaptation.

Acknowledgment. E. Bartocci and D. Ničković acknowledge the partial support of the EU ICT COST Action IC1402 on Runtime Verification beyond Monitoring (ARVI) and of the HARMONIA (845631) project, funded by a national Austrian grant from Austrian FFG under the program IKT der Zukunft. E. Bartocci acknowledges the partial support of the Austrian National Research Network S 11405-N23 (RiSE/SHiNE) of the Austrian Science Fund (FWF). G. Fainekos acknowledges the support of the NSF CAREER award 1350420.

References

1. Abbas, H., Fainekos, G.: Computing descent direction of MTL robustness for non-linear systems. In: Proceedings of ACC 2013: The 2013 American Control Conference, pp. 4405–4410 (2013)
2. Abbas, H., Fainekos, G.E., Sankaranarayanan, S., Ivancic, F., Gupta, A.: Probabilistic temporal logic falsification of cyber-physical systems. ACM Trans. Embed. Comput. Syst. **12**(s2), 95:1–95:30 (2013)

3. Abbas, H., Hoxha, B., Fainekos, G., Ueda, K.: Robustness-guided temporal logic testing and verification for stochastic cyber-physical systems. In: Proceedings of the 4th Annual IEEE International Conference on Cyber Technology in Automation, Control and Intelligent, pp. 1–6. IEEE (2014)

4. Abbas, H., Mittelmann, H., Fainekos, G.E.: Formal property verification in a conformance testing framework. In: Proceedings of MEMOCODE 2014: The 12th ACM-IEEE International Conference on Formal Methods and Models for System Design, pp. 155–164. IEEE (2014)

5. Abbas, H., Rodionova, A., Bartocci, E., Smolka, S.A., Grosu, R.: Quantitative regular expressions for Arrhythmia detection algorithms. In: Feret, J., Koeppl, H. (eds.) CMSB 2017. LNCS, vol. 10545, pp. 23–39. Springer, Cham (2017). https://doi.org/10.1007/978-3-319-67471-1_2

6. Abbas, H., Winn, A., Fainekos, G.E., Julius, A.A.: Functional gradient descent method for metric temporal logic specifications. In: Proceedings of ACC 2014: The American Control Conference, pp. 2312–2317. IEEE (2014)

7. Akazaki, T., Hasuo, I.: Time robustness in MTL and expressivity in hybrid system falsification. In: Kroening, D., Păsăreanu, C.S. (eds.) CAV 2015. LNCS, vol. 9207, pp. 356–374. Springer, Cham (2015). https://doi.org/10.1007/978-3-319-21668-3_21

8. Alur, R., Feder, T., Henzinger, T.A.: The benefits of relaxing punctuality. J. ACM **43**(1), 116–146 (1996)

9. Annapureddy, Y.S.R., Fainekos, G.E.: Ant colonies for temporal logic falsification of hybrid systems. In: Proceedings of IECON 2010: The 36th Annual Conference on IEEE Industrial Electronics Society, pp. 91–96 (2010)

10. Annpureddy, Y., Liu, C., Fainekos, G., Sankaranarayanan, S.: S-TaLiRo: a tool for temporal logic falsification for hybrid systems. In: Abdulla, P.A., Leino, K.R.M. (eds.) TACAS 2011. LNCS, vol. 6605, pp. 254–257. Springer, Heidelberg (2011). https://doi.org/10.1007/978-3-642-19835-9_21

11. Asarin, E., Caspi, P., Maler, O.: Timed regular expressions. J. ACM **49**(2), 172–206 (2002)

12. Aydin-Gol, E., Bartocci, E., Belta, C.: A formal methods approach to pattern synthesis in reaction diffusion systems. In: Proceedings of CDC 2014: The 53rd IEEE Conference on Decision and Control, pp. 108–113. IEEE (2014)

13. Bartocci, E., Aydin-Gol, E., Haghighi, I., Belta, C.: A formal methods approach to pattern recognition and synthesis in reaction diffusion networks. IEEE Trans. Control Netw. Syst. **PP**(99), 1–12 (2016)

14. Bartocci, E., Bonakdarpour, B., Falcone, Y.: First international competition on software for runtime verification. In: Bonakdarpour, B., Smolka, S.A. (eds.) RV 2014. LNCS, vol. 8734, pp. 1–9. Springer, Cham (2014). https://doi.org/10.1007/978-3-319-11164-3_1

15. Bartocci, E., Bortolussi, L., Loreti, M., Nenzi, L.: Monitoring mobile and spatially distributed cyber-physical systems. In: Proceedings of MEMOCODE 2017: The 15th ACM-IEEE International Conference on Formal Methods and Models for System Design, pp. 146–155. ACM (2017)

16. Bartocci, E., Bortolussi, L., Milios, D., Nenzi, L., Sanguinetti, G.: Studying emergent behaviours in morphogenesis using signal spatio-temporal logic. In: Abate, A., Šafránek, D. (eds.) HSB 2015. LNCS, vol. 9271, pp. 156–172. Springer, Cham (2015). https://doi.org/10.1007/978-3-319-26916-0_9

17. Bartocci, E., Bortolussi, L., Nenzi, L.: A temporal logic approach to modular design of synthetic biological circuits. In: Gupta, A., Henzinger, T.A. (eds.) CMSB 2013. LNCS, vol. 8130, pp. 164–177. Springer, Heidelberg (2013). https://doi.org/10.1007/978-3-642-40708-6_13

18. Bartocci, E., Bortolussi, L., Nenzi, L., Sanguinetti, G.: System design of stochastic models using robustness of temporal properties. Theor. Comput. Sci. **587**, 3–25 (2015)

19. Bartocci, E., Bortolussi, L., Sanguinetti, G.: Data-driven statistical learning of temporal logic properties. In: Legay, A., Bozga, M. (eds.) FORMATS 2014. LNCS, vol. 8711, pp. 23–37. Springer, Cham (2014). https://doi.org/10.1007/978-3-319-10512-3_3

20. Bartocci, E., Corradini, F., Berardini, M.R.D., Entcheva, E., Smolka, S.A., Grosu, R.: Modeling and simulation of cardiac tissue using hybrid I/O automata. Theor. Comput. Sci. **410**(33–34), 3149–3165 (2009)

21. Bartocci, E., Corradini, F., Merelli, E., Tesei, L.: Model checking biological oscillators. Electr. Notes Theor. Comput. Sci. **229**(1), 41–58 (2009)

22. Bartocci, E., Corradini, F., Merelli, E., Tesei, L.: Detecting synchronisation of biological oscillators by model checking. Theor. Comput. Sci. **411**(20), 1999–2018 (2010)

23. Bartocci, E., Falcone, Y., Bonakdarpour, B., Colombo, C., Decker, N., Havelund, K., Joshi, Y., Klaedtke, F., Milewicz, R., Reger, G., Rosu, G., Signoles, J., Thoma, D., Zalinescu, E., Zhang, Y.: First international competition on runtime verification: rules, benchmarks, tools, and final results of CRV 2014. Int. J. Softw. Tools Technol. Transf., 1–40, April 2017

24. Bartocci, E., Grosu, R., Karmarkar, A., Smolka, S.A., Stoller, S.D., Zadok, E., Seyster, J.: Adaptive runtime verification. In: Qadeer, S., Tasiran, S. (eds.) RV 2012. LNCS, vol. 7687, pp. 168–182. Springer, Heidelberg (2013). https://doi.org/10.1007/978-3-642-35632-2_18

25. Bartocci, E., Liò, P.: Computational modeling, formal analysis, and tools for systems biology. PLoS Comput. Biol. **12**(1), 1–22 (2016)

26. Basin, D., Caronni, G., Ereth, S., Harvan, M., Klaedtke, F., Mantel, H.: Scalable offline monitoring. In: Bonakdarpour, B., Smolka, S.A. (eds.) RV 2014. LNCS, vol. 8734, pp. 31–47. Springer, Cham (2014). https://doi.org/10.1007/978-3-319-11164-3_4

27. Basin, D., Harvan, M., Klaedtke, F., Zălinescu, E.: MONPOLY: monitoring usage-control policies. In: Khurshid, S., Sen, K. (eds.) RV 2011. LNCS, vol. 7186, pp. 360–364. Springer, Heidelberg (2012). https://doi.org/10.1007/978-3-642-29860-8_27

28. Bauer, A., Küster, J.-C., Vegliach, G.: From propositional to first-order monitoring. In: Legay, A., Bensalem, S. (eds.) RV 2013. LNCS, vol. 8174, pp. 59–75. Springer, Heidelberg (2013). https://doi.org/10.1007/978-3-642-40787-1_4

29. Bauer, A., Leucker, M., Schallhart, C.: Monitoring of real-time properties. In: Arun-Kumar, S., Garg, N. (eds.) FSTTCS 2006. LNCS, vol. 4337, pp. 260–272. Springer, Heidelberg (2006). https://doi.org/10.1007/11944836_25

30. Bauer, A., Leucker, M., Schallhart, C.: Comparing LTL semantics for runtime verification. J. Logic Comput. **20**(3), 651–674 (2010)

31. Bortolussi, L., Milios, D., Sanguinetti, G.: U-check: model checking and parameter synthesis under uncertainty. In: Campos, J., Haverkort, B.R. (eds.) QEST 2015. LNCS, vol. 9259, pp. 89–104. Springer, Cham (2015). https://doi.org/10.1007/978-3-319-22264-6_6

32. Brim, L., Dluhos, P., Safránek, D., Vejpustek, T.: STL*: Extending signal temporal logic with signal-value freezing operator. Inf. Comput. **236**, 52–67 (2014)

33. Brim, L., Vejpustek, T., Safránek, D., Fabriková, J.: Robustness analysis for value-freezing signal temporal logic. In: Proceedings of HSB 2013: The Second International Workshop on Hybrid Systems and Biology. EPTCS, vol. 125, pp. 20–36 (2013)

34. Bufo, S., Bartocci, E., Sanguinetti, G., Borelli, M., Lucangelo, U., Bortolussi, L.: Temporal logic based monitoring of assisted ventilation in intensive care patients. In: Margaria, T., Steffen, B. (eds.) ISoLA 2014. LNCS, vol. 8803, pp. 391–403. Springer, Heidelberg (2014). https://doi.org/10.1007/978-3-662-45231-8_30

35. Cameron, F., Wilson, D.M., Buckingham, B.A., Arzumanyan, H., Clinton, P., Chase, H.P., Lum, J., Maahs, D.M., Calhoun, P.M., Bequette, B.W.: Inpatient studies of a Kalman-filter-based predictive pump shutoff algorithm. J. Diabetes Sci. Technol. **6**(5), 1142–1147 (2012)

36. Cameron, F., Fainekos, G., Maahs, D.M., Sankaranarayanan, S.: Towards a verified artificial pancreas: challenges and solutions for runtime verification. In: Bartocci, E., Majumdar, R. (eds.) RV 2015. LNCS, vol. 9333, pp. 3–17. Springer, Cham (2015). https://doi.org/10.1007/978-3-319-23820-3_1

37. Chakarov, A., Sankaranarayanan, S., Fainekos, G.: Combining time and frequency domain specifications for periodic signals. In: Khurshid, S., Sen, K. (eds.) RV 2011. LNCS, vol. 7186, pp. 294–309. Springer, Heidelberg (2012). https://doi.org/10.1007/978-3-642-29860-8_22

38. Cobelli, C., Man, C.D., Sparacino, G., Magni, L., Nicolao, G.D., Kovatchev, B.P.: Diabetes: Models, signals and control (methodological review). IEEE Rev. Biomed. Eng. **2**, 54–95 (2009)

39. D'Angelo, B., Sankaranarayanan, S., Sanchez, C., Robinson, W., Finkbeiner, B., Sipma, H., Mehrotra, S., Manna, Z.: LOLA: runtime monitoring of synchronous systems. In: Proceedings of TIME 2005: The 12th International Symposium on Temporal Representation and Reasoning, pp. 166–174. IEEE (2005)

40. Deshmukh, J.V., Donzé, A., Ghosh, S., Jin, X., Juniwal, G., Seshia, S.A.: Robust online monitoring of signal temporal logic. In: Bartocci, E., Majumdar, R. (eds.) RV 2015. LNCS, vol. 9333, pp. 55–70. Springer, Cham (2015). https://doi.org/10.1007/978-3-319-23820-3_4

41. Deshmukh, J.V., Donzé, A., Ghosh, S., Jin, X., Garvit, J., Seshia, S.A.: Robust online monitoring of signal temporal logic. Formal Methods Syst. Des. **51**(1), 5–30 (2017)

42. Deshmukh, J.V., Majumdar, R., Prabhu, V.S.: Quantifying conformance using the Skorokhod metric. In: Kroening, D., Păsăreanu, C.S. (eds.) CAV 2015. LNCS, vol. 9207, pp. 234–250. Springer, Cham (2015). https://doi.org/10.1007/978-3-319-21668-3_14

43. Dokhanchi, A., Hoxha, B., Fainekos, G.: On-line monitoring for temporal logic robustness. In: Bonakdarpour, B., Smolka, S.A. (eds.) RV 2014. LNCS, vol. 8734, pp. 231–246. Springer, Cham (2014). https://doi.org/10.1007/978-3-319-11164-3_19

44. Dokhanchi, A., Hoxha, B., Fainekos, G.E.: Metric interval temporal logic specification elicitation and debugging. In: Proceedings of MEMOCODE 2015: The 13th ACM/IEEE International Conference on Formal Methods and Models for Codesign, pp. 70–79. IEEE (2015)

45. Dokhanchi, A., Zutshi, A., Sriniva, R.T., Sankaranarayanan, S., Fainekos, G.: Requirements driven falsification with coverage metrics. In: Proceedings of EMSOFT: The 12th International Conference on Embedded Software, pp. 31–40. IEEE (2015)

46. Donzé, A.: Breach, a toolbox for verification and parameter synthesis of hybrid systems. In: Touili, T., Cook, B., Jackson, P. (eds.) CAV 2010. LNCS, vol. 6174, pp. 167–170. Springer, Heidelberg (2010). https://doi.org/10.1007/978-3-642-14295-6_17

47. Donzé, A., Clermont, G., Legay, A., Langmead, C.J.: Parameter synthesis in nonlinear dynamical systems: application to systems biology. In: Batzoglou, S. (ed.) RECOMB 2009. LNCS, vol. 5541, pp. 155–169. Springer, Heidelberg (2009). https://doi.org/10.1007/978-3-642-02008-7_11

48. Donzé, A., Fanchon, E., Gattepaille, L.M., Maler, O., Tracqui, P.: Robustness analysis and behavior discrimination in enzymatic reaction networks. PLoS ONE 6(9), e24246 (2011)

49. Donzé, A., Ferrère, T., Maler, O.: Efficient robust monitoring for STL. In: Sharygina, N., Veith, H. (eds.) CAV 2013. LNCS, vol. 8044, pp. 264–279. Springer, Heidelberg (2013). https://doi.org/10.1007/978-3-642-39799-8_19

50. Donzé, A., Krogh, B., Rajhans, A.: Parameter synthesis for hybrid systems with an application to simulink models. In: Majumdar, R., Tabuada, P. (eds.) HSCC 2009. LNCS, vol. 5469, pp. 165–179. Springer, Heidelberg (2009). https://doi.org/10.1007/978-3-642-00602-9_12

51. Donzé, A., Maler, O.: Robust satisfaction of temporal logic over real-valued signals. In: Chatterjee, K., Henzinger, T.A. (eds.) FORMATS 2010. LNCS, vol. 6246, pp. 92–106. Springer, Heidelberg (2010). https://doi.org/10.1007/978-3-642-15297-9_9

52. Donzé, A., Maler, O., Bartocci, E., Nickovic, D., Grosu, R., Smolka, S.: On temporal logic and signal processing. In: Chakraborty, S., Mukund, M. (eds.) ATVA 2012. LNCS, pp. 92–106. Springer, Heidelberg (2012). https://doi.org/10.1007/978-3-642-33386-6_9

53. Dreossi, T., Dang, T., Donzé, A., Kapinski, J., Jin, X., Deshmukh, J.V.: Efficient guiding strategies for testing of temporal properties of hybrid systems. In: Havelund, K., Holzmann, G., Joshi, R. (eds.) NFM 2015. LNCS, vol. 9058, pp. 127–142. Springer, Cham (2015). https://doi.org/10.1007/978-3-319-17524-9_10

54. Drusinsky, D.: Monitoring temporal rules combined with time series. In: Hunt, W.A., Somenzi, F. (eds.) CAV 2003. LNCS, vol. 2725, pp. 114–117. Springer, Heidelberg (2003). https://doi.org/10.1007/978-3-540-45069-6_11

55. Eisner, C., Fisman, D.: A Practical Introduction to PSL. Springer, Heidelberg (2006). https://doi.org/10.1007/978-0-387-36123-9

56. Eisner, C., Fisman, D., Havlicek, J.: A topological characterization of weakness. In: Proceedings of PODC 2005: The 24th Annual ACM Symposium on Principles of Distributed Computing, pp. 1–8. ACM (2005)

57. Eisner, C., Fisman, D., Havlicek, J., Lustig, Y., McIsaac, A., Van Campenhout, D.: Reasoning with temporal logic on truncated paths. In: Hunt, W.A., Somenzi, F. (eds.) CAV 2003. LNCS, vol. 2725, pp. 27–39. Springer, Heidelberg (2003). https://doi.org/10.1007/978-3-540-45069-6_3

58. Fainekos, G.E., Giannakoglou, K.C.: Inverse design of airfoils based on a novel formulation of the ant colony optimization method. Inverse Prob. Eng. 11(1), 21–38 (2003)

59. Fainekos, G.E., Girard, A., Pappas, G.J.: Temporal logic verification using simulation. In: Asarin, E., Bouyer, P. (eds.) FORMATS 2006. LNCS, vol. 4202, pp. 171–186. Springer, Heidelberg (2006). https://doi.org/10.1007/11867340_13
60. Fainekos, G.E., Pappas, G.J.: Robustness of temporal logic specifications. In: Havelund, K., Núñez, M., Roşu, G., Wolff, B. (eds.) FATES/RV 2006. LNCS, vol. 4262, pp. 178–192. Springer, Heidelberg (2006). https://doi.org/10.1007/11940197_12
61. Fainekos, G.E., Pappas, G.J.: Robustness of temporal logic specifications for continuous-time signals. Theor. Comput. Sci. **410**(42), 4262–4291 (2009)
62. Fainekos, G.E., Sankaranarayanan, S., Ueda, K., Yazarel, H.: Verification of automotive control applications using S-TaLiRo. In: Proceedings of ACC 2012: The 2012 American Control Conference, pp. 3567–3572. IEEE (2012)
63. Falcone, Y., Ničković, D., Reger, G., Thoma, D.: Second international competition on runtime verification. In: Bartocci, E., Majumdar, R. (eds.) RV 2015. LNCS, vol. 9333, pp. 405–422. Springer, Cham (2015). https://doi.org/10.1007/978-3-319-23820-3_27
64. Ferrère, T.: Assertions and measurements for mixed-signal simulation. Ph.D. thesis. Université Grenoble-Alpes, France (2016)
65. Ferrère, T., Maler, O., Ničković, D., Ulus, D.: Measuring with timed patterns. In: Kroening, D., Păsăreanu, C.S. (eds.) CAV 2015. LNCS, vol. 9207, pp. 322–337. Springer, Cham (2015). https://doi.org/10.1007/978-3-319-21668-3_19
66. Finkbeiner, B., Sipma, H.B.: Checking finite traces using alternating automata. Formal Methods Syst. Des. **24**(2), 101–127 (2004)
67. Grosu, R., Batt, G., Fenton, F.H., Glimm, J., Le Guernic, C., Smolka, S.A., Bartocci, E.: From cardiac cells to genetic regulatory networks. In: Gopalakrishnan, G., Qadeer, S. (eds.) CAV 2011. LNCS, vol. 6806, pp. 396–411. Springer, Heidelberg (2011). https://doi.org/10.1007/978-3-642-22110-1_31
68. Grosu, R., Smolka, S.A., Corradini, F., Wasilewska, A., Entcheva, E., Bartocci, E.: Learning and detecting emergent behavior in networks of cardiac myocytes. Commun. ACM **52**(3), 97–105 (2009)
69. Haghighi, I., Jones, A., Kong, Z., Bartocci, E., Grosu, R., Belta, C.: SpaTeL: a novel spatial-temporal logic and its applications to networked systems. In: Proceedings of HSCC 2015: The 18th International Conference on Hybrid Systems: Computation and Control, pp. 189–198. IEEE (2015)
70. Havelund, K., Rosu, G.: Monitoring Java programs with Java pathexplorer. Electron. Not. Theoret. Comput. Sci. **55**(2), 200–217 (2001)
71. Ho, H.-M., Ouaknine, J., Worrell, J.: Online monitoring of metric temporal logic. In: Bonakdarpour, B., Smolka, S.A. (eds.) RV 2014. LNCS, vol. 8734, pp. 178–192. Springer, Cham (2014). https://doi.org/10.1007/978-3-319-11164-3_15
72. Hovorka, R.: Continuous glucose monitoring and closed-loop systems. Diabet. Med. **23**(1), 1–12 (2005)
73. Hoxha, B., Bach, H., Abbas, H., Dokhanci, A., Kobayashi, Y., Fainekos, G.: Towards formal specification visualization for testing and monitoring of cyber-physical systems. In: International Workshop on Design and Implementation of Formal Tools and Systems, DIFTS 2014 (2014)
74. Hoxha, B., Dokhanchi, A., Fainekos, G.: Mining parametric temporal logic properties in model based design for cyber-physical systems. Int. J. Softw. Tools Technol. Transf. (2017). (in press)

75. Hoxha, B., Mavridis, N., Fainekos, G.E.: VISPEC: a graphical tool for elicitation of MTL requirements. In: Proceedings of IROS 2015: The 2015 IEEE/RSJ International Conference on Intelligent Robots and Systems, pp. 3486–3492. IEEE (2015)

76. MathWorks, Inc.: Test generated code with SIL and PIL simulations, cf. https://www.mathworks.com/help/ecoder/examples/software-and-processor-in-the-loop-sil-and-pil-simulation.html

77. Jaksic, S., Bartocci, E., Grosu, R., Kloibhofer, R., Nguyen, T., Ničković, D.: From signal temporal logic to FPGA monitors. In: Proceedings of MEMOCODE 2015: The 13th ACM/IEEE International Conference on Formal Methods and Models for Codesign, pp. 218–227. IEEE (2015)

78. Jakšić, S., Bartocci, E., Grosu, R., Ničković, D.: Quantitative monitoring of STL with edit distance. In: Falcone, Y., Sánchez, C. (eds.) RV 2016. LNCS, vol. 10012, pp. 201–218. Springer, Cham (2016). https://doi.org/10.1007/978-3-319-46982-9_13

79. Jensen, J.C., Chang, D.H., Lee, E.A.: A model-based design methodology for cyber-physical systems. In: Proceedings of IEEE Workshop on Design, Modeling, and Evaluation of Cyber-Physical Systems (CyPhy), pp. 1666–1671. IEEE (2011)

80. Jiang, Z., Pajic, M., Alur, R., Mangharam, R.: Closed-loop verification of medical devices with model abstraction and refinement. Int. J. Softw. Tools Technol. Transfer **16**(2), 191–213 (2014)

81. Jiang, Z., Pajic, M., Moarref, S., Alur, R., Mangharam, R.: Modeling and verification of a dual chamber implantable pacemaker. In: Flanagan, C., König, B. (eds.) TACAS 2012. LNCS, vol. 7214, pp. 188–203. Springer, Heidelberg (2012). https://doi.org/10.1007/978-3-642-28756-5_14

82. Juniwal, G., Donzé, A., Jensen, J.C., Seshia, S.A.: CPSGrader: synthesizing temporal logic testers for auto-grading an embedded systems laboratory. In: Proceedings of EMSOFT 2014: The 2014 International Conference on Embedded Software, pp. 24:1–24:10. IEEE (2014)

83. Kalajdzic, K., Bartocci, E., Smolka, S.A., Stoller, S.D., Grosu, R.: Runtime verification with particle filtering. In: Legay, A., Bensalem, S. (eds.) RV 2013. LNCS, vol. 8174, pp. 149–166. Springer, Heidelberg (2013). https://doi.org/10.1007/978-3-642-40787-1_9

84. Kane, A.: Runtime monitoring for safety-critical embedded systems. Ph.D. thesis, Carnegie Mellon University, College of Engineering (2015)

85. Kapinski, J., Jin, X., Deshmukh, J., Donzé, A., Yamaguchi, T., Ito, H., Kaga, T., Kobuna, S., Seshia, S.: ST-Lib: a library for specifying and classifying model behaviors. In: SAE Technical Paper. SAE International (2016)

86. Kowalski, A.: Pathway to artificial pancreas revisited: moving downstream. Diabetes Care **38**, 1036–1043 (2015)

87. Koymans, R.: Specifying real-time properties with metric temporal logic. Real-Time Syst. **2**(4), 255–299 (1990)

88. Lee, E.A.: Cyber physical systems: design challenges. In: Proceedings of ISORC 2011: The 11th IEEE International Symposium on Object and Component-Oriented Real-Time Distributed Computing, pp. 363–369, May 2008

89. Lee, I., Kannan, S., Kim, M., Sokolsky, O., Viswanathan, M.: Runtime assurance based on formal specifications. In: Proceedings of PDPTA 1999: The International Conference on Parallel and Distributed Processing Techniques and Applications, pp. 279–287. CSREA Press (1999)

90. Lemire, D.: Streaming maximum-minimum filter using no more than three comparisons per element. Nord. J. Comput. **13**(4), 328–339 (2006)

91. Luo, Q., Zhang, Y., Lee, C., Jin, D., Meredith, P.O.N., Şerbănuţă, T.F., Roşu, G.: RV-Monitor: efficient parametric runtime verification with simultaneous properties. In: Bonakdarpour, B., Smolka, S.A. (eds.) RV 2014. LNCS, vol. 8734, pp. 285–300. Springer, Cham (2014). https://doi.org/10.1007/978-3-319-11164-3_24
92. Maahs, D.M., Calhoun, P., Buckingham, B.A., et al.: A randomized trial of a home system to reduce nocturnal hypoglycemia in type 1 diabetes. Diabetes Care 37(7), 1885–1891 (2014)
93. Majumdar, R., Prabhu, V.S.: Computing the Skorokhod distance between polygonal traces. In: Proceedings of HSCC 2015: The 18th International Conference on Hybrid Systems: Computation and Control, pp. 199–208. ACM (2015)
94. Majumdar, R., Prabhu, V.S.: Computing distances between reach flowpipes. In: Proceedings of HSCC 2016: The 19th International Conference on Hybrid Systems: Computation and Control, pp. 267–276. ACM (2016)
95. Maler, O.: Some thoughts on runtime verification. In: Falcone, Y., Sánchez, C. (eds.) RV 2016. LNCS, vol. 10012, pp. 3–14. Springer, Cham (2016). https://doi.org/10.1007/978-3-319-46982-9_1
96. Maler, O., Nickovic, D.: Monitoring temporal properties of continuous signals. In: Lakhnech, Y., Yovine, S. (eds.) FORMATS/FTRTFT 2004. LNCS, vol. 3253, pp. 152–166. Springer, Heidelberg (2004). https://doi.org/10.1007/978-3-540-30206-3_12
97. Maler, O., Ničković, D.: Monitoring properties of analog and mixed-signal circuits. STTT 15(3), 247–268 (2013)
98. Maler, O., Nickovic, D., Pnueli, A.: Checking temporal properties of discrete, timed and continuous behaviors. In: Avron, A., Dershowitz, N., Rabinovich, A. (eds.) Pillars of Computer Science. LNCS, vol. 4800, pp. 475–505. Springer, Heidelberg (2008). https://doi.org/10.1007/978-3-540-78127-1_26
99. Man, C.D., Raimondo, D.M., Rizza, R.A., Cobelli, C.: GIM, simulation software of meal glucose-insulin model. J. Diabetes Sci. Tech. 1(3), 323–330 (2007)
100. Mobilia, N., Donzé, A., Marc Moulis, J., Fanchon, E.: Producing a set of models for the iron homeostasis network. In: Proceedings of HSB 2013: The Second International Workshop on Hybrid Systems and Biology. EPTCS, vol. 125, pp. 92–98 (2013)
101. Nelder, J.A., Mead, R.: A simplex method for function minimization. Comput. J. 7, 308–313 (1965)
102. Nenzi, L., Bortolussi, L., Ciancia, V., Loreti, M., Massink, M.: Qualitative and quantitative monitoring of spatio-temporal properties. In: Bartocci, E., Majumdar, R. (eds.) RV 2015. LNCS, vol. 9333, pp. 21–37. Springer, Cham (2015). https://doi.org/10.1007/978-3-319-23820-3_2
103. Nghiem, T., Sankaranarayanan, S., Fainekos, G.E., Ivancic, F., Gupta, A., Pappas, G.J.: Monte-carlo techniques for falsification of temporal properties of non-linear hybrid systems. In: Proceedings of HSCC 2010: The 13th ACM International Conference on Hybrid Systems: Computation and Control, pp. 211–220. ACM (2010)
104. Nguyen, L., Kapinski, J., Jin, X., Deshmukh, J., Butts, K., Johnson, T.: Abnormal data classification using time-frequency temporal logic. In: Proceedings of HSCC 2017: The 20th ACM International Conference on Hybrid Systems: Computation and Control, pp. 237–242. ACM (2017)
105. Nguyen, T., Bartocci, E., Ničković, D., Grosu, R., Jaksic, S., Selyunin, K.: The HARMONIA project: hardware monitoring for automotive systems-of-systems. In: Margaria, T., Steffen, B. (eds.) ISoLA 2016. LNCS, vol. 9953, pp. 371–379. Springer, Cham (2016). https://doi.org/10.1007/978-3-319-47169-3_28

106. Nguyen, T., Ničković, D.: Assertion-based monitoring in practice – checking correctness of an automotive sensor interface. In: Lang, F., Flammini, F. (eds.) FMICS 2014. LNCS, vol. 8718, pp. 16–32. Springer, Cham (2014). https://doi.org/10.1007/978-3-319-10702-8_2

107. Nickovic, D.: Checking timed and hybrid properties: theory and applications. Ph.D. thesis. Université Joseph Fourier, Grenoble, France (2008)

108. Nickovic, D., Maler, O.: AMT: a property-based monitoring tool for analog systems. In: Raskin, J.-F., Thiagarajan, P.S. (eds.) FORMATS 2007. LNCS, vol. 4763, pp. 304–319. Springer, Heidelberg (2007). https://doi.org/10.1007/978-3-540-75454-1_22

109. Pajic, M., Mangharam, R., Sokolsky, O., Arney, D., Goldman, J., Lee, I.: Model-driven safety analysis of closed-loop medical systems. IEEE Trans. Ind. Inform. **10**(1), 3–16 (2014)

110. Pnueli, A.: The temporal logic of programs. In: Proceedings of the 18th Annual Symposium on Foundations of Computer Science, pp. 46–57. IEEE (1977)

111. Raman, V., Donzé, A., Sadigh, D., M. Murray, R., Seshia, S.A.: Reactive synthesis from signal temporal logic specifications. In: Proceedings of the HSCC 2015: The 18th International Conference on Hybrid Systems: Computation and Control, pp. 239–248. ACM (2015)

112. Reger, G., Hallé, S., Falcone, Y.: Third international competition on runtime verification. In: Falcone, Y., Sánchez, C. (eds.) RV 2016. LNCS, vol. 10012, pp. 21–37. Springer, Cham (2016). https://doi.org/10.1007/978-3-319-46982-9_3

113. Rizk, A., Batt, G., Fages, F., Soliman, S.: On a continuous degree of satisfaction of temporal logic formulae with applications to systems biology. In: Heiner, M., Uhrmacher, A.M. (eds.) CMSB 2008. LNCS (LNAI), vol. 5307, pp. 251–268. Springer, Heidelberg (2008). https://doi.org/10.1007/978-3-540-88562-7_19

114. Rodionova, A., Bartocci, E., Ničković, D., Grosu, R.: Temporal logic as filtering. In: Proceedings of HSCC 2016: The 19th International Conference on Hybrid Systems: Computation and Control, pp. 11–20. ACM (2016)

115. Sankaranarayanan, S., Fainekos, G.: Falsification of temporal properties of hybrid systems using the cross-entropy method. In: Proceedings of HSCC 2012: The 15th ACM International Conference on Hybrid Systems: Computation and Control, pp. 125–134. ACM (2012)

116. Sankaranarayanan, S., Kumar, S.A., Cameron, F., Bequette, B.W., Fainekos, G.E., Maahs, D.M.: Model-based falsification of an artificial pancreas control system. SIGBED Rev. **14**(2), 24–33 (2017)

117. Sankaranarayanan, S., Miller, C., Raghunathan, R., Ravanbakhsh, H., Fainekos, G.E.: A model-based approach to synthesizing insulin infusion pump usage parameters for diabetic patients. In: Proceedings of the 50th Annual Allerton Conference on Communication, Control, and Computing, pp. 1610–1617. IEEE (2012)

118. Selyunin, K., Jaksic, S., Nguyen, T., Reidl, C., Hafner, U., Bartocci, E., Nickovic, D., Grosu, R.: Runtime monitoring with recovery of the SENT communication protocol. In: Majumdar, R., Kunčak, V. (eds.) CAV 2017. LNCS, vol. 10426, pp. 336–355. Springer, Cham (2017). https://doi.org/10.1007/978-3-319-63387-9_17

119. Selyunin, K., Nguyen, T., Bartocci, E., Grosu, R.: Applying runtime monitoring for automotive electronic development. In: Falcone, Y., Sánchez, C. (eds.) RV 2016. LNCS, vol. 10012, pp. 462–469. Springer, Cham (2016). https://doi.org/10.1007/978-3-319-46982-9_30

120. Short, M., Pont, M.J.: Hardware in the loop simulation of embedded automotive control system. In: Proceedings of 2005 IEEE Intelligent Transportation Systems, pp. 426–431. IEEE, September 2005

121. Steil, G.M.: Algorithms for a closed-loop artificial pancreas: the case for proportional-integral-derivative control. J. Diabetes Sci. Technol. **7**, 1621–1631 (2013)

122. Steil, G., Panteleon, A., Rebrin, K.: Closed-sloop insulin delivery - the path to physiological glucose control. Adv. Drug Deliv. Rev. **56**(2), 125–144 (2004)

123. Stoma, S., Donzé, A., Bertaux, F., Maler, O., Batt, G.: STL-based analysis of TRAIL-induced apoptosis challenges the notion of type I/type II cell line classification. PLoS Comput. Biol. **9**(5), e1003056 (2013)

124. Ulus, D., Ferrère, T., Asarin, E., Maler, O.: Timed pattern matching. In: Legay, A., Bozga, M. (eds.) FORMATS 2014. LNCS, vol. 8711, pp. 222–236. Springer, Cham (2014). https://doi.org/10.1007/978-3-319-10512-3_16

125. Ulus, D., Ferrère, T., Asarin, E., Maler, O.: Online timed pattern matching using derivatives. In: Chechik, M., Raskin, J.-F. (eds.) TACAS 2016. LNCS, vol. 9636, pp. 736–751. Springer, Heidelberg (2016). https://doi.org/10.1007/978-3-662-49674-9_47

126. Vijayaraghavan, S., Ramanathan, M.: A Practical Guide for SystemVerilog Assertions. Springer, New York (2006). https://doi.org/10.1007/b137011

127. Watterson, C., Heffernan, D.: Runtime verification and monitoring of embedded systems. IET Softw. **1**(5), 172–179 (2007)

128. Weinzimer, S., Steil, G., Swan, K., Dziura, J., Kurtz, N., Tamborlane, W.: Fully automated closed-loop insulin delivery versus semiautomated hybrid control in pediatric patients with type 1 diabetes using an artificial pancreas. Diabetes Care **31**, 934–939 (2008)

129. Xiaoqing, J., Donzé, A., Deshmukh, J.V., Seshia, S.A.: Mining requirements from closed-loop control models. In: Proceedings of HSCC 2013: The ACM International Conference on Hybrid Systems: Computation and Control, pp. 43–52. ACM (2013)

130. Yaghoubi, S., Fainekos, G.: Hybrid approximate gradient and stochastic descent for falsification of nonlinear systems. In: Proceedings of ACC 2017: The 2017 American Control Conference, pp. 529–534. IEEE (2017)

131. Yamaguchi, T., Kaga, T., Donzé, A., Seshia, S.A.: Combining requirement mining, software model checking, and simulation-based verification for industrial automotive systems. In: Proceedings of FMCAD 2016: The 16th International Conference on Formal Methods in Computer-Aided Design, pp. 201–204 (2016)

132. Yang, H., Hoxha, B., Fainekos, G.: Querying parametric temporal logic properties on embedded systems. In: Nielsen, B., Weise, C. (eds.) ICTSS 2012. LNCS, vol. 7641, pp. 136–151. Springer, Heidelberg (2012). https://doi.org/10.1007/978-3-642-34691-0_11

Runtime Verification for Decentralised and Distributed Systems

Adrian Francalanza[1], Jorge A. Pérez[2,3], and César Sánchez[4(✉)]

[1] CS@ICT, University of Malta, Msida, Malta
adrian.francalanza@um.edu.mt
[2] University of Groningen, Groningen, The Netherlands
j.a.perez@rug.nl
[3] CWI, Amsterdam, The Netherlands
[4] IMDEA Software Institute, Madrid, Spain
cesar.sanchez@imdea.org

Abstract. This chapter surveys runtime verification research related to distributed systems. We report solutions that study how to monitor system with some distributed characteristic, solutions that use a distributed platform for performing a monitoring task, and foundational works that present semantics for decomposing monitors or expressing specifications amenable for distributed systems.

We will identify some characteristics that distinguish distributed monitoring from centralised monitoring, and characteristics that allow to classify distributed runtime verification works based on features of the executing platforms, the specification language and the system description. Then, we will use these characteristics to describe and compare the distributed runtime verification solutions proposed in the research literature.

Keywords: Monitoring distributed systems · Distributed monitoring
Decentralised monitoring · Monitor decomposition

1 Introduction

This chapter surveys works on runtime verification (RV) related to distributed computing systems. Distributed computing is the area of computer science devoted to the study of *distributed systems*: computational artifacts that run in execution units placed at different locations, and that exchange information using a communication infrastructure, such as a computer network (see Coulouris [38], Garg [62], Attiya and Welch [4]).

Since distributed systems encompass many different but related classes of systems, the terminology has not been uniformly used. We begin by clarifying what we mean in this chapter by different terms and conventions commonly used in distributed computing, particularly with respect to monitoring.

The computational units that form a distributed system are typically able to execute processes simultaneously, under true concurrency. Each computational

© Springer International Publishing AG, part of Springer Nature 2018
E. Bartocci and Y. Falcone (Eds.): Lectures on Runtime Verification, LNCS 10457, pp. 176–210, 2018.
https://doi.org/10.1007/978-3-319-75632-5_6

unit can run more than one *process*, and independently manage a set of local resources, typically including local memory and a local clock. We call each of these computational units a *location*.

There are two large classes of distributed systems, according to the way in which processes communicate and synchronize: systems that can use shared memory, and systems that can only use some form of message passing as means of communication. It is nowadays widely accepted to refer to the former as *parallel systems* and to the latter as distributed systems, and here we follow this convention. Additionally, some systems assume the existence of a shared clock (also called global clock) among the computational units, which is another usual classification criteria. When one assumes the existence of a global clock, the distributed system is usually called synchronous or *decentralised system*. If the global clock is not assumed then the system is called asynchronous distributed system or simply a *distributed system*. Sometimes the communication infrastructure within the distributed system is simple, as in the case of buses or broadcast communication, but it is often the case that the network *topology* is relevant for the study of a given class of distributed systems. We follow the convention that, unless specified otherwise, all execution units can talk to all other execution units directly.

In practice, components of distributed systems can fail independently. Locations are typically the units of failure, modeling crashes on the execution platform that cause all processes in the location to stop their execution. Moreover, messages in message passing systems can arrive out-of-order, be duplicated or lost, or experience unbounded delays. The nature of the failures and the high independence of failure between the different components is another factor of complexity when dealing with distributed systems. Unless stated, it is common in distributed systems to assume that the system under study presents no failures. We follow this convention here too.

Due to their concurrent nature and to the other aspects of distribution, it is well-known that distributed systems are notoriously difficult to design and reason about. Throughout the years researchers have proposed many techniques to increase the reliability of distributed algorithms and systems, including dynamic solutions. These efforts include the development of runtime verification techniques for distributed computing, which we report here. We will use *distributed runtime verification* to refer to the broad area of research that studies runtime verification in connection with distributed or decentralised systems. This includes the monitoring of distributed systems as well as the use of distributed systems for monitoring. Due again to these intrinsic difficulties, distributed runtime verification is a very active area of research and new results will be produced in the near future.

Terminology. A distributed and decentralised monitoring setting is typically built from subsystems, which we identify with processes for the discussion in this chapter. We use $P_1, P_2, \ldots$ to refer to processes. Processes execute independently and occasionally synchronize or communicate with each another via the underlying communication platform.

Processes are partitioned across locations, meaning that every process is located at exactly one location for any given instance. We use $l, k, \ldots$ to refer to locations. When two processes are co-located at the same location, we say that they are *local* to one another. Otherwise, we say that they are *remote*. Processes may interact and communicate with both local and remote processes. Remote communication is typically assumed to be more expensive than its local counterpart.

A *local trace* (or simply a *trace*), denoted $T_1, T_2, \ldots$ constitutes a log of past behavior used for monitoring purposes. A trace consists of a totally ordered set of trace *events*, each describing discrete computational steps of the monitored system. The ordering of trace events is necessary for the monitoring of temporal properties. A trace can describe events corresponding to a single process or else a group of processes. Although a particular location may host a number of traces (e.g., one per process hosted), we assume that a local trace cannot span across locations.

A monitoring task can be performed *online*, while the system under analysis is running, or *offline* by analysing the log after the system has finished its execution. Here we consider both kinds of solutions.

In runtime verification, monitors are created from specifications, but we will use monitoring and runtime verification interchangeably in this chapter. In online runtime verification, *monitors*—denoted as $M_1, M_2, \ldots$—are computing entities that check at runtime for the satisfaction or violation of correctness properties of the running system. Different monitors can be created to verify different properties simultaneously, and also in a modular fashion, which generally leads to better separation of concerns. The checking that the monitors perform is carried out by analysing the traces generated by the executing processes. Similar to processes, monitors are hosted by a single location for any given instance. We allow monitors to analyse multiple traces in order to generate composite traces. We do not put restrictions on whether a monitor is allowed to analyse local or remote traces, but highlight the fact that remote trace analysis may carry additional overhead costs and entail higher security risks. Monitors are allowed to communicate with one another, which gives the flexibility for property checking to be carried out in a decentralised or choreographed manner (see Sects. 4.2 and 4.4).

The rest of the chapter is organised as follows. Section 2 presents a collection of reasons that have been proposed in the literature to motivate the study of distributed runtime verification problems. Section 3 identifies a number of characteristics that are relevant in the study of the solutions proposed; these characteristics serve as a basis to classify and compare the proposed solutions. Section 4 contains a description of the different ways to organize the activities carried out by the monitoring infrastructures. Section 5 describes a collection of solutions proposed in the literature, classified according to the attributes described in the preceding sections. Finally, Sect. 6 presents current challenges and concluding remarks. The following diagram illustrates the dependencies between the sections.

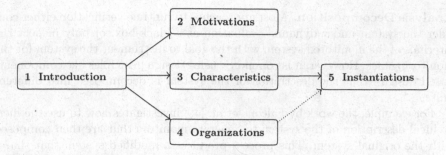

Essentially, Sect. 5 contains the description and comparison of relevant work, using the classification characteristics extracted in Sect. 3.

2 Motivation and Scenarios

In this section we justify the study of distributed runtime verification. We present different scenarios that motivated research related to distributed runtime verification, according to the problem that these efforts were trying to solve. The list we present here is not intended to be exhaustive but its purpose is to give some practical justifications for the study of distributed runtime verification. Similarly, we do not claim that the papers cited are necessarily the first work to propose the study of a similar class of problems. The works mentioned below are further discussed in Sect. 5.

Observing Distributed Computations. The obvious setting where distributed monitoring arises is when the system under scrutiny is itself distributed. One important problem related to observing distributed computations is that of detecting global predicates, which is recognised as an important problem since the early ages of distributed computing (Cooper and Marzullo [37]).

It is known that checking general predicates is hard, since one has to store and enumerate all interleavings of the local processes. The so-called *computation slices* can be used for a more efficient detection (see Mittal et al. [79], Alagar and Venkatesan [1], Chauhan et al. [30]). Computation slices are abstractions of the distributed computation that guarantee the following: the predicate is present in a slice of a computation c if the predicate occurred in some state of c. This approximation is precise enough to detect the predicate. If an algorithm is too general and does not exploit the structure of the predicate under consideration, predicate detection can involve a long runtime and large memory overhead (Chauhan et al. [30]). Hence, best current solutions for predicate detection consider only fragments of the possible space of global predicates (for example the so-called linear, relational, regular and co-regular, and stable fragments) to gain efficiency. Even though most techniques for predicate detection (Cooper and Marzullo [37], Mittal et al. [79], Alagar and Venkatesan [1]) send all local events to a central process for inspection of its interleavings, some modern approaches (see Chauhan et al. [30]) consider purely distributed detection. Based on Chauhan et al. [30], Mostafa and Bonakdarpour [80] adapt the work to check whether properties defined using LTL are satisfied.

Analysis Decomposition. Most approaches to runtime verification either consider the system under dynamic evaluation as a black-box, or only inspect the internals of the monitored system with the goal to instrument the system for the monitoring task. However, it is common—using design principles like component-based design—that the description of the system is decomposed into different units.

For example, the work by Falcone et al. [49] investigates how to use the hierarchical description of the system to generate monitors that are then composed with the original system. This process produces a modified system that shares the original decomposition (and implements its functionality) and also includes the monitors embedded. Within this setting, the authors study how to compile a given design into either a centralised or a decentralised platform by deciding the placement of components using different deployment possibilities. Although the work by Falcone et al. [49] does not specifically target distributed systems, the solution obtained from the compilation of the modified system can lead to a distributed monitoring solution if the target platform is distributed.

A similar approach is exemplified by Cassar and Francalanza [23, 24], where a framework for monitoring asynchronous component-based systems is presented. Again, the authors do not treat the system under scrutiny as a single monolithic block, but identify its constituent sub-components in the form of independently computing entities, called actors. The resulting monitoring setup generated is also localised to sub-components of the system, mirroring its non-monolithic structure. Even though actor systems are not necessarily executed in distributed fashion, the asynchronous nature of the code generated and its localisation lead to a straightforward distribution.

Exploiting Parallelism. Another justification for studying runtime verification in the context of distributed systems is the exploitation of parallel executing units to perform a monitoring task. For example, Berkovich et al. [14] propose to use additional hardware (a GPU parallel execution platform) to minimize the impact of online monitors on execution time overhead, reducing the intrusiveness. Moreover, the works by Francalanza and Seychell [59, 60] report performance gains in terms of lower overheads when monitors are specified as concurrent entities and executed over the prevalent multi-core and multi-processor architectures. This gain is obtained because the concurrent monitors exploit better the resources of the underlying processing units.

Fault Tolerance. Handling failures in distributed systems is challenging because different components can fail independently (e.g., nodes crashing) and the communication can miss, duplicate or reorder messages or incur in unbounded delays (Francalanza and Hennessy [58]). Even worse, there can be complicated failure dependencies between components, and the resulting failure patterns can be difficult to predict and explain.

At the same time, failure tolerance can be achieved by replicating components that perform a certain task, including monitors. For example, Fraigniaud et al. [53] study the problem of distributed monitoring with failures, where events can be observed from more than one monitor, but the nodes where the monitors execute can crash. The distributed monitoring algorithm then tries to reach a verdict among the surviving monitors.

The work by Basin et al. [7] targets the incomplete knowledge caused by network failures and message corruptions and attempts to handle the resulting disagreements. A subsequent work investigates how to handle network failures, and proposes algorithms that can reach verdicts when some information is missing and messages are reordered (see Basin et al. [8]). Since message losses are also considered, this approach can also model node crashes, which are simulated by all messages from the crashed node being lost.

Efficiency. In many distributed systems scenarios, a simple monitoring solution can be obtained by implementing a central monitor that all other entities communicate with. However, distribution itself can be exploited to coordinate the monitoring task more efficiently. Many works attempt to provide more efficient solutions by exploiting the locality in the observations to also perform partially the monitoring task. For example, the works by Falcone et al. [49] and by Cassar and Francalanza [23, 24], already mentioned, exploit the hierarchical structure of the system to generate local monitors. On the other hand, Cassar et al. [25] and Francalanza and Seychell [59, 60] exploit the structure and semantics of the correctness property from which the monitors are synthesised to generate monitor organisations that use the underlying hardware efficiently. Concretely, the generated monitors minimize idle computing units and improve memory management via redundant monitor deallocations and monitor network reorganisations. These works pursue a more efficient monitoring where less communication and execution overhead is needed.

The pursuit of lowering overheads has also led Colombo et al. [36] to consider distribution as a means of offloading part of the monitoring computation to the computing resources of another machine. They provide handles that allow the specifier to dictate whether a property is to be runtime-checked locally, as inlined code within the monitored system, or remotely via an independent monitoring unit located on a separate machine. In separate work Colombo et al. [32] investigate various instrumentation techniques in Enterprise-Service Bus (ESB) distributed architectures, so as to determine which of them lead to lower monitoring overheads.

As observed by Bauer and Falcone [11] and in Francalanza et al. [57], when atomic observations of the monitored system occur locally, one can organize the monitors hierarchically according to the structure of the original specification. This can lead to substantial savings in communication overheads because a verdict of a subformula can often be reached further down hierarchically. From the practical point of view, Bauer and Falcone [11] claim that many cyber-physical systems, like distributed systems found in the automotive and avionics industries, fulfill the requirement that both observations and their placement to local nodes are known at deployment time.

In the context of multithreaded programs with shared memory, the work of Luo and Roşu [73] proposes to decompose a given property into local decentralised monitors for each of the threads, which again helps to reduce monitoring overheads.

Monitoring Expressivity. Some approaches borrow directly monitoring languages from non-distributed computing, and study how to exploit or adapt the methods for distributed systems. Other approaches present new formalisms or extend existing ones with specific capabilities for distributed systems. For example, Sen et al. [89,90] propose a method to check for violations of safety properties in distributed systems, using a variation of LTL that is suitable to describe (past time) properties of distributed systems. This extension essentially allows to express the knowledge of particular agents. The work in Francalanza et al. [57] proposes and formalizes a migrating monitor setup so as to better handle the open-ended and dynamic nature of distributed systems. This helps monitoring to adapt to locations that are learnt dynamically and to varying correctness specifications over the course of long-running distributed computations.

The efficiency of migrating monitors is investigated by Bauer and Falcone [11] for fixed-location setups. The subsequent work Colombo and Falcone [34] extends these results and compares them to choreographic solutions (see Sect. 4.4).

Testing and Enforcement. Testing multithreaded programs is in general a challenging task because often concurrency errors arise only under specific interleavings and execution conditions, which are hard to cause and reproduce due to the non-determinism introduced by the scheduler. The work by Luo and Roşu [73], already mentioned, presents an *enforcement* mechanism that exploits user-specified properties to generate local monitors that can influence the executions. This approach either (1) attempts to improve testing by forcing promising schedules that can lead to violations; or (2) prevents violations of the specified property by blocking individual threads whose execution may lead to a violation. This kind of enforcement is otherwise typically implemented using ad-hoc manual synchronisation. The monitoring generation described in [73] includes the decomposition of the property into local decentralised monitors for each of the threads.

3   Characteristics of Distributed Runtime Verification

In this section we capture some challenges that distributed systems impose on monitoring and the main difficulties that must be tackled by solutions to distributed runtime verification. We begin in Sect. 3.1 by describing some key characteristics of distributed system monitoring, particularly following a historical perspective. Overall, we consider 14 characteristics, denoted (C1)–(C14). Some of them (in particular (C1)–(C5)) are common to most distributed monitoring solutions, but are not typically a concern for non-distributed systems. Other criteria are not oblivious to all distributed monitoring cases, but identify aspects that will allow us to extract some classification dimensions, according to the approach taken by each solution. Most of these characteristics are also either unique to distributed systems or more challenging and important in distributed systems than in non-distributed systems. The classification aspects are listed later in Sect. 3.2.

3.1 Common Characteristics

Already in the late 1980s, Joyce et al. [70] identified five issues in monitoring distributed systems, in an early attempt to characterize the key constraints that distinguish monitoring in sequential settings from monitoring in distributed systems:

(C1) The fact that distributed systems have *many foci of control*;
(O2) The presence of *communication delays* among nodes, which makes it difficult to determine a system's state at any given time;
(C3) The inherent *non-determinism* in distributed and asynchronous systems;
(C4) The fact that monitoring a distributed system *alters its behavior*;
(C5) The *complexity of the interactions* between the system and the system developer.

Aspect (C1) captures the idea that a distributed system is composed of processes running independently in distributed execution units. Issue (C2) refers to one of the aspects of message passing systems. We will later refer to this aspect that allows to distinguish between systems that are not synchronised (see **Global Clock** below) and where messages can be unboundedly delayed or be lost (see **Failures** below). Not all current research in distributed monitoring assumes that messages can suffer independent delays. Issue (C3) refers to the non-deterministic and asynchronous nature common to many distributed systems. Issue (C4) refers to the intrusiveness of monitoring in the system under analysis, which is not a unique characteristic of monitoring distributed systems. We consider here intrusiveness as a key characteristic (see **Intrusiveness** below). Finally, issue (C5) refers to the additional complexity (when compared with non-distributed systems) for the engineer exercising the monitoring infrastructure, in terms of deploying the monitors and collecting and analysing the reported data. We do not develop (C5) further in this chapter as we focus on runtime verification, and not on software engineering aspects.

Another work that explores monitoring distributed systems and identifies common and classifying criteria, by Francalanza et al. [56,57], extracts the following characteristics:

(C6) Difficulties in keeping a *global state*;
(C7) Confidentiality of the information collected and communicated;

(C8) Trace analysis *locality*;
(C9) *Dynamic* aspects of specifications;
(C10) Locations constitute *units of failure*.

Maintaining a global state in a distributed system under observation is impractical for several reasons, captured by aspect (C6). One reason is that sometimes it is even theoretically impossible to build and maintain a global view, due to the lack of global clocks, asynchrony, message loss and reordering, etc. Even when it is theoretically possible, it is common that the volume of event messages that are required to build such a global view would substantially increase the monitoring overhead, making it impractical. Most works recognize that although such a central solution would greatly simplify monitoring, it is either too complex or too intrusive. This difficulty will be captured as **Global Clock** and **Failures** below.

Aspect (C7) is related to security (also mentioned by Falcone et al. [46]). Every time a trace of events is communicated across locations, the confidentiality of the information contained may be compromised. Solutions that encode and decode this information can further increase the monitoring overhead. However, we will not discuss this security aspects in this chapter.

Aspect (C8) refers to where the monitors are placed and where the events from the observed system are collected. Ideally, local monitors should analyse events locally and then communicate analysis summaries across locations. On the other hand, placement sometimes involves additional restrictions. For example, certain locations may not allow monitoring to be carried out locally due to resource constraints. Placement is often at odds with locality, which sometimes involves dynamic aspects. There are cases when it is difficult to anticipate the location where certain computations will be executed because this location depends on some runtime information that is hard to infer statically. Aspect (C8) is related to the distribution of the monitoring process, and in particular refers to the preference of decentralizing it (see **Centralisation** below).

Aspect (C9) considers that in long-running applications without a central authority, correctness specifications may not be all available prior to deployment. Some specifications are added at runtime, while the system is already executing, which disables the static placement of monitors. Dynamic aspects of monitoring are considered in (C8) and (C9), caused by either unpredictable aspects at deployment time, or constraints in the execution platform which restrict installing monitors dynamically. Finally, aspect (C10) considers again the issue of failures (see **Failures** below).

In a recent short paper, Bonakdarpour et al. [20] discuss the following four issues as distinctive, characteristic challenges of distributed runtime verification:[1]

(C11) *Modeling* a distributed RV system (particularly the system under observation);

---

[1] The distributed RV considered in Bonakdarpour et al. [20] is a general monitoring solution that runs on an infrastructure that is unreliable and unable to solve consensus.

(C12) Defining and evaluating distributed correctness *specifications*;
(C13) Using different *verdicts* on the state of the monitored system;
(C14) Giving semantics to the different verdicts.

Aspect (C11) concerns both the actual implementation of a distributed systems's description (including whether it is used in the monitoring process, see issue **Exploiting System Description** below), as well as efforts devoted to describing the monitoring solutions (see Sect. 4). It is well-known that describing precisely the semantics of distributed systems is more difficult than when centralised systems are considered. Aspect (C12) is related to the formalism used to describe monitors (see **Distributed Specifications**). Finally, the last two issues (C13) and (C14) are more specific to the solution provided in [20]. The first issue (C13) states that local monitors need to emit verdicts from richer domains, not just Boolean values, due to the necessary amount of information that needs to be collected and combined. This aspect has already been witnessed in monitoring non-distributed systems using LTL_3 (see Bauer et al. [13]), where the semantics of LTL for finite traces is expressed using a 3 valued domain (the third value captures the possibility of expressing an *unknown* verdict, which may become later true or false when new observations are made). Issue (C13) refers to the use of multi-valued domains as verdicts emitted the local monitors in the distributed systems. Issue (C14) refers to how these multiple verdicts can be combined during the creation of a final verdict.

3.2   Distinguishing Characteristics

We now list six dimensions that will allow us to distinguish the different lines of research and classify the solutions proposed.

Exploiting System Description. Most work in RV focuses on building monitors that can analyse any system (under some general assumptions), that is, the system is consider as a black-box that emits the necessary signals to the monitors. On the other hand, some other approaches exploit the system's description to generate specialised monitors. Examples of system's descriptions proposed include models of the system, abstractions or even full descriptions as programs. In this case, the monitors generated are only guaranteed to be correct for the specific system analysed, and in case a different system is finally deployed with the monitor, the verdicts of this monitor may not be correct. On the other hand, solutions that consider the system as a black-box generate monitors that are correct for every system (that fulfills some general assumptions) at the price of potentially less efficiency. For example, algorithms that generate monitors as finite state machines from LTL specifications work for all systems as sources of traces. If the monitor can rule out certain paths using concrete facts of the system under observation, obtained by static analysis for example, then the monitor can be specialised into a smaller finite state machine.

In some cases only certain aspects of the system description are used to build the solution, like the number of distributed nodes, the location of the individual predicates emitted by the running system, or the topology of the network.

Centralisation. Even if the system under observation is intrinsically distributed, the monitoring task can be performed in a central location that collects information from the remote units. However, solutions with a *central monitor* have many drawbacks from the points of view of overhead, efficiency, tolerance to faults and security. For these reasons, many solutions attempt to divide the monitors into local monitors and perform part of the monitoring activities locally, in a distributed fashion.

Global Clock. There are two large classes of distributed runtime verification techniques depending on whether it is assumed that all nodes have access or not to a global clock (or to perfectly-synchronised local clocks). In case a global clock is assumed, the system under analysis is equivalent to a synchronous system (following distributed computing terminology). In this case, we call the problem *decentralised monitoring*. Similarly, when monitors do not have access to a global clock we refer to the problem as *distributed monitoring*. Another characteristic feature of monitoring distributed systems is *asynchrony*, both between the monitors and the distributed system under scrutiny, and among the distributed monitors themselves.

Monitoring a distributed system often amounts to monitoring a message passing system. We reserve the term non-distributed systems for those systems that have a global clock and direct access shared memory between all computational units. For example, parallel systems (as defined above) are non-distributed systems with several concurrent execution units.

Distributed Specifications. One key classification criteria is whether the specification language from which monitors are generated has specific features for distributed systems, that is whether the formalism allows to refer to characteristics of the distributed platform. Some approaches borrow directly a language originally proposed for non-distributed systems, like LTL, and attack the problem of monitoring distributed systems against specifications written in this language. Other approaches start by introducing a modified specification language with some distributed feature, and then develop specific monitoring algorithms for this language.

Failures. In practice, both non-distributed and distributed systems are subject to failures. However, failures in distributed systems can be more subtle than in non-distributed systems due to the physical independence of the executing units. Even though most monitoring solutions assume that no component can fail, some approaches consider the possibility of some part of the distributed system failing. In particular, some of the failing aspects considered are network delays in the transmission of the messages, message loss or duplication, message corruption and node crashes. Even though Byzantine failures have been thoroughly studied in distributed systems, this aspect has received little attention in the area of monitoring distributed systems.

Intrusiveness. As already identified in early surveying efforts (see (C4) above), the monitoring process typically modifies the behavior of the monitored system. Naturally, most works focus on the effectiveness of the monitoring solution proposed, that is, on proving that the monitoring process actually detects the intended property. Some research also considers the efficiency of the combined solution (in terms of running time, number of messages, etc.) and in some few cases how the monitoring process affects the running system (that is, how intrusive monitoring is). Moreover, some works are intrusive *on purpose*, trying to reduce the intrinsic non-determinism of the running system with the goal of avoiding failures (like in enforcement) or provoking failures (for testing purposes).

4   Monitor Organisations

In this section we explain and compare the various ways in which monitoring distributed system activities can be organised. The various monitoring organisations can be explained in terms of the different configurations used to compose these components together as a monitoring infrastructure contributing towards a common goal.

The analysis of correctness properties concerning different processes, possibly spanning across different locations, often requires the aggregation of traces into composite traces. We will generally assume that the composition of two remote traces does not necessarily yield a total ordering among the events of the resulting composite trace, but instead gives a partial ordering. Monitors can communicate with each other to coordinate the monitoring task.

4.1   Traditional Monitoring

A traditional monitoring setup, depicted in Fig. 1, typically consists of a group of processes (P_1, P_2 and P_3 in the figure) that reside at one location (l). These processes generate a single local trace (T_1) that is analysed by a single monitor (M_1), also located at the same location. Even if these processes execute concurrently and are subject to a different interleaving every time the system is executed, the monitoring setup will always report a trace with a total ordering of events reflecting the executed interleaving.

4.2   Decentralised Monitoring

As depicted in Fig. 2, a decentralised monitoring setup resembles traditional monitoring in that all process executions and trace events are governed by a single global clock. Moreover, processes and monitors can communicate using synchronous channels, and computations are totally ordered. Consequently, traces can also be totally ordered, either explicitly as one data structure or locally by using time-stamps.

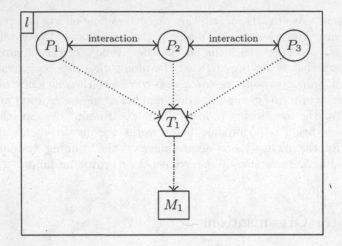

Fig. 1. A traditional (centralised) monitoring setup where processes P_1, P_2 and P_3 generate a single trace T_1 observed by a single monitor M_1. The interaction between processes illustrate that processes may communicate or synchronize, even though it is not assumed that they do (as P_1 with P_3 in the figure).

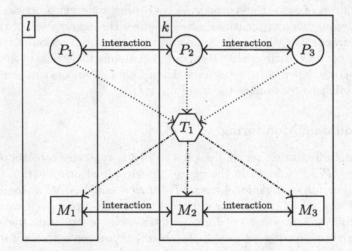

Fig. 2. In a decentralised monitoring setup the synchronised trace T_1 can be processed by several independent monitors. Now monitors can interact (like M_1 and M_2, and M_2 and M_3) but are not required to (like M_1 and M_3). Also, monitors and processes can be placed at different locations that share a global clock (l and k in the figure).

In contrast to traditional monitoring which is typically performed by a single monolithic monitor, monitoring in a decentralised and distributed setup is decomposed into different sub-components (M_1, M_2, M_3) reflecting the fact that a global correctness property may be decomposed into smaller properties.

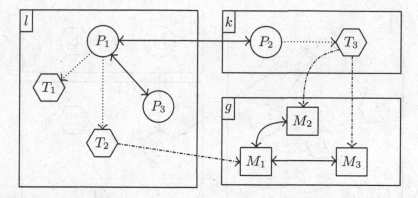

Fig. 3. In an orchestrated monitoring setup, traces are independently produced locally at the location of processes, but can be processed by remote monitors.

For instance, in cases where trace events may be attributed to different system units (e.g. classes or objects), each monitor may selectively analyse events pertaining to a particular unit entity (e.g. all the method call invocations on a particular object) and then communicate aggregate monitoring information to other monitors in order to verify a global property. It is common that sub-monitors reflect some decomposition of the specification, but sometimes sub-monitors are obtained directly by the placement of parts of the specification into locations without much decomposition.

There are also cases in which the correctness properties are inherently separate and concern only a subset of processes as in the case of parametric monitoring where the property can be evaluated independently for different parameter instances (see, e.g., Chen and Roşu [31]). In this case, monitoring may be decentralised in a natural manner without the need for the individual monitors to communicate.

4.3   Orchestrated Monitoring

Orchestrated and choreographed monitoring approaches are used in settings where more than one process is dispersed across more than one location. The set of processes generate more than one trace that can only be partially ordered due to the absence of a global clock.

In an orchestration all monitoring is ultimately performed *centrally* by a single monitor, accessing the respective trace events from different locations. The approach is depicted in Fig. 3, which shows two sub-systems located at l and k, each producing local traces of events (T_1, T_2 and T_3 respectively), subsequently analysed by monitors M_1, M_2 and M_3 from a remote location g. Each of these monitors analyse an independent correctness property.

On the one hand, the centralisation of the analysis simplifies the logic of the monitor, which is conducive to a decrease in errors in the monitor code itself. However, these benefits come at a cost in distributed settings such as the one

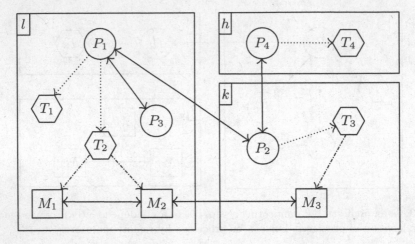

Fig. 4. In an choreographed monitoring setup, traces are independently produced locally at the location of processes and can be processed by different monitors independently.

depicted in Fig. 3. First, the approach leads to a substantial increase in the volume of trace information which has to be transmitted remotely for monitoring. The considerable increase in communication overhead across locations affects monitoring scalability when the number of processes and locations increases. The approach is also susceptible to data exposure when the trace events transmitted across locations contain private information. Adding additional security layers via mechanisms such as encryption further increases the monitoring overhead. Finally, the architecture poses a security risk by exposing the monitor as a central point of attack from which sensitive information can be tapped. Nevertheless, restricted forms of the orchestrated monitoring approach can be suitable when dealing with public information that is communicated over a relatively safe medium.

4.4   Choreographed Monitoring

A choreographed monitoring approach also targets system settings consisting of multiple processes dispersed across more than one location. In contrast to orchestrated monitoring, choreography-based approaches push the runtime verification activities locally to the location where the traces are generated, as shown in Fig. 4. The diagram depicts four processes, located at three locations l, k, and h, each generating local traces, with monitors M_1, M_2 placed at l, and M_3 placed at k. The monitor decomposition is not only due to the independence of the correctness properties being checked. In fact, monitors M_2 and M_3 could be verifying the same global property and eventually interact with each other in order to synchronize their monitoring effort.

The appeal of localizing monitoring is the potential minimisation of data exposure and communication overhead. By verifying locally, we avoid having to transmit trace information to a remote monitor. Moreover, localised monitors typically require less communication than remote monitoring using a central monitor. However, choreography is more complex to instrument, since correctness properties need to be decomposed into coordinated local monitors. Furthermore, choreographed monitoring is also more intrusive, by burdening the monitored subsystems with additional local computation, and is thus applicable only when the hosting locations allow local instrumentation of monitoring code.

5   Instantiations

In this section we describe and compare research solutions proposed in the literature, using the characteristics captured in Sect. 3 and the organisations described in Sect. 4. To ease the description we group the papers as follows:

- Decentralised Monitoring
- Distributed Monitoring
- Fault Tolerance
- Monitor Decomposition
- Predicate Detection for Distributed Systems
- Intrusiveness
- Behavioral Type Systems for Distributed Monitoring

Other features cross-cut papers across different characteristics and are mentioned in each particular case. Tables 1 and 2 summarize the papers according to the main characteristics considered. In the characteristics shown in the tables, **Global Clock, Failures, System Description, Distributed Specs** and **Intrusiveness** are directly characteristics captured in Sect. 3. **Asynchronous Msgs** refers to whether the underlying platform is a message passing system. **Asynchronous Msgs, Decentralised Monitoring** and **Distributed Monitoring** are characteristics considered within **Global Clock** in Sect. 3.

The entries **LTL** and **Predicate Detection** are included because these specification languages have been thoroughly considered in many works. Finally, **Types** refer to a line of research based on process algebras and session types.

Decentralised Monitoring. Bauer and Falcone [11,12] study the problem of decentralised monitoring. The starting point is a specification expressed in LTL without any specific extension for distributed systems, except for the static mapping of atomic predicates to individual processes. Note that individual state predicates of the specification may be split into more than one process. The solution synthesizes a monitor for each process, under the assumption that components communicate synchronously with a global clock. Each component has a local monitor attached, and emits events synchronously after every global clock tick. By design, the solution to a verdict is taken as combination of the execution of the local monitors, lacking a central decision-making point. This work is later generalised by Falcone et al. [46] beyond LTL to cover all regular languages.

Table 1. State-of-the-art on distributed monitoring. Each paper is classified according to the characteristics considered (part 1).

Publication	year	Global Clock	Asynchonous Msgs	Decentralised Monitoring	Distributed Monitoring	Failures	System Description	Distributed Specs.	LTL	Predicate Detection	Intrusiveness	Types
Bauer and Falcone [11]	2012	✓	·	✓	·	·	·	·	✓	·	·	·
Bauer and Falcone [12]	2016	✓	·	✓	·	·	·	·	✓	·	·	·
Colombo and Falcone [33]	2014	✓	·	✓	·	·	·	·	✓	·	·	·
Colombo and Falcone [34]	2016	✓	✓	✓	·	·	·	·	✓	·	·	·
Falcone et al. [46]	2014	✓	·	✓	·	·	·	·	·	·	·	·
Bartocci [6]	2013	✓	✓	✓	·	·	·	·	✓	·	·	·
Sen et al. [89]	2004	·	✓	·	✓	·	·	✓	✓	·	·	·
Francalanza et al. [56]	2011	·	✓	·	✓	·	✓	·	·	·	·	✓
Francalanza et al. [57]	2013	·	✓	·	✓	·	✓	·	·	·	·	✓
Basin et al. [7]	2013	✓	·	·	·	✓	·	·	·	·	·	·
Basin et al. [8]	2015	✓	✓	·	✓	✓	·	·	·	·	·	·
Fraigniaud et al. [53]	2014	·	✓	·	✓	·	·	·	✓	·	·	·
Bonakdarpour et al. [19]	2016	·	✓	·	✓	·	·	·	✓	·	·	·
Falcone et al. [49]	2015	·	·	·	·	·	✓	·	·	·	·	·
Bonakdarpour et al. [17]	2010	·	✓	·	·	·	✓	·	·	·	·	·
Bonakdarpour et al. [18]	2010	·	✓	·	·	·	✓	·	·	·	·	·
Berkovich et al. [14]	2015	✓	·	·	·	·	·	·	✓	·	✓	·
Francalanza and Seychell [59]	2013	·	✓	·	✓	·	·	·	·	·	·	·
Francalanza and Seychell [60]	2015	·	✓	·	✓	·	·	·	·	·	·	·
Attard and Francalanza [3]	2016	·	✓	·	✓	·	·	·	·	·	·	·
Chase and Garg [29]	1998	·	✓	·	·	·	·	·	·	✓	·	·
Cooper and Marzullo [37]	1991	·	✓	·	·	·	·	·	·	✓	·	·
Garg and Waldecker [64]	1994	·	✓	·	·	·	·	·	·	✓	·	·
Garg and Mittal [63]	2001	·	✓	·	·	·	·	·	·	✓	·	·
Mittal and Garg [78]	2005	·	✓	·	·	·	·	·	·	✓	·	·
Mittal et al. [79]	2007	·	✓	·	·	·	·	·	·	✓	·	·
Sen and Garg [88]	2007	·	✓	·	·	·	·	·	·	✓	·	·
Ogale and Garg [83]	2007	·	✓	·	·	·	·	·	✓	✓	·	·
Chauhan et al. [30]	2013	·	✓	·	✓	·	·	·	·	✓	·	·
Mostafa and Bonakdarpour [80]	2015	·	✓	·	✓	·	·	·	✓	✓	·	·
Sen and Garg [86]	2003	·	✓	·	·	·	·	·	✓	✓	·	·
Luo and Roşu [73]	2013	✓	·	✓	·	·	✓	·	·	·	✓	·
Cassar and Francalanza [22]	2014	·	✓	·	✓	·	·	·	·	·	✓	·
Zhang et al. [93]	2016	·	✓	·	✓	·	·	·	·	·	✓	·
Colombo et al. [36]	2012	·	✓	·	·	·	·	·	·	·	✓	·

Table 2. State-of-the-art on distributed monitoring. Each paper is classified according to the characteristics considered (part 2).

Publication	year	Global Clock	Asynchonous Msgs	Decentralised Monitoring	Distributed Monitoring	Failures	System Description	Distributed Specs.	LTL	Predicate Detection	Intrusiveness	Types
Colombo et al. [35]	2011	·	✓	·	✓	·	·	·	·	·	✓	·
Cassar and Francalanza [24]	2016	·	✓	·	✓	·	·	·	·	·	✓	·
Bocchi et al. [15]	2013	·	✓	·	✓	·	·	✓	·	·	·	✓
Bocchi et al. [16]	2017	·	✓	·	✓	·	·	✓	·	·	·	✓
Hu et al. [67]	2013	·	✓	·	✓	·	·	✓	·	·	·	✓
Demangeon et al. [41]	2015	·	✓	·	✓	·	·	✓	·	·	·	✓
Neykova et al. [82]	2013	·	✓	·	✓	·	·	✓	·	·	·	✓
Neykova et al. [81]	2014	·	✓	·	✓	·	·	✓	·	·	·	✓
Jia et al. [69]	2016	·	✓	·	✓	·	·	✓	·	·	✓	✓
Di Giusto and Pérez [42]	2015	·	✓	·	✓	✓	·	✓	·	·	✓	✓
Di Giusto and Pérez [43]	2016	·	✓	·	✓	✓	·	✓	·	·	✓	✓
Castellani et al. [26]	2014	·	✓	·	✓	✓	·	✓	·	·	✓	✓
Castellani et al. [27]	2016	·	✓	·	✓	✓	·	✓	·	·	✓	✓
Mezzina and Pérez [75]	2016	·	✓	·	✓	·	·	✓	·	·	✓	✓
Mezzina and Pérez [76]	2017	·	✓	·	✓	·	·	✓	·	·	✓	✓

The main advantage of a decentralised solution over a non-distributed one is that not all events must be sent to the location of the central monitor. The challenge is that local monitoring must be performed with only partial observations of the global trace. The algorithm progresses by rewriting the specification at each node, with the partial information available. When local monitors are unable to evaluate a specification given their local view of the computation, they communicate their residual formulas to the other monitors. An alternative approach would use a central monitor that receives information about the local states of all other locations. One of the main practical concerns is how the decentralised approach compares with this alternative central approach. The empirical evaluation reported by Bauer and Falcone [11,12], Falcone et al. [46] suggests that the overhead introduced is lower in the distributed solution. There is also an economic advantage in the decentralised solution, because in a distributed solution there is no need to add a central processor. Practical applications of this approach involve monitoring the behavior of embedded systems that are distributed by nature, like cars and airplanes where the different distributed components are known upfront. These include typical field-busses like EtherCAT, ProfiBus and

ProfiNet (also known as "Industrial Ethernet" [50]). In these systems, processes communicate over a synchronous bus, so the global clock assumption is justified.

Bartocci [6] extends the work by Bauer and Falcone [11] to real-time embedded systems by considering the maximum duration of the computation and communication. The main result is the ability to calculate a sampling ratio above which the decentralised monitoring process is guaranteed to generate the correct outcome.

The works by Colombo and Falcone [33,34] start from similar assumptions and goals: there is a global clock and one local monitor per executing component. The number of executing components is also known upfront. The work in [34] removes the assumption of instantaneous communication from Colombo and Falcone [33] and enables a solution with reliable messages with any delay. Still, a global clock is assumed because the specification logic is LTL and individual predicates sensed are totally ordered. The solution proposed is a choreographed decentralised monitoring algorithm, where each local monitor senses a collection of local predicates. The local monitors use the rewriting approach (also known as formula progression) by which the state of the monitor is the LTL formula that results by expanding the LTL formula to the residual formula in the next state, simplified with the acquired knowledge. A key element in the solution is that a network of monitors is statically built by assigning each subformula of the original formula to a node in the distributed system. The hierarchical description inherent by the sub-formula relation in turn dictates the communication pattern between the local monitors. Consider a formula ψ and let φ be a sub-formula of ψ. The monitor M_1 for φ informs the monitor M_2 for ψ about the verdict of φ which, in turn, is used by M_2 to compute the verdict of ψ. If a synchronous clock is assumed, the root formula verdict is guaranteed to be reached within at most k steps of delay, where k is the height of the original formula.

Distributed Monitoring. Sen et al. [89] propose a method to detecting violations of safety properties in an asynchronous distributed system, where no global clock is assumed. The method proposed generates, given a specification, local monitors for all distributed nodes. These local monitors communicate only by piggybacking additional information in the messages sent by existing processes in the system, so the shape of the history of messages exchanged is not modified by the actions taken by the monitors. The logic used in Sen et al. [89] extends past time LTL with features for distributed systems, in particular an operator $@_j\varphi$, which captures the most recent value of formula φ according to process j.

The algorithm uses vector clocks (see Lamport [71], Mattern [74] and Fidge [51,52]) to transmit the most recent value of sub-formulas needed to compute the outcome of their containing formulas. Then, at deployment time, the monitor specification is decomposed into local monitors that collect information locally and compute the current value of formulas, based on this local information and on the information received in messages about the causal past of remote processes. This approach allows to generate monitors without inspecting the internal behavior of each process.

Francalanza et al. [56,57] present a formal model for distributed monitoring. System computations are described as π-calculus processes (Milner et al. [77]) hosted at different locations and interacting with one another via message passing. When systems compute, they generate residual trace events that are only locally ordered (with respect to the other events generated at the same location) but globally unordered (with respect to events generated at other locations), thereby modeling the absence of global clocks. Distributed monitors, also residing a different locations, are then tasked with analysing local traces and interacting with one another in order to perform a global analysis of system computation. The model is equipped with a bisimulation-based equivalence relation that is used to reason about different distributed monitoring strategies such as those discussed in Sect. 4. The model is also used to define and evaluate a new migrating monitor strategy that better handles the dynamic nature of open distributed systems.

Fault Tolerance. Not many works attack the problem of monitoring distributed systems considering that components can fail. Notable exceptions are the works by Basin et al. [7,8], and by Fraigniaud et al. [53] and Bonakdarpour et al. [19].

Basin et al. [7] present a policy language, a variant of FOLTL with three-valued semantics, and an algorithm that allows to reason about incomplete knowledge and handle disagreements. The main practical motivation is to handle errors in the observed trace, for example due to corruption or loss of part of logs files in complex IT systems, crashes in running systems, or network failures. Another motivation is to reconcile different views or verdicts obtained from monitors that observe different parts of the logs. The key idea is to equip the execution with features to enable monitors to distinguish between an event not being observed and the event not existing at all. The authors claim that any approach that solves this problem must satisfy that, once a definite verdict is given, providing more compatible information cannot retract the definite verdict. They manage to provide a complete algorithm for a fragment of the policy language. A similar work on compliance checking is Garg et al. [61]. Even though these works do not explicitly handle distributed systems, they handle runtime verification under incomplete information and incorrect information, which can be used to encode problems for distributed systems.

Influenced by [7], Basin et al. [8] consider the problem of monitoring distributed systems in the presence of network failures. The authors also consider the case that the monitor itself is distributed for the purposes of efficiency, performing the monitoring computation closer to the observation point and reducing the communication overhead. The paper [8] deals with Metric Temporal Logic (MTL), a logic that allows to express real-time properties. The algorithm is designed based on the *timed asynchronous* model for distributed systems (see Cristian and Fetzer [39]), which assumes the availability of highly-synchronised local clocks but permits crash failures in the processes and in the network. Another assumption is that components are known at deployment time.

In [8] processes time-stamp their observation before communicating them to the local monitors. The time-stamp allows components to compute precise delays between events, and to totally order the events. It is interesting to point out that even without failures, reliable asynchronous networks allow messages to arrive in different orders. Forcing messages to arrive in order requires buffering messages to ensure proper delivery order, which in turn prevents the early detection of some violations that would be possible with out-of-order delivery. The algorithm in Basin et al. [8] uses a richer value to encode the absence of knowledge when evaluating part of the specification. When the missing information is finally received, the monitor can precisely resolve the uncertainty. Sometimes, a monitor can reach a precise verdict only with the partial information received in a timely manner. Consequently, the algorithm can monitor MTL properties tolerating the out-of-order arrival of partial observations.

Concerning organisation, the monitors in [8] are distributed in a directed acyclic graph (DAG) where each monitor handles a subformula of the given formula, and children nodes handle subformulas of the formula handled by their parent node. The root of the DAG handles the original formula. During execution, messages are sent from children to parent monitors to inform about the verdicts reached in the subformula handled at the given point in time. When a process performs an atomic observation it also equips the time-stamp with an additional sequence number, which is locally unique. This sequence number allows monitors to infer the existence or absence of unknown intermediate samples between two observations. Intermediate nodes can also send heart-beat messages, which serve the purpose of informing about the absence of verdicts and the health of the intermediate node. Heart-beats also allow to infer the existence or absence of intermediate meaningful observations or verdicts, and in turn compute timeouts.

The problem of distributed monitoring for asynchronous distributed systems with node crashes is considered by Fraigniaud et al. [53] and Bonakdarpour et al. [19]. Monitors can either work correctly or fail, but after a fail, monitors do not perform any action for the reminder of the execution. The solution is based on the asynchronous "wait-free" communicating infrastructure. It is well known from the research area of distributed algorithms that the wait-free model of computation (see Attiya and Welch [4]) can simulate many other models of crash-fail asynchronous distributed systems. The main result in [19,53] is an algorithm and a lower-bound on the number of different verdicts that monitors need to communicate with each other to correctly detect the violation of an LTL property. The lower bound on the number of verdicts reveals that monitors need to communicate complex information in order to compute a global outcome. The final verdict reached by the cooperating monitors, in turn, will be that of LTL$_3$. The following three options are possible: (1) the property is satisfied in all continuations; (2) the property is violated in all continuations; (3) the outcome is unknown. These papers do not assume that the observations of the distributed monitors are disjoint. Even though monitors may only be observing part of the global input alphabet, several monitors may overlap in their partial observation.

Monitor Decomposition. Falcone et al. [49] target the problem of monitoring component based-systems, that is, systems that are described by the composition of components. More precisely, in [49] systems are described using the Behavior-Interaction-Priority (BIP) component-based framework (see Basu et al. [9]). Even though this paper does not attack explicitly the problem of monitoring a distributed system, it is nowadays well understood that component-based descriptions can be compiled into distributed implementations (see Bonakdarpour et al. [17,18]). Consequently, the monitors generated at the component level following [49] are attached to the system generating a modified BIP description that can subsequently be compiled into a distributed system.

Monitor decomposition for decentralised monitoring can also be inferred from the specification formula from which a monitor is synthesised. This line of research is explored extensively by Francalanza and Seychell [59,60] and Attard and Francalanza [3] for both safety and co-safety properties of logics involving conjunctions, disjunctions and recursion. Conjunctions and disjunctions are synthesised into concurrent monitors that analyse sub-parts of the system, whereas recursion leads to the dynamic generation of concurrent monitors, generated lazily only when required to minimize monitoring overheads. In every case, the concurrent monitors generated lead to self-contained localised monitoring that can be readily distributed. The automated synthesis function is proved correct in each of these cases (see Francalanza et al. [55] for the correctness proof in [3]). The work by Cassar et al. [25] considers a refined implementation where the concurrent sub-monitors cooperate among themselves and reorganize their interconnection so as to optimize the resources used for monitoring, thus reducing monitoring overheads.

Predicate Detection for Distributed Monitoring. Predicate detection (see Chase and Garg [29]) consists on checking whether a certain predicate occurred during the distributed execution, or more formally, whether the predicate holds in some *consistent cut* of the execution. In this context, predicates are state formulas (and consequently safety properties) even though some work has extended predicate detection to richer temporal formulas (see below for details).

All algorithms for predicate detection assume that the collection of executing processes is known a-priori, that processes do not fail and that all messages eventually arrive. Predicate detection can be performed offline, when all events are available before the detection algorithm starts running, or online, when one event at a time is processed. There are three main techniques for predicate detection. The first technique uses the global snapshots proposed by Chandy and Lamport [28], which can only detect *stable* predicates, which are predicates that remain true after becoming true (like termination, but unlike mutual exclusion). The second technique consists in an explicit construction of the lattice of global states proposed by Cooper and Marzullo [37]. This technique can detect unstable predicates but it is exponential in the number of local states and processes. Finally, the third technique exploits the specific structure of the predicate to provide efficient solutions. Examples include conjunctions of local predicates (Garg and

Waldecker [64]) and relational predicates of the form $\sum_i x_i < C$, where x_i are local variables.

Even if one had access to all the local histories of the execution of all processes, detecting a predicate is hard because—for general Boolean formulas—one needs to enumerate and search all possible interleavings of the local executions. Chase and Garg [29] show that detection of 2-CNF predicates is an NP-hard problem, even when assuming a central monitor. A solution to this explosion problem is a technique called *slicing* (see [63]). Slices are abstractions of the computation that guarantee that the predicate is detected in a slice if and only if the predicate holds in some consistent cut of the original computation. Computing a slice for a general predicate is still an NP-hard problem, shown by Mittal and Garg [78], but when efficient slices exist, these are much smaller than actual explicit histories. Consequently, a line of work has focused on identifying classes of predicates for efficient slicing procedures exist. These slices are based on fragments of the logic used to express the global state predicates. These fragments include regular, co-regular, linear, relational and stable predicates (see Mittal and Garg [78], Mittal et al. [79], Sen and Garg [88], Ogale and Garg [83]). Some of these solutions construct the slices offline, assuming that the whole histories are available to the slicing algorithms, while others work online, building the slice incrementally. Similarly, most of the solutions are still centralised (Cooper and Marzullo [37], Mittal et al. [79], Sen and Garg [88], Mittal et al. [79]) in the sense that all histories are sent to a central monitor that computes the slice and detects the predicate.

The first distributed solution to slice-based predicate detection is by Chauhan et al. [30]. The solution is online and distributed, in the sense that the slicing is computed by the distributed monitors. The guarantee is that if the predicate exists in a consistent cut of the computation, then it is detected by some monitor. The algorithm exploits both the structure of the property ([30] study regular properties) and epistemic information about what the knowledge that the different monitors acquire.

Also, even though most approaches are restricted to state predicates (or more precisely, fragments of the propositional logic for state predicates), some approaches tract richer temporal properties. For example, Sen and Garg [87], Ogale and Garg [83] present methods for sliced based predicate detection for a fragment of temporal logic that includes invariants (AG) and possible reachable (EF) operators, which extends the applicability beyond safety properties into a subclass of CTL formulas called Regular CTL (see Sen and Garg [86]). The restrictive use of negation in [87] is relaxed in [83]. Even though the work in [83,87] is applicable to a richer fragment of temporal logic, these algorithms work with a central monitor.

More recently, Mostafa and Bonakdarpour [80] provide a solution for monitorable LTL_3 temporal properties, but in this case extending the work of Chauhan et al. [30] so the solution obtained is distributed. This solution inserts additional messages in the network and is not restricted to only piggybacking information in existing messages.

Intrusiveness. It is often desirable that the monitoring process perturbs the execution of the system under analysis in the least possible manner. Typically, either the system is instrumented by embedding monitors in the code itself, or monitors and processes share resources because they execute in the same platform. These changes affect the behavior of the system, sometimes in a significant manner.

Berkovich et al. [14] propose to use additional hardware, and in particular a GPU parallel execution platform, to minimize the impact of online monitoring. The authors show how to generate parallel monitors from temporal logic specifications and evaluate empirically that the obtained parallel monitors together with the additional GPU hardware alleviate the effect of monitoring on the execution of the original system. This is a parallel solution (and not a message passing distributed solution) to reduce the intrusiveness of monitoring.

Other times, it is desirable that the monitoring process perturbs the execution of the system. One example is runtime enforcement, where the objective of the "monitoring" is to guarantee that the system stays within a safe region of states. Consequently, the enforcement system uses the information provided by the monitor to prevent an error before it occurs (see the chapter in this monograph about runtime enforcement). Another example is testing of multithreaded programs, which is in general a very hard task, due to the non-deterministic nature of the execution of concurrent programs, and the difficulty to reproduce erroneous behaviors. In this context it is desirable to guide the system towards executions that are more likely to produce an error. The work by Luo and Roşu [73] consists of an *enforcement* mechanism that uses user-specified monitors to generate local monitors. Such local monitors block individual threads that violate the specified properties. This enforcement pursues two objectives: (1) to guarantee the enforcement of properties in a multi-threaded program in a systematic way, which is typically implemented using ad-hoc synchronisation manually; and (2) to force schedules that test properties during the testing of multithreaded programs. The monitor generation described in Luo and Roşu [73] includes the decomposition of the property into local decentralised monitors for each of the threads.

The body of work by Roşu and Havelund [85], Cassar and Francalanza [22], Zhang et al. [93] explores the idea of decoupling the execution of monitors from the systems under scrutiny. This approach uses a mixture of synchronous and asynchronous monitoring, in order to obtain a feasible instrumentation setup that distribute monitors and systems at different locations, such as in the case of Colombo et al. [36] and other orchestrated monitoring setups. Asynchronous monitoring, used in various monitoring tools such as Colombo et al. [35], Francalanza and Seychell [60], Zhang et al. [93], Attard and Francalanza [3], minimizes monitor intrusiveness because it requires less instrumentation effort. Moreover, Cassar and Francalanza [22], Zhang et al. [93] show that this method of instrumentation can substantially reduce monitoring overhead. By using hybrid solutions, they also show how one need not compromise on the timeliness of detections.

Cassar and Francalanza [23, 24] extend the concept of non-intrusiveness to runtime adaptation via hybrid asynchronous monitoring. The goal is to design monitors that intervene with the execution of the system under scrutiny, and apply these interventions (i.e. system adaptations) with minimal overheads. In particular, the work [24] implements a framework where the monitors for system components can act at varying degrees of synchrony with respect to the observed components. Some parts of the system can be executed in a decoupled fashion with their monitors when no adaptations on that sub-system are required. Later, these sub-systems can be incrementally synchronised with the respective monitor when an adaptation is about to be applied. The entire framework is implemented atop a completely asynchronous actor computational model, which eases the distribution over remote locations.

Behavioral Type Systems for Distributed Monitoring. In this subsection we describe the work in process calculus related to studying the monitoring of distributed systems. Many large-scale systems consist of heterogeneous, distributed software artifacts (processes) that interact following some precise protocols. In these communication-centric settings, processes communicate asynchronously, without a global clock, and are prone to local failures. These characteristics make distributed monitoring a suitable approach to enforce system correctness by complementing the static verification techniques that are typically applied individually to each process. As we detail next, monitoring for communication-centric systems is an instance of the choreographed monitoring organisation described in Sect. 4.

A productive research strand to the analysis of communication-centric software systems uses *process calculi* (such as the π-calculus) as minimal specification languages. These formal calculi provide an unambiguous setting in which the communication correctness of these systems can be compositionally established. In particular, coupling process calculi with so-called *behavioral type systems* allows to (statically) enforce safety and liveness properties associated to protocol conformance. Rather than classifying data values, behavioral types define abstractions of the protocols that a communication entity (say, a socket or a channel) should respect throughout its execution (see Hüttel et al. [68] for a survey).

Several works have explored the interplay of behavioral types and mechanisms for distributed monitoring. In particular, monitoring frameworks based on *session types*, a particular class of behavioral types, have been put forward. Session types organize a series of communication actions corresponding to the same reciprocal protocol into a structure called *session* (see Honda et al. [65]). While typed process frameworks for binary session types can analyse two-party protocols, more general type theories for multiparty session types cover the case of protocols with three or more participants (Honda et al. [66]). Both binary and multiparty session types start to make their way into mainstream programming languages and frameworks (Ancona et al. [2]). In the multiparty case, a global type entirely describes the intended communication scenario. By projecting this global type onto each protocol participant, one may obtain its corresponding local type, which abstracts a participant's contribution to the protocol. This collection of local types thus offers a key reference for obtaining correct implementations for all participants.

Communication-centric systems often comprise components made available as grey- and black-boxes, with limited communication interfaces. As such, static verification techniques are unsuitable for their validation. Motivated by this observation, several works develop abstract frameworks based on process calculi in which monitors are terms of the specification language. The formal semantics of these calculi uses these monitor terms to enable process behavior according to the intended protocol. Rather than a logical specification (say, an LTL formula), each monitor uses a behavioral type (e.g., a local protocol) to guide a participant's behavior. These works define a special case of choreographed monitoring: the coupling of processes and monitors at the same level of abstraction makes the notion of local trace implicit. Monitors do not communicate to each other, nor perform autonomous actions. The global type through its projections is used to synthesize a monitor for each participant. This way, even untyped processes can be used to implement a protocol participant as long as they offer the right communication actions at the right time, in accordance with the governing local protocols.

Based on this general setup, Bocchi et al. [15,16] develop a monitored π-calculus with dynamic usage of multiparty session types, offering local and global safety assurance of distributed components. In their model, a network is a collection of processes (one per participant) that communicate via asynchronous message passing. Each participant is equipped with a trusted monitor that guards the run-time behavior of both the principal and its environment— this is realised by the evaluation of incoming and outgoing messages. Monitors regulate the creation of sessions and movement of messages within sessions. This dynamic checking can be switched off when processes have been statically verified. A series of queues shared between principals is assumed to support message passing, together with a global transport that abstracts distributed communication.

Building upon Bocchi et al. [15] and Bocchi et al. [16], the works by Hu et al. [67], Demangeon et al. [41] propose a dynamic verification framework for multiparty session types that admit interruptions. This a practical framework, which relies on the Scribble protocol language, an implementation of multiparty session types (see Yoshida et al. [92]), to specify global protocols, and on a Python API for conversation programming. In this framework, the monitor that tracks the progress of each participant within a session is represented using a finite state machine (FSM), generated from the local type. By independently monitoring each session endpoint at runtime, this framework ensures global communication safety even in the presence of asynchronous interruptions.

Other works on a practical strand are [81,82]. Neykova et al. [82] propose a toolchain for designing deadlock-free multiparty global protocols. Using automatically generated monitors for each session endpoint, this toolchain can detect illegal communication actions and mistaken message types that go against protocol conformance. The work by Neykova et al. [81] extends preceding works with timed information: Scribble specifications are extended with clocks, resets, and clock predicates that constrain the occurrence of protocol interactions.

Recent work by Jia et al. [69] introduces a framework for monitoring interacting processes that follow binary session protocols, building upon a logically motivated theory of session types. As in several of the works mentioned above, in this framework monitors are placed next to communication endpoints.

A distinguishing aspect is blame assignment: in case processes deviate from the prescribed session protocols, monitors may halt the execution, raise an alarm, and assign blame. The authors prove that their dynamic monitoring is not intrusive in the sense that it does not change the behavior of well-typed processes. Also, they show that in case of alarm one of an indicated set of possible culprits must have been compromised.

Finally, we mention some works in which the concept of monitor as a process term, in the sense just described, has been exploited. Even though the main purpose of these works is not run-time verification, they can be seen as applications of choreographed monitoring. Di Giusto and Pérez [42], Di Giusto and Pérez [43] use this kind of monitors to support the run-time adaptation of session-typed processes in both binary and multiparty settings. There is exactly one monitor per session. By combining monitor information and event-based constructs, one may specify the reaction to unanticipated circumstances (for example, local failures) by means of adaptation steps. An associated type system ensures communication safety and consistency properties: while safety guarantees absence of run-time communication errors, consistency ensures that adaptation steps do not disrupt already established session protocols. In a similar line, the monitors defined by Castellani et al. [26,27] play a dual role: they enforce run-time adaptation policies, and ensure secure information flow in multiparty exchanges. Recent work by Mezzina and Pérez [75,76] uses monitors as the memories required to support models of concurrency in which actions are reversible and causally consistent.

6   Challenges and Conclusion

6.1   Challenges

We list here some challenges for future research in distributed runtime verification.

Fault Tolerance. One of the key characteristics of distributed systems is that, in practice, different parts of the system can fail independently. However, most approaches consider that the system does not fail. Some future problems include the following.

The theoretical approach by Fraigniaud et al. [53], Bonakdarpour et al. [19] (discussed in Sect. 5) has two major obstacles to become practical:

- First, after the distributed verdicts are emitted, there is a phase in which a global function is applied to the collection of verdicts emitted. This function must be implemented somehow by a central computational infrastructure which must receive all verdicts and produce an outcome. However, a general implementation of this function requires a non-failing central monitor. But the existence of such a central unit would greatly simplify the initial monitoring problem, and in fact, the basic starting point of [19,53] is to design distributed fault tolerant solutions.
- Second, the work [19] only presents an algorithm for the processing of a one letter observation, under the assumption that the processes are perfectly synchronised at the beginning of such an observation. To process a subsequent observation, the monitors that survive the first round must somehow re-synchronize, but again, a synchronisation procedure would provide a much simpler solution to the monitoring problem at hand. In summary, A general fault-tolerant solution for sequences of observations is still an open problem.

Also, there are very few results in runtime verification that can handle network failures (most notably, the work by Basin et al. [8]). It would be very interesting to extend these approaches to other logics and distributed system assumptions.

Global Atomic Observations. Specification formalisms for non-distributed systems assume that atomic predicates are testable, which is not a restriction. In distributed systems, in general, predicates are global in the sense that they can involve different parts of the system. Then, not all global predicates are Boolean combinations of local predicates. For example, one restriction of the work by Bauer and Falcone [11] is that the individual global observations are Boolean combinations of local observations performed in each of the processes, whose observations do not overlap. More formally, each process j can emit a collection of local propositions AP_j (such that $AP_j \cap AP_i = \emptyset$ whenever $i \neq j$). The alphabet of atomic observations is then $\Sigma_j = 2^{AP_j}$. Note how the global alphabet $\Sigma = 2^{\cup_i AP_i}$ is strictly larger, in general, than $\cup_i \Sigma_i$ because it can contain relational symbols like $p_i \vee p_j$ where p_i and p_j are local observations at different processes. We use *relational observations* to refer to atomic propositions whose truth value depends on the observations made at more than one process. For example, consider the numeric variables x_i and y_j where the sub-index indicates the process at which the variable is observed (P_i and P_j resp). The atomic predicate $x_i < y_j$ cannot be evaluated at P_i or P_j alone, and it cannot be decomposed into a Boolean combination of local predicates either.

As discussed earlier, even though research in predicate detection has considered classes of predicates richer than individual observations (regular, linear, etc.) and has characterised that detecting a predicate in 2-CNF is already NP-hard, it would be interesting to extend other techniques for decentralised and distributed monitoring beyond combinations of local predicates.

Monitor Orchestrations. Colombo and Falcone [34] present a choreographed decentralised monitoring solution obtained from a network of local monitors, which is statically computed by mapping every subformula to a distributed system node. There are many possible ways to create such a network, even if one restricts the map (as in [34]) to one of the nodes with the highest number of propositions locally involved in the subformula, because there can be more than one such node. Even though all choices could lead to a correct monitoring solution, for a given trace of execution, the choice of network has an impact in the communication overhead. For every input trace, one could calculate a-posteriori the best network in the sense of the network that would have produced the lowest overhead. However, even for the fixed parameter assumed in [34] (e.g., static number of locations, fixed specifications, no dynamic remote spawning of new computation, the assumption of a global clock) it is not clear how to precompute an optimal network, even how to approximate it. Nevertheless, there are alternatives worth investigating. One plausible solution is to exercise the system in a test-bed to obtain input traces and compute the optimal network for the observed set of traces, with the assumption that the traces after deployment will involve similar communication flows. However, this kind of approach is not considered in [34].

Adequate solutions to this problem are probably even harder to come up with when proper distributed system constraints are considered, such as computation asynchrony, distributed clocks, and the possibility of partial failure. In practical settings, cases may even arise whereby one has to content with conflicting criteria. For instance, certain locations may not allow monitor processing and analysis to be carried out locally, forcing events to be communicated remotely to the analysing monitor. This, in turn, may conflict with confidentiality and security concerns.

Monitorability and Correctness. In general, the use of runtime analysis impinges on the extent to which a correctness property can be verified.

This aspect is often referred to as *monitorability*. One of the first works that introduces a notion of monitorability by defining classes of reactive languages that can be monitored is Viswanathan [91]. Later, D'Angelo et al. [40] defined monitorability for stream runtime verification on finite traces as the class of specifications for which efficient monitors can be generated. Pnueli and Zaks [84] formalised monitorability for LTL as the possibility of a finite trace to be extended to a finite witness of a specification satisfaction or violation. A similar notion was presented by Bauer et al. [13] and proved equivalent by Falcone et al. [48]. This notion was generalised to ω-regular languages by Falcone et al. [47] and Bauer [10], and later extended by Diekert et al. [44]. The tight complexity of this notion of monitorability was finally captured in [5]. An alternative definition of monitorability is given by Francalanza et al. [55] where the fragment of formulas of a given branching time logic that can be monitored at runtime is captured.

Decentralised and distributed monitoring introduces further restrictions and raises additional issues that may affect the monitorability of certain correctness properties. A first solution to decentralised monitorability was given recently by El-Hokayem and Falcone [45], but further work will be necessary to study its full applicability and possible extensions.

Concurrent and distributed systems are notoriously hard to get right and these complications extend also to distributed runtime verification: errors arise only for particular sequences of events that are hard to simulate using pre-deployment techniques such as testing, and are also hard to trace and reproduce for analysis once they occur. It is thus imperative to continue to extend existing work on developing methods for ascertaining the correctness of the decentralised and distributed monitoring setups constructed along the lines of [16,49,54].

6.2 Conclusion

In this chapter we have surveyed the literature on runtime verification for distributed systems. After showing some practical motivations that have justified the study of monitoring techniques for distributed and decentralised systems, we identified a series of features that characterize and that allow to classify the different problems and approaches. These criteria include whether the solution involves or exploits the description of the system under analysis, whether there is a single central monitor or the monitoring task is distributed, whether there is an assumption on a global clock, and whether the system tolerates failures or perturbs the execution. Finally, we showed a comprehensive list of results proposed in the literature and listed some challenges for future work.

Acknowledgments. We are grateful to the anonymous reviewers for their useful remarks and suggestions, which led to significant improvements.

Financial Acknowledgements. This work was partially supported by COST Action IC1402 (Runtime Verification beyond Monitoring). César Sánchez is funded in part by Spanish MINECO Project "RISCO (TIN2015-71819-P)" and by EU H2020 project 731535 "Elastest". Pérez is also affiliated to the NOVA Laboratory for Computer Science and Informatics (NOVA LINCS – PEst/UID/CEC/04516/2013), Universidade Nova de Lisboa, Portugal.

References

1. Alagar, S., Venkatesan, S.: Techniques to tackle state explosion in global predicate detection. IEEE Trans. Softw. Eng. (TSE) **27**(8), 704–714 (2001)
2. Ancona, D., Bono, V., Bravetti, M., Campos, J., Castagna, G., Deniélou, P., Gay, S.J., Gesbert, N., Giachino, E., Hu, R., Johnsen, E.B., Martins, F., Mascardi, V., Montesi, F., Neykova, R., Ng, N., Padovani, L., Vasconcelos, V.T., Yoshida, N.: Behavioral types in programming languages. Found. Trends Program. Lang. **3**(2–3), 95–230 (2016)
3. Attard, D.P., Francalanza, A.: A monitoring tool for a branching-time logic. In: Falcone, Y., Sánchez, C. (eds.) RV 2016. LNCS, vol. 10012, pp. 473–481. Springer, Cham (2016). https://doi.org/10.1007/978-3-319-46982-9_31
4. Attiya, H., Welch, J.L.: Distributed Computing: Fundamentals, Simulations and Advanced Topics. Wiley, Hoboken (2004)

5. Baader, F., Lippmann, M.: Runtime verification using the temporal description logic ALC-LTL revisited. J. Appl. Logic 12(4), 584–613 (2014)
6. Bartocci, E.: Sampling-based decentralized monitoring for networked embedded systems. In: Bortolussi, L., Bujorianu, M.L., Pola, G. (eds.) Proceedings of the 3rd International Workshop on Hybrid Autonomous Systems (HAS 2013). EPTCS, vol. 124, pp. 85–99 (2013)
7. Basin, D., Klaedtke, F., Marinovic, S., Zălinescu, E.: Monitoring compliance policies over incomplete and disagreeing logs. In: Qadeer, S., Tasiran, S. (eds.) RV 2012. LNCS, vol. 7687, pp. 151–167. Springer, Heidelberg (2013). https://doi.org/10.1007/978-3-642-35632-2_17
8. Basin, D.A., Klaedtke, F., Zalinescu, E.: Failure-aware runtime verification of distributed systems. In: Proceedings of FSTTCS 2015, pp. 590–603 (2015)
9. Basu, A., Bozga, M., Sifakis, J.: Modeling heterogeneous real-time components in BIP. In: Proceedings of the 4th IEEE International Conference on Software Engineering and Formal Methods (SEFM 2006), pp. 3–12. IEEE Computer Society (2006)
10. Bauer, A.K.: Monitorability of ω-regular languages. arXiv:1006.3638v1 (2010)
11. Bauer, A., Falcone, Y.: Decentralised LTL monitoring. In: Giannakopoulou, D., Méry, D. (eds.) FM 2012. LNCS, vol. 7436, pp. 85–100. Springer, Heidelberg (2012). https://doi.org/10.1007/978-3-642-32759-9_10
12. Bauer, A.K., Falcone, Y.: Decentralised LTL monitoring. Formal Methods Syst. Des. 48(1–2), 49–93 (2016)
13. Bauer, A.K., Leucker, M., Schallhart, C.: Runtime verification for LTL and TLTL. ACM Trans. Softw. Eng. Methodol. 20, 14:1–14:64 (2011)
14. Berkovich, S., Bonakdarpour, B., Fischmeister, S.: Runtime verification with minimal intrusion through parallelism. Formal Methods Syst. Des. 46(3), 317–348 (2015)
15. Bocchi, L., Chen, T., Demangeon, R., Honda, K., Yoshida, N.: Monitoring networks through multiparty session types. In: Proceedings of FMOODS/FORTE 2013, pp. 50–65 (2013)
16. Bocchi, L., Chen, T., Demangeon, R., Honda, K., Yoshida, N.: Monitoring networks through multiparty session types. Theor. Comput. Sci. 669, 33–58 (2017)
17. Bonakdarpour, B., Bozga, M., Jaber, M., Quilbeuf, J., Sifakis, J.: Automated conflict-free distributed implementation of component-based models. In: Proceedings of the IEEE 5th International Symposium on Industrial Embedded Systems (SIES 2010), pp. 108–117. IEEE (2010)
18. Bonakdarpour, B., Bozga, M., Jaber, M., Quilbeuf, J., Sifakis, J.: From high-level component-based models to distributed implementations. In: Proceedings of EMSOFT 2010, pp. 209–218. ACM (2010)
19. Bonakdarpour, B., Fraigniaud, P., Rajsbaum, S., Rosenblueth, D., Travers, C.: Decentralised asynchronous crash-resilient runtime verification. In: Proceedings of the 27th International Conference on Concurrency Theory (CONCUR 2016). LIPIcs, vol. 59, pp. 16:1–16:15. Schloss Dagstuhl - Leibniz-Zentrum fuer Informatik (2016)
20. Bonakdarpour, B., Fraigniaud, P., Rajsbaum, S., Travers, C.: Challenges in fault-tolerant distributed runtime verification. In: Margaria, T., Steffen, B. (eds.) ISoLA 2016, Part II. LNCS, vol. 9953, pp. 363–370. Springer, Cham (2016). https://doi.org/10.1007/978-3-319-47169-3_27
21. Carbone, M. (ed.): Proceedings of the Third Workshop on Behavioural Types (BEAT 2014). EPTCS, vol. 162 (2014)

22. Cassar, I., Francalanza, A.: On synchronous and asynchronous monitor instrumentation for actor systems. In: Proceedings of FOCLASA 2014, vol. 175, pp. 54–68 (2014)

23. Cassar, I., Francalanza, A.: Runtime adaptation for actor systems. In: Bartocci, E., Majumdar, R. (eds.) RV 2015. LNCS, vol. 9333, pp. 38–54. Springer, Cham (2015). https://doi.org/10.1007/978-3-319-23820-3_3

24. Cassar, I., Francalanza, A.: On implementing a monitor-oriented programming framework for actor systems. In: Ábrahám, E., Huisman, M. (eds.) IFM 2016. LNCS, vol. 9681, pp. 176–192. Springer, Cham (2016). https://doi.org/10.1007/978-3-319-33693-0_12

25. Cassar, I., Francalanza, A., Said, S.: Improving runtime overheads for detector. In: Buhnova, B., Happe, L., Kofron, J. (eds.) Proceedings of the 12th International Workshop on Formal Engineering approaches to Software Components and Architectures (FESCA 2015). EPTCS, vol. 178, pp. 1–8 (2015)

26. Castellani, I., Dezani-Ciancaglini, M., Pérez, J.A.: Self-adaptation and secure information flow in multiparty structured communications: a unified perspective. In: [21], pp. 9–18

27. Castellani, I., Dezani-Ciancaglini, M., Pérez, J.A.: Self-adaptation and secure information flow in multiparty communications. Formal Asp. Comput. **28**(4), 669–696 (2016)

28. Chandy, K.M., Lamport, L.: Distributed snapshots: determining global states of distributed systems. ACM Trans. Comput. Syst. **3**(1), 63–75 (1985)

29. Chase, C.M., Garg, V.K.: Detection of global predicates: techniques and their limitations. Distrib. Comput. **11**(4), 191–201 (1998)

30. Chauhan, H., Garg, V.K., Natarajan, A., Mittal, N.: A distributed abstraction algorithm for online predicate detection. In: IEEE 32nd Symposium on Reliable Distributed Systems (SRDS 2013), pp. 101–110. IEEE Computer Society (2013)

31. Chen, F., Roşu, G.: Parametric trace slicing and monitoring. In: Kowalewski, S., Philippou, A. (eds.) TACAS 2009. LNCS, vol. 5505, pp. 246–261. Springer, Heidelberg (2009). https://doi.org/10.1007/978-3-642-00768-2_23

32. Colombo, C., Dimech, G., Francalanza, A.: Investigating instrumentation techniques for ESB runtime verification. In: Calinescu, R., Rumpe, B. (eds.) SEFM 2015. LNCS, vol. 9276, pp. 99–107. Springer, Cham (2015). https://doi.org/10.1007/978-3-319-22969-0_7

33. Colombo, C., Falcone, Y.: Organising LTL monitors over distributed systems with a global clock. In: Bonakdarpour, B., Smolka, S.A. (eds.) RV 2014. LNCS, vol. 8734, pp. 140–155. Springer, Cham (2014). https://doi.org/10.1007/978-3-319-11164-3_12

34. Colombo, C., Falcone, Y.: Organising LTL monitors over distributed systems with a global clock. Formal Methods Syst. Des. **49**(1–2), 109–158 (2016)

35. Colombo, C., Francalanza, A., Gatt, R.: Elarva: a monitoring tool for Erlang. In: Khurshid, S., Sen, K. (eds.) RV 2011. LNCS, vol. 7186, pp. 370–374. Springer, Heidelberg (2012). https://doi.org/10.1007/978-3-642-29860-8_29

36. Colombo, C., Francalanza, A., Mizzi, R., Pace, G.J.: polyLARVA: runtime verification with configurable resource-aware monitoring boundaries. In: Eleftherakis, G., Hinchey, M., Holcombe, M. (eds.) SEFM 2012. LNCS, vol. 7504, pp. 218–232. Springer, Heidelberg (2012). https://doi.org/10.1007/978-3-642-33826-7_15

37. Cooper, R., Marzullo, K.: Consistent detection of global predicates. In: Proceedings of the ACM/ONR Workshop on Parallel and Distributed Debugging, pp. 163–173 (1991)

38. Coulouris, G.: Distributed Systems: Concepts and Design. Addison-Wesley, Boston (2011)
39. Cristian, F., Fetzer, C.: The timed asynchronous distributed system model. IEEE Trans. Parallel Distrib. Syst. **10**(6), 642–657 (1999)
40. D'Angelo, B., Sankaranarayanan, S., Sánchez, C., Robinson, W., Finkbeiner, B., Sipma, H.B., Mehrotra, S., Manna, Z.: LOLA: runtime monitoring of synchronous systems. In: Proceedings of the 12th International Symposium of Temporal Representation and Reasoning (TIME 2005), pp. 166–174. IEEE CS Press (2005)
41. Demangeon, R., Honda, K., Hu, R., Neykova, R., Yoshida, N.: Practical interruptible conversations: distributed dynamic verification with multiparty session types and python. Formal Methods Syst. Des. **46**(3), 197–225 (2015)
42. Di Giusto, C., Pérez, J.A.: An event-based approach to runtime adaptation in communication-centric systems. In: Hildebrandt, T., Ravara, A., van der Werf, J.M., Weidlich, M. (eds.) WS-FM 2014-2015. LNCS, vol. 9421, pp. 67–85. Springer, Cham (2016). https://doi.org/10.1007/978-3-319-33612-1_5
43. Di Giusto, C., Pérez, J.A.: Event-based run-time adaptation in communication-centric systems. Formal Aspects Comput. **28**(4), 1–36 (2016)
44. Diekert, V., Muscholl, A., Walukiewicz, I.: A note on monitors and Büchi automata. In: Leucker, M., Rueda, C., Valencia, F.D. (eds.) ICTAC 2015. LNCS, vol. 9399, pp. 39–57. Springer, Cham (2015). https://doi.org/10.1007/978-3-319-25150-9_3
45. El-Hokayem, A., Falcone, Y.: Monitoring decentralized specifications. In: Proceedings of the 26th ACM SIGSOFT International Symposium on Software Testing and Analysis (ISSTA 2017), pp. 125–135. ACM (2017)
46. Falcone, Y., Cornebize, T., Fernandez, J.-C.: Efficient and generalized decentralized monitoring of regular languages. In: Ábrahám, E., Palamidessi, C. (eds.) FORTE 2014. LNCS, vol. 8461, pp. 66–83. Springer, Heidelberg (2014). https://doi.org/10.1007/978-3-662-43613-4_5
47. Falcone, Y., Fernandez, J.-C., Mounier, L.: Runtime verification of safety-progress properties. In: Bensalem, S., Peled, D.A. (eds.) RV 2009. LNCS, vol. 5779, pp. 40–59. Springer, Heidelberg (2009). https://doi.org/10.1007/978-3-642-04694-0_4
48. Falcone, Y., Fernandez, J.C., Mounier, L.: What can you verify and enforce at runtime? STTT **14**(3), 349–382 (2012)
49. Falcone, Y., Jaber, M., Nguyen, T.H., Bozga, M., Bensalem, S.: Runtime verification of component-based systems in the BIP framework with formally-proved sound and complete instrumentation. Softw. Syst. Model. **14**(1), 173–199 (2015)
50. Felser, M.: Real-time Ethernet - industry prospective. Proc. IEEE **93**(6), 1118–1129 (2005)
51. Fidge, C.: Timestamps in message-passing systems that preserve the partial ordering. In: Proceedings of the 11th Australian Computer Science Conference, pp. 55–66 (1989)
52. Fidge, C.: Logical time in distributed computer systems. Computer **24**(8), 28–33 (1991)
53. Fraigniaud, P., Rajsbaum, S., Travers, C.: On the number of opinions needed for fault-tolerant run-time monitoring in distributed systems. In: RV (2014)
54. Francalanza, A.: A theory of monitors. In: Jacobs, B., Löding, C. (eds.) FoSSaCS 2016. LNCS, vol. 9634, pp. 145–161. Springer, Heidelberg (2016). https://doi.org/10.1007/978-3-662-49630-5_9
55. Francalanza, A., Aceto, L., Ingolfsdottir, A.: Monitorability for the Hennessy-Milner logic with recursion. FMSD **51**(1), 1–30 (2017)

56. Francalanza, A., Gauci, A., Pace, G.J.: Distributed system contract monitoring. In: Pimentel, E., Valero, V. (eds.) Proceedings of the Fifth Workshop on Formal Languages and Analysis of Contract-Oriented Software, FLACOS 2011, Málaga, Spain, 22–23 September 2011. EPTCS, vol. 68, pp. 23–37 (2011)

57. Francalanza, A., Gauci, A., Pace, G.J.: Distributed system contract monitoring. J. Logic Algebraic Program. 82(5–7), 186–215 (2013)

58. Francalanza, A., Hennessy, M.: A theory of system behaviour in the presence of node and link failure. Inf. Comput. 206(6), 711–759 (2008)

59. Francalanza, A., Seychell, A.: Synthesising correct concurrent runtime monitors. In: Legay, A., Bensalem, S. (eds.) RV 2013. LNCS, vol. 8174, pp. 112–129. Springer, Heidelberg (2013). https://doi.org/10.1007/978-3-642-40787-1_7

60. Francalanza, A., Seychell, A.: Synthesising correct concurrent runtime monitors. FMSD 46(3), 226–261 (2015)

61. Garg, D., Jia, L., Datta, A.: Policy auditing over incomplete logs: theory, implementation and applications. In: Proceedings of CCS 2011, pp. 151–162 (2011)

62. Garg, V.K.: Elements of Distributed Computing. Wiley-IEEE Press, New York (2002)

63. Garg, V.K., Mittal, N.: On slicing a distributed computation. In: Proceedings of the 21st IEEE International Conference on Distributed Computing Systems (ICDCS 2001), pp. 322–329. IEEE CS Press (2001)

64. Garg, V.K., Waldecker, B.: Detection of weak unstable predicates in distributed programs. IEEE Trans. Parallel Distrib. Syst. 5(3), 299–307 (1994)

65. Honda, K., Vasconcelos, V.T., Kubo, M.: Language primitives and type discipline for structured communication-based programming. In: Hankin, C. (ed.) ESOP 1998. LNCS, vol. 1381, pp. 122–138. Springer, Heidelberg (1998). https://doi.org/10.1007/BFb0053567

66. Honda, K., Yoshida, N., Carbone, M.: Multiparty asynchronous session types. J. ACM 63(1), 9:1–9:67 (2016)

67. Hu, R., Neykova, R., Yoshida, N., Demangeon, R., Honda, K.: Practical interruptible conversations - distributed dynamic verification with session types and python. In: [72], pp. 130–148

68. Hüttel, H., Lanese, I., Vasconcelos, V.T., Caires, L., Carbone, M., Deniélou, P., Mostrous, D., Padovani, L., Ravara, A., Tuosto, E., Vieira, H.T., Zavattaro, G.: Foundations of session types and behavioural contracts. ACM Comput. Surv. 49(1), 3:1–3:36 (2016)

69. Jia, L., Gommerstadt, H., Pfenning, F.: Monitors and blame assignment for higher-order session types. In: Bodík, R., Majumdar, R. (eds.) Proceedings of the 43rd Annual ACM SIGPLAN-SIGACT Symposium on Principles of Programming Languages, POPL 2016, St. Petersburg, FL, USA, 20–22 January 2016, pp. 582–594. ACM (2016)

70. Joyce, J., Lomow, G., Slind, K., Unger, B.W.: Monitoring distributed systems. ACM Trans. Comput. Syst. 5(2), 121–150 (1987)

71. Lamport, L.: Time, clocks and the ordering of events in distributed systems. Commun. ACM 21(7), 558–565 (1978)

72. Legay, A., Bensalem, S. (eds.): RV 2013. LNCS, vol. 8174. Springer, Heidelberg (2013). https://doi.org/10.1007/978-3-642-40787-1

73. Luo, Q., Roşu, G.: EnforceMOP: a runtime property enforcement system for multithreaded programs. In: ISSTA. ACM, New York (2013)

74. Mattern, F.: Virtual time and global states of distributed systems. In: Proceedings of the Workshop on Parallel and Distributed Algorithms, pp. 215–226. Elsevier (1989)

75. Mezzina, C.A., Pérez, J.A.: Reversible sessions using monitors. In: Orchard, D.A., Yoshida, N. (eds.) Proceedings of the Ninth Workshop on Programming Language Approaches to Concurrency- and Communication-cEntric Software (PLACES 2016). EPTCS, vol. 211, pp. 56–64 (2016)

76. Mezzina, C.A., Pérez, J.A.: Reversibility in session-based concurrency: a fresh look. J. Log. Algebraic Methods Program. **90**, 2–30 (2017)

77. Milner, R., Parrow, J., Walker, D.: A calculus of mobile processes, I. Inf. Comput. **100**(1), 1–40 (1992)

78. Mittal, N., Garg, V.K.: Techniques and applications of computation slicing. Distrib. Comput. **17**(3), 251–277 (2005)

79. Mittal, N., Sen, A., Garg, V.K.: Solving computation slicing using predicate detection. IEEE Trans. Parallel Distrib. Systems (TPDS) **18**(12), 1700–1713 (2007)

80. Mostafa, M., Bonakdarpour, B.: Decentralized runtime verification of LTL specifications in distributed systems. In: Proceedings of the 2015 IEEE International Parallel and Distributed Processing Symposium (IPDPS 2015), pp. 494–503. IEEE Computer Society (2015)

81. Neykova, R., Bocchi, L., Yoshida, N.: Timed runtime monitoring for multiparty conversations. In: [21], pp. 19–26

82. Neykova, R., Yoshida, N., Hu, R.: SPY: local verification of global protocols. In: [72], pp. 358–363

83. Ogale, V.A., Garg, V.K.: Detecting temporal logic predicates on distributed computations. In: Pelc, A. (ed.) DISC 2007. LNCS, vol. 4731, pp. 420–434. Springer, Heidelberg (2007). https://doi.org/10.1007/978-3-540-75142-7_32

84. Pnueli, A., Zaks, A.: PSL model checking and run-time verification via testers. In: Misra, J., Nipkow, T., Sekerinski, E. (eds.) FM 2006. LNCS, vol. 4085, pp. 573–586. Springer, Heidelberg (2006). https://doi.org/10.1007/11813040_38

85. Roşu, G., Havelund, K.: Rewriting-based techniques for runtime verification. Autom. Softw. Eng. **12**(2), 151–197 (2005)

86. Sen, A., Garg, V.K.: Detecting temporal logic predicates in distributed programs using computation slicing. In: Papatriantafilou, M., Hunel, P. (eds.) OPODIS 2003. LNCS, vol. 3144, pp. 171–183. Springer, Heidelberg (2004). https://doi.org/10.1007/978-3-540-27860-3_17

87. Sen, A., Garg, V.K.: Partial order trace analyzer (POTA) for distributed programs. ENTCS **89**(2), 22–43 (2003). Proceedings of Workshop on Runtime Verification (RV 2003)

88. Sen, A., Garg, V.K.: Formal verification of simulation traces using computation slicing. IEEE Trans. Comput. **56**, 511–527 (2007)

89. Sen, K., Vardhan, A., Agha, G., Rosu, G.: Efficient decentralized monitoring of safety in distributed systems. In: Proceedings of ICSE 2004. IEEE CS Press (2004)

90. Sen, K., Vardhan, A., Agha, G., Rosu, G.: Decentralized runtime analysis of multithreaded applications. In: Proceedings of the 20th IEEE International Parallel and Distributed Processing Symposium (IPDPS 2006). IEEE (2006)

91. Viswanathan, M.: Foundations for the run-time analysis of software systems. Ph.D. thesis, University of Pennsylvania (2000)

92. Yoshida, N., Hu, R., Neykova, R., Ng, N.: The scribble protocol language. In: Abadi, M., Lluch Lafuente, A. (eds.) TGC 2013. LNCS, vol. 8358, pp. 22–41. Springer, Cham (2014). https://doi.org/10.1007/978-3-319-05119-2_3

93. Zhang, T., Gebhard, P., Sokolsky, O.: SMEDL: combining synchronous and asynchronous monitoring. In: Falcone, Y., Sánchez, C. (eds.) RV 2016. LNCS, vol. 10012, pp. 482–490. Springer, Cham (2016). https://doi.org/10.1007/978-3-319-46982-9_32

Industrial Experiences with Runtime Verification of Financial Transaction Systems: Lessons Learnt and Standing Challenges

Christian Colombo(✉) and Gordon J. Pace

Department of Computer Science, University of Malta, Msida, Malta
{christian.colombo,gordon.pace}@um.edu.mt

Abstract. The chapter will focus on experiences the authors had in applying runtime verification in industrial settings, in particular on financial transaction systems. We discuss how runtime verification can be introduced in the software development lifecycle and who are the people to be involved and when. Furthermore, we investigate what kind of properties have been found useful in practise and how these were monitored to keep intrusion to a minimum. Next, we describe two significant case studies which have been successfully carried out in the past, and conclude by outlining a number of challenges which we believe still need to be addressed for runtime verification to become more mainstream in industrial settings.

1 Introduction

As software systems increased in size and complexity, it was quickly recognised that many problems which arise in system development can be addressed by adopting a well-defined, more rigorous process, moving from an individual-based craft view of programming to a process (and team) based engineering approach [28]. Different software engineering processes have been advocated and adopted by industry, and today it is unthinkable that any non-trivial software be developed in an ad-hoc manner. These software engineering processes have shaped the organisation of industry, and any novel element part of the software development process stands little chance of being adopted in the short-term unless it finds a home as part of this organisational structure. Runtime monitoring and verification have been advocated as very industry-friendly techniques, especially due to their scalability to large systems, and accessibility to traditionally trained software engineers. Surprisingly, however, the literature describing the use of runtime verification in industry and evidence of its adoption remains

The Open Payments Ecosystem has received funding from the European Union's Horizon 2020 research and innovation programme under grant number 666363.
Project GOMTA financed by the Malta Council for Science & Technology through the National Research & Innovation Programme 2013.

E. Bartocci and Y. Falcone (Eds.): Lectures on Runtime Verification, LNCS 10457, pp. 211–232, 2018.
https://doi.org/10.1007/978-3-319-75632-5_7

sparse and far between. Use of formal methods (and in particular runtime verification) in the literature tends to consider the adoption of formal tools throughout the development process—for instance, in [27] one of the few papers which reports on the experience of integrating runtime verification into the development process of an industry-grade project, model checking is initially used to verify at the design and code level, thus providing formal properties to be used with the runtime verification tool, an unrealistic assumption in most industrial settings.

One can argue that dynamic monitoring and verification has featured in software development since the first software systems—adding auxiliary code to check what the system is doing, and assertions to check predicates in order to identify and report or react to unexpected behaviour, is nothing but a primitive form of runtime monitoring and verification. More recent structured approaches to runtime verification, which focus on separating the concerns of system development and the specification of monitors and verification code, allow for greater independence between the process of system and monitor development. However, the integration of runtime verification in standard software engineering practice remains a little explored area. Although some work (e.g. [36]) does look at how the development process can be adapted to incorporate runtime analysis concerns, a shift in existing software engineering practice is difficult to achieve, and thus, integration into existing practice is crucial to widespread industrial adoption of runtime verification.

In the past decades, as software dependability became increasingly important, testing was promoted to a first-class concern in the development process, with approaches such as test-driven development becoming the norm in many settings. It is natural to ask whether runtime verification can simply piggyback onto the integration of testing in the software engineering process. The most important common concern between testing and runtime verification is the development of oracles able to flag unexpected system behaviour. However, the two also differ substantially in other aspects, making their merging in the software engineering process difficult. The fact that, unlike testing, runtime verification code (sometimes) is intended to be executed alongside the system post-deployment puts extra demands on this code, and requires a spread in the concern of software engineering from mainly the development time towards the runtime [6]. Also, although oracles and verification checks have a similar goal, in practice tests tend to hard code input behaviour and output pairs, whereas in runtime verification it is necessary to abstract the oracle to all potential input behaviour. These differences indicate that depending on the quality assurance infrastructure already existent in most software companies, adopting runtime verification might not be as straightforward as one might hope.

In this chapter, we present a number of industrial case studies which we have been involved in, and discuss what worked and what issues arose in the process. A secondary aim of the chapter is to assess, albeit in a qualitative and anecdotal manner, the challenges runtime verification faces before it can be adopted in the industry. Furthermore, it is worth noting that all case studies discussed in this chapter are in the financial software sector.

Case studies 1 and 2 were carried out with two different companies[1]. Both cases were the outcome of employees from the companies attending research talks and showing interest in adopting aspects of the runtime technologies we spoke about. We then set up a process of giving hands-on talks on site to company employees about the more pragmatic aspects of runtime verification. This was followed by being on their site to work on an initial proof-of-concept implementation with the hope of bootstrapping the use of runtime verification in a more widespread fashion within the companies' products.

Despite the limited technological success of these initial experiences, the collaboration has led to two formal projects being setup with one of the companies, indicating that the technology does hold promise to the industry. *Project 1*[2] [13] is an ongoing project GOMTA (Generation Online Monitors from Tests) between the University of Malta and Ixaris Ltd. in which the focus was to address one of the challenges identified in our initial collaboration—that of specifying appropriate properties for runtime verification. *Project 2*[3] [4,5] is another ongoing project with Ixaris Ltd, where the runtime verification aspect is more ambitious, since runtime verification is integrated as a core part of the compliance engine of the OPE (Open Payments Ecosystem) platform. Also of interest is that the development of the platform and the compliance engine are being done concurrently, unlike the other use cases, in which integration of runtime verification was attempted *a posteriori* to the system development.

All these use cases are discussed in more detail in the rest of the chapter.

2   Financial Transaction Systems

Over the past years, we have worked on various industrial financial transaction systems. In this section we combine the common aspects into a single description, highlighting any differences only when necessary. Although financial transaction systems face various challenges, from fraud and security, to functional correctness, all the work we discuss focusses on the functional correctness, since various third-party tools already address issues such as fraud detection and security effectively.

The transaction systems we interacted with, handle credit card transactions and are thus composed of two sub-systems: one which handles the part of the transaction taking place between the customer and the transaction system, and another handling the transaction between the transaction system and the bank. These will be referred to as the transaction handling system and the processor communication system respectively.

---

[1] Due to non-disclosure agreements, one of the companies cannot be named. However, it is worth noting that both companies had a R&D team of 50–100 persons.

[2] https://www.um.edu.mt/ict/cs/research/projects/gomta.

[3] https://www.openpaymentsecosystem.eu.

A transaction is processed by going through a number of states such as authorisation, communication with the user interface, inserting the transaction in the database and communicating with the commercial entity involved in the transaction. Each type of transaction will have its particular chain of states through which it must go to be successfully completed. Similarly, system user accounts also go through a cycle of events including registration, logging in, performing financial activities, suspension, etc. The interaction between these two life cycles as well as its implications on the amount limits are among the most commonly specified properties:

Life cycles. Entities in a transaction system, particularly users and transactions, go through a life cycle of stages. Each stage will determine how the entity can behave and stages it can transition to in the future. For example, *a user who has been suspended should not be allowed to perform any financial transactions*. Similarly, *a transaction which is in the processing stage, should not be modifiable*.

Real-time. A transaction system typically has real-time aspects such as *a transaction should not take longer than 500 milliseconds to complete*. Naturally, real-time properties can also be related to life cycles, e.g., *once a user has been inactive for three months, then the account should be frozen*.

Amount and frequency limits. Other commonly occurring properties in financial transaction systems involve amounts and frequencies of transactions and transaction amounts, e.g., *a user cannot transfer more than €2000 a week*. These limits may also be related to the life cycle, e.g., *a user who has registered but has not yet been fully approved, cannot withdraw more than €100 per week from the account*.

Other. There are a number of other properties which are difficult to classify under the previous headings. For example, to ensure adherence to VISA regulations, the transaction system cannot store credit card numbers. Another practical property is to ensure that a transaction is not initiated twice by the user mistakenly clicking the submit button twice.

3   Runtime Verification from a Process and Software Engineering Point of View

While making runtime verification attractive to industry necessarily requires the investigation of the appropriate process and software engineering practices, these elements remain largely unexplored in the literature.

The software testing community has had to solve a similar problem when it came to integrating testing in the development life cycle of software, requiring years of experimentation with different setups. To some extent engineering of properties for monitoring is similar to the engineering of test oracles in that both are meant to tag behaviour as good or bad by observing the system's behaviour. However, there is a major difference between the two, namely that test oracles are typically designed to handle only the test case it has been written for. On the other hand, a monitor oracle needs to be generic enough to handle any observed behaviour. This makes the problem significantly different and given the lack of published material on this topic in the context of runtime verification, in this section we simply give some anecdotal reporting on what we have done and how it worked out.

3.1 Process Engineering Challenges

The first problem when introducing a new verification technique such as runtime verification within a software company is to identify the people who will be interacting with the technique. This section will analyse a number of questions which arise from process engineering point of view.

Engineering the Properties. When attempting to start the process of engineering properties for our industrial partners, a number of questions started to emerge:

Which properties are worth monitoring?

A number of discussions were needed with our industrial partners simply to identify which properties are worth the effort of monitoring. At first the example properties which were being suggested were deemed to be superfluous given the way the system had been engineered. For example checking that the balance is correct after a transaction was well tested, would have simply wasted resources to monitor it. Similarly, properties found in runtime verification literature at the time—mainly focusing on properties extracted from the Javadoc of Java libraries such as those concerning iterators, maps, etc. [9, 10]—while useful, were not deemed to warrant the introduction of runtime verification technology (opting instead to use code reviews, etc to eliminate such standard bugs).

Following more discussions and involvement of different people in the organisation, it started to emerge that the most useful properties were those which crosscut the system across its modules or history. The crosscutting nature of properties such as: *"ensure the credit card numbers are never stored inside our system"*, *"ensure a user does not carry out any transaction when suspended"*, or *"the user should follow a particular cycle throughout its lifetime"*, made it hard to check them (without monitoring) in a straightforward manner, i.e., without cluttering the code and risking introducing additional bugs in the process.

Experience 3.1. Taken from case studies #1, #2.

▶ **Which properties are useful to monitor.** Identifying which properties are to be monitored might in itself be a challenging aspect for the success of a runtime verification project. If the involved people do not see the benefit of monitoring, then it is likely that monitoring will be sidelined. Our case studies have taught us that a number of meetings might be required before the right kind of properties are identified for monitoring (Experience 3.1). Even the notion of a property itself is usually alien in the context of the software development industry (typically the word *property* is taken to refer to an object attribute). However, once the initial communication hurdles are overcome, appropriate system-wide properties—typically having a temporal aspect—start to emerge.

▶ **Who is responsible?** Once a number of example properties are identified, the next challenge is to identify who would be responsible to express them

---

Which team will host the runtime verification engineer?
One of the interesting characteristics which emerged from both case study #1 and #2 was how many times the researcher had to change the team he was working with: In the case of the first case study, the researcher was first placed with the security team. Soon it was realised that the runtime checking of functional aspects had little to do with security. Next, the researcher was placed within the development team: This move facilitated the familiarisation of the researcher with the system code, but did little to help him understand the properties of interest. Next, the researcher had a meeting with the system architects and this proved to be a swift way of obtaining a bird's eye view of the system, including some of its main properties. Finally, the researcher found it best to work closest to the testing team whose system-level tests were closest to what the runtime monitors were expected to do. A similar experience of moving from one team to another could be recounted for the second case study. The situation was however different in that testing was mostly carried out by the developers themselves. This meant that developers were mainly responsible for testing their own modules while there was a dedicated team for quality assurance (QA) which performed some testing and dealt with customer issues. This time the researcher found it best to interact with the QA team to identify the properties of interest. The main difference between the kind of properties identified by the QA team and those identified by interacting with the architects is that the former are more likely to actually be violated at runtime (e.g., a fee which is charged twice to the customer), while the others are more fundamental but usually highly unlikely to be violated (e.g., the sequence of states a customer goes through: from registered, to active, to suspended, etc).

Experience 3.2. Taken from case studies #1, #2.

> **Who will write the properties?**
> In both case study #1 and #2, when developers were asked to write
> properties to be monitored at runtime, they felt that they were simply
> redoing work already done while at the same time their view of the
> system was focused on their particular module, making it difficult to
> capture system-wide properties. Instead, runtime verification moni-
> tors were more naturally expressed by high level testers/QA person-
> nel who view properties as a concise way of expressing complex sys-
> tem properties and providing them with a kind of dashboard through
> property violation reporting. Furthermore, since the people writing
> the properties were not the same ones who programmed the system,
> this approach yielded better results in identifying bugs.

Experience 3.3. Taken from case studies #1, #2.

in a monitorable format. As Experience 3.2 shows, when the runtime verification engineer started to work at the site of our industrial partner, it was
not straightforward to pinpoint the team which could most naturally handle
property writing. The issues involved were not limited to who has the knowledge of the system at the right level of abstraction, but also who is willing to
do the work while finding it beneficial (Experience 3.3). The conclusion of our
case studies was that the people who tick all the identified boxes in a software
development organisation are the QA personnel who have a vested interest in
ensuring that the system as a whole works as expected. Runtime verification
provides them with a methodological approach of specifying properties and a
way of automatically checking them.

▶ **In what format should properties be expressed?** Identifying an appropriate format for expressing the properties is crucial to enable the identified
personnel to express the properties. Admittedly, we have not experimented
with different specification languages. However, our use of automata-flavoured
notation (more specifically [24]) has proved effective with non-academics who
used it.

Engineering the Verification Code. Once the properties are available, the
next challenge is to engineer the corresponding code to check for their violation.
Typically, the purpose of writing the properties formally is to exploit some runtime verification tool which is able to generate the code for the properties automatically. On the other hand, programming the verification code from scratch
is also an option, but this would mean that the property engineering step is
skipped. Furthermore, taking this option would also usually mean that the code
would not be separate from the system code, and consequently, this is programmed directly by the programmers (in the case of our first experience (see
Experience 3.4) since the testing team was closely involved in the development

process and had ample experience in writing system-wide scripts, it was responsible for integrating the runtime verification code). If the verification code is not integrated with the system—usually when the verification does not take place in sync with the system—then the code can be maintained by a team other than that of the system developers, e.g., the QA team (this was the case with the second experience mentioned in Experience 3.4).

Who manages the verification code?

In the first experience, since runtime verification was carried out in an online fashion, the testing team had to be involved to help set up the necessary scripts to integrate the monitoring within the system code. The reason for involving the testing team was that they had ample experience with launching the system through script writing. Unfortunately, the system was never updated after the introduction of runtime verification code, meaning that we cannot comment further on this experience regarding the management of synthesis and synthesised code.

In the second experience, runtime verification was carried out in an offline fashion and therefore this could be fully managed by the QA team with little involvement from the development team in case required logs were missing or in an unexpected format.

Experience 3.4. Taken from case studies #1, #2.

Considering the option of automated synthesis, two separate choices have to be made: (i) concerning the synthesis code and (ii) concerning the synthesised code. If the latter is to be integrated with the system, then one would typically expect the system developers to be responsible for it. However, if the generated code is to be used separately from the system, then once more there is the option of involving other teams. As for the synthesis code, since this does not directly interact with the system and it would probably be a third party tool, then its management need not be tied to the system developers' team.

Recommended procedure for introducing runtime verification. Based on our experience, in an ideal scenario, we recommend the following procedure when introducing runtime verification in a company not familiar with the technology:

Initial meetings. An initial meeting where an overview of the system and teams involved (including architects, developers, and QA) is provided by the company. Next, another meeting where the ideas behind runtime verification are presented to the teams by the runtime verification engineers.

Information gathering. Following the meetings, all relevant specifications, architectural designs, etc. should be made available to the runtime verification engineers. This is then followed up with meeting with relevant parties to fill in any gaps in such documents.

Meeting with QA. The QA team can provide information regarding the kind of problems they worry about the most on a day-to-day basis. These are usually the areas where runtime verification can be useful. Properties can then be composed based on these revelations.

Implementation phase. Once properties are at hand, input is likely to be required the system architects and developers.

Testing phase. Finally, when monitors are running, one would likely need to verify any detected violations with the QA team. It is probable that the first issues encountered would be the result of miscommunicated requirements, requiring fine-tuning of the properties.

Delegation phase. If monitors are running as expected, then it would be the right time for the responsibility to pass on from the runtime verification engineers to the teams in their respective roles: the architects to ensure the monitoring code is well integrated in the system design, the developers to manage the code, and QA personnel to maintain the properties.

3.2   Monitor Design Challenges

A significant challenge from a software engineering point of view with respect to runtime verification is to keep the concern separate from the system's logic while at the same time making it easy to integrate the two.

Furthermore, this has to be achieved while keeping the runtime overhead to a minimum. The following subsections deals with elements one should be aware of when designing the verification code. It is worth noting that many of these elements are interconnected and one choice influences others. One important starting factor when considering these options is that of what properties one is interested in, and when and how one is to react to their violation. Such considerations already restricts architecture choices, and event extraction mechanisms.

Architecture Design. One important question to be addressed is that of how the high-level architecture combining the system and the verification units is designed. In both case studies 1 and 2, the verification modules were developed *a posteriori*, and had to be integrated to systems which had been in production for various years, which proved to be an extra challenge in that limited architectural choices were available.

▶ **Synchronous vs. asynchronous vs. offline monitoring.** One major choice to make when integrating runtime verification and the system-under-scrutiny, is whether the composition of the two is (i) *online synchronous*, in that after each relevant step, the system will pause for the verification component to complete and announce compliance before proceeding further, or (ii) *online asynchronous*, in which the monitor is running with the system but steps of the system are checked asynchronously i.e., the system continues as the monitor does its verification; or (iii) *offline*, in which the system simply dumps relevant information during its execution, and the verification is carried out completely independently of the system, possibly even after the system has finished executing. The choice of architecture impacts how much the monitors can help the system react to errors, but also the overheads of the deployed monitoring. We had different experiences with possible composition approaches, as discussed in Experience 3.5.

▶ **Managing communication between system and monitors.** When monitoring takes place in a white box fashion, i.e., with full knowledge and access of the system code, monitors might be inlined directly along with the system code. This is typically done through the use of aspect-oriented programming [31] although it is common to write assertions by hand. To keep concerns more separate, e.g., if the system and the monitor are running on different resources and/or implemented in different technologies, one might opt for a less tightly coupled form of communication such as the use of TCP/IP [19]. When monitoring in a black box fashion, the separation between system and monitors is naturally bigger and thus less direct ways of communication would be typically employed. For example, the monitor might use a tracing facility at the virtual machine level to pick up events of interest. Similarly, the monitor might be able to indirectly detect system API calls by tapping into the system's communication channel. Opting for even less interaction, the monitor might simply process logs which the system would have saved in a database or text file during its execution.

Event Extraction Design. Runtime monitoring requires an awareness of the system behaviour, typically by capturing relevant events[4]. In what follows, we describe three kinds of software events and outline ways these can be captured and communicated to the monitor:

▶ **Method-call-based events.** Method calls frequently provide the right correspondence between the system's behaviour and the monitor events of interest. For example if the monitor is interested in money transfers, probably one can easily find a method which performs the money transfer, providing access to the parameter representing the amount being transferred. Method entry and exit points are typically captured through aspect-oriented programming (this was the case with our case studies, see Experience 3.6), or a tracing mechanism which the virtual machine provides.

▶ **Communication events.** While in Java it feels natural to capture method call entry or exit, other programming languages or system organisations may provide different useful points of interest. A prevalent one of these is message communication in the case of languages such as Erlang [18] or organisations such as the service-oriented architecture [17]. Once again, such communication can be captured using similar techniques, as applicable, such as aspect-oriented programming and tracing.

---

[4] Other than software events, one may for example capture the state of the hardware, or perform regular sampling of the variables. However, in this chapter we focus on the more commonly used software events.

How to synchronise between the system and the monitors?
In case study 1, we started by implementing online synchronous verification on a sandboxed system. However, in the second case study we had to forgo synchrony due to (i) lack of trust impeding the integration of the runtime verification tool as part of the development toolset; (ii) fear of overheads due to online monitoring impacting the system, particularly at times of peak transaction traffic. The solution initially adopted to enable verification was, in both use cases, to adopt an offline policy [1, 25, 26]. Given that the interested events of the systems were already logged by systems in use by both companies, it was simply a matter of accessing existing logs and connecting them with our runtime verification tool.[a] The results were sufficiently convincing that the monitoring was considered to be adopted on a nightly basis, running it on the logs of the day. This led to the realisation that an important feature of a runtime verifier is efficient bootstrapping—starting up the verification process in a fast manner, without having to rerun full historic traces every time. This led to a solution which was effective enough to be used in the nightly verification process [22]. The use of offline monitoring also enabled further trust in the verification package, which enabled further investigation, even if online overheads were still considered prohibitive since they were not planned for in the original system design. Financial systems typically handle *long-lived transactions*—financial transactions which last far too long to justify locking of resources (e.g., user's bank account) in order to ensure consistency. The solution practically universally adopted in this industry is that of using *compensations*, effectively computations which can approximate the undoing of part of a transaction. In this manner, transactions are allowed to proceed unchecked, and in case of a late discovered failure, the transaction is "rewound" to just before the event that broke consistency constraints. This led to the development of a novel quasi-synchronous runtime verification [23, 24] in which the monitor was deployed asynchronously (though online) with the system, but upon identifying a violation, compensations were triggered to enable recovery in the state of the system where the violation actually occurred.

---

[a] It is worth noting that although the required events were logged, many events unnecessary for our properties were also logged, so using the logs as a starting point for identifying points-of-interest in the system is not necessarily a useful procedure.

Experience 3.5. Taken from use cases #1, #2.

▶ **Events-by-design.** Rather than relying on naturally occurring execution points in the system (such as method call entry/exit points and communication events), another option is to explicitly plan points-of-interest when to raise an event in the system design. From a monitoring point of view, this approach naturally represents the most straightforward one as the system emits events automatically without the need to capture them. At their most basic, such events may take the form of logging events in a text file or database. In other cases, events might be broadcast to interested subscribers, one of which might be the monitor.

How to capture system events?
In both case studies, the events of interest could be directly mapped to method calls. For this reason, it was natural to opt for method-call-based events. Furthermore, given the maturity of tools supporting aspect-orientation, we chose a well-known aspect-oriented extension for Java, AspectJ. A significant difference between the two case studies is that the first was carried out online while the second was carried out offline by connecting to a database. We note that AspectJ could not be used to directly interact with an SQL database. However, by using a Java event replayer we were able to use AspectJ for both case studies.

Experience 3.6. Taken from use cases #1, #2.

Verification Design Challenges. Having events of interest reaching the monitor, we now focus on how the monitor will process them. The main concern in this respect is how to keep the runtime overheads to a minimum and avoid memory leaks which might cause the monitor to take more resources to the detriment of the system.

▶ **Keeping runtime work to a minimum.** One choice when designing the verifier is whether to explore the monitored logic a priori to avoid having to unfold it during runtime. For example in the case of LTL [34], one would generate the equivalent automaton such that at runtime one would simply need to move from one state to another rather than rewriting the formula. The approach we took in our case studies (see Experience 3.7) is to some extent even more extreme as we chose to allow the users to program the properties directly as automata[5]. In this way, we pass on the control of (most of) the overheads to the user.

---

[5] Users all had an undergraduate degree which covered automata and they did not have full formal training in using formal logics such as LTL, they were comfortable using automata.

▶ **Bounded resources and garbage collection.** If the chosen specification language supports monitoring using bounded memory, one may carefully implement the verifier such that the resource boundedness is exploited. The approach adopted for the case studies was to have a fixed set of user-defined states and thus memory leaks can only be introduced by the user through the Java code which can be used in transition conditions and actions.

Furthermore, another concern is the garbage collection of monitors—unused monitors can cause a memory leak. In general it is not trivial to identify monitors which can be discarded, since monitors are typically stateful and discarding part of the state might lead to incorrect monitoring. For our case studies (Experience 3.7) we chose to allow the user to explicitly mark states as *accepting*, meaning that once an automaton reaches that state it can be garbage collected.

How to design the verifier?

For both case studies we used the runtime verification tool Larva [25] to generate the monitors. Two important choices in the generated verification code were: (i) to use explicit automata, meaning that at runtime only simple if-conditions are evaluated (apart from conditions and actions explicitly programmed by the user); and (ii) to generate a hashing function for monitors (building on the user-defined hashing function of the monitored object) so that monitor lookup takes place in constant time. The first case study, in particular, served as the first testbed for the Larva tool and several modifications were introduced based on the experience. One such modification is the introduction of *accepting states*, i.e., states which signify property satisfaction and hence that that particular automaton can be garbage collected. Providing a means of garbage collection proved crucial to have monitors which are usable in real-life.

Experience 3.7. Taken from use cases #1, #2.

3.3 Conclusions

In this section we have presented the main challenges we have encountered when introducing runtime verification into an environmental setting. The challenges fall under two clear categories (i) how the introduction of monitoring will impact the management of the software design and development process, and (ii) the technical challenges as to how to capture events and process them, i.e. the monitoring architecture, for the system at hand. A number of observations we made from our experiences were the following:

1. Companies do not trust new software easily, especially if it interacts with their live system at runtime.
2. Overheads are a worry, even when they might not be a real concern.
3. A major challenge is to have existing company structures organised to fit their current software engineering process absorb runtime verification without reorganisation.
4. Attractive, low-cost applications of monitoring have been found to be statistics gathering and user interface traversal analysis.

4   Challenges in Adoption of Runtime Verification

After presenting the challenges and design issues involved in introducing runtime monitoring in industry, this section presents a number of proposals and describes how these are being taken on board in two ongoing projects:

Project 1—OPE. The Open Payments Ecosystem (OPE) is an EU-funded Horizon 2020 project, aiming at creating a single pan-European cloud-based marketplace allowing third party developers to create payments applications and service providers (e.g., banks) to provide a range of services (e.g., card authorisation, ACH transfer, Swift) to support these applications. As a core component of the OPE infrastructure, is a verification engine which allows for matching applications with service providers based on their requirements, and to runtime verify the behaviour of these applications to ensure compliance to legislation, risk restrictions and other rules as required.

Project 2—GOMTA. The GOMTA project—Generating Online Monitors from Tests Automatically—is a project funded by the Malta Council for Science and Technology (MCST). The project aims to facilitate the adoption of runtime monitoring by saving the user the specification of the properties, extracting them instead from the test suite.

4.1   Challenge 1: Monitoring Overhead

Based on our experience with industrial case studies, monitoring overheads (primarily time, but also memory) have proved to be a major challenge and hurdle in the adoption of runtime verification in industrial-grade systems. The runtime verification community has focussed on the use of techniques at two different levels of abstraction: system level monitoring vs. business logic. The former, focussing on elements of lower-level code and libraries (e.g., iterators), implies higher requirement of low overheads of monitoring due to the denser spread of events, while the latter can make do with higher overhead per event since the events being monitored are typically substantially sparser. Industry tends to invest substantial resources in identifying the right infrastructure and libraries, with trustworthiness being one of the important metrics used. Due to this, it was observed that the use of runtime verification techniques was seen by the industrial collaborators solely as a means of verifying their business logic. This reduces the requirements as to what are reasonable overheads, but it is worth noting different issues related to overheads which have been identified in the past use cases:

Worst-case overheads: The main concern with overheads is how large they can grow per event. However, given that runtime verification is a technique which (may) use the history of the system to deduce correctness, a concern is also that certain properties might require more time to check as the history grows longer, unless techniques such as incrementally verifiable properties are used to ensure this does not happen.

Variability of overheads: Another concern is that the overheads might change as the system evolves, leading to variability in quality-of-service measures over time.

Overhead spikes: In many transaction systems, there are (sometimes predictable) spikes of usage. For instance, on the payment portal of an online betting service, one gets high numbers of transactions just before an important sports event. This results in a proportionate spike in overheads, but is also the moment when fast reactivity is of high importance. A decrease in transaction processing speed could have a proportionately decrease in income. Catering for these moments of high server stress through hardware redundancy is only part of the solution here, and techniques to deal with monitoring in the presence of such spikes is a challenge still to be addressed.

Throughput: In a financial transaction system, all the concerns above are ultimately transaction, rather than event centric. In other words, transaction throughput is a key measure used by this industry. This means than looking at overheads at the quantum of transactions (which are variable compounds of events) gives a better hold on the applicability of the techniques in this domain.

Many techniques have been developed in the runtime community to address the issue of overheads. From the adoption of additional hardware for verification e.g., using GPUs [8,33] or FPGAs [30] to adaptive techniques to manage monitors through measures of criticality e.g., [7], much runtime verification literature is concerned with this issue. From a more pragmatic perspective, it is still the case that choosing which architecture to adopt—in particular whether online or offline monitoring—is largely motivated by the requirements on overheads.

Work on the use of static analysis techniques in order to partially verify requirements and thus alleviating runtime verification overhead is also showing promising results e.g., [3,11,14,15,29,35,37]. Recently, we have started adopting such a technique (in ongoing project 1—see Experience 4.1), which uses static analysis to reduce dynamic properties, thus lowering overheads.

> **Combining static and dynamic analysis**
> In the OPE project, one important functionality of the framework is to enable a developer to submit a payment app (or rather a model of the app), which is automatically matched with an appropriate service provider, based on capabilities, risk analysis and other aspects. In order to perform this matching, static analysis of the model submitted by the developer is performed [4].
> This gave the opportunity to include further static analysis to reduce runtime verification overheads in the compliance engine, which has to check that (i) the application adheres to the model supplied by the user; and (ii) that it does not violate legislation, service provider risk limits, etc. For example, according to English legislation, the customer should always have the possibility of redeeming money from his or her account after closure. Using the app model, we statically check that this possibility is in fact supported—noting that this would otherwise have to be runtime checked frequently (even when no redemption is carried out). Moreover, regulations also state that money redemption should occur at par value and without delay. However, it is not possible to statically verify that these hold as the model does not contain this level of detail, which leaves parts to be checked dynamically (in this case, for example, timely redemption is not statically verifiable at the level of abstraction of the model). These remaining checks are delegated to be carried out through runtime monitoring.

Experience 4.1. Taken from ongoing project #1.

4.2 Challenge 2: Proposals for Runtime Verification from the Software Engineering Point of View

Introducing runtime verification within a software development life cycle presents a number of challenges as highlighted in the previous section. In what follows, we attempt to address them below by describing different approaches we have adopted in ongoing projects.

Monitoring as part of system design. One of the main drawbacks of our previous experiences was that monitoring was not included in the original design of the system being monitored. Instead, monitoring had to be somehow retrofitted into the system architecture. In the OPE project (see Experience 4.2) runtime verification was included from the start and used to ensure the reliability of the framework.

Monitor architecture. The underlying system architecture naturally has a direct effect on the monitor architecture. In traditional monolithic systems, without significant effort, the choice is usually limited to online or offline monitoring. System architectures which allow submodules to be more decoupled such as actor systems and those based on the service-oriented architecture, allow more monitoring options. The OPE (see Experience 4.3) is based on a micro-services architecture and therefore it was natural to have monitoring as a service and the system may decide to wait or not for the monitor verdict depending on the context.

Extracting events. Identifying system execution points of interest and intercepting them through aspect-oriented programming proved to be a non-trivial task in previous case studies. Having predefined, clearly specified events makes it significantly more straightforward for components within the system to communicate as the events serve as a common interface; not least for the monitor. In the OPE project (see Experience 4.3), events from each micro-service are published with the monitor simply listening out for the relevant ones.

Monitoring as part of the system design
In past case studies the monitor has always been introduced after the system had already been developed. On the contrary, in the OPE the compliance unit (of which runtime verification plays a major role) was part of the initial design of the framework. This saved the OPE execution environment from having to be inundated with checks to cater for the legislation. The design, in turn, was taken into consideration when choosing the implementation framework and as further elaborated in Experience 4.3, incorporating the monitor in the OPE was straightforward.

Experience 4.2. Taken from ongoing project #1.

Monitoring architecture in a micro-services architecture
Being programmed as a monolithic Java system, previous case studies relied on aspect-oriented programming to embed the runtime verification code, resulting in either fully synchronous or completely offline monitoring. By contrast the OPE is organised in terms of micro-services, making it relatively easy to have asynchronous monitoring on the live system: on the one hand, introducing the monitoring service was as straightforward as adding any other service to the system; while on the other hand, using the native communication infrastructure, all services can report events to the monitoring service.

Experience 4.3. Taken from ongoing project #1.

4.3   Challenge 3: Communication and Formalisation of Properties

One of the initial hurdles of introducing runtime verification in industry is that of expressing the system properties in a formal fashion. To address this problem, we are working on two fronts:

> **Developing a controlled natural language**
> The OPE project is concerned with alleviating the administrative
> burdens of creating financial applications. As such, there are various
> laws and directives which need to be taken into consideration (e.g., the
> Electronic Money Directive and the Anti-Money Laundering Regula-
> tions). The main challenge with encoding such legislation into formal
> properties is that they are regularly updated, and that lawyers need
> to be involved to confirm that what is being specified corresponds
> to the law. Using a controlled natural language enabled us to have a
> communication language with the non-technical lawyers, and at the
> same time technical people would not need to be involved each time
> the legislation is updated.

Experience 4.4. Taken from ongoing project #1.

Using a controlled natural language. One way of easing the difficulty of
expressing correctness properties is by providing a specification language
which does not require its users to have a background in formal methods.
While automata have been useful in previous experiences, their expressivity
is substantially limited except through the use of additional Java code on
the transitions. One way of lifting this limitation without impinging on the
understandability of the language is through the use of controlled natural
languages [32]. These allow the creation of a custom language whose expressivity matches that required in the context while the learning curve can be
kept to a minimum. We have experimented with the use of controlled natural
languages in such contexts in more academic projects [12,13,20] before, but

> **Generating monitors automatically**
> While none of our industrial partners had been using runtime verifi-
> cation before our collaboration, they both had a formidable test suite
> with good coverage of the system's functionality. This realisation led
> us to consider extracting monitors from tests. While the investigation
> is still in its early phases, initial experiments using the Daikon invari-
> ant inference engine suggest that a number of properties can indeed
> be extracted from tests automatically: depending on some quality
> attributes of the test suite such as branch coverage, we were able to
> exceed 70% specification recall, although admittedly precision is still
> below 30% [17].

Experience 4.5. Taken from ongoing project #2.

the OPE project (Experience 4.4) was the first industrial-project setting in which we have used this approach, and which has so far proved to be effective. **Generating monitors automatically.** Another approach being explored to simplify property specification is to attempt to extract them automatically or otherwise from available information already present in tests. There has been some previous work on automated monitor synthesis from tests e.g. [2,26], although these approaches work at a level of abstraction which is not always available in real-life case studies. For instance, [26] requires model-based test case generators which are infrequently used in industry. There is some initial work to start from the (universally used in industry) unit tests, but it is still unclear how much can be achieved automatically. On the other hand, as a means of supporting manual property writing, there is no denying that tests contain much information which can be used for property writing (Experience 4.5).

5   Conclusions

In this chapter we have presented an anecdotal view of the use of runtime verification in an industrial setting. Although we focussed on our experiences in the domain of financial transaction systems, much of the observations are not domain-specific, and can be extrapolated for other application domains.

The challenges encountered can mostly be split into two categories—firstly how runtime verification can be fitted into existing software engineering practices and management structures, and secondly technical ones, particularly tailoring the right runtime verification flavour to match the requirements and system at hand. We have found that some such choices tend to pave the way for smoother adoption of monitoring technologies—for instance, starting with offline verification using existing system behaviour logs can be an excellent way of showing potential benefit without having to surpass the hurdle of introducing new code into the system. Finally, we have identified the major challenges which we believe are still to be addressed before runtime verification can find a foothold in industry, enabling its widespread use.

References

1. Abela, P., Colombo, C., Pace, G.J.: Offline runtime verification with real-time properties: a case study. In: University of Malta Workshop in ICT (WICT 2009) (2009)
2. Artho, C., Barringer, H., Goldberg, A., Havelund, K., Khurshid, S., Lowry, M.R., Pasareanu, C.S., Rosu, G., Sen, K., Visser, W., Washington, R.: Combining test case generation and runtime verification. Theor. Comput. Sci. **336**(2–3), 209–234 (2005). https://doi.org/10.1016/j.tcs.2004.11.007
3. Artho, C., Biere, A.: Combined static and dynamic analysis. Electr. Notes Theor. Comput. Sci. **131**, 3–14 (2005). https://doi.org/10.1016/j.entcs.2005.01.018

4. Azzopardi, S., Colombo, C., Pace, G.: A model-based approach to combining static and dynamic verification techniques. In: Margaria, T., Steffen, B. (eds.) ISoLA 2016, Part I. LNCS, vol. 9952, pp. 416–430. Springer, Cham (2016). https://doi.org/10.1007/978-3-319-47166-2_29

5. Azzopardi, S., Colombo, C., Pace, G.J., Vella, B.: Compliance checking in the open payments ecosystem. In: De Nicola, R., Kühn, E. (eds.) SEFM 2016. LNCS, vol. 9763, pp. 337–343. Springer, Cham (2016). https://doi.org/10.1007/978-3-319-41591-8_23

6. Baresi, L., Ghezzi, C.: The disappearing boundary between development-time and run-time. In: Proceedings of the FSE/SDP Workshop on Future of Software Engineering Research, FoSER 2010, pp. 17–22. ACM, New York (2010). http://doi.acm.org/10.1145/1882362.1882367

7. Bartocci, E., Grosu, R., Karmarkar, A., Smolka, S.A., Stoller, S.D., Zadok, E., Seyster, J.: Adaptive runtime verification. In: Qadeer, S., Tasiran, S. (eds.) RV 2012. LNCS, vol. 7687, pp. 168–182. Springer, Heidelberg (2013). https://doi.org/10.1007/978-3-642-35632-2_18

8. Berkovich, S., Bonakdarpour, B., Fischmeister, S.: GPU-based runtime verification. In: 27th IEEE International Symposium on Parallel and Distributed Processing, IPDPS 2013, Cambridge, MA, USA, 20–24 May 2013 (2013). https://doi.org/10.1109/IPDPS.2013.105

9. Bodden, E., Hendren, L., Lam, P., Lhoták, O., Naeem, N.A.: Collaborative runtime verification with tracematches. J. Log. Comput. **20**(3), 707–723 (2010). https://doi.org/10.1093/logcom/exn077

10. Bodden, E., Hendren, L., Lhoták, O.: A staged static program analysis to improve the performance of runtime monitoring. In: Ernst, E. (ed.) ECOOP 2007. LNCS, vol. 4609, pp. 525–549. Springer, Heidelberg (2007). https://doi.org/10.1007/978-3-540-73589-2_25

11. Bodden, E., Lam, P., Hendren, L.: Clara: a framework for partially evaluating finite-state runtime monitors ahead of time. In: Barringer, H., et al. (eds.) RV 2010. LNCS, vol. 6418, pp. 183–197. Springer, Heidelberg (2010). https://doi.org/10.1007/978-3-642-16612-9_15

12. Calafato, A., Colombo, C., Pace, G.J.: A controlled natural language for tax fraud detection. In: Davis, B., Pace, G.J.J., Wyner, A. (eds.) CNL 2016. LNCS (LNAI), vol. 9767, pp. 1–12. Springer, Cham (2016). https://doi.org/10.1007/978-3-319-41498-0_1

13. Cauchi, A., Colombo, C., Francalanza, A., Micallef, M., Pace, G.J.: Using gherkin to extract tests and monitors for safer medical device interaction design. In: Proceedings of the 8th ACM SIGCHI Symposium on Engineering Interactive Computing Systems, EICS 2016, Brussels, Belgium, 21–24 June 2016, pp. 275–280. ACM, New York (2016). http://doi.acm.org/10.1145/2933242.2935868

14. Centonze, P., Flynn, R.J., Pistoia, M.: Combining static and dynamic analysis for automatic identification of precise access-control policies. In: 23rd Annual Computer Security Applications Conference (ACSAC 2007), Miami Beach, Florida, USA, 10–14 December 2007, pp. 292–303 (2007). https://doi.org/10.1109/ACSAC.2007.14

15. Chimento, J.M., Ahrendt, W., Pace, G.J., Schneider, G.: STaRVOORS: a tool for combined static and runtime verification of Java. In: Bartocci, E., Majumdar, R. (eds.) RV 2015. LNCS, vol. 9333, pp. 297–305. Springer, Cham (2015). https://doi.org/10.1007/978-3-319-23820-3_21

16. Chircop, L., Colombo, C., Micallef, M.: Exploring the link between automatic specification inference and test suite quality (2017). Submitted for publication

17. Colombo, C., Dimech, G., Francalanza, A.: Investigating instrumentation techniques for ESB runtime verification. In: Calinescu, R., Rumpe, B. (eds.) SEFM 2015. LNCS, vol. 9276, pp. 99–107. Springer, Cham (2015). https://doi.org/10.1007/978-3-319-22969-0_7

18. Colombo, C., Francalanza, A., Gatt, R.: Elarva: a monitoring tool for erlang. In: Khurshid, S., Sen, K. (eds.) RV 2011. LNCS, vol. 7186, pp. 370–374. Springer, Heidelberg (2012). https://doi.org/10.1007/978-3-642-29860-8_29

19. Colombo, C., Francalanza, A., Mizzi, R., Pace, G.J.: polyLARVA: runtime verification with configurable resource-aware monitoring boundaries. In: Eleftherakis, G., Hinchey, M., Holcombe, M. (eds.) SEFM 2012. LNCS, vol. 7504, pp. 218–232. Springer, Heidelberg (2012). https://doi.org/10.1007/978-3-642-33826-7_15

20. Colombo, C., Grech, J.-P., Pace, G.J.: A controlled natural language for business intelligence monitoring. In: Biemann, C., Handschuh, S., Freitas, A., Meziane, F., Métais, E. (eds.) NLDB 2015. LNCS, vol. 9103, pp. 300–306. Springer, Cham (2015). https://doi.org/10.1007/978-3-319-19581-0_27

21. Colombo, C., Pace, G.J.: Fast-forward runtime monitoring — an industrial case study. In: Qadeer, S., Tasiran, S. (eds.) RV 2012. LNCS, vol. 7687, pp. 214–228. Springer, Heidelberg (2013). https://doi.org/10.1007/978-3-642-35632-2_22

22. Colombo, C., Pace, G.J., Abela, P.: Compensation-aware runtime monitoring. In: Barringer, H., et al. (eds.) RV 2010. LNCS, vol. 6418, pp. 214–228. Springer, Heidelberg (2010). https://doi.org/10.1007/978-3-642-16612-9_17

23. Colombo, C., Pace, G.J., Abela, P.: Safer asynchronous runtime monitoring using compensations. Formal Methods Syst. Des. **41**(3), 269–294 (2012). https://doi.org/10.1007/s10703-012-0142-8

24. Colombo, C., Pace, G.J., Schneider, G.: Dynamic event-based runtime monitoring of real-time and contextual properties. In: Cofer, D., Fantechi, A. (eds.) FMICS 2008. LNCS, vol. 5596, pp. 135–149. Springer, Heidelberg (2009). https://doi.org/10.1007/978-3-642-03240-0_13

25. Colombo, C., Pace, G.J., Schneider, G.: LARVA – safer monitoring of real-time Java programs (tool paper). In: Seventh IEEE International Conference on Software Engineering and Formal Methods, SEFM 2009, Hanoi, Vietnam, 23–27 November 2009, pp. 33–37 (2009). https://doi.org/10.1109/SEFM.2009.13

26. Falzon, K., Pace, G.J.: Combining testing and runtime verification techniques. In: Machado, R.J., Maciel, R.S.P., Rubin, J., Botterweck, G. (eds.) MOMPES 2012. LNCS, vol. 7706, pp. 38–57. Springer, Heidelberg (2013). https://doi.org/10.1007/978-3-642-38209-3_3

27. Giannakopoulou, D., Pasareanu, C.S., Lowry, M., Washington, R.: Lifecycle verification of the NASA ames K9 rover executive. Technical report, NASA (2004). http://ti.arc.nasa.gov/publications

28. Hoare, C.: Programming is an engineering profession. In: Wallis, P. (ed.) State of the Art Report 11, No. 3: Software Engineering, pp. 77–84. Pergamon/Infotech (1983). Also Oxford PRG Monograph No. 27; and IEEE Softw. **1**(2)

29. Hu, R., Yoshida, N.: Hybrid session verification through endpoint API generation. In: Stevens, P., Wąsowski, A. (eds.) FASE 2016. LNCS, vol. 9633, pp. 401–418. Springer, Heidelberg (2016). https://doi.org/10.1007/978-3-662-49665-7_24

30. Jaksic, S., Bartocci, E., Grosu, R., Kloibhofer, R., Nguyen, T., Nickovic, D.: From signal temporal logic to FPGA monitors. In: 13th ACM/IEEE International Conference on Formal Methods and Models for Codesign, MEMOCODE 2015, Austin, TX, USA, 21–23 September 2015, pp. 218–227 (2015). https://doi.org/10.1109/MEMCOD.2015.7340489

31. Kiczales, G., Lamping, J., Mendhekar, A., Maeda, C., Lopes, C., Loingtier, J.-M., Irwin, J.: Aspect-oriented programming. In: Akşit, M., Matsuoka, S. (eds.) ECOOP 1997. LNCS, vol. 1241, pp. 220–242. Springer, Heidelberg (1997). https://doi.org/10.1007/BFb0053381

32. Kuhn, T.: A survey and classification of controlled natural languages. CoRR abs/1507.01701 (2015). http://arxiv.org/abs/1507.01701

33. Medhat, R., Bonakdarpour, B., Fischmeister, S., Joshi, Y.: Accelerated runtime verification of LTL specifications with counting semantics. In: Falcone, Y., Sánchez, C. (eds.) RV 2016. LNCS, vol. 10012, pp. 251–267. Springer, Cham (2016). https://doi.org/10.1007/978-3-319-46982-9_16

34. Pnueli, A.: The temporal logic of programs. In: 18th Annual Symposium on Foundations of Computer Science, Providence, Rhode Island, USA, 31 October–1 November 1977, pp. 46–57 (1977). https://doi.org/10.1109/SFCS.1977.32

35. Smaragdakis, Y., Csallner, C.: Combining static and dynamic reasoning for bug detection. In: Gurevich, Y., Meyer, B. (eds.) TAP 2007. LNCS, vol. 4454, pp. 1–16. Springer, Heidelberg (2007). https://doi.org/10.1007/978-3-540-73770-4_1

36. Tamura, G., et al.: Towards practical runtime verification and validation of self-adaptive software systems. In: de Lemos, R., Giese, H., Müller, H.A., Shaw, M. (eds.) Software Engineering for Self-Adaptive Systems II. LNCS, vol. 7475, pp. 108–132. Springer, Heidelberg (2013). https://doi.org/10.1007/978-3-642-35813-5_5

37. Wonisch, D., Schremmer, A., Wehrheim, H.: Zero overhead runtime monitoring. In: Hierons, R.M., Merayo, M.G., Bravetti, M. (eds.) SEFM 2013. LNCS, vol. 8137, pp. 244–258. Springer, Heidelberg (2013). https://doi.org/10.1007/978-3-642-40561-7_17

Author Index

Printed in the United States
By Bookmasters